VOLUNTARY ASSOCIATIONS IN THE GRAECO-ROMAN WORLD

VOLUNTARY ASSOCIATIONS IN THE GRAECO-ROMAN WORLD

Edited by John S. Kloppenborg and Stephen G. Wilson

London and New York

First published 1996
by Routledge
11 New Fetter Lane, London EC4P 4EE

Simultaneously published in the USA and Canada
28 West 35th Street, New York, NY 10001

Typeset in 10/12pt Monotype Garamond
Set by Datix International Limited, Bungay, Suffolk
Printed and bound in Great Britain by
TJ Press (Padstow) Ltd, Padstow, Cornwall

British Library cataloguing in Publication data
A catalogue record for this book is available from the British Library

Library of Congress Cataloging in Publication Data
A catalogue record for this book has been applied for

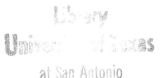
ISBN 0–415–13593–1

CONTENTS

CONTENTS

FIGURES

CONTRIBUTORS

Roger Beck is Professor in the Department of Classics at the University of Toronto.

Wendy Cotter is Assistant Professor in the Department of Theology at Loyola University of Chicago.

Valerie Heuchan is a Ph.D. candidate at the Centre for Religious Studies at the University of Toronto.

John S. Kloppenborg is Associate Professor in the Faculty of Theology at the University of St. Michael's College.

Wayne O. McCready is Associate Professor and Chair of the Department of Religious Studies at the University of Calgary.

B. Hudson McLean is Dean of Theology of St. John's College, University of Manitoba.

Steve Mason is Professor and Chair of the Department of Classics and Ancient Mediterranean Studies at Pennsylvania State University.

Sharon Lea Mattila is a Ph.D. candidate in the Divinity School of the University of Chicago.

Harold Remus is Professor in the Department of Religion and Culture at Wilfrid Laurier University.

Peter Richardson is Professor in the Department of Religion at the University of Toronto.

Eileen Schuller is Professor in the Department of Religion at McMaster University.

Torrey Seland is Associate Professor in Biblical Studies at Volda College, Norway.

S. G. Wilson is Professor in the Department of Religion at Carleton University.

PREFACE

Most of the essays in this volume originated as contributions to a seminar on voluntary associations sponsored by the Canadian Society of Biblical Studies during the period 1988–1993. All but one of the contributors were attached to Canadian universities as faculty or graduate students and were involved in the work of the seminar. When, through the wonders of electronic mail, it was discovered that Torrey Seland had been working on voluntary associations and Philo, the editors invited him to contribute his essay, which was so obviously pertinent.

The book is dedicated to three past Presidents of the Canadian Society of Biblical Studies, all of whom reached the traditional age of retirement at the time we decided to collect and publish the essays. In addition to serving as President, each has contributed enormously to the Society over the years, and it is particularly fitting that we are able to honor them with a book of essays by a number of their friends and colleagues. The individual tributes provide some sense of the high regard in which are held.

John Kloppenborg would like to thank the Collegium of the University of St. Michael's College for granting a research leave, during which time much of the editing on this volume was completed. He also gratefully acknowledges the Theological Scholarship and Research Award granted by the Association of Theological Schools of the United States and Canada which made the sabbatical possible. The editors would like to thank Mr. Richard Ascough who rendered various services during the final editorial stages.

ABBREVIATIONS

ABD	*The Anchor Bible Dictionary*
AGJU	Arbeiten zur Geschichte des antiken Judentums und des Urchristentums
ALGHJ	Arbeiten zur Literatur und Geschichte des hellenistischen Judentums
ANRW	*Aufstieg und Niedergang der römischen Welt*
ASR	*American Sociological Review*
ATR	*Anglican Theological Review*
BA	*Biblical Archaeologist*
BAG	W. Bauer, W. Arndt, F. W. Gingrich. *A Greek–English lexicon of the New Testament.* Chicago: University of Chicago Press, 1952
BAR	*Biblical Archaeology Review*
BCH	*Bulletin de correspondance Hellénique*
BCHSup	Bulletin de correspondance Hellénique supplément
BE	*Bulletin épigraphique* (in *Revue des études grecques*)
BEFAR	Bibliothèque des écoles françaises d'Athènes et de Rome
BETL	Bibliotheca ephemeridum theologicarum lovaniensium
BGU	*Ägyptische Urkunden aus den Königlichen Museen zu Berlin. Griechische Urkunden*
BJRL	*Bulletin of the John Rylands University Library*
BJS	Brown Judaic Studies
BR	*Biblical Research*
BTB	*Biblical Theology Bulletin*
BZ	*Biblische Zeitschrift*
CBQ	*Catholic Biblical Quarterly*
CBQMS	Catholic Biblical Quarterly Monograph Series
CDH	P. Bruneau. *Recherches sur les cultes de Délos à l'époque hellenistique et à l'époque impériale.* Paris: E. de Boccard, 1970
CE	P. Roussel. *Les cultes égyptiens à Délos du III^c au Ier siècles av. J. C.* Paris and Nancy: Berger; Levrault, 1916.
Choix	F. Durrbach, ed. *Choix d'inscriptions de Délos.* Paris: E. Leroux, 1921

CIJ	J.-B. Frey, ed. *Corpus inscriptionum iudaicarum.* Roma: Pontificio Istituto di Archeologia Cristiana, 1936-1952
CIL	*Corpus inscriptionum latinarum.* 17 vols. Berlin: G. Reimer, 1863–1974
CIRB	V. V. Struve, ed. *Corpus inscriptionum Regni Bosporani: Korpus bosporskikh nadpisei.* Moscow and Leningrad: Nauka, 1965
CPJ	V. Tcherikover, ed. *Corpus Papyrorum Judaicarum.* 3 vols. Cambridge, Mass.: Harvard University Press, 1957
CR	*Classical Review*
CRINT	Compendia Rerum Iudaicarum ad Novum Testamentum
DCA	P. Roussel. *Délos, colonie athénienne.* Paris: E. de Boccard, 1916
DJD	Discoveries in the Judaean Desert
EAD	*L'Exploration Archéologique de Délos.* Paris: E. de Boccard, 1909–85
EPRO	Etudes préliminaires aux religions orientales dans l'Empire romain
GD	P. Bruneau and G. Daux. *Guide de Délos,* 2d ed. Paris: E. de Boccard, 1965
G&R	*Greece and Rome*
GRBS	*Greek, Roman and Byzantine Studies*
HDR	Harvard Dissertations in Religion
HNT	Handbuch zum Neuen Testament
HR	*History of Religions*
HTR	*Harvard Theological Review*
ID	F. Durrbach, P. Roussel, M. Launey, A. Plassart, and J. Coupry, eds. *Inscriptions de Délos.* 7 vols. Paris: Librairie ancienne Honoré Champion, 1926-1973
IDB	*Interpreter's Dictionary of the Bible*
IG	*Inscriptiones Graecae, consilio et auctoritate Academiae Litterarum Borussicae editae.*
IGR	Cagnat, René L. *et al.* eds. *Inscriptiones graecae ad res romanas pertinentes.* 4 vols. Paris: E. Leroux, 1901–27.
ILS	H. Dessau. *Inscriptiones latinae selectae.* 3 vols in 5. Berlin: Weidmann, 1892-1916
IRD	J. Hatzfeld, "Les Italiens résidant à Délos," *BCH* 36 (1912) 5–218
JAAR	*Journal of the American Academy of Religion*
JAC	*Jahrbuch für Antike und Christentum*
JBL	*Journal of Biblical Literature*
JEA	*Journal of Egyptian Archaeology*
JJP	*Journal of Juristic Papyrology*
JJS	*Journal of Jewish Studies*
JMS	*Journal of Mithraic Studies*
JQR	*Jewish Quarterly Review*
JRH	*Journal of Religious History*
JSJ	*Journal for the Study of Judaism*

JSNT	*Journal for the Study of the New Testament*
JSNTSup	Journal for the Study of the New Testament, Supplement
JSOTSup	Journal for the Study of the Old Testament, Supplement
JSPSup	Journal for the Study of the Pseudepigrapha, Supplement
JTS	*Journal of Theological Studies*
KEK	Kritisch-exegetischer Kommentar über das Neue Testament
LCL	Loeb Classical Library
LSAM	F. Sokolowski, *Lois sacrées de l'Asie Mineure*. Paris: E. de Boccard, 1955
LSJ	Liddell–Scott–Jones. *Greek–English Lexicon*
MDAIA(A)	*Mitteilungen des Deutschen Archäologischen Instituts. Athenische Abteilung*
NEAEHL	E. Stern and A. Lewinson-Gilboa, eds. *The New Encyclopedia of Archaeological Excavations in the Holy Land.* 4 vols. Jerusalem: Israel Exploration Society & Carta; New York and Toronto: Simon & Schuster, 1993.
NedTTs	*Nederlands theologisch tijdschrift*
Neot	*Neotestamentica*
NovT	*Novum Testamentum*
NovTSup	Novum Testament Supplements
NTAbh	Neutestamentliche Abhandlungen
NTOA	Novum Testamentum et orbis antiquus
NTS	*New Testament Studies*
OCD	*Oxford Classical Dictionary*
OGIS	W. Dittenberger. *Orientis graeci inscriptiones selectae.* 2 vols. in 3. Leipzig: S. Hirzel, 1903–5
OLP	*Orientalia lovaniensia periodica*
OLZ	*Orientalische Literaturzeitung*
PEQ	*Palestine Exploration Quarterly*
PW	*Pauly–Wissowa, Real-Encylopädie der classischen Altertumswissenschaft*
RA	*Revue archéologique*
RAC	*Reallexikon für Antike und Christentum*
RB	*Revue biblique*
REG	*Revue des études grecques*
RevQ	*Revue de Qumran*
RGVV	Religiongeschichtliche Versuche und Vorarbeiten
RIG	Charles Michel. *Recueil d'inscriptions grecques.* Bruxelles: Lamertin, 1900; repr. Hildesheim: G. Olm, 1976.
RSR	*Recherches de science religieuse*
SBLDS	Society of Biblical Literature Dissertation Series
SBLMS	Society of Biblical Literature Monograph Series
SBLTT	Society of Biblical Literature Texts and Translations
ScEs	*Science et esprit*
SEG	*Supplementum epigraphicum graecum*
SJLA	Studies in Judaism in Late Antiquity
SNTSMS	Society for New Testament Studies Monograph Series

SPB	Studia Post-Biblica
SR	*Studies in Religion/Sciences religieuses*
ST	*Studia theologica*
Syll²	Wilhelm Dittenberger, ed. *Sylloge Inscriptionum Graecarum*. 2d ed. 3 vols. Lipsiae: S. Hirzel, 1898–1901
Syll³	Wilhelm Dittenberger, ed. *Sylloge Inscriptionum Graecarum*. 3d ed. 4 vols. Lipsiae: S. Hirzel, 1915–24
TAPA	*Transactions of the American Philological Association*
TDNT	*Theological Dictionary of the New Testament*
TLZ	*Theologische Literaturzeitung*
TS	*Theological Studies*
VigChr	*Vigiliae Christianae*
YCS	Yale Classical Studies
ZNW	*Zeitschrift für die neutestamentliche Wissenschaft*
ZPE	*Zeitschrift für Papyrologie und Epigraphik*
ZTK	*Zeitschrift für Theologie und Kirche*
ZWT	*Zeitschrift für wissenschaftliche Theologie*

Qumran literature

CDC	(Cairo) Damascus Covenant
1QS	*Serek hayyahad,* Manual of Discipline
1QpPs37	Pesher on Psalm 37

Josephus

Ag. Apion	*Against Apion (Contra Apionem)*
Ant.	*Jewish Antiquities (Antiquitates Judaicae)*
Life	*Life (Vita)*
War	*War of the Jews (Bellum Judaicum)*

Philo

Abr.	*On Abraham (De Abrahamo)*
Agric.	*On Husbandry (De agricultura)*
Cher.	*On the Cherubim (De cherubim)*
Confus.	*On the Confusion of Tongues (De confusione linguarum)*
Congr.	*On the Preliminary Sacrifices (De congressu quaerendae eruditionis gratia)*
Dec.	*On the Decalogue (De decalogo)*
Ebr.	*On Drunkenness (De ebrietate)*
Flacc.	*Flaccus (In Flaccum)*
Fuga	*On Flight and Finding (De fuga et inventione)*
Gig.	*On the Giants (De Gigantibus)*

Immut.	*On the Unchangeableness of God (Quod Deus immutabilis sit)*
Jos.	*Joseph (De Josepho)*
Leg. All.	*Allegorical Interpetation (Legum allegoriae)*
Legat.	*Legatio ad Gaium*
Migr.	*On the Migration of Abraham (De migratione Abrahami)*
Mutat.	*On the Change of Names (De mutatione nominum)*
Opf.	*On the Creation (De opficio mundi)*
Plant.	*On Noah's Work as a Planter (De plantatione)*
Post.	*On the Posterity of Cain (De posteritate Caini)*
Praem.	*On Rewards and Punishments (De praemiis et poenis)*
Prob.	*Every Good Man is Free (Quod omnis probus liber sit)*
Prov.	*On Providence (De providentia)*
QG	*Questions and answers on Genesis (Questiones in Genesim)*
Quod omnis	*Every Good Man is Free (Quod omnis probus liber sit)*
Sacr.	*On the Sacrifices of Abel and Cain (De sacrificiis Abelis et Caini)*
Somn.	*On Dreams (De somnis)*
Spec. Leg.	*On the Special Laws (De specialibus legibus)*
Virt.	*On the Virtues (De virtutibus)*
Vita cont.	*On the Contemplative Life (De vita contemplativa)*
Vita Mosis	*On the Life of Moses (De vita Mosis)*

Other

Dig.	Digesta Justiniana

DEDICATIONS

AN OPEN LETTER TO LLOYD GASTON

Dear Lloyd,

It is my great honour and pleasure to write a brief dedication to you on behalf of your friends in the Canadian Society of Biblical Studies. This volume, the outcome of a recent Society seminar, is the most appropriate way to honour you as you reach retirement.

Your contribution to the Society has been influential and profound, as a member of the Executive and as President, but above all perhaps as a witty, provocative and eccentric contributor to the annual debates and discussions. I am sure that I am not alone in finding myself unable to think about the problem of Judaism in the Fourth Gospel without automatically thinking of lobsters. And if you do not carry me all the way with your brilliant and complex arguments about Paul, I cannot think about him without having to take scrupulous account of them.

Above all, however, we admire your combination of serious learning and puckish humour. It is a rare combination. Your insistence that scholarship should be interesting in conception and amusing in execution has rubbed off on us all. And, of course, your gracious, enthusiastic, but often unobtrusive encouragement of our own ideas has been more influential than you would care to recognize.

It is with the greatest respect and affection that I, on behalf of all your friends in Canada, dedicate this volume to you.

Stephen G. Wilson

AN OPEN LETTER TO WILLIAM KLASSEN

Dear Bill,

You already know, I expect, the affection in which you are held by your colleagues across Canada. Through the past score or so years you have been involved in all the activities of the Canadian Society of Biblical Studies. You have been an ideal colleague, whether in seminars, in individual concerns, or in the health and well-being of the whole group.

We honour you particularly for your broad knowledge of Hellenistic philosophical traditions, of the Cynics and Stoics in particular. You have always championed the underdog, as your recent fascination with Judas Iscariot demonstrates. And you have been passionately concerned for peace-making and the ethics behind it, often juxtaposed in your work with your similar (some might say contradictory!) interest in zealotism. When to these wide interests in Christian origins are added your almost equally strong interests in the Anabaptist wing of the Reformation and in mental health and psychiatry, most of us stand in awe.

I know of no one who gets as much of a "high" from the joy of discovery in research. Yet over the years you have managed, apparently almost effortlessly, to balance an active research program with other more practical pursuits, whether administration or fund-raising. Your peripatetic tendencies are almost legendary, whether on student tours – as I know all too well – or in our own professional life as you have moved from Elkhart to Winnipeg to Vancouver to Jerusalem to Toronto to Waterloo and now back to Jerusalem – and all of that after you already had tenure!

In honouring you in this way we want merely to say thank you and to offer you our best wishes on your so-called retirement.

Peter Richardson

AN OPEN LETTER TO HAROLD REMUS

Dear Harold,

This volume is dedicated to you at your retirement in honour of your years of teaching and your scholarly contributions in Canada and beyond.

You immersed yourself in scholarship with studies in English, Greek, German, Patristics, and Christian origins. The results have been a major contribution to the study of the period, reflected best in *Pagan–Christian Conflict over Miracle in the Second Century*. Your career has also had its miraculous dimension.

It has been full of major publishing responsibilities which you have miraculously survived and thrived on. While thickly immersed in writing your doctorate, you were already contributing to the well-being of the field, as when you researched and edited *A Study of Graduate Education in Religion*, the famous Welch Report. And you have been an editor of *Lutheran World*, Fortress Press, and Director of the Wilfrid Laurier University Press and executive officer for the Council on the Study of Religion. You founded and managed *Religious Studies Review* and managed *Studies in Religion/Sciences religieuses* as well as being on the advisory board of countless journals: *Zygon, Dialog, The Journal of Ritual Studies*, to name but a few. You have helped religious studies in Canada to understand itself better through your work on the advisory board of that multi-volume study and in particular on your work on Ontario.

But the most important new aspect of your career, you waited until your Presidential address to show us I no doubt, your new lucrative, post-retirement career – channelling Abraxas.

We don't know whether it was by miracle or magic that, while you were doing all these tasks, you continued to participate in scholarly activities, not least in the Canadian Society of Biblical Studies. You helped us understand the classical world, Hellenistic backgrounds of Christianity, and the social-scientific study of religion. Your colleagues thank you for your miraculous career; we did not want you to think that you could retire without our noting it.

With gratitude and affection,

Alan F. Segal

1

VOLUNTARY ASSOCIATIONS

An overview

S. G. Wilson

A brief overview of the papers in this volume provides an opportunity to do a number of things. First, to consider the nature and significance of the multitude of overlapping terms used of and by associations in the Hellenistic era. Second, to offer some reflections on the pertinence and utility of those modern concepts – some with ancient equivalents, some without – which have become familiar in recent sociological discussion of religious groups and which are drawn on casually or deliberately by various authors in this volume. Finally, to draw together some of the common themes and issues that arise when these essays are looked at broadly and as a whole.

The term "voluntary association" has become common parlance among those involved in a Canadian Society of Biblical Studies seminar in recent years.[1] The initial impulse of the seminar was to understand how discrete Jewish and Christian communities fitted into patterns of communal life already established in Graeco-Roman society. The aim was to cast the net as widely as possible and "voluntary association" was chosen as the term that most naturally and comprehensively captured the range of phenomena that we wished to study. The most common ancient terms – such as *collegium, secta, factio, thiasos, eranos, koinon* – like their modern counterparts "club" or "guild," are broad in scope but not quite broad enough. The term "association" was already well established in discussions of the ancient phenomena, and the addition of the adjective "voluntary" (which others have used too) was designed to distinguish them from institutions such as the state, city, or family, where membership was automatic – a question of birth rather than choice. It also distinguishes them from the official collegia and sacred sodalities run by the state, even though the participants in at least one of these, the Augustales, may have included privileged freedmen who belonged to private associations too (Kloppenborg, chapter 2). The distinction between voluntary and involuntary associations cannot be too rigid, since membership in a synagogue, family cult, or trade guild may have been for different reasons more or less obligatory. The term "private association," which some prefer, is a possible alternative, though it too would have required careful definition.

The term "voluntary association" has nevertheless served us well. It has

1

encouraged us to look both at terms (for example, *philosophia*, *ekklēsia*, *hairesis*) and at phenomena (for example, mystery cults, Asclepieia, Therapeutae, Qumran, synagogues) that have not often been brought into the discussion of ancient associations, thus broadening the comparative base and enriching our sense of the range and variety of such groups. This in turn raises questions about the utility and accuracy of subsuming all of these phenomena under one label – questions to which we shall later return.

It is possible that the term could cause some confusion for those familiar with its use in modern socio-political discourse. There is, of course, some overlap. "Voluntary association" in this context also refers to groups that people opt to join. Moreover, the circumstances that are thought to encourage their proliferation (social dislocation), some of their organizational features (elaborate hierarchies), as well as the needs they purportedly meet (as "fictive" families, or as mediators between the individual and the state), are all things that have been observed about their counterparts in the ancient world.

Yet the term "voluntary association" is also connected in modern discussion with another set of issues. It is used mostly, though not exclusively, with reference to the United States, designated by both Weber and de Tocqueville as the supreme example of a society organized around voluntary associations. In this context the term refers to almost any group organized to further the interests of its members, to lobby, transform, even resist the state or any other major vested interest. Voluntary associations are thus seen as the ideal vehicle for defending the democratic principle of liberty and the cause of pluralism. Historically, and even more broadly, anything from universities to unions, churches to charities, can be seen as organizations that have at one time furthered these aims, even though they have often ended up becoming part of the very establishment they set out to challenge.[2]

The impulse to reform, to speak for the unheard, to advance the cause of liberty and democracy, are not aims that we immediately associate with ancient associations – understandably so when we cast things in this modern way. Yet we should not assume that ancient associations were entirely introverted, passive and indifferent to political affairs. It is true that many associations were organized in a manner that both reflected and reinforced the existing social order, for example family or household cults such as we find in the Agrippinilla inscription, or collegia that structured themselves as miniature city-states.[3] And, according to R. Beck (chapter 10), the Mithras cult was a home for social conformists. We are also warned not to liken ancient guilds to modern unions though, as J. Kloppenborg notes (chapter 2), we find a few instances of guild members going on strike or threatening a work-stoppage. This last example may point to an occasional, if modest amount of political activity. The link between patrons and associations could also have a political dimension, as when members were called out to support their patron for political office (the Isis cult at Pompeii; Isodorus in Alexandria, Philo *Flacc.* 137-38).[4] Such actions may have tended to reinforce rather than to reform existing political structures, but they were nevertheless a collective attempt to assert influence on the course of political affairs. Then again, W. Cotter (chapter 5) has shown how collegia were often suspected of harboring socially disruptive elements and were for this reason banned. Was this due just to Roman conservatism and paranoia, or did they have good reason for their suspicions? Philo certainly thinks so, and he describes intrigue and conspiracy as normal features of association life (*Legat.* 312-13, *Flacc.* 4, *Spec. Leg.* 4.46-47; Seland, chapter 7). Philo, of course, speaks scathingly about the activities of pagan associations (particularly their drunken carousing) and contrasts them with the sober pursuit of virtue in Jewish gatherings. Perhaps he exaggerates, or perhaps the conspiracies he alludes to were personal rather than political and nothing more than alcoholically induced fantasies. But it just may be that he gives us a glimpse of a feature of association life that the Romans had good reason to suspect.

One thing that limited the political influence of collegia/*thiasoi* was that they were normally local organizations. They were linked only loosely to a larger network, and contacts were casual and informal. Travelers, for example, might for a while join in the activities of a sister association when on the road or join permanently if they settled down. We also know of troupes of performers (musicians, actors) who moved from one Dionysiac centre to another offering their services. The Dionysos mystery cult, like others, spread widely, sometimes through a deliberate decision; but once established, local cults remained largely autonomous and could take quite divergent forms from one locality to another.[5] Two groups that did belong to more active networks, churches and synagogues, were concerned mostly to protect their privileges or to encourage circumstances that allowed them to run their internal affairs without interference. Their aim was not to overthrow the existing political system, but to find their niche within it – even if on their own terms. So while some aspects of early Christian communal life, for example, could be seen as politically or socially destabilizing, in fact most early Christian writers call on their members to support the state (Rom. 13; 1 Pet. 2). It is true that some Jews and Christians envisaged the overthrow of the state in the end times, and that the Judaean and North African Jews anticipated this outcome in a series of revolts against Rome in the first and second centuries CE. These uprisings were, however, driven more by a revolutionary than a reformist impulse, were limited geographically and temporally, and were atypical of the experience of the majority of Jews under Roman rule.

Yet neither Jews nor Christians were entirely quietist. As can be seen in their apologetic literature, they were not unwilling to pillory the religious practices and social mores of pagan society and at the same time boast of the superiority of their own. In this, as in their trans-local organization, they were more like the philosophers, whose promotion of good living as well as right thinking, philanthropy as well as piety, could involve sharp criticism of the ruling classes. Thus, despite their prestige and respect for their learning, philosophers were also mistrusted and occasionally expelled or put to death (Mason, chapter 3). So it could be argued that philosophers, and Jews and Christians to the degree that they

3

were like them, come closer to the reformist impulse of modern associations than do some other ancient groups. This forges a link between the use of "voluntary association" as a term to describe ancient and modern phenomena, even when it is clear that important differences of emphasis remain.

While it might be objected that lumping schools, guilds, cults, synagogues and churches together adds more confusion than clarity, the truth is that in the ancient world the boundaries and the terminology were fluid. We know, for example, of Jews and Christians who tried to persuade their readers that their tradition as a whole or sub-groups within them should be viewed as schools of thought (*haireseis* or *proaireseis*) or as *philosophia* in general (for example, Philo; Josephus; Luke–Acts; second-century apologists; see Mason, chapter 2, and Heuchan). *Hairesis* in this context refers of course to an identifiable group or viewpoint within a larger philosophical or medical matrix (the pejorative sense of a deviant or erroneous tendency is a later, mainly Christian and Jewish, usage).[6] At the same time we know that philosophical schools were on occasions likened to *thiasoi* and that some of them, particularly the Epicureans, enjoyed an organized communal life, which included regular banquets and religious rites in addition to the pursuit of learning. Others, such as the Stoics and the school of Epictetus, gathered daily for study and reflection, but apparently for little else.[7]

Other terminological links abound. Jewish communities, largely organized around the synagogue and led by figures such as the *archisynagōgos*, recall the use of *synagōgē* as a self-designation by some pagan associations as well as the penchant for describing leaders and officials in compounds using *archi-* or *-archēs*. More distinctive Jewish groups, such as the celibate monastic group near Alexandria described by Philo, are called by him Therapeutae, the same term used to describe the members of some Graeco-Roman associations (as on Delos; McLean, chapter 11). Similarly, a connection between Christian groups and collegia, at least on a terminological level, is indicated by the use of *ekklēsia* and *episkopos* as group or leadership designations in some associations.[8]

Pointing to such coincidences in terminology in the ancient sources does not in itself prove anything. The coincidences may, after all, be coincidental. As S. Walker-Ramisch (chapter 8) points out with reference to the community envisaged by the Damascus Document, similar terminology and even similar organizational structures can be adopted by groups with radically different ideologies and purposes. Yet they do suggest that, despite the manifest differences between them, these groups can usefully be considered together as part of a broad social phenomenon. It is important to note the limits of this claim: we are suggesting analogies between the various associations and not, as has so often been done in the past, genealogical relationships or influences.[9]

That Jewish communities can be compared with Graeco-Roman associations has been suggested in passing by others, but P. Richardson (chapter 6) has now fully and persuasively made the case that pre-70 synagogues were in all respects analogous to collegia, while enjoying greater imperial protection.[10] It is significant that both Philo and Josephus, our best-preserved ancient Jewish witnesses, draw our attention to this, even if they also insist on significant differences (Josephus *Ant.* 14.215-16, 235-36, 259-60; Philo *Legat.* 312, 316; Seland, Richardson, chapters 7 and 6). That early Christian groups can be viewed likewise has been a more controversial proposition, though the discussion has been driven more by theological or confessional presuppositions than exact observation. Kloppenborg's recent essay has shown clearly that the similarities are many and the differences less sharply defined than has commonly been claimed,[11] and despite his emphasis on a number of differences W. McCready (chapter 4) allows for significant points of connection too. B. H. McLean (chapter 11) has also made a strong case for thinking that the churches on Delos patterned themselves (at least architecturally and perhaps ritually) on the many other local associations on that island.

Some other terms with a modern flavor have also been introduced. The least controversial of these is the concept of "networks," a form of microsociological analysis that emphasizes dynamic rather than static aspects of society and that focuses on precisely that space between the individual and society which voluntary associations are commonly thought to inhabit. Compared with some other concepts there are fewer problems moving from modern to ancient applications, though ancient sources do not often provide a wealth of detail, and when they do, it is usually confined to the activities of the upper classes. H. Remus (chapter 9) has struck a rich vein of information about Aelius Aristides' association with the sanctuary of Asclepius at Pergamum, and uses the insights of network analysis to uncover the social dynamics at work. He suggests that we should distinguish between informal social networks and formally organized associations. He recognizes that the two may overlap, but rightly insists that in principle they may diverge – networks may be different from and work independently of connections forged in an association. At the same time it is clear from his own description that Aristides shares with most of the significant figures in his circle a devotion to Asclepius and the sanctuary at Pergamum. As he says, "Asclepius is, one might say, the key networker among his friends."[12] Thus Aristides and his friends and acquaintances form a network within an association whose focus is Asclepius. That they are part of a largely aristocratic network as well opens up a dimension of their participation in this cult that has not often been so clearly and richly documented. In this case network and association complement each other and point to the way in which the life of associations functioned within a larger nexus of social relationships. That they could be complementary, particularly in the way that well-connected members could act not only as patrons but as conduits of influence on behalf of the association and its other members, has been noted by others too.[13]

The term "cult," occasionally introduced in these essays in connection with ancient voluntary associations, is also routinely used by sociologists of religion. In this case the use of a common term could lead to confusion. For one thing the sociological use is ill-defined. Sometimes it is used as a synonym for "new religious movement," at other times for "sect," both terms which have themselves resisted consensual definition. It is well known, for example, that defining the concept sect (usually in terms of a church–sect dichotomy) and establishing a typology that is both comprehensive and accurate, has taxed sociologists at least since the time of Weber. And, despite active debate, there is no apparent consensus on the matter. The more recent label, new religious movement, has proven almost as elusive. In the more useful schemes, sects are distinguished from cults/new religious movements. The latter, it is suggested, emphasize the personal and the affective, simple but rigid dogma, and are usually loosely organized around a charismatic leader. But even here the distinctions are sometimes unclear. This is partly because the different terms are used to label identical or at least overlapping phenomena, a problem exacerbated by the tendency of cults to transmute into sects and sects into denominations or even churches.[14]

It is interesting to note that at one point Weber, distinguishing between church and sect in terms of their modes of membership and consequent forms of social organization, suggests that sects could be defined as voluntary associations with restricted membership and churches as compulsory associations with universalist aspirations (1968:56). Some of the groups we have looked at might loosely qualify as sects using this definition. The Therapeutae and the society envisaged by the Damascus Document come to mind (although S. Walker-Ramisch concludes that it is precisely its sectarian ideals that separate CDC from pagan associations). Yet the broader Judaism of which they were a part was itself fragmented and only some Jews had a genuinely universalist vision. Early Christian groups, which we have not considered in any detail, have in recent literature often been likened to sects too. Thus it might be argued that when the author of Matthew uses *ekklēsia* (16:18; 18:17) to describe his community he may be likening it to other voluntary associations, since some of them use the same label, but he may also be expressing a sense of sectarian identity in the broader context of synagogue Judaism. However, quite apart from the lack of consensus in modern discussions of sectarianism, as a sociological category it is of limited value in analyzing voluntary associations because a sect is typically defined over and against a larger, mainstream entity, in this case a church. For many of the associations we have looked at there is no equivalent entity with which to contrast them. The dominance of the church–sect distinction in modern discussions of sectarianism, usually with reference to a historically limited period, makes it a particularly treacherous and problematic category to transfer to the ancient world.[15]

To return to the term "cult," S. Mason (chapter 3) notes a distinction made between cult and philosophy by A. D. Nock in his famous book on conversion (1933). In comparison with philosophy, cults, Nock argued, were characterized by emotion rather than reason, ritual rather than morality, experience rather than instruction, personal gods rather than divinity at large, shared rather than professional leadership, and casual allegiance rather than absolute commitment. Nock also noted that some of these distinctions began to break down in the first century CE as the philosophical schools became more overtly religious. His emphasis on the personal and affective nature of ancient cults resonates with modern sociological descriptions of cults or new religious movements. Yet, comparing in the other direction, many of the features thought to characterize modern cults – exclusivism, dogma, and charismatic leadership are just the most obvious examples – are different enough to suggest that modern attempts to identify and define cults are of limited value in considering the ancient phenomena, at least as Nock describes them.

The examples that Nock primarily has in mind in his discussion are, of course, the mystery cults. One thing that distinguished them in comparison with other pagan associations was intense religious devotion, which was indeed their main purpose and function. Yet B. H. McLean (chapter 11), who distinguishes between the congregational and cultic aspects of the associations on Delos, demonstrates what other essays also repeatedly note: that all associations had a religious or cultic dimension. In the examples from Delos (with the exception of the Samaritan or Jewish synagogue) this is clear from the architectural evidence for dedicated sanctuaries either outside or within the general place of assembly. In this sense the term "cult," used roughly as a synonym for an element of religious devotion, is an apt description of a ubiquitous feature of ancient associations, as indeed of ancient life in general.

It is a now commonplace, but important, observation that in the ancient world religion was not merely one component of human experience (as we tend to think of it) but rather was inextricably bound up with all aspects of life. With a few exceptions, people unquestioningly accepted religious beliefs and practices as part of their everyday routine. Yet we should not conclude from this that all individuals or groups were equally devout. The associations we have looked at give a sense of the range of possibilities. As far as we can tell, in all cases religious devotion was in some form or another integrated into the life of the group. For some, as for those in synagogues, churches, or mystery cults, it was central, the chief reason why the association was formed in the first place, even though there were doubtless different levels of devotion within each community. In extreme cases, as with the Therapeutae, the devotees abandoned ordinary life for a secluded, monastic existence, the better to pursue their spiritual path. For others, however, it seems highly likely that religious rituals were seen as a necessary but minor part of their routine, one expression of a group solidarity that was more importantly rooted in social or commercial interests.

In her essay S. Walker-Ramisch (chapter 8) offers the most thoroughgoing attempt to define ancient associations with the help of modern counterparts. In both cases, she notes, they are voluntary, part-time, private, and formally organized; they serve a variety of manifest and latent purposes; and, especially during times of rapid social change, they cater to the needs of individuals when governments or kinship groups fail. There are, however, important differences: ancient associations were invariably religious, local rather than trans-local in their organization, and they tended to support the existing political order. She also concludes that the group envisaged by the Damascus Document, despite many points of congruence with pagan associations, cannot be placed in the same category. The "sectarian" ideology of CDC (by which she means its exclusivism and its antagonism to the existing socio-political order), exhibits ideals quite different from that of the collegia.

This conclusion sharply highlights the problem of definition. The issue at stake is partly methodological, partly terminological. By its very nature, sociological enquiry tends to emphasize the general rather than the particular, the common rather than the idiosyncratic. To foster comparisons, within or across cultures, sociologists typically make use of abstractions – models or ideal types – that allow them to grasp complex social phenomena. But the majority of them are fully aware that they are working with abstractions, and that these abstractions have constantly to be reshaped and redefined in response to the specific examples to which they are applied. There is thus ideally a constant, reciprocal interaction between the abstract and the specific, between the general pattern and the local example. In her conclusion Walker-Ramisch veers towards one of these poles – the local and specific – and suggests that the distinctive traits of the community envisaged by CDC exclude it from the general category collegia. Local phenomena are, she argues, to be seen in their local context and produce local truths.

There are several things that can be said about this. The first is that the emphasis on differences rather than similarities and the decision to exclude one local example from the general category are arbitrary. The exclusion of CDC privileges a particular ideological element (which she rightly notes had social repercussions) as the decisive factor. But there are other ways of construing things (equally arbitrary, of course) – placing emphasis on similarities rather than differences, and highlighting things other than the attitude to the outside world, for example. This latter approach is not uncommon in the study of new religious movements, which are thought to have enough in common to be considered collectively, but whose attitudes towards a number of things – including the world outside their sect – can vary widely.[16]

This points, secondly, to another issue, this time one of definition. What belongs or does not belong in a category depends to some degree on how broadly it is defined. The differences Walker-Ramisch notes between ancient and modern associations, and the exclusion of CDC from the rank of typical associations because of its "sectarian" ideology, rest on a model that draws its notion of ancient associations from the evidence for pagan collegia/*thiasoi* alone. That is to say, it excludes from the comparative base other Jewish, Christian, and pagan organizations that might broaden the category sufficiently to allow the inclusion of CDC. We know, for example, of Jewish and Christian groups that had "sectarian" tendencies not too dissimilar from those of CDC, and there were no doubt ascetic devotees in the various mystery cults who effectively cut themselves off from and disdained the world, as did the Therapeutae and, to a lesser extent, the members of certain philosophical schools.

It is also important to note Walker-Ramisch's further conclusion: that Jewish

organizations must be understood in terms of the distinctive historical experience and cultural traditions of Judaism, despite any similarities they may appear
to have with other organizations, and that even among Jewish organizations
there were differences in the way they responded to Roman rule. One implication of the last point is that CDC is not representative of Jewish groups as a
whole and that others, diaspora synagogue communities for example, might well
fit more readily into the pattern of ancient associations even as more narrowly
defined.

In all this there is, thirdly, a significant warning. In our enthusiasm for finding
connections between ancient associations it is easy to ignore the differences between them, the peculiar and distinctive ways in which associations that in many
respects looked alike organized and presented themselves. This is particularly
true when the category "voluntary association" is opened up to include a larger
range of groups than usual. That there were differences – in ideology, organization, membership, and purpose – both between and within the larger categories
we are dealing with goes without saying. And, as Kloppenborg shows, it is no
easy matter to provide a clear taxonomy for one group of associations (collegia/
thiasoi), let alone for them all. Our purpose in drawing them together under one
broad concept is not to blur or deny these differences, to create a homogeneous
category so broad that it applies to everything in general and nothing in particular. Nor is it to imply that when we have viewed particular groups in this way
we have said all there is to be said about them. It is rather to point to the significant overlap between these groups as social phenomena, how they looked to
others and how they aspired to be seen in terms of the social categories available
to them at the time.

What points of connection do these essays suggest apart from the ones already discussed? Most clearly that all associations were formally organized. Rules
for entry and standards of behavior were commonplace requirements, if quite
varied. Joining some guilds seems to have been a fairly undemanding matter, a
case of being in the appropriate trade, on the right street and being voted in.
Other associations, such as the mystery cults or churches, had more elaborate
initiation rituals. At one end of the scale, rules of behavior meant no more than
the regulation of communal activities – which was as far as many collegia went –
but at the other end it could extend to a comprehensive ethical vision for life as a
whole (synagogues, churches, philosophical schools). And while in some groups
the initial process of entry was sufficient to open up full membership, in others
(Mithraism is a classic example) there were carefully delineated stages through
which members progressed.

It has frequently been noted that Graeco-Roman associations did not demand
the exclusive allegiance of their members. There may be one or two exceptions,
where exclusive commitment was required,[17] and many people may in fact have
belonged to only one association as a matter of choice or practicality (the spare
time of an average person was probably quite limited). Yet in principle there was
usually nothing to stop a person belonging to or being the patron of more than

9

one guild or mystery cult, each of which may have honored a different deity. Equally there is evidence that shows that some cult centres, for example Mithraea, were not averse to honoring deities other than the one who was their chief object of devotion (see MacMullen 1981:92).

In contrast it is said that Jews, Christians – and to some extent philosophical schools – made exclusive demands on the loyalty of their members. For Jews and Christians this may in principle have been true, but the reality was as always less tidy. Philo, for example, warns his fellow Jews about the dangers of joining in pagan symposia, clubs, and schools, and notes that some became apostates in this way. Clearly some Jews were socially adventurous and, despite his warnings, Philo surprisingly suggests that he (and others who were morally mature) could participate in certain pagan gatherings providing they did not drink or eat to excess. How Philo and other Jews dealt with the religious element in associations, as well as in the gymnasia and theatres, remains obscure.

Evidence for Christians crossing theoretically exclusive boundaries can also be found. Some Christian Judaizers found the attractions of synagogue life irresistible, as the classic instance of Chrysostom's Antioch shows, and others seem to have considered participation in pagan associations socially necessary (1 Cor. 8–10) or politically expedient (Rev. 2–3). The philosophical schools, according to Nock, required a commitment akin to conversion (Mason, chapter 3). Even so, it is striking how eclectic philosophy was in the Graeco-Roman era and how easy it was to explore one school after another (Justin is a good example). Commitment to one school may often have been temporary, and may for the while have excluded participation in other schools, though not in principle from other types of association.

Once established, voluntary associations seem invariably to have developed an organizational hierarchy. At an early stage, as in the Pauline churches and some of the mystery cults, the organization may have been informal and ad hoc, but eventually some kind of formal structure was assumed. This was no doubt in part a result of the almost inevitable tendency of human groups to bureaucratize as they become established and grow, but it was also in part a love of ranks and titles for their own sake – for in many instances these appear to have proliferated artificially and bore little relationship to power or responsibility. It is impossible to generalize further about the precise functions, titles, and roles of the leaders, since the variety within and among the different types of association was almost without limit.

It is often noted that membership in associations was confined largely to the lower classes – typically the urban poor, slaves, and freedmen. This is generally true, though it can also give a misleading impression. For one thing it tells us only that they catered to all but an elite minority. For another, the categories slave and freedman cover a wide range of people, from the abjectly poor and beholden to the relatively wealthy and influential. The privileged few it is true had access to state-run sodalities and, Remus (chapter 9) suggests, in general they had no need for associations, the benefits of which they already enjoyed by virtue of their position and power. Yet things were not quite so clear-cut as this. While Aristides and his aristocratic friends were clearly part of a social network of equals they were also devotees in the cult of Asclepius at Pergamum, which was itself an association and in which they may simply have been an upper-class clique. Other associations (the Iobacchoi) also had a largely upper-class membership. Many associations benefited from wealthy patrons. In some cases patrons apparently took little part in the life of an association besides providing financial support and appointing the leaders; but in others they had a more active role. This is perhaps most clearly seen in associations based in a household, where the patrons were leaders as well as providers (for example, the Pauline churches), or perhaps more obviously when the association was itself a household cult. In the latter case the membership could run from the senatorial class at the top to slaves at the bottom, as the Agrippinilla inscription shows.

It has been noted that while some associations preserved and reinforced the social distinctions of everyday life (different rules for slaves and citizens, for example), in others all members were in principle treated as equals.[18] Indeed, it may be that this was precisely one of the elements of association life that caught the attention of state authorities and led to the suspicion that they were a potentially subversive force. Yet the example of the Christian churches shows us that even where there was a self-conscious attempt to be inclusive and to dissolve in principle some of the standard social distinctions (slave/free, male/female), the reality was that the hierarchical structures of society tended to be reflected in the organization of the associations too.

Pertinent to this and of particular interest in a number of essays is the role of women in voluntary associations. In some, such as the Mithras cult, philosophical schools, or various trade guilds, membership was exclusively male. There were on the other hand some Graeco-Roman associations whose membership was exclusively female (Kloppenborg, chapter 2), others in which they had a significant role (Dionysos cults), and yet others in which their role may have been confined to their position as spouses or benefactors. The evidence for Christian and Jewish groups is also mixed. In both cases, of course, women were usually members, though the evidence from Qumran is in this respect ambiguous, as E. Schuller (chapter 13) shows. There is more controversy over the roles they performed. Paul's letters and those of his followers, to take well-known examples, show that the earliest churches had female leaders but that soon after Paul's time (if not during it) attempts were made to minimize their public role. It has traditionally been assumed that Jewish groups were organized along patriarchal lines, yet the evidence that names women as *archisynagōgos* and the like – not all instances of which can be explained as honorific titles enjoyed by virtue of their spouse's position or their patronage of a synagogue – suggests otherwise (Brooten 1982). And while in public meetings in the synagogues men and women were usually segregated, as they were in most Christian and Graeco-Roman associations (S. Mattila, chapter 14), we cannot assume either that Jewish women were inactive or insignificant in synagogue life or that their experience

11

was uniform across the empire. The Therapeutae are a particularly interesting example: a monastic community of both men and women who seem to have been equally involved in the most important aspects of communal life, a feature that V. Heuchan (chapter 12) suggests may have derived in part from the influence of the Isis cult – an association in which women played a central role as well. The evidence is, however, somewhat mixed, and the claim that "men and women were equal" is not clear from her own analysis. There was segregation during worship, which seems to have been led by men, and to some degree at common meals. And many of the women were virgins (unlike the men who had left their families and distributed their possessions to others). To call this equality is perhaps to use a somewhat loaded modern term and to overlook the patriarchal framework in which the community lived (to which the segregation points). Even so, it is noteworthy that Philo, in his description of the group, resists his normal inclination to denigrate women/the female principle and subordinate them to men/the male principle (see Wegner 1991b). Since he was apparently enchanted by the serious dedication of this group, he may simply have reported what he saw even though it did not fit his own predilections. If P. Richardson (chapter 6) is right, it may be that the temple at Leontopolis employed female priests, a startling takeover of a role traditionally reserved for males. The evidence for philosophical schools is mixed: the Epicureans welcomed women, even though some found this mildly scandalous; and while the Stoic schools were usually all-male preserves, some individuals, such as Musonius, advocated the same education (including the study of philosophy) for men and women.[19]

Communal eating and drinking are a fairly constant feature of life in associations. For some this may have been the chief reason for their existence – to eat and drink well and to socialize in convivial company, often to the accompaniment of music and entertainment. Indeed, Graeco-Roman associations were notorious for their drunken excesses, a feature that the somewhat prudish Philo frequently harps on (and probably exaggerates). Philo contrasts the fasting and sobriety of Jews on the annual day of atonement with the excesses of other associations (*Spec. Leg.* 2.145-46), but tells us little about what went on at other regular Jewish gatherings. He does note that the Therapeutae ate communally and eschewed alcohol (*Vita Cont.* 40-47). They had special feast (and fast) days too, but their communal meals, like those of the Qumran covenanters, were a routine part of their communal living arrangements and thus somewhat unlike the occasional meals of other associations. There is extensive evidence that prayer and Torah-reading were central activities in the synagogue, but rather less about other aspects of communal life. Nevertheless, it appears that communal feasting played an important role at Delos and Sardis, since the imperial decrees mentioned by Josephus specifically allow for the collection of funds for that purpose (Josephus *Ant.* 14.214-16, 260-61). Christians, too, are known to have met for ordinary meals (Agape feasts, 1 Cor. 11) as well as a regular sacramental meal that may at times have been celebrated simultaneously. Sacramental meals were also common in the mystery cults (Beck, chapter 10).

In some associations (Dionysos cults) sacrificial rites were an important part of communal gatherings; in others they played little or no role (Mithraism). In Judaism sacrifices were normally performed only in Jerusalem (and for a while in Leontopolis). This is probably what Philo is referring to when he mentions the collection of funds to pay for sacrifices and sacred envoys (*Legat.* 312-13), but the meaning is uncertain. Josephus' reference to sacrifices in Sardis (supra) could refer to sacrifices in the local synagogue, but also perhaps to some sort of communal meal (Cohen 1987a:165-66). This evidence merely confirms what was already noted above: that all associations, in one form or another and to a greater or lesser degree, had a religious or cultic focus.

Many associations arranged for the burial of their members. Kloppenborg questions the common view that many Graeco-Roman associations were set up primarily for this purpose, except perhaps after the time of Hadrian. Even in the latter case, he suggests, the social life of the association was probably more important than making arrangements for the dead. Nevertheless, it was a task that many pagan, Jewish and Christian associations took upon themselves, acting not only as an extended family during mourning, but more importantly guaranteeing a burial plot that would be kept sacred and undisturbed after death.

It is estimated that most associations were relatively small in number, typically fifteen to twenty at one end of the scale and up to two hundred at the other. Their size would have been constrained by the places in which they met. Many of them – churches, synagogues, collegia, schools – met in the room of a house, often that of their patron or one of their wealthier members. The overlap between associations and households is thus considerable, not only because some were set up exclusively for the members of a particular household but also because many of them met under the auspices of a householder. Sometimes meeting places were purpose-built or bequeathed by a sympathetic patron, and they could be quite grandiose – as with the synagogues at Alexandria or Sardis, for example.[20]

We turn finally to more speculative matters: the needs which associations met and the benefits they conferred; and the reasons why they proliferated in the Hellenistic-Roman era. It is widely noted that as social organizations they took up the slack between the individual and the state, providing fictive families for those uprooted from clan or family and fictive polities for those excluded from political power. This, it is claimed, is to be connected with the breakdown of traditional social and political institutions during the Hellenistic era. It is true that their small size, intimate relations, and convivial gatherings could have been substitutes for family and clan; and opportunities to lead and organize, together with conferred grades, ranks and titles, could have satisfied needs that were not met in the outside world. Much the same is said of modern associations. Yet there is little hard evidence to prove that this was the case. Moreover, sweeping statements about the disruptions and trends of the Hellenistic era are suspect by virtue of their very generality. The Hellenistic-Roman era was a very long period of time and its effects varied widely from place to place, but as historians we are all too prone to compress hundreds of years and vastly varying types of human experience into a few brief clichés. We often read, for example, that it was an era of individualism – a suspiciously modern concept to start with and one that could at any rate account for only a limited portion of the ancient evidence at best.

Some observations, it is true, are based on common sense – that some people relish ranks and titles whoever confers them, or that transient populations look instinctively to familiar organizations (guild, cult, church) to pick up the threads of their social and religious life. It is probable too that the need for associations was less marked in small, stable rural communities where the community effectively functioned as an association. And associations were, in the ancient world, typically urban phenomena. It would, however, be a mistake to suppose that the motive for joining these groups was always compensatory, making up for something otherwise lacking in family or political life. Many of their members, I would assume, had a stable family life and no great interest in politics (and it has been suggested that in the modern world those with satisfactory primary group ties are more likely to join associations).[21] Those associations based on a household, for example, were an expression of family life, not a substitute for it. The reasons why people found associations attractive were doubtless many, but we should never underestimate the basic and instinctive desire of most people to socialize with those with whom they share things in common – devotion to a deity, a trade or skill, a similar background, or even just a love of eating and drinking in good company.

NOTES

1 The relation of the papers to this seminar of the Canadian Society of Biblical Studies is explained in the Preface. As it turned out, while a number of studies considered Jewish examples, few focused on early Christian groups. Some of those that did have been set aside for a volume that is promised from the group studying inscriptional evidence at the University of Toronto under the direction of John S. Kloppenborg and B. Hudson McLean.

2 See the essays in Robertson 1966; Pennock and Chapman 1969. The first volume has a number of essays on religious groups, such as the Anabaptists of the Reformation period – a good example of how an original association (the early church) became part of the establishment in the post-Constantinian era and, in turn, spawned another generation of protest (the Anabaptists, or left-wing Protestants). Many of these essays note how easily associations become bureaucratized, rigid and oligarchic as they move away from the idealistic days of their founding. For a historical perspective on the importance of associations in the history of Western societies see Chapman 1969. A useful survey, from both an anthropological and sociological perspective, can be found in the articles on voluntary associations by Banton (1968) and Sills (1968).

3 On the Agrippinilla inscription see McLean 1993a.

4 White 1991a:16–18.

5 See Henrichs 1982:151–55; and in the same volume Tran 1982:110–11. In an as yet unpublished paper presented to the Canadian Society of Biblical Studies annual meeting in 1995, Richard Ascough has challenged the prevailing consensus on the question of trans-

local links by arguing that the collegia/*thiasoi* had more, and the churches in the early period fewer, trans-local links than is usually recognized.

6 See Desjardins 1991.
7 See Culpepper 1975:95 (on *thiasoi*) and 101–44 (on the Epicurean and Stoic schools). See further Mason and Heuchan–Richardson in this volume.
8 See particularly Kloppenborg 1993. He notes the terminological links, especially between churches and collegia, while noting the plethora of terms connected with ancient associations.
9 See further Kloppenborg 1993:224–30; and the important discussion of Smith 1990.
10 See, in addition to Richardson's references, Kraabel 1987 (repr. 1992b).
11 See Kloppenborg 1993, esp. 231–38. Also Wilken 1984:44.
12 See below, p. 160.
13 White 1991a:6.
14 Throughout this paragraph I am indebted to the fine paper delivered early in the seminar by Lorne L. Dawson, "Reflections on Sociological Theories of Sects and New Religious Movements," the bulk of which was subsequently published as Dawson 1992.
15 Some of the problems of applying sectarian concepts to early Christianity are discussed by Holmberg 1990:77–117.
16 See the examples considered by A. J. Blasi in his comparison of new religious movements with early Christianity in Blasi 1989:189–96. He also notes that they range from local to international organizations.
17 For example, P. Lond. 2710 (first century BCE; Egypt [Zeus Association]), pointed out to me by John Kloppenborg.
18 For examples see Kloppenborg 1993:234–36.
19 Culpepper 1975:110-11, 129-30. On Musonius see Klassen 1984. Mason suggests (but without documentation) that women played a prominent role in the schools.
20 On the size of collegia and their connection with households see Kloppenborg (in this volume). Also Maier 1991:15-28.
21 Sills 1968:373. He notes that in some instances (in Africa for example) rapid detribalization and urbanization may spur the establishment of compensatory social groups.

2

COLLEGIA AND *THIASOI*

Issues in function, taxonomy and membership

John S. Kloppenborg

INTRODUCTION

The term "collegium" compasses two main types of associations, the official Roman sacerdotal colleges and sacred sodalities on the one hand, and private associations on the other. The distinctions between the two types are both legal and social. The sacerdotal colleges and sacred sodalities were established by an act of the senate or imperial edict and frequently had important competences and responsibilities within the apparatus of government. They also drew upon the elite for their members. By contrast, private associations had no official functions as instruments of government; their existence was tolerated rather than encouraged; and their membership was for the most part drawn from the non-elite: freedmen, slaves, *peregrini* and resident aliens.

To the first type of collegium belong the four principal priestly colleges (*sacerdotum quattuor summa collegia*; Suetonius, *Augustus* 100):

1   the *collegium pontificum*, which from the time of Julius Caesar consisted of six-teen members, and throughout most of the principate had the emperor as Pontifex Maximus;[1]
2   the *Augures*, also consisting of sixteen members and responsible for determin-ing the advisability of public actions;[2]
3   the *XV viri sacris faciundis*, fifteen in number (since the time of Sulla) and charged with the custody of the Sibylline books and the supervision of for-eign cults;[3] and
4   the *VII viri epulones* who retained this name even after Julius Caesar increased their number to ten[4] and who oversaw various public festivals.[5]

There were in addition several lesser priestly colleges or *sodalitates*: the *Fetiales*, responsible for treaties and declarations of war,[6] the ancient *Fratres Arvales* which had been revived by Augustus about 21 BCE and whose twelve members were drawn from senatorial families, the *Salii* (priests of Mars) and the *Luperci* who officiated at the Lupercalia festival in February. After the death of Augustus in 14 CE the *sodales Augustales* was founded, patterned on an older and rather ob-scure *sodales Titi*,[7] and this provided the precedent for the formation of other minor priestly colleges following the deaths of Claudius (*sodales Aug. Claudiales*), Vespasian (*sodales Flaviales*) and Hadrian (*sodales Hadrianales*).

The important distinction between the *Augustales* and the other priestly colleges was that the *Augustales* were open to freedmen, who were barred from the other collegia as well as from the magistracies and cities councils. This college afforded a means by which successful freedmen could receive honours comparable with those accorded to decurions and magistrates: they had the right to special seats at public events, to carry the insignia of authority and to wear the *toga praetexta*.[8] From Ostia alone there are over 200 names of *Augustales* who were freedmen also belonging to guilds of woodworkers, barge operators, grain merchants, millers, and of the imperial house.[9]

The *sodalitates sacrae* represent a slightly different form of official collegium charged with matters of the public cult. The members of these collegia were not called priests but *cultores*. While in the earlier period of the republic these sodalities seem to have been identified with various families (*gentes*), they were later organized either by profession or by physical location. An example of the first type is the *collegium mercatorum* or *Mercurialium*, perhaps composed of merchants in whose care the rites were celebrated in the temple of Mercury at the foot of the Aventine Hill.[10] To the second type belonged the *collegium Capitolinorum*, which put on the games in honour of Jupiter Capitolinus and which consisted of residents of the Capitol hill.[11]

A parallel distinction may be made for Greek associations, between the small groups (*thiasoi*) that comprised some or all of the Attic phratries (kinship groups)[12] and the numerous associations that existed outside civic organizations, and often among the metic population of Greek cities.

PRIVATE ASSOCIATIONS

Voluntary associations – *collegia* in Latin, *thiasoi, koina, orgeones, eranoi*, and a variety of other terms in Greek – are essentially phenomena of the Hellenistic period, of the urban centres and of the urban poor. Although the mention of *hieron orgeones* and *thiasotai* in Solon's laws indicates that associations were in existence in sixth-century Athens,[13] it was the age after Alexander that witnessed the striking proliferation of these associations. The evidence is widespread. Inscriptions are extant from virtually every locale in the ancient world and from every period from the fourth century BCE to the later Roman Empire. This suggests that voluntary associations represented a cultural institution integral to Hellenistic and Roman society where they played a significant role in mediating various kinds of social exchange.

The reasons for the growth of such associations are not especially difficult to grasp. The ties that bound a citizen to the polis were weakened by the relative ease of travel and by the diminished influence that local inhabitants had over their own affairs. Significant dislocations of persons resulted from the establishment of trading conventicles in foreign territories, from the slave markets, and from the Roman practice of settling veterans in cities near the frontiers. Each of these forces separated individuals and groups from their *patriae* and created the need for social arrangements that would replace the older structures of the family, the deme, the tribe, and the polis. It might be said that voluntary associations compensated for the demise of the importance of the polis by imitating civic structures. The association afforded each member a say in who joined the group and how the group was run, fellowship and conviviality, and perhaps the opportunity to become an officer or magistrate – in short, to participate in a *cursus honorum* to which he or she could never aspire outside of the association.

TAXONOMY

It is especially difficult to arrive at a clear taxonomy of associations in the Hellenistic and imperial periods. This is due in part to a rather bewildering array of terms used in both Greek and Latin to designate these organizations, coupled with a striking lack of consistency on the part of ancient authors in the use of the terms. For example, the terms *factio* and *coetus* are normally used pejoratively in contexts that imply political subversion.[14] Tertullian, however, refers to the gathering of Christians as a *coetio Christianorum* and *factio Christiana* and expressly promotes these associations as *licitae factiones* (*Apol.* 38.1; 39.1, 20). At least one other association referred to itself as a *factio artium* (*CIL* X 3479). Such vagaries make difficult any meaningful distinctions among the terms. The difficulties of taxonomy are exacerbated by the fact that in a very large number of instances, all that is known of an association is its name. We are left to guess as to what members did at their meetings or what benefits they derived from membership. A further complicating factor is that in some cases our informants were not members of the associations about which they speak. It is not always clear, for example, that the way in which a Roman jurist such as Marcianus or an emperor such as Trajan understood the purpose and functioning of a collegium would coincide significantly with how the collegium thought of itself.

It is usual in discussing Roman private associations to distinguish three types: funerary collegia (*collegia tenuiorum*), religious clubs (*collegia sodalicia*) and professional associations. In Greek, the terminology is extremely varied, but one can at least distinguish religious clubs and professional associations. As sensible as these distinctions seem, closer inspection indicates that often the boundaries are blurred and the nomenclature misleading. In a sense, most, perhaps all, associations were "religious" inasmuch as piety was fully embedded in other dimensions of ancient culture.[15] It is true that some collegia used such names as the Poseidoniastai, Dionysiastai or Asclepiastai without adding any additional qualifications such as "the association (*koinon*) of the Beirut Poseidoniast wholesale merchants, shippers and receivers."[16] But the lack of qualifying terms does not necessarily imply that the collegium in question had mainly cultic interests. A comparison of two inscriptions from associations of Zeus illustrates the problem. The first, from Philadelphia (Lydia) in the second or first century BCE, describes the activities of a cult association which include monthly sacrifices, purifications, "mysteries," a strict code of conduct, and the ritual touching of the college's stele.[17] But to judge from the *lex collegii* of the guild of Zeus Hypsistos in Heracleopolis [Egypt] from perhaps fifty years later,[18] the cultic functions of this ostensibly religious guild did not go much beyond the usual prayers and libations prior to the more serious matter of drinking.

Terminology can also be misleading when it comes to professional associations. These collegia no less than religious clubs honored the appropriate deities. A woodcutters' guild (*collegium dendrophorum*), for instance, would naturally have as its patronal deity Silvanus (for example, the *cultores Silvani dendrophori, CIL* VI 642 [97 CE]) or the Great Mother (for example, *collegium dendrophorum Matris deum m(agnae) I(daeae) et Attis, CIL* VI 641 [time of Hadrian]). However, it would be a mistake to conclude from the fact that professional associations were organized on the basis of a common economic pursuit, that these collegia had as their primary purpose the control of wages or the monopolization of trade sectors, or any other economic goal. Of this there is little evidence. Professional collegia were almost entirely local; although *collegia dendrophorum* were perhaps to be found in every city of the empire, there is no indication of trans-local linkages. At most the association might extend over an island or a nome in Egypt (Tod 1932:81).[19]

The benefits sought by professional collegia were for the most part unconnected with their work. These included above all patronage in support of the common meals. And perhaps a wealthy patron might be persuaded to purchase buildings for the group's meetings or a common burial ground. As Ramsay MacMullen observes, collegia were more interested in the pursuit of honour than of economic advantage (1974:76).

This statement might be qualified, if only slightly, by fragmentary evidence which suggests that at least on some occasions, collegia withdrew services or rioted, probably in order to protest at wage or commodity price changes. A bakers' strike at Ephesus (*c.* 200 CE) evidently led to a riot and to a proconsular restriction on factitious meetings: "Therefore I order the bakers not to hold meetings as a faction nor to be leaders in recklessness."[20] The action of the bakers seems not to have been directed at employers or owners in the manner of modern industrial action, but was instead a more generalized expression of grievance, perhaps about grain or bread prices.[21] Two other inscriptions attest to threats of work stoppage on public buildings at Pergamon (mid II CE),[22] and Miletus (II CE).[23] In the latter instance, which takes the form of an oracular question and response from Didyma, it would appear that the contractors responsible for the arches and vaulting over the columns were concerned that they might incur a loss owing to poor supervision of the project, and enquire of the oracle whether they should abandon their work and seek other employment. The oracle, needless to say, counsels against a withdrawal of services and suggests instead the employment of an expert adviser along with sacrifices to Athena (the patroness of skills) and Heracles. But such evidence of "industrial action" is sparse and does not gainsay the conclusion that although collegia might occasionally exert pressure on civic governance, their *raison d'être* was not principally economic but social.

Collegia tenuiorum (collegia funeraticia)

Funerary collegia raise a special set of questions. For obvious reasons, no collegium identified itself as a *collegium tenuiorum*; that designation derives from the jurist Marcianus.[24] Instead, they invoked the names of their gods (for example, *cultores Dianae et Antinoi, collegium salutare Dianae et Antinoi, CIL* XIV 2112 [136 CE]) or their masters or benefactors (for example, *collegium magnum tribunorum divae Augustae, CIL* VI 4305 [time of Claudius]). It is for this reason that a few authors (Kornemann; Waszink) treat funerary collegia as a sub-type of religious clubs.

Since Mommsen it has been usual to argue that *collegia tenuiorum* received a general concession from the Senate which permitted them to constitute themselves without individual approval so long as they abided by certain restrictions.[25] The principal basis for this conclusion is the striking similarity between Marcianus' references to imperial mandates and provincial directives on the formation of collegia for the indigent[26] and the *lex collegii* of the *cultores Dianae et Antinoi* from Lanuvium and dated at 136 CE.[27] This important inscription not only provides a set of by-laws and feast days of the society, but quotes a *senatusconsultum*:

> Clause from the *Senatusconsultum* of the Roman People:
> These are permitted to assemble, convene, and maintain a society: those who desire to make monthly contributions for funerals may assemble in such a society, but they may not assemble in the name of such a society except once a month for the sake of making contributions to provide burial for the dead.

Waltzing has convincingly argued that the words "quibus coire convenire collegiumque habere liceat" make sense only if they are taken as introducing a general regulation rather than a special dispensation of the Senate. If the Lanuvium association had received a special Senate permission, this surely would have been mentioned specifically (1895–1900, 1:143).

More problematic is the issue of the dating of this *senatusconsultum*. Waltzing took the view that this law was in effect since the early principate and probably from the time of Augustus.[28] As evidence he pointed to the existence of funerary collegia in Rome and the Italian peninsula during the first century, arguing that this creates the presumption that they were officially permitted.[29] Unfortunately, the concession formula, *quibus ex S. C. coire licet*, is not attested prior to the second quarter of the second century.[30] Moreover, a careful examination of the inscriptions that Waltzing cites shows that none falls clearly into the class of a *collegium tenuiorum*: three appear to be connected with the imperial cult (*CIL* X 1238; VI 471; VI 958) and had a mainly religious function, as Waltzing himself later admits,[31] one was evidently a college of timber dealers (*collegium Silvani: CIL*

X 444) and the nature of the other two is unclear (*conlegium pietatis*: *CIL* XII 286; conlegium honoris et virtutis: *CIL* XII 4371). It is *possible*, even likely, that they arranged burial for their members; but that does not necessarily mean that this was their *raison d'être*.

Waltzing's conclusion is in part based upon the supposition that many collegia devoted to a divinity, all collegia which employ the term *salutare* in their name, and most which designate members as *cultores* were in fact funerary. He concluded that in the long run most colleges assumed a funerary function as their principal role. Even in the case of religious collegia:

> comme tous les collèges, ils songèrent en même temps aux funérailles, et, plus tard, ce qui était l'accessoire devint le principal: le culte céda le pas aux funérailles sans jamais disparaître.[32]

Waltzing is not the only advocate of this. Kornemann, following Schiess (1888), argued that a variety of names disguised funerary collegia. All associations which are named for a divinity, all which use the epithet *salutare*, all *collegia domestica* consisting of slaves or freedmen, all *collegia familiae publicae*, and probably the *collegia iuvenum* (1901:388). The difficulty with this is, as Waszink (1978:108) rightly notes, that there is no epigraphical or literary evidence to support this supposition nor, indeed, is there much clear evidence of first-century collegia representing themselves as *primarily* funerary.

With regard to the Lanuvium inscription Eliachevitch points out that the fact that the paragraph (*kaput*) of the *senatusconsultum* dealing with *collegia tenuiorum* is quoted in full suggests that it was at the time something of a novelty. He infers from this that it must have come into force only slightly before the founding of the collegium in 133 CE.[33] Two facts could be adduced in support of his conclusion. First, none of the later inscriptions that employ the concession formula follows the example of the Lanuvium collegium in citing the entire paragraph of the *senatusconsultum*; for the period after 133 it was apparently sufficient to use the abbreviation, "quibus coire convenire collegiumque habere liceat."[34] And second, Trajan's letters to Pliny in regard to the petition of Amiseni (*Epistulae* 10.93) and the *collegium fabri* in Nicomedia (*Epistulae* 10.34) reveal an extreme reluctance to permit *any* associations in the territories in which Roman law applied. He forbade the *collegium fabri* even though they were to serve the customary function of firefighters, and allowed the Amiseni to assemble only because Roman law did *not* apply to them, and then only with the proviso that they meet for the purpose of assisting the indigent. It is with Hadrian and his reforms of the legal system[35] that there seems to be a loosening of Trajan's restrictions. Perhaps significantly, it is in the period after Hadrian that most of the *collegia salutare* are found.[36]

What I am suggesting is that during the first century, *collegia tenuiorum* did not exist as such, although, to be sure, many, perhaps most, associations took care of the burial of their members. It was only with Hadrian that the notion of a collegium established *solely* for the sake of burial entered the realm of Roman law.

That it was something of a legal fiction, exploited by groups who for other reasons wished to meet, is tacitly admitted by Waltzing[37] and confirmed by the contents of the Lanuvium inscription. While the first part of the *lex* deals with the rights and obligations of the collegium in matters pertaining to the deaths of members, about one-half deals with the schedule of banquets and etiquette at festive occasions. Although the *senatusconsultum* restricted meetings to one per month and stipulated that the meetings were for the purpose of making the monthly contribution, it is clear that several of their meetings were banquets in which business was not transacted.[38] It is even possible that banquets were held in addition to the monthly business meetings.[39] Samuel Dill comments that it did not take much ingenuity to multiply occasions for feasts by honoring the birthdays of the collegium's gods, its various patrons and perhaps the emperor too (1905:259).

The collegium of Aesculapius and Hygia from Rome (153 CE)[40] provides an even better example of an association with a nominal funerary function. There is only one reference to burial in the lengthy inscription, no indication of monthly dues, and no details of the conditions under which burial grants were made. Instead, the attention is focused upon the periodic banquets and the distribution of bread, wine, and money from the sum of 25,000 sesterces given the association by its benefactors, Marcellina and her brother (?) P. Aelius Zeno. For their part the benefactors were assured perpetual and grateful remembrance of her husband, Flavius Apollonius, an imperial procurator, and the collegium members enjoyed regular gifts of from 1–6 denarii (depending upon rank in the collegium) and regular banquets and social occasions.

To view the phenomenon of so-called *collegia tenuiorum* in this way relieves one of the anomalies produced when one compares Greek and Roman associations. Both Erich Ziebarth and Franz Poland observed that associations devoted *solely* to the burial of members and the collection of monies for that purpose are unattested in Greek.[41] This observation has been confirmed more recently in P. M. Fraser's study of Rhodian funerary monuments, which attest to the widespread existence of professional, religious, and gentilitial associations (*koina*) that saw to the burial of their members and often owned burial-grounds, but not to the existence of *collegia funeraticia*.[42]

Thus the usual classification of collegia by their supposed principal activities appears problematic, and we must, it seems, be prepared for a messy taxonomy. The principal activities of an association with a theophoric name might range from cultic (in the case of the Zeus association from Philadelphia) to social; the professional collegia seem to have been mainly social clubs which perhaps on rare occasions flexed some political muscle.[43] But one cannot in principle exclude the possibility that professional collegia occasionally leaned in the direction of cultic associations too. Both kinds of clubs might take responsibility for the burial of members although this was not likely to have been their sole purpose prior to the time of Hadrian, and even after Hadrian the notion of a funerary collegium was probably something of a legal fiction.[44]

MEMBERSHIP

Perhaps a better taxonomy of collegia would be based on the profile of their membership, especially since the actual functions of various collegia overlapped to a substantial degree. It would seem that the majority of associations, with the exception of the priestly sodalities, were composed of the urban poor, slaves, and freedmen.

The most basic locus of organization was in the household itself. We have inscriptions from several hundred *collegia domestica* associated with the imperial household, the house of Livia, and various private households. Many of these inscriptions take the form of funerary monuments bearing a formula such as:

Ex domo Scriboniae Caesar(is) libertorum libertar(umque) et qui in hoc monument(um) contulerunt.

(CIL VI 26032 [I BCE or CE])

What these domestic collegia did besides arranging the burial of their members is not always clear, although they, like other voluntary associations, elected persons to magistracies and other positions of honour,[45] and conferred special honours upon their own members and upon benefactors (normally the master or mistress of the household). Pliny remarks of his own slaves and *liberti/ae*, "nam servis res publica quadam et quasi civitas domus est" ("for slaves the household takes the place of city and commonwealth," *Epistulae* 8.16). The civic honours and achievements from which they were legally debarred were available to them within the association. It was also probably to the advantage of masters and mistresses of large households to permit their slaves and freedmen to organize collegia. This would effectively discourage them from joining outside associations in which the owner might not have much influence. Such was probably the case with the household "collegium quod est in domo Sergiae L(uci) f(iliae) Paullinae" from which a series of inscriptions, all of them funerary, come.[46] The similarity between this (apparently technical) phrase and the *hē kat' oikon autōn ekklēsia* which occurs in the Pauline corpus (Rom. 16:5, Col. 4:15) allows the possibility that some of Paul's churches began as domestic collegia.

Professional associations are widely attested in both Greek and Latin. Although Numa (715–673 BCE) is said to have founded Roman *koinōnia* and *synodoi* of artisans as a means of breaking down national rivalries (Plutarch, *Numa* 17), they proliferated almost uncontrollably in the Hellenistic and imperial periods. Among Poland's list of 1,200 associations and Waltzing's almost 2,500 collegia, many fall into the class of associations organized around a common profession. The degree to which the state had an interest in the organization of certain collegia is disputed: Waltzing took the view that collegia enjoyed no special privileges,[47] but Rostovtzeff has pointed out that those connected with the grain trade in Rome – grain shippers (*navicularii*), merchants (*negotiatores*) and measurers (*mensores frumentarii*), longshoremen (*lenuncularii*), and shipwrights (*fabri navales*) – were probably recognized as agents of the state.[48] Certainly, Claudius favored the *negotiatores frumentarii* by insuring them against losses at sea, and the *fabri navales* by exemption from the Lex Papia Poppaea, citizenship, and, in the case of women, application of the *ius trium liberorum*.[49] Additionally, the associations of carpenters (*fabri*), rag dealers (*centonarii*) and timber cutters (*dendrophori*), collectively known as the *collegia tria* or *collegia omnia*, normally served as firefighters (except in Rome) and it was to the state's obvious advantage to provide for (and regulate) such organizations, as Pliny's correspondence with Trajan indicates. Finally, as has already been noted, many of the members of these guilds became *Augustales*, which suggests something more than tolerance on the part of the state. However, other Roman guilds and the numerous associations in the East were tolerated or ignored.

Membership in professional associations was probably not only a function of common profession, but also of location. In cities of the empire, crafts and trades tended to cluster for quite practical reasons, with the result that streets and squares often bore the names of the trades practiced there.[50] This meant on the one hand that the claim of a collegium to be "the entire craft of carpenters" (*lignari universi*, *CIL* IV 960) was probably not far wrong,[51] and, on the other, that occasionally someone might belong to a guild in virtue of his location rather than his trade.[52] If the descriptions in Acts are regarded as Lukan idealizations,[53] it is quite conceivable that Paul regularly began his activities in the context of the local tentmaker's guild. Indeed Acts 18:3 uses the term *homotechnon* which is attested along with *synergasia* and *syntechnia* in conjunction with professional guilds (Poland 1909:122).

As I have noted above, professional associations seem to have served a mainly social function although, like domestic collegia, they too often saw to the burial of their members. In some instances, the collegium owned a burial plot and members who were in good standing could be buried there by permission of the club's decurion.[54] In some instances it would appear that the burial place was privately owned, but managed and policed by the guild to which the deceased belonged. Such is the case in an inscription from Ephesus about the time of Claudius:

> This tomb and the area around it and the subterranean vault belongs to M. Antonius Hermeias, silversmith, and Claudia daughter of Erotion, his wife. No one is to be put in this tomb except the aforementioned. If anyone does dare to put in a corpse or to excise this text, he shall pay the silversmiths at Ephesus 1,000 denarii. Responsibility for this tomb rests with the association (*synedrion*) of silversmiths, and Erotion dedicated 50,000 denarii. The legacy was provided in the 6th month, on the appointed day.[55]

Membership in professional guilds is likely to have been relatively homogeneous not only with respect to the trade and the quarter of the city from which members were drawn, but also with respect to gender. Whereas domestic collegia clearly had women members, the evidence for the presence of women in professional associations is ambiguous. There were, of course, some collegia composed solely of women, for example the *sociae mimae* (*CIL* VI 10109). It has normally been assumed that, for obvious reasons, there were few, if any, women in artisan guilds.[56] That did not prevent women from patronizing such associations, however. An inscription from Regium Julium (Calabria) dated to 79 CE provides a good example:

> Ob munificientiam earum quae dendrophoros honoraverunt honos decretus est eis q(uae) i(nfra) s(criptae) s(unt): Claudia Justa [. . .]iva sac(erdos) S[. . .]ia Faustina sac(erdos), Sicin [.]ivocepta, Amullia Primigenia, Satria Pietas, Claudia Ptolemais, Terentia Athenais.
>
> (*CIL* X 7)[57]

The ambiguity arises because of the occurrence of the title *mater collegii* in connection with professional guilds.[58] While Liebenam thought that the titles *pater* and *mater* were equivalent to *patronus* and *patrona* (1890:218), there is no real evidence of this. Waltzing prefers the view that the titles are purely honorific, given to persons of the same social standing as those in the collegium.[59] The difficulty with this view is that in the collegium of Aesculapius and Hygia, for example, the *pater* and *mater* are mentioned in the list of persons to whom special distributions are made on feast days. They are named after the *quinquennalis* and before the *immunes* and *curatores*, which implies that they are members of the collegium in some official position (*CIL* VI 10234.10–12).[60] It is possible that the titles *mater* and *pater* functioned differently in professional associations than they did in cultic collegia, but until unequivocal evidence of this is forthcoming the strong possibility remains that even in professional guilds women were both members and officials.

The most inclusive type of voluntary association was probably the collegium organized around the cult of a deity. The association of Zeus in Philadelphia describes its membership with the formula "men and women, freeborn and slaves (*oiketai*)."[61] This is not to say that every such group had this policy: some associations were restricted to a particular ethnic group or gender; some were restricted to women,[62] while in others women served only as priestesses but did not seem to belong to the general membership.[63]

There is considerable variability in the size of collegia. Poland's survey of collegia in and outside Attica from the fourth century BCE to the third century of the common era indicates that most collegia ranged between 15 and 100 members. Some professional associations from Rome and Ostia register numbers between 200–300,[64] surprising perhaps in view of Pliny's assurances that the *collegium fabrum* in Nicomedia would be limited to 150. But most of the Ostian collegia were connected with the grain trade (either *lenuncularii* or *fabres navales*) and it is perhaps correct to conclude with Rostovtzeff that such associations had a special relation to the state and enjoyed certain exemptions and privileges. It would appear that most other collegia had fewer than 100 members.[65]

ORGANIZATION

As has already been mentioned, the organization of Roman voluntary associations was normally patterned on that of the city and the army. It is quite common to find collegia divided into *centuriae* or *decuriae* although these terms had apparently lost their numeric significations. In many collegia, the group of decurions functioned as the administrative body. Other associations appear to have had a more differentiated leadership, with *magistri* or *quinquennales* as the highest positions, then other officials variously named *mater collegii, pater collegii, curator, honoratus, immunis, quaestor, sacerdos* and *scriba*. Where lists of officials (*album*) are extant, they normally begin with the patrons, but they, presumably, were in many instances only nominal members of the collegium. It is of interest, however, that patrons of collegia were often senators (in Rome) or civic officials or civic patrons (in other cities) which at least informally tied the collegia to the interests of the polis.[66]

The leadership of Greek associations was even more varied. In cultic associations the titles *hiereus, archiereus, archimystēs* and *archithiasitēs* (or *thiasarchēs*) are common. In a more general sense, the president of an association could be called the *archisynagōgos* or *epimelētēs*. The term *prostatēs* (or *epistatēs*) is found in several senses. Occasionally, *prostatēs* is found in the sense of the Latin *patronus*;[67] but more often it connotes an official of the collegium itself, especially in Egypt.[68] There are in addition a large number of titles – *patēr, matēr, presbys, tamias, grammateus, hypēretēs, diakonos* – and a host of more specialized terms. In general it would appear that Greek associations, though they had much more varied terminology for leaders than Latin collegia, tended towards a smaller group of leaders, in some cases having only a single president/patron.[69]

CONCLUSION

In classifying Greek and Roman voluntary associations it seems most appropriate to distinguish them on the basis of their respective membership bases, rather than by their ostensible functions. Thus we arrive at three groupings: those associated with a household, those formed around a common trade (and civic locale), and those formed around the cult of a deity. It is likely that burial of members was a task undertaken by many of these collegia, but their primary purposes were more likely to have been social or cultic. As a polis writ small, the collegium provided a social setting in which persons who normally could never aspire to participation in the *cursus honorum* of the city and state could give and receive honors, enjoy the ascribed status that came with being a *quinquennalis* or *mater*, have a feeling of control over at least the destiny of the collegium, and enjoy regular banquets. The collegium, whether domestic, professional, or cultic, also afforded the elite an opportunity to display largesse in the form of benefactions given to collegia. The collegia involved would then be expected to reciprocate by honoring and, perhaps more than occasionally, supporting the interests of their patron/a. And in the case of the professional associated with municipal services and especially the grain trade, collegia became invaluable instruments of the state. The collegium, therefore, provided not only an effective means by which to structure social relationships within the mass of urban poor, but it also served the equally crucial function of mediating relationships between the enormous body of non-elite and the tiny aristocratic elite in the cities of the empire.

NOTES

1 Livy, *Periocha* 89; Dio Cassius 42.51.4; 51.20. The number of *pontifices* had gradually increased from five (Cicero, *De Republica* 2.26) to eight or nine (Livy 10.6.6) to fifteen.
2 Livy 10.6.7–8 and *Periocha* 89; Dio Cassius 42.51.4.
3 Tacitus, *Annales* 3.64 (*quindecemviri*); Livy 6.37.12 (*decemviri*).
4 Dio Cassius 43.51.9; Tacitus, *Annales* 3.64.
5 See in general, Kornemann 1901:380–480, esp. 381–83; Waltzing 1895–1900, 1:34–35.
6 Livy 36.3.7; Cicero, *De Legibus* 2.21; Tacitus, *Annales* 3.64.
7 Tacitus, *Annales* 1.54; Suetonius, *Claudius*, 6. Tacitus connects the *sodales Titi* with the Sabine king Titus Tatius but little else is known of them.
8 Garnsey and Saller 1987:121.
9 Frank 1940, 5:246; Waltzing 1895–1900, 4:214–16.
10 Livy 2.27.5; Ovid, *Fasti* 5.669–93; Cicero, *Epistulae ad Quintum fratrem* 2.5.2. See Kornemann 1901:384; Waltzing 1895–1900, 1:35. A full study in now available by Combet-Farnoux 1980. That the *Mercurales* had any connection with merchants is doubted by Fisher 1988b:1200.
11 Livy 5.50.4; 52.11; Cicero, *Epistulae ad Quintum fratrem* 2.5.2.
12 Poland 1909:18-20; Schmitt-Pantel 1990:205.
13 The text is preserved in Gaius' commentary on the Law of the Twelve Tables (*Digesta* 47.22.4). *Hetairiai* (political clubs) played a role in the turmoil at the time of the Peloponnesian War (Thucydides 3.82).
14 Sallust, *Jugurtha* 31: "haec inter bonos amicitia, inter malos factio est." Pliny, *Epistulae* 10.34: "eas civitas eiusmodi factionibus esse vexatas." Tertullian, *Apologia* 40: "illis nomen factioni accommodandum est qui in odium bonorum et proborum conspirant." See Waltzing 1895–1900, 1:134–35.
15 See, for example, Poland 1909:5–6. On the issue of "religion" as an embedded aspect of culture, see Malina 1986b:92–101.
16 From Delos: *ID* 1520 (153/52 BCE); *ID* 1774 (*c.* 110 BCE); *ID* 1778 (after 88 BCE). On associations on Delos, see McLean in this volume.
17 Dittenberger, *Syll*[3] 985; see Barton and Horsley 1981:7–41.
18 P. Lond. 2710; see Nock *et al.* 1936.
19 While there is little to suggest extra-local links between professional associations, there are some important exceptions. Richard Ascough points out associations of traders and shippers naturally might have connections with other associations in other locales. More importantly, he adduces decrees of *thiasotai* of Bendis in Salamis and Piraeus which seem to suggest connections between these two cult associations, and IG X/2 255 (first/second century CE) which indicates a relationship between a Sarapis association in Opus and one

in Thessalonica. Some of the groups of Dionysiac artists also claimed to be "universal" or "worldwide" (*oikoumenē*; cf. I Ephesus 22.)

20 The inscription was published by Buckler 1923:30–31 (cf. *SEG* IV 512). An improved edition (I Eph. 215) is available in Wankel and Engelmann 1979–84, no. 215.

21 The price of grain had been regulated at least since the time of Augustus (Suetonius, *Augustus* 42). Further adjustments were made by Tiberius (Tacitus, *Annales* 2.87) and Nero (ibid. 15.39) and Diocletian. On the latter see Graser 1933–40, 5:305–421.

22 Buckler 1923:33.

23 Buckler 1923:34–35; Pleket 1964:34 (no. 20).

24 *Digesta* 47.22.3.2: "servos quoque licet in collegio tenuiorum recipi volentibus dominis" ("It is legal for slaves to be admitted to a collegium of the indigent with the consent of their owners"). A century earlier, Trajan's response to the request of the Amiseni to establish an *eranos* uses similar vocabulary: "possumus . . . non impedire, eo facilius, si tali collatione, non ad turbae et illicitos coetus, sed ad sustinendam tenuiorum inopiam utuntur" ("We cannot oppose it; especially if [the] contributions are employed, not for the purpose of riot and faction, but for the support of the indigent") (Pliny, *Epistulae* 10.93).

25 Mommsen 1843:87–91; Kornemann 1901:410; Waltzing 1895–1900, 1:141–53; Waszink 1978:106.

26 *Digesta* 47.22.1: "Mandatis principalibus praecipitur praesidibus procinciarum, ne patiantur esse collegia sodalicia neve militis collegia in castris habeant. Sed permittitur tenioribus stipen menstruam conferre, dum tamen semel in mense coeant, ne sub praetextu huiusmodi illicitum collegium coeat."

27 *CIL* XIV 2112; Waltzing 1895–1900, 3:642–46; ET, Lewis and Reinhold 1966b:273–75.

28 Waltzing 1895–1900, 1:148. He is followed by La Piana 1927:241.

29 *CIL* X 1238 (Nola, time of Augustus): Laurinienses cultores Augusti; *CIL* VI 471 (Rome; 68 CE): imaginum domus Augustae cultores; (see also *CIL* VI 958 [Rome; 108 CE]: cultores Larum et Imaginum domus Augustae); *CIL* X 444 (Lucania, time of Domitian): collegium Silvani; *CIL* XII 286 (Gallia Narbonensis, early I CE): conlegium pietatis; *CIL* XII 4371 (Gallia Narbonensis, early I CE): conlegium honoris et virtutis; *CIL* XIV 3659 (Tibur, early I CE): collegium.

30 In Rome: *CIL* VI 85 (198): me(n)sor(es) mach(niarii) f(rumenti) p(ublici); *ILS* 4075 (206 CE): collegi(um) dendrophor(um); *CIL* VI 1872 (206 CE): corp(us) piscatorum et urinatorum; outside Rome: *CIL* XIV 168, 169, 256 (Ostia, 195 CE): corpus fabrorum navalium Ostiensium; *CIL* XIV 10: corpus pell(ionum) (Ostia, II CE); CIL IX 2213 (Telesia, early III CE): colleg(ium) fabrum tignuar(iorum); *CIL* X 1642 (Puteoli, 139 CE): collegium scabillariorum; *CIL* X 1647 (Puteoli, 161 CE) scabillariores; *CIL* X 3699, 3700 (Cumae, 251 CE): dendrophori; *CIL* V 7881 (Provincia Alpium Maritimarum, early III CE) collegial tria = collegia fabrum centonariorum dendrophororum.
    A similar formula from more than a century before (first century BCE) is, however, attested in an inscription quoting the *Lex Iulia*: "Dis Manibus. Collegio symphoniacorum qui sacris publicis praestu sunt, quibus senatus c(oire) c(onvocari) c(ogi) permisit e lege Iulia ex auctoritate Aug(usti) ludorum causa" (*CIL* VI 2193 = *ILS* 4966). It is doubtful, however, whether the *Lex Iulia* applied outside Rome. See Liebenam 1890:32, 225–26: "Das julische Gesetz wurde später für das übrige Italien und die Provinzen ebenfalls giltig erklärt; der Zeitpunkt dieser Erweiterung ist nicht zu bestimmen, ebensowenig ist mit Sicherheit zu sagen, ob dieselbe durch ein allgemeines Reichsgesetzt oder, was wahrscheinlicher ist, durch schrittweise erlassene Verfügungen geschah."

31 Waltzing 1895–1900, 1:263: "on trouve, au commencement du premier siècle, des *cultores* qui paraissent exclusivement associés pour le culte; tels sont les *Cultores Aug(usti) Laurinienses* qui existaient à Nola, sous le règne d'Auguste."

32 Waltzing 1895–1900, 1:260–63. Similarly, La Piana 1927:237–38.

33 Eliachevitch 1942:261–62. His argument is accepted by Waszink 1978:107.

34 See above, n. 30.

35 See the paper by Cotter 1989:19–21 (and in this volume). Of particular significance is *BGU* 1074 (Oxyrhynchus, 275 CE), which indicates that Hadrian reviewed and reconfirmed the privileges of an association of Dionysos after it had been established by Augustus and reconfirmed by Tiberius.

36 *CIL* XIV 2112 (Lanuvium, 136 CE); VI 338 (159 CE); VI 1013 (Rome, 165–171 CE); XIV 2653 (Tusculum, II CE); Waltzing 1895–1900, 3:313 (no. 1332) (Rome; time of Hadrian); *CIL* VI 404 (Rome, 122 CE); VI 978 (Rome, time of Hadrian). Only *CIL* XII 4449 (Gallia Narbonensis, I CE) comes from the first century and the reading [collegium sa]lutare [f]amilia[e] is based on the restoration of a lacuna. Waltzing (1895–1900, 4:203) also cites *CIL* VI 542 (Rome, 112 CE), but this does not contain the term salutare, while in *CIL* VI 543 (Rome, 115 CE), the term modifies Silvanus: sancti Silvani Salutaris sacrum.

37 Waltzing 1895–1900, 1:150: "Il est possible que bien des collèges d'artisans, peut-être aussi des collèges religieux, s'arbitrèrent sous l'apparence légale de collèges funéraires."

38 *CIL* XIV 2112, 2.23: "Item placuit, si quis quid queri aut referre volet, in conventu referat, ut quieti et hilares diebus sollemnibus epulemur" ("It was voted further that if anyone wishes to make a complaint or to discuss business, he should bring it up at the business meeting so that we may banquet in peace and good cheer on the solemn (festival) days").

39 The inscription from Luciania (*CIL* X 444, time of Domitian) lists two feasts for the month of July (5 Julias, 12 Julias). Waltzing (1895–1900, 1:152 n. 5), following Schiess (1888, n. 339) suggests an emendation of 5 Julias to 5 Junias in order to space the feasts one month apart. This, of course, presupposes that the *senatusconsultum* was in effect under Domitian.

40 *CIL* VI 10234: Lex collegii Aesculapi et Hygiae. See Waltzing 1895–1900, 3:268–71 (no. 1083). This collegium was limited to 60 members.

41 Ziebarth 1896, 17; Poland 1909:56, 503–504.

42 Fraser 1977:58–70, esp. 59–60. Only fragmentary evidence from Rough Cilicia (perhaps mid-first century CE) might be interpreted to imply the existence of associations devoted exclusively to the burial of members. See Bean and Mitford 1970:nos 197, 198, 201, 202, 205. A series of five grave inscriptions indicates a common burial place for several evidently unrelated persons, bearing the customary stipulation that anyone making unauthorized burials is to pay the *koinon* a fine. The editors suggest that the graves belonged to a colony of craftsmen (p. 178). Moreover, the inscriptions mentioning burial were all found *in situ* in a burial plot; this is not the place that an association would be expected to state its rule; obviously, only matters pertaining to burial would be given there.

43 Trajan's letter to Pliny (*Epistulae* 10.34) recalls disturbances in Bithynia provoked by collegia. The nature of the disturbances is unclear. Tacitus' report in *Annales* 14.17 of the dissolution of collegia in Pompeii suggests that they had provoked disturbances at the gladiatorial games.

44 There may, of course, have been exceptions. See the pathetic notice of Artemidorus, magister of the *collegium Jovis Cerneni*, and Valerius, its quaestor, announcing the dissolution of a collegium (*CIL* III 924–27; Alburnus Major, 167 CE). Of the original 54 members, only 17 remained, the co-magister had never attended a meeting, the collegium's coffers were now empty, and its membership had not bothered to attend the prescribed meetings or to contribute their monthly fees. It concludes: "si quis defunctus fuerit, ne putet se collegium habere aut ab eis aliquem petitionem funeris habiturum."

45 The titles *quinquennalis, decurio, sacerdos, honoratus, curator, mater, pater, scriba* are all attested. See Waltzing 1895–1900, 3:162–76.

46 *CIL* VI 9148, 9149, 10260–64; Waltzing 1895–1900, 3:253, 274–75.

47 Waltzing 1895–1900, 1:162–81.

48 Rostovtzeff 1926:148–49, 532.

49 Suetonius, *Claudius* 18.2–19.

29

50 See MacMullen 1974: Appendix A.2 (pp. 132–35.)

51 For other instances see Poland 1909:122; Waltzing 1895–1900, 1:169.

52 See MacMullen 1974:176 n. 61.

53 See Stowers 1984:59–82.

54 The formula "ex permisso decurionum locus datus" acknowledging permission to use a plot for purposes of burial appears in several Roman inscriptions, *CIL* VI 7297, 7303 (58 CE), 7304, 7373, 7379, 7387 – most of them from mid-first-century Rome. See also VI 8744 (Rome, 126 CE). For Greek examples, see Poland 1909:503–505.

55 I Ephesus 2212 (Engelmann 1980: no. 2212); Horsley 1987, 4:7–10.

56 An inscription from Milan (*CIL* V 5869 [III CE]) honors Germanus Stator Marsianus, patron and curator of the *collegium fabrum et centonariorum* and Cissonia Aphrodite his wife, also a patron. It is unclear whether she too was a guild member. See the discussion by Waltzing 1895–1900, 1:348–49.

57 See also *CIL* III 1207; V 4411; IX 2687; IX 5450; XI 1356.

58 *CIL* IX 2687 (*mater collegii centonariorum*); III 7505; XIV 69 (*c. dendrophorum*); XIV 256 (*corporis fabrum navalium*); for other examples see Waltzing 1895–1900, 4:369–70.

59 Waltzing 1895–1900, 1:448; also Kornemann 1901:425.

60 An analogous problem arises in the evaluation of the term *mater synagogi* which, until Brooten's study (1982) was regularly taken to be an honorific title, it being (apparently) self-evident that women could not have served in leadership roles. Brooten's study, and those of van der Horst (1991) and Cohen (1980) have challenged the purely honorific interpretation of this title.

61 *Syll*[3] 985; Barton and Horsley 1981:8–9.

62 Foucart 1873, 5–7; Horsley 1987, 4:15.

63 Poland 1909:292–93.

64 A *collegium fabrum tignuariorum* in Rome in the early third century had a membership of about 1200 (*CIL* VI 1060).

65 See Waltzing 1895–1900, 4:270–80.

66 See also the election slogans from Pompeii, in which various collegia endorse the favorite candidate, presumably one of their patrons. *CIL* IV 206; 113; 710; 960; 826; 864; 336; 677; 743; 497; 7164; 7273; 7473, etc.

67 *IGR I 1114 = Poland 1909:575 (no. B 461, 17* BCE): *ton heauton patrōna kai euergetēn*. The statutes of the Iobacchi (*IG* II[2] 1368; 178 CE) indicate that the patron, the priest and the arch-bacchus had to approve the statutes. See Tod 1932:86. See, now, the list of members of a synagogue published by Reynolds, Tannenbaum and Erim (1987) which mentions a Iael (male or female?) as *prostatēs*. On the issue of gender, see Brooten 1991 and Williams 1992.

68 See San Nicolò 1913–15, 2:95–96; Poland 1909:363–66; Lajtar 1992. For the feminine form, *prostatis*, see, for example, Kayser 1994:224–26 (no. 70; I CE; Alexandria).

69 For example, the association of Zeus in Philadelphia seems to have had only their patron, Dionysos, as a leader.

3

PHILOSOPHIAI
Graeco-Roman, Judean and Christian[1]

Steve Mason

My interest in the philosophical schools of antiquity results from my work on Josephus, for the Judean historian makes a sustained effort to portray Judaism for his Greek and Roman readers as a national philosophy with its own schools. This effort raises at least three questions: (1) What was there about the structure or status of *philosophiai* in antiquity that led Josephus to appropriate this category for Judaism? (2) To what degree was he justified in making such an association? (Did others do so? On what basis?) And (3) if the philosophical connection was part of an apologetic strategy for Josephus, did the same strategy occur to some early Christians? Obviously, such questions raise formidable issues; this paper is a report on work in progress.

We shall look first at the constitution and status of philosophical schools in the Roman empire, then at Judaism as philosophy, and finally at the Christian repudiation and adoption of philosophy as a self-description. We confine our scope to the first two centuries of the common era.[2]

GRAECO-ROMAN SOCIETY

As far as we know, Pythagoras (sixth century BCE) was the first to establish a philosophical school in the sense in which we shall be using the term, as an identifiable group committed to the teachings and manner of life prescribed by the founder.[3] He was followed by Plato, Diogenes, and Aristotle (fourth century), then by Epicurus and Zeno (early third century).[4] Throughout the period of our interest, all of the schools founded by these men continued to flourish, although a broadly conceived "Stoicism" exercised the dominant influence.[5] Our primary concern is not with their distinctive features or metaphysics, however, but with what they had in common – their structural similarities, their social and legal status.

The shape of a philosophy

In the early decades of the third century CE, Diogenes Laertius tried to map out the whole development of Greek philosophy. Others had done so before him, but his is the only effort that has survived. Since he made extensive use of the earlier manuals, we may conclude that his portrayal was fairly typical of current schemes.[6]

A noteworthy feature of those schemes is the depiction of philosophical schools as *diadochai*, or "successions."[7] Already in the second century BCE, several authors undertook to write histories of philosophy and at least four of them chose to call their books *diadochai*.[8] Their claim was that each philosophical school had passed on or handed down (*paradidōmi/tradere*) the original precepts of its founder from one head (*scholarchēs*) to another.[9] Bickerman observes: "The great task of disciples would be to transmit faithfully the teaching of the school" (1980:263). The founders themselves came to be highly revered, sometimes deified, and stories of their miraculous births and deeds circulated widely.[10]

Diogenes, doubtless following his sources, goes so far as to claim that all philosophy can be divided into two different "successions." The Ionian succession, beginning with Thales and Anaximander, includes the pre-Socratics and the Athenians, and culminates in the New Academy and Stoicism; the Italian succession, initiated by Pythagoras, ends with Epicurus (1.13–15). Diogenes also broadly classifies the schools into two classes: the dogmatists, who make assertions, and the sceptics, who suspend judgement (1.16). So the term *diadochē* was commonly used in our period to describe both the entire philosophical programme and the traditions of particular schools.

In the early empire, the succession model for philosophical schools became increasingly appropriate as they largely abandoned not only innovative thinking but even serious attempts at reinterpreting their own traditions; they seem now to have focused their efforts on applying their various traditions to moral philosophy (see, for example, Meredith 1991:288–91). Epictetus and Plutarch are striking examples. This widely noted phenomenon has often been attributed to the Romans' philosophical ineptitude or, less charitably, to their credulity. But Nock argues that some basic Roman social values were fundamentally opposed to radical philosophy:

> The tendency to conservatism [in philosophy] was greatly strengthened by the rise of Rome, which glorified parental authority, the wisdom of age, and the value of ancestral custom, and had a horror of innovation.
>
> (1933:161)

Such values placed the philosophical enterprise in a peculiar social position, as we shall see; the point here is only that in the Roman period the philosophical schools developed fully whatever incipient tendencies they may have had toward conservatism.

This absence of originality did not, however, mean that the schools had no usefulness in the empire. If the aristocracy was not looking for an atmosphere of free investigation and discussion, it did require from philosophy a sure basis for living, a system that would provide some ground for judgements as to right and wrong. So one of Lucian's characters claims that he had gone to the philo-sophers in order to find "a plain, solid path in life" (*hodon haplēn kai bebaion tou biou, Menippus* 4). Plutarch alleges that philosophy, as distinct from superstition, offers a way that is "both safe" (*asphalōs*) and expedient" (*kai sympherontōs, De Superstitione* 171E). And Justin explains that his youthful philosophical quest was only satisfied when he found a "philosophy which is secure and profitable" (*asphalē te kai symphoron, Dial.* 8.1). A key word in the literature of the various schools is *eudaimonia/felicitas* – "good spirits," "well being," or "happiness" – which Aristotle had identified as the chief end (*telos*) of human life.[11] Epictetus complains that people "want the things that conduce to happiness (*ta pros eudai-monia pheronta*) but they are looking for them in the wrong places!" (3.23.34). Each school had its own recipe for *eudaimonia* but many philosophers were pre-pared to say that philosophy in general, the philosophical life, was the way to happiness.[12] In accord with the basic values of imperial Rome, then, philo-sophical schools of our period were less interested in original research than in the "marketing" or dissemination of what they already had: a venerable body of tradition about how to find happiness.

This preoccupation with practical ethics can be illustrated in the various syn-onyms for "philosophical school" that turn up in the literature. In addition to *hairesis* and *secta*, we often find *agōgē* (way), *hodos* (path, road), *askēsis* (discipline), *disciplina*, and, simply, *bios* (life); these terms indicate that philosophy consisted as much in one's actions as in one's beliefs. Joining a philosophical school was not an abstract exercise or simply another activity such as music or farming (Dio 70.1–10); it often involved what Nock calls "conversion": a radical break with one's previous way of living and the resolute adoption of a new path. Dio of Prusa is a famous example of such profound conversion – in his case from out-spoken rhetorical opposition to philosophy.[13] Diogenes (4.16) recounts the story of Polemo, who wandered, drunk, into the lecture-hall of Xenocrates: he was so moved by the philosophical challenge that he threw himself into the new way of living and even became the next head of the school. Something like evangelical fervor drove many philosophers of the day, and the words *epistrophē, conversio*, and *metanoia* routinely characterize the acceptance of philosophy.[14] Epictetus views the lecture hall as a "hospital" for sick souls (3.21.20) and he insists that, if a lecture does not bring about a change in behavior on the part of the hearer, "cutting him to the quick," it has failed in its purpose (3.23.37).[15]

Although the schools differed in their prescriptions for right behavior, there seems to have been a broad consensus that philosophy, any philosophy, helped to inculcate the bedrock social values of piety toward the gods (*eusebeia, pietas*) and justice (*ta dikaia, dikaiosynē, iustitia*) or philanthropy toward humanity.[16] Sometimes, the linking of these two values seems jarring, as in Persius' descrip-tion of the benefits of (Stoic) philosophy:

O poor wretches, learn, and come to know the causes of things, what we are, for what life we are born, what the assigned order is, where the turning point of the course is to be rounded gently, what limit to set on money, for what it is right to pray, what is the use of hard cash, how much you ought to spend on your country and on those near and dear to you, what kind of man god ordered you to be and where as a man you are placed.

(Persius 3.66)

Avoiding extravagance, of course, was only a concern for the privileged classes, so this observation indicates the status of the philosophers' clientele. What many people wanted from philosophy was not, evidently, some new hypothesis about the nature of things, but rather a solid basis for social values that were already considered axiomatic. Nock says, "it was left for philosophy to give a *raison d'être* for the disciplined life" (1933:167). Robert Wilken points out that sarcophagi from the period often present an *orans* (female figure with hands raised in prayer) on one side, and a *kriophoros* (shepherd carrying a kid) on the other, with a philosopher seated in the middle. The art signifies that the person buried has lived a philosophical life – one of both piety and philanthropy (1984:81).

Accordingly, two of the most popular philosophical themes were attacks on luxury and pretense. Seneca (though wealthy himself) summarizes the philosopher's teaching:

We talk much about despising money and we give advice on this subject in the lengthiest of speeches, that mankind may believe true riches to exist in the mind and not in one's bank account, and that the man who adapts himself to his slender means and makes himself wealthy on a little sum, is the truly rich man.

(*Epistulae* 108.11)

He claims that when the philosophers utter proverbs against greed such as, "The poor lack much: the greedy man lacks all," or "He needs but little who desires but little," the crowds break out in thunderous applause – even the wealthy and the greedy (*Epistulae* 108.9, 11–12)![17] Plutarch and Epictetus make similar remarks.[18] The philosopher's attack on pretense was an ethical application of the Platonic distinction between seeming (*dokein*) and being (*einai*), between opinion (*doxa*) and knowledge (*epistēmē*) (cf. Dio 68). Luxury and sham were particularly contemptible in those who claimed to practice philosophy. Seneca devotes one of his moral epistles to the theme of "practicing what you preach." He says:

Philosophy teaches us to act, not to speak; it exacts of every man that he should live according to his own standards, that his life should not be out of harmony with his words . . . . This, I say, is the highest duty and the highest proof of wisdom, that deed and word should be in accord . . . .

(*Epistulae* 20.2)[19]

Merely seeming to be something was the trait of rhetoricians and sophists.[20] Dio observes: "It is absurd that we should know and pass upon every man's life on the strength of what he says (*legei*) rather than of what he does (*apo tōn ergōn*)"

(70.3). And Plutarch begins his *De stoicorum repugnantiis* with the same insistence "that the philosopher's life be in accord with his theory" (1). Epictetus (3.26.8–23) and Lucian (*Hermotimus* 9–19) inveigh, from different perspectives, against mere pretenders to the philosophic life.

The litmus tests of genuine philosophic practice were clear to everyone: utter simplicity of life; tranquillity of mind in all circumstances; disdain for common values, opinions, and sensual delights; disregard for social conventions and status, demonstrated in bold speech before one's social betters; and, especially, fearlessness in the face of death. Pompous teachers who failed these tests, the last in particular, were exposed as fakes (cf. Epictetus 3.26.37–39).

Social and legal status

If we turn now to consider the status of the philosophical schools in Graeco-Roman society, we find that their situation was complicated, again, by the conservative values of the aristocracy. As cheerleader for the accepted mores, philosophy was welcome enough among the educated class; but when its call for whole-hearted commitment sounded like fanaticism, or when its social criticism was too sharp, its proponents found themselves vulnerable.

On the one hand, philosophy continued to enjoy something of the prestigious role that it had inherited from Greek and Hellenistic society. Just as Plato, Aristotle, and Zeno had been retained by kings, so also the careers of Cicero, Seneca, Musonius Rufus, Epictetus, and Marcus Aurelius demonstrate the continued prominence of philosophy in education and government. Philosophy represented the highest level of education – after elementary tutoring, grammar, and rhetoric – attained by a very few.[21] Nock observes: "From the beginning of the first century B.C. till late in the Empire few doubted that philosophy was the natural crown of education" (1933:177). The availability of philosophers for private hire, the frequency of public lectures on philosophy, and the widespread denunciation of impostors and charlatans in the extant literature confirm that philosophy maintained considerable stature throughout the early principate.

On the other side, however, and precisely because of its old ties to the establishment, philosophy had a tremendous potential for subversion – a fact that was not lost on emperors.[22] In the first century, philosophy often found a home in the vestigial republican opposition to autocratic rule. Under Nero, several philosophers were killed (among them Seneca) or exiled because, according to the historian Dio Cassius, they could not endure that emperor's tyranny. Some plotted against him; others were simply uncooperative.[23] Vespasian is a good example of imperial ambivalence toward philosophy, for he put philosophers on the public payroll as teachers of "Latin and Greek learning" (65.12.1a) but then lost his (otherwise noted) patience with the Cynic Demetrius and several others; in 71 CE, he expelled from the city all philosophers except Musonius Rufus (65.13.2). Our reporter's sentiments become clear when he complains that one of the offenders behaved "as if it were the function of philosophy to insult those in power, to stir up the multitudes, to overthrow the established order of things."[24] Vespasian's advisor is said to have complained that philosophers "look down on everybody"; they are never satisfied with society as it is (65.13.1). Under Domitian such freedom of expression, especially as it concerned the emperor, was most unwelcome. Dio of Prusa, convert to philosophy, and others were exiled. In 93 CE, Domitian reportedly executed several prominent citizens "on the charge of philosophizing."[25] Clearly, many philosophers were not content with a role as pillars of the status quo; they were suspected of nurturing subversive ideas. With all of their talk about freedom (*eleutheria*) and equality, and with their belief in frank speaking (*parrhēsia*),[26] they proved a thorn in the flesh of the autocratic *princeps*. Who could forget that Cato, Brutus, and Cassius – the opponents of Julius Caesar – had all been practitioners of philosophy?[27]

But the fear of "too much philosophy" was not confined to emperors; it pervaded the aristocracy. Seneca recounts how, as a young man, he became enamored of Pythagoreanism and took on its disciplines, including the vegetarian diet, for an entire year. At that point, however, his renowned father counseled him to quit the practice because, as Seneca says, his father "detested philosophy" (*Epistulae* 108.22).[28] When we recall the stature of Seneca's father and brother – Gallio, proconsul of Achaia in Paul's day – we have reason to suspect that this opposition to serious philosophizing was common among the upper class. Indeed, a similar story is told by Tacitus of his famous father-in-law Agricola: "in early life he was inclined to drink more deeply of philosophy than is permitted a Roman and a Senator," though in this case it was Agricola's mother who advised him to leave it for politics (*Agricola* 4.3).

This aristocratic mistrust of philosophy evidently stemmed, then, from the belief that it encouraged a reprehensible withdrawal from civic life. The rhetorician Quintilian belittles philosophy because its devotees cloister themselves in "porches and gymnasia" rather than making themselves useful in public affairs.[29] Plutarch must argue against the grain that, as he titles one essay, *A Philosopher Ought to Converse with Those in Power*. Both Seneca (*Epistulae* 56) and Dio (*Discourse* 20) concur that the philosopher's true retirement is internal, and so can be found even in the midst of city turmoil. Seneca, despite his belief that retirement from society is sometimes necessary for the philosopher (*Epistulae* 7–8), takes pains to avoid the charges of novelty, innovation, and subversion (*Epistulae* 5.2):

> The mere name of philosophy, however quietly pursued, is an object of sufficient scorn; and what would happen if we should begin to separate ourselves from the customs of our fellow-men?

He requires that philosophers live outwardly normal lives, adapting harmoniously to the larger culture.[30] In spite of such disavowals, however, the Socratic image of the philosopher as relentless gadfly seems to have lingered in the consciousness of Roman society. Tertullian later summarizes a common view when he says of philosophers:

They howl against your customs, rites, cults, and ceremonies openly, publicly, and with every kind of bitter speech, some of them flaunting their
freedom unpunished against the very emperors.

(*Ad Nationes* 1.4)

Indeed, the values of the schools *were* different from those of the establishment,
and so the potential for at least intellectual subversion was always present.[31]

The Roman ambivalence toward philosophical schools doubtless explains, at
least in part, two of the salient features of philosophy in that period, namely its
eclecticism and the *topos* of the "adolescent quest for truth." By all accounts
eclecticism was rampant, both in the borrowing of the schools from each other
and in the various "customized" philosophies that individuals cobbled together
for themselves.[32] Of Seneca, who is usually considered a Stoic, Momigliano says:
"Even the trained student of today finds it difficult to disentangle the Platonic
from the Stoic, the Epicurean from the Cynic element in Seneca's philosophy."[33]
Likewise, numerous sources from our period recount a young person's investigation of all of the philosophical schools before either settling on one or, just as
often, leaving philosophy altogether for public life.[34]

If we take into account the experiences of Seneca and Agricola, we might
conclude that eclecticism was a useful protection against philosophical excess
for the conservative aristocracy. That is to say: some knowledge of philosophical
issues and vocabulary was deemed essential for persons of breeding, but actual
commitment to the regimen of a particular school smacked of fanaticism. Ramsay
MacMullen captures the prevailing attitude toward the schools when he observes, "Specialization in one school . . . belonged to pedants, not to gentlemen"
(1966:47). And Nock observes, "Of course, anything like conversion would be a
breach of etiquette: it would mean *superstitio*, unreasonable enthusiasm characteristic of the lower orders" (1933:162). Dedicated commitment to a philosophical
school was largely for slaves, freedmen, and women.

Among the nobility, devotion could be excused as youthful idealism, as in
Seneca's case, but to extend such zeal beyond adolescence was repugnant to men
of affairs. Eclecticism might also have a practical cause. Lucian's character Lyci-
nus advises against serious commitment to one school because of (a) the multiplicity of schools and (b) the impossibly long period required for mastery, and
hence happiness (*Hermotimus* 25–50). So the eclecticism and youthful experimentation that characterized our period seem to have been defense mechanisms on
the part of the aristocracy. These devices allowed them to recognize in principle
the value of a generalized Philosophy, as the undergirding of the social order,
while at the same time obviating any threat to that order: they embraced philosophy only to the extent that it could be accommodated to the needs of state
and society.

Philosophia, cult, collegium, and conversion

We close this section with an overview of the relationship between philosophical schools and two other pertinent social categories in ancient Rome: cult and collegium. Two papers in this volume deal with the substantial overlaps between cult and collegium;[35] it remains to explore the connections between these organizational types and the philosophical schools and to ponder the implications for the issue of "conversion" to philosophy.

It was a large part of Nock's purpose in his book *Conversion* to elucidate the relationship between philosophy and cult. His overriding thesis was that these two kinds of groups had distinct social functions, engaged in different activities, and met different psychological needs. Cults, by far the more popular of the two, were primarily local groups. Their whole emphasis was experiential, emotional, and focused on the group's particular rituals. Their services included some speaking, but this was primarily liturgical recitation; there is little evidence of teaching or preaching in these groups. Although their meetings began with a formal *prorrhesis*, dismissing the unworthy and calling for the others to purify themselves, they did not (apparently) engage much in moral exhortation. Indeed, they had no professional leadership, but rather an annually rotating priesthood, and no canonical writings. What they provided was an immediate, individual encounter with a caring god, a means of escape from Fate's grasp, and the assurance of bliss in the hereafter. Yet for all that, the cults did not require exclusive or absolute devotion from their membership; inscriptions show us people with numerous allegiances. Perhaps one reason for this openness was that the mysteries did not attempt to work out a comprehensive code of living, so there was no possibility of conflict with other such codes.

The philosophical schools, according to Nock, met an entirely different kind of need: they were for those who sought the keys to life's mysteries through reasoned analysis. They were very much occupied with moral exhortation and teaching; they had authoritative texts that they expounded; they were run by professional teachers who were masters of their traditions; and they were concerned not with devotion to one God, but with understanding the whole class of "divinity" and its relationship to human affairs. The schools did, moreover, advocate a comprehensive code of behavior – a discipline that included matters of diet, work, money, sex, and friendships; hence Nock's claim that only philosophy required "conversion" of its members.

In Nock's view, these two fundamentally different kinds of group existed in harmony because they had little to do with each other. They were not in competition, for one might belong to several mystery cults and also indulge an interest in philosophy; these were two different aspects of one's life. The Pythagoreans seem to have been an exception to the rule, since they combined philosophic and cultic aspects from the beginning. Nock argues, however, that, from the end of the first century CE, the dichotomy between cult and school began slowly to break down, as the schools became more overtly religious in character. The final plank in his argument is that a factor in the success of Christianity was its ability to fuse the two categories, so that it could satisfy the whole spectrum of social, intellectual, and psychological needs.

The relationship between philosophical school and collegium is the topic of an essay by Robert Wilken (1972). He points out both similarities and differences between these groups. One of the chief differences is that, whereas the collegia were consistently small and locally defined, as in an association of butchers or devotees of Diana, the schools had a world-wide presence and members from any region would have been trained in the same writings and traditions; although they had no official headquarters, the schools were in this respect universal organizations.

Wilken observes that the schools sometimes took the form of collegia in a given locale. Although we have little clear evidence of their social structures, it appears that disciples often lived with their master as they studied with him, thus forming a voluntary association. Indeed, Strabo (17.1.8) mentions an association of philosophers in connection with the Museion at Alexandria. Tertullian seems to classify the philosophical schools as associations, for he cites the Epicureans as an example of a *secta* that had not been banned, unlike the politically threatening ones (*Apologia* 38.1, 5). And the Pythagoreans offer an example of a school that lived permanently as a collegium. Although some schools locally took the form of collegia, it is not clear whether they all did. In any case, if the schools were considered collegia, they were presumably old enough to have been exempt from the laws proscribing such associations.[36]

Wilken's concern is to show that the second-century Christian apologists, in pleading for recognition of Christianity as either a philosophical school (Justin) or as a collegium (Tertullian), were merely using the most plausible social categories of the day in order to help secure the position of the church in the empire.

Having identified philosophical schools as "voluntary associations," which often use the language of conversion, we must consider the mechanics of that conversion, in particular the lecture or tract designed to attract converts to philosophy: the *logos protreptikos* (Marrou 1956:206–207). Although scholars have found examples of this genre in part of Plato's *Euthydemus*, the chief exemplar is thought to have been Aristotle's *Protreptikos* (Diogenes Laertius 5.22.12), which is preserved only in fragments. According to Diogenes, philosophers of all schools wrote *protreptikoi* – Aristippus (2.85.5), Plato (3.60.4), Theophrastus (5.49.18), Demetrius of Phaleron (5.81.13), Antisthenes (6.2.1), Monimus (6.83.14), Persaeus the student of Zeno (7.36.15), Posidonius (7.91.8), Ariston of Chios (7.163.7), Cleanthes (7.175.9), and Epicurus (10.28.13) – but none of these texts has survived. Cicero's fragmentary *Hortensius* is famous largely for its role in persuading the young Augustine to take up philosophy (*Confessions* 3.4.7). An extant Greek inscription mentions a competition for composing *logoi protreptikoi* in the Athenian ephebate (*IG* II[2] 2119). The evidence is thus enough to indicate that *logoi protreptikoi* constituted a recognized class of philosophical writing throughout our period.

Unfortunately, the dearth of surviving early examples is matched by a complete absence of theoretical discussion in either the handbooks of rhetorical theory or exercise manuals (*progymnasmata*). David Aune reasonably suggests that this deficiency results from the ancient stand-off between rhetors and philosophers: the rhetors simply did not recognize exhortations to philosophical conversion (1991:280). Our only course now is to rely on contemporary scholars who have proposed syntheses of the phenomenon based upon inductive analyses of early fragments and later texts.

Mark D. Jordan (1986) attempts to eke out a generic definition of philosophic protreptic from four examples: the Socratic "interludes" in Plato's *Euthydemus*, Aristotle's *Protreptikos* (hypothetically reconstructed from fragments), Seneca's *Epistula* 90 (which sets out to correct Posidonius' lost *Protreptikos*), and Iamblichus' later (fourth-century) *Protreptikos* – the second volume of his *Collection of Pythagorean Teachings*. Acknowledging the paucity of hard evidence, Jordan settles for this situational definition: writers of protreptic try to persuade interested parties, who are still vulnerable to persuasion by others, of a higher level of commitment to their own schools. In his own words:

> [E]ach author confronts a hearer whose choice is the target of many other persuasions. The unity of philosophic protreptic. . . would seem to lie in the [sic] this exigence, in the hearer's moment of choice before ways-of-life. . . . Protreptics are just those works that aim to bring about the firm choice of a lived way to wisdom.
>
> (Jordan 1986:330)

Jordan notes that the address to an individual, such as Aristotle's writing a *protreptikos* for Themison, King of Cyprus, gives the treatise that concrete urgency appropriate to protreptic. He also shows the importance of polemical contrast (*sygkrisis*) in repudiating all claims to knowledge other than those being advocated by the author (1986:321).

Also helpful is the summary portion of Aune's essay arguing that Paul's letter to the Romans is a *logos protreptikos* (1991:279–80). He observes that, "The central function of *logoi protreptikoi*, within a philosophical context, was to encourage conversion. . . . However, *logoi protreptikoi* also characteristically included a strong element of dissuasion (*apotrepein*) or censure (*elenchein*) aimed at freeing the person from erroneous beliefs and practices" (1991:280). This combination of persuasion and dissuasion is sometimes complemented by "an optional section, consisting of a personal appeal to the hearer, inviting the immediate acceptance of the exhortation" (1991:283).

Aune mentions several late Hellenistic–Roman and Christian examples of the genre including Lucian's *Wisdom of Nigrinus*. Although Aune does not discuss this text, it may serve as a concrete example for our purposes.

Although Lucian frames the *Nigrinus* as a dialogue at beginning and end, the bulk of it is given to the speech of "Character B," who has just returned from Rome, where he met the otherwise unknown Platonist philosopher Nigrinus. The encounter has suddenly changed his life, transforming him into a happy and blissful (*eudaimōn te kai makarios*) man. He says: "Don't you think it wonderful, by Zeus, that instead of being a slave, I am free; instead of being poor, I am truly wealthy; instead of being ignorant and blind, I have become sound?" (1). Character A then implores him not to hoard jealously (*oude phthonein*) the source of such bliss from a friend. In response to the request, Character B recalls in detail the speech of Nigrinus that pierced his soul and led him to embrace philosophy (35–37). That speech is essentially a *sygkrisis*, contrasting the worldly values so prevalent in Rome with the philosophical life, free of luxury and sham, that prevails in Athens. To choose (*proaireomai*) the Athenian life (*bion*) is to choose a life of toil (14, 33), but one which alone brings happiness. Character B's praise of the philosophic life does not include an explicit appeal for the conversion of his friend, but we are not surprised when Character A insists at the end that he must join his friend in a "change of heart" (*epaschon en tē psychē*, 38).

JUDAISM AS PHILOSOPHY

Both Judaism and Christianity found it difficult to explain themselves in social terms to the Graeco-Roman world; for this purpose, both would at times exploit the category of "philosophy." In the case of Judaism, however, outside observers had already suggested this connection before Judean authors made any attempt to do so.

Outside observers of Judaism

Already in the fourth century BCE, several Greek writers commented on the philosophical character of the Judeans as a nation. Aristotle himself, according to a tradition attributed to one of his disciples, asserted:

> These people are descended from the Indian philosophers. The philosophers, they say, are in India called Calani, in Syria by the territorial name of Jews [or Judeans, *Ioudaioi*]; for the district which they inhabit is known as Judaea.
>
> (Cited in Josephus, *Ag. Apion* 1.179)

Theophrastus and Megasthenes (both *c.* 300 BCE) likewise considered the Judeans a nation of philosophers, like the "Brahmins"; they thought that both were descendants of the Persian Magi.[37] From comments in Hecataeus of Abdera and Strabo, it seems that the basis for this claim was the Judeans' "philosophical" view of God, that is, as One, ineffable and invisible, who could not be represented in images (Diodorus Siculus 40.3.4; Strabo 16.2.35).

But in the Roman empire, this theoretical association of the Judeans with philosophy would doubtless have been underscored by the social fact that they seemed to behave as a philosophical school, not as a cult. That is to say, the cultic aspects of Judaism – temple, sacrifice, priesthood – were visible only in Jerusalem and only before 70; what the rest of the world saw was the synagogue/ *proseuchē*, which served as a place for study, discussion of sacred texts, and moral exhortation. Judeans were well known for their disciplined way of life, restraint from certain foods, calendar observance, and close community, separate from the rest of society. Joining the group did indeed require "conversion" – the adoption of an entirely new regimen – and there is considerable evidence that Judaism welcomed such converts.[38] If Acts provides a realistic picture, noted speakers in a synagogue would draw large audiences from the general public.[39] So, as Nock suggests, the synagogue "would remind outsiders of a philosophical school rather than a temple."[40]

It is nevertheless significant that our Roman sources tend to treat Judaism not as a philosophy but as a cult. They tell us that Judeans were expelled from Rome in 139 BCE for trying to "infect Roman customs with the cult of Jupiter Sabazius"; a further expulsion in 19 CE linked the Judeans with Egyptian cultists.[41] The standard term for Judean religious practices in the Roman literature is *superstitio*, which normally describes alien cults.[42]

Judean authors

Perhaps it was partly because of the outsiders' inclination to view Judaism as an alien cult that various Judean authors tried to preserve the more generous classification as "philosophy" for their tradition. This effort was well underway by the mid-second century BCE, with Aristobulus of Alexandria. In the surviving fragments, he claims that Pythagoras, Socrates, and Plato all borrowed heavily from the laws of Moses for their views of God and nature (in Eusebius, *Praep. Evang.* 13.12.1, 4).[43] He presents Judaism as a philosophical school on a par with the others:

> For it is agreed by all the philosophers that it is necessary to hold holy opinions concerning God, a point our philosophical school (*hairesis*) makes particularly well. And the whole constitution of our law is arranged with reference to piety (*eusebeia*) and justice (*dikaiosynē*) and temperance (*egkrateia*) and the rest of the things that are truly good.

> (13.12.8)

4 Maccabees, also perhaps from Alexandria, sets out to prove the thesis that the "devout reason" is master of the passions. The author begins: "The subject that I am about to discuss is most philosophical. . . . So it is right for me to advise you to pay earnest attention to philosophy" (1:1). Most interesting is an exchange between Eleazar the priest and Antiochus IV, in which the priest is called upon to defend his philosophy of Judaism (5:4). Antiochus objects that "it does not seem to me that you are a philosopher when you observe the *devotion* (*thrēskeia*) of the Judeans" (5:7). By repeatedly preferring to call Judaism a *thrēskeia*, he

links it with superstition, in which taboos are observed through fear (cf. 5:13). But it is hardly a philosophy: the Judeans' refusal to act in accord with nature, especially their abhorrence of such a natural delight as pork (5:8), makes Judaism unreasonable and anti-philosophical. Eleazar responds, however, that the divine law is wholly in accord with nature, and that it specifies the foods most suitable to human life: "You scoff at our philosophy as though living by it were irrational, but it teaches us self-control, so that we master all the pleasures and desires, and it also trains us in courage" (5:23). It is Eleazar's "philosophical reason" (*philosophos logos*) that will not permit him to eat pork (5.35).

With Philo of Alexandria and Flavius Josephus, the portrayal of Judaism as philosophy comes to fullest expression.

One need not examine the entire Philonic corpus to realize that Philo wants to bring Judaism into the philosophical mainstream.[44] Words built on the root *philosoph-* occur some 212 times in his writings. Everywhere he employs the concepts, techniques, and jargon of philosophy in his day. Moses, he argues, had a first-rate education in all branches of knowledge, but also had unique insight into God and nature (*Vita Mosis* 1.21–24). His laws therefore accord perfectly with natural law (2.52). Indeed, Moses was the ideal philosopher–king envisaged by Plato (2.2). What Moses produced was not material for pettifoggery among the schools, "but the true philosophy which is woven from three strands – thoughts, words, and deeds – united into a single piece for the attainment and enjoyment of happiness" (*eudaimonia*, 2.212). Accordingly, what Judeans do on the sabbath when they meet together is "philosophize":

> The Judeans every seventh day occupy themselves with the philosophy of their fathers (*patrion philosophian*), dedicating that time to the acquiring of knowledge and the study of the truths of nature. For what are our places of prayer. . . but schools (*didaskaleia*) of prudence and courage and temperance and justice [the cardinal virtues]?
>
> (2.216)

Philo claims that the purpose of the Judean law is to promote piety (*eusebeia*) toward God and justice (*dikaiosynē*) toward one's fellows; we have seen that these were the bedrock values of Graeco-Roman civilization (*Dec.* 2, 52; *Spec.Leg.* 4.135). He devotes one of his works to a thorough defense of the Stoic proposition "that every good man is free," but in his argument praises Moses' law as the means of achieving such freedom:

> The legislator of the Judeans in a bolder spirit went to a further extreme and in the practice of his "naked" philosophy [gymnosophy?], as they call it, ventured to speak of him who was possessed by love of the divine and worshipped the Self-existent only . . . .
>
> (*Quod omnis* 43)

Philo devotes another work to demonstrating that the Judean Therapeutae are the most philosophical of all people, both in their beliefs about God and in their discipline of life.[45] This tract borrows the common image of the philosophical school as a hospital for the soul.

In the case of Josephus, we have an even more deliberate argument – because it is plainly directed at Gentile readers (*Ant.* 1.5; 20.262) – that Judean culture embodies the highest aspirations of philosophy. That Josephus always thought this way seems clear from his earliest extant writing, the *Judean War*, in which he discusses at some length the several "schools" (*haireseis*) among the Judeans who "philosophize" (2.119, 166), portraying the Essenes as the most exemplary school (2.119, 161). Just as Diogenes would later distinguish between dogmatic and sceptical schools, Josephus sets up the Pharisees as dogmatists and the Sadducees as sceptics (2.162–65). But in the *War*, philosophical themes are subordinate to Josephus' cultic apologetic, to the effect that lassitude in the observance of temple ritual led to its destruction (cf. Lindner 1972). In his later writings, conversely, the cultic-priestly themes yield some ground to his philosophical agenda. We can sketch only a few signal points here.

Josephus' later writings are directed at a benevolent Gentile readership, represented in the preface to *Antiquities* by Ptolemy II Philadelphus and the patron Epaphroditus, who are very eager to learn of Judean philosophy and who love the truth (1.12; *Ag. Apion* 2.196). Josephus will follow the magnanimous example of the high priest Eleazar, who authorized the translation of the Septuagint because he did not wish to "hoard jealously" (1.11: *oude phthonein* – the same phrase as used by the character in *Nigrinus*!) the good things of Judaism from others. He means to show that the Judean laws, in marked contrast to the grotesque mythologies of other nations (1.15), accord with the laws of nature (1.19) and are "highly philosophical" (1.25). He appeals directly to the reader (*parakalō*, 1.15, 24) to judge whether his history does not show the unique efficacy of these laws: the just are always rewarded with happiness (*eudaimonia*),[46] and the wicked always punished (1.14, 20). Other systems cannot deal effectively with human vice (1.22–23; *Ag. Apion* 2.190–219; 276–77). Although the Judeans are a uniquely happy nation (cf. 4.114), their happiness can be shared by all readers, for their God "watches over *all things*" (1.20). Great rulers such as Cyrus, Artaxerxes, and Alexander happily acknowledge his providence. Josephus recounts the misfortunes of Judeans in Seleucia (*Ant.* 18.345–49) and the story of Gaius Caligula's death at length (cf. *Ant.* 303–306; 19.201–11) to show the universality of God's reach in punishing the wicked. On the other side, he celebrates both the conversion of the royal house of Adiabene (*Ant.* 20.17–96) and the general influence of Judean culture around the world.

Judean philosophy covers every aspect of behavior – diet, friendship, and life-style – from the cradle to the grave (*Ag. Apion* 2.171–74). It avoids the common problem of superficial pretense by its unique combination of word (*logos*) and action (*askēsis*, *Ag. Apion* 2.172–74). Moses, its founder, entrusted his laws to the priests, who have preserved them with scrupulous accuracy ever since, and who now have the responsibility to teach them regularly to the people (*Ant.* 1.14; 3.286). Interestingly enough, Josephus employs the vocabulary of "succession" (*diadochē*) to describe Judean high priests: they are the successors (*diadochoi*) who hand down (*paradidōmi*) unchanged the original teachings of the founder, Moses.[47] Thus the Judeans fulfill Plato's ideal of a populace that knows its laws (*Ag. Apion* 2.257). Indeed, Pythagoras, Plato, and Aristotle all borrowed from Moses' scheme (*Ag. Apion* 1.162, 165, 175–82).

Moses was not the only important philosopher in Judean history for Josephus. Louis H. Feldman has studied at least two dozen of the major characters in his paraphrase of the Bible (*Ant.* 111) and finds significant philosophical themes in many of these reinterpretations.[48] Abraham, according to Josephus, carefully studied heavenly bodies and was the first to conclude that the ultimate power, God, was one (1.154–57). While in Egypt, Abraham even taught astronomy and arithmetic to the Egyptians; so, their renowned abilities in these areas actually come from the Judeans (1.166–67). After Moses came Solomon, who was thoroughly acquainted with nature; he surpassed all ancient philosophers in wisdom (8.42–44).

Throughout his portrayal of Judean culture Josephus often pauses to reflect on philosophical issues: the folly of the Epicureans who deny providence (*Ant.* 10.277–81), or the roles of fate, fortune, and human will in the case of Herod (*Ant.* 16.395–401). While narrating some biblical scene, he typically points out who acted virtuously and who was guilty of vice (for example, *Ant.* 4.387; 6.93; 8.252; cf. Attridge 1976:121–40). In his hands, the episode of the Midianite women becomes a parable of Judean discipline: those Judeans who remain true to their heritage, like Lucian's philosopher Nigrinus, lead an ascetic life impervious to the sensual delights around them (*Ant.* 4.137–55). He often employs the bedrock philosophical concepts of piety toward God and justice toward humanity. These are, he says, the values that Judaism teaches (*Ant.* 7.384; 12.56, 121; 14.315; *Ag. Apion* 2.171, 181), what John the Baptist taught (*Ant.* 18.117), what the Essenes swear to practice (*War* 2.139), what the great kings of Israelite history represented (*Ant.* 7.338, 342, 356, 374; 9.236). Josephus' Pharisees, Sadducees, and Essenes continue to appear as *haireseis* or *philosophiai*, who mainly debate such philosophical issues as the survival of the soul and the relationship between fate and free will (*Ant.* 13.171–73; 18.12–20). His Stoic-like Pharisees condemn luxury (*Ant.* 18.12; cf. *Life* 12); his Pythagorean-like Essenes (*Ant.* 15.371) share all things in common and are perfect masters of their souls (*Ant.* 18.18–20). Josephus' own life story even includes the obligatory "adolescent quest for truth" – an experimentation with each of the schools (*Life* 10–12). He admits that he did become a philosophical "zealot" for a short time in his youth but, like Seneca, he properly abandoned that exercise for serious worldly affairs (*politeuesthai, Life* 12).

Josephus knows well the acid tests of true philosophy: simplicity and discipline, mastery of the passions, composure in the face of adversity, harmony of word and deed, and genuine contempt of death. These are precisely the aspects of Judaism that he highlights throughout the *Antiquities* and especially in the extended peroration of *Ag. Apion* (2.145–296). He stresses the ungrudging welcome that Judeans offer those who choose to join them – not as casual visitors but as complete converts to their laws (*Ag. Apion* 2.209–10, 261). For him, Judaism is a way of life (*bios*), a philosophy, that one can and should choose (*proaireomai*) (*Ag. Apion* 2.258). His later works, then, have a broadly protreptic character, commending Judaism to the interested reader.

Although Josephus was often accused by older scholarship of misrepresenting the Pharisees, Sadducees, and Essenes as philosophical schools, as a more or less ad hoc concession to his readers,[49] that portrayal plainly fits with deep currents in his work. Interestingly enough, Bickerman has shown that rabbinic tradition also presents itself according to the model of the philosophical school (1980). Bickerman argues that the "chain of tradition" described in *m. 'Abot* 1 represents the (earlier) Pharisees' self-understanding as a philosophical school. There is a striking formal resemblance between the short, pithy sayings attached to each of the "successors" in *m. 'Abot* 1 and those attributed by Diogenes Laertius to the Greek philosophers. Morton Smith contends on other grounds that the Pharisees, at least, spoke and behaved as philosophers (1956:79–81). And Jacob Neusner has worked out a thorough reinterpretation of the Mishnah as a philosophical statement.[50]

Now an obvious problem is this: the *Antiquities* was completed in 93/94 CE, but that was precisely the year in which Domitian expelled the philosophers from Rome. Why would Josephus, who is now living in Rome, seek to present Judaism as a philosophy when philosophers are in such difficult straits? It is impossible to be certain, but the solution may lie in his careful distinction of Judean culture from Greek and Roman. He does not present Judaism as a philosophical school *within* Graeco-Roman society, but argues rather that the Judeans have a distinct culture with its own philosophical schools. Judean philosophy is not implicated at all, therefore, in the sordid conspiracies of imperial Rome. It represents an ideal: what everyone likes about philosophy, but without the grubby realities of obnoxious Cynics and moralizing Stoics.

CHRISTIANITY AS PHILOSOPHY

It is well known that the second-century Christian apologists Justin Martyr and Athenagoras, who both presented themselves as philosophers, depicted Christianity for outsiders as the "true philosophy." But it is sometimes suggested that this portrayal was a novel strategy, as Wilken claims:

> Justin's somewhat innocent identification of Christianity with a philosophical school was a radical departure from earlier Christian views. Few of his contemporaries and none of his predecessors would have felt at all comfortable with such an understanding of Christianity.[51]

Wilken also thinks that Galen (*c.* 150 CE) was one of the first outsiders to think of Christianity in these terms.[52] I propose, on the contrary, that already in its first generation, Christianity looked like a philosophical school (though a bad one) to some observers, that some first-generation Christians, whose voices have been lost, might well have seen themselves as a philosophical school, that Luke–Acts begins to take up pronounced philosophical themes in its narratives, and that, consequently, the efforts of Justin and Athenagoras are not cut out of whole cloth.

The first generation

In the very earliest Christian writing we possess, 1 Thessalonians, we meet Paul on his first preaching tour through Greece. He claims that he has faced considerable opposition in both Philippi and Thessalonica (2:12) and now vigorously defends himself against a series of charges – lying, deceit, impurity, flattery, greed – that seem to have provided the basis for the outside hostility (2:3–12). Concerned that his recent converts will not falter in the face of continued opposition, he has sent Timothy to visit the group; now, on Timothy's return, he tries to remove any lingering suspicions that they might have about him, based on the outsiders' criticisms.

The charges against which Paul defends himself are those that were routinely leveled against the Cynics and other wandering philosophers of his day, namely:[53] he has flattered the people (perhaps with his message of exclusive salvation for them, 1:9–10) in order to take their money and leave town, never to be seen again.[54] Such charges explain both his insistence that he has repeatedly tried to visit them (2.18) and his effusive assurances of love and concern (2:7–8, 11–12, 19; 3:9–10). They also explain his "reminder" that he worked to support himself while in Thessalonica, so as not to burden them financially.[55] Paul was thus viewed by others as a wandering philosopher. The well-known parallels between some of his key motifs and moral maxims and those of the Hellenistic philosophers, as well as his use of the "Cynic–Stoic diatribe" style in Romans would only have strengthened this impression.[56]

To be sure, it does not seem that Paul envisioned his own work as a species of philosophy. He wages a forceful attack on the wisdom sought by the Greeks (for example, 1 Cor. 1:20–21). His whole aeon-ending vision seems to preclude philosophy as a worthwhile pursuit. And the only reference to philosophy in a letter of the Pauline tradition decries "philosophy and empty deceit and human tradition, according to the elements of the world and not according to Christ" (Col. 2:8). This attack would later serve Tertullian's denunciation of Greek learning (*Praescript. haer.* 7). The first point needs to be qualified, since philosophers such as Seneca and Epictetus were just as concerned as Paul to distinguish empty philosophical speech from the effective cure of souls.[57] From Socrates onward, philosophers routinely denounced rhetoric – usually by means of powerful rhetoric, as did Paul. Nevertheless, Paul's conception of the "new creation" in Christ, before which all prior categories dissolve (2 Cor. 5.17; Gal. 6.15), seems logically to leave little room for even the best of Greek wisdom. Although Paul might have been seen as a wandering philosopher by some outsiders, therefore, and his writing reflects the moral ethos of his day, he did not himself attempt to portray Christianity as a philosophy.

Yet it is Paul's very vehemence in denouncing wisdom and rhetoric that allows us obliquely to glimpse *other Christians* who perhaps did view themselves and their master Jesus as somewhat like philosophers. In 1 Corinthians 1–4, where he denounces the wisdom of this world, he repeatedly stresses that he proclaims not only Christ, but him *crucified* (1:17, 23; 2:2). Since he also insists that wisdom teaching empties "the cross" of its power (1:17), the conclusion lies near to hand that his opponents espoused a kind of allegiance to Jesus that did not feature, to Paul's satisfaction, either his saving death or resurrection (cf. 15:12). Indeed, the context would suggest that they esteemed Jesus primarily as a teacher of *knowledge* – knowledge about how to live so as to find happiness (1 Cor. 1:5, 19–30; 4:8–13; 8:1; 13:8–12). Such an emphasis on happiness through the wisdom taught by Jesus may find rough parallels in various texts that arguably have first-generation roots but did not ultimately become part of the main tradition: the early strata of Q, the letter of James, and the *Gospel of Thomas*.[58] It is plausible that this view of Jesus as exalted teacher had its roots in Judean circles associated with James (cf. *Gos. Thom.* 12 and the letter of James), in which case Paul's Judean (Jewish) and wisdom-advocating opponents would have a shared origin.

The second generation

Among the second generation of Christian groups – say, from 65/70 to the end of the first century – some are well on their way to assuming the form of a philosophical school. One could put forward several candidates for the role of founder of Christian philosophy. Most obviously, if the metaphysical aspects of philosophy are in view, the author of Hebrews displays a knowledge of Platonic themes in his interpretation of Jesus as eternal high priest of the heavenly tabernacle. Critics have found many parallels to the language of Philo in this author (cf. Thompson 1982).

Again, the pastoral epistles could be read as handbooks of Christian moral philosophy. Unlike any other first-century Christian text, they characteristically speak of Christian belief as "the teaching" (*hē didaskalia*) – sometimes qualified by "good" or "healthy" – that must now be "guarded" (1 Tim. 1:10; 4:6, 13; 6:1; 2 Tim. 1:13; 3:10; 4:3; Tit. 1:9; 2:1); the end of this teaching is *eusebeia*, for which one should train (*gymnazō*) oneself (1 Tim. 4:7). They launch the typical philosophers' attacks on those who teach for base profit (Tit. 1:11), and on those who retail in empty speech and old stories (*mythoi*) (1 Tim. 1:46; 4:7; 2 Tim. 2:14; 3:23; Tit. 3:9). The Pastorals are largely constituted of standard moral exhortations for each class of society, discussing even details of dress and demeanor for various social groups within the community (1 Tim. 2:8–3:13). Filled with common lists of virtues and vices, they denounce luxury (1 Tim. 6:5, 17–19), insist on an accord between words and deeds (1 Tim. 2:10; 2 Tim. 3:10; Tit 3:7), adduce suffering as proof of truth (2 Tim. 3:10–13), and offer a reliable (*pistos*) way among competing claims (2 Tim. 2:11; Tit. 3:8).

In the space available here, however, I should like to point out the strong philosophical tone of a less obvious text: Luke–Acts, which accounts for about one quarter of the canonical New Testament. Some philosophical overtones have been identified in Luke–Acts by various scholars, for example C. H. Talbert and Robert L. Brawley.[59] I would propose a more comprehensive reading of Luke–Acts as a philosophical statement, thus: the author implies that the young church should be viewed as another Judean philosophical school. Although he never makes this claim explicit, the cumulative evidence is overwhelming when read in its first-century context.

In the preface to his gospel, first, Luke uses several terms that suggest a philosophical school. The first is *paradidōmi*: he will record the acts of Jesus, "even as those who were from the beginning eyewitnesses and ministers of the word handed them down to us" (Luke 1:2). At Luke's time of writing, the deeds and sayings of Jesus have already become a *paradosis* that must be carefully preserved; this recalls the concern of the philosophical schools to maintain their various *paradoseis* or *diadochai*. Second, Luke writes so that Theophilus might come to realize the "certain ground" (*asphaleia*) of what he has been taught, in the midst of competing Christian claims. Although this word is characteristic of historical prefaces, we have also seen that philosophers used it to describe their efforts, namely: to provide a sure basis, among many competing claims and promises, for living. What Luke offers as a distinctive basis for *asphaleia* is an emphasis on proper sequence (*kathexēs*, 1:3), which has the effect of clarifying Jesus' own teaching, the successive revelations to the church, Christian relations with Judaism, proper behavior for Gentile Christians, and much else. Finally, the verb *katēcheō* identifies the implied reader as a *student*: we are in an atmosphere of teaching and learning (cf. Beyer 1965).

Luke does not need to call the characters in his story "philosophers" for the first-century reader to understand their philosophical overtones. John the Baptist leads an ascetic life, repudiates the privileges of birth from Abraham, demands a change of thinking (*metanoia*), insists upon ethical behavior and simplicity (Luke 3:2–14). Before long, however, his fearless speech lands him in trouble with an ostensibly powerful ruler – in reality a pretender, a reed shaken by the wind who prefers soft clothing and comfort (3:19–20; 7:24–25). And the established philosophers of the day, the Pharisees and "legists," blithely ignore John's teaching (7:30). These images were familiar to Luke's readers: whatever else he was, John was a Jewish philosopher. Josephus presents him in much the same way (*Ant.* 18.116–19).

Similarly, notwithstanding Jesus' classically Jewish, messianic, and prophetic identifications in Luke–Acts, he appears in first-century Galilee as a philosopher, a teacher who calls students to a radically new way of life. In spite of humble origins among the poor (Luke 2:7, 24), this teacher is quickly recognized because of his effective teaching. Other teachers respect and consult him (5:17; 7:36;

11:37; 13:31; 14:1; 17:20), though he sharply criticizes them and prefers to teach among the socially undesirable fringe groups. His message has a powerful ethical thrust. He demands that the wealthy jettison their ingrained social conventions and include social outcasts in their lives (14:7–14)! He requires that his own followers leave their homes and sell their goods (9:23–25, 57–62; 12:32–34, 49–53; 14:25–33). This ascetic behavior is necessary if they are to be effective salt (14:34–35) – a metaphor, like that of the gadfly, which emphasizes their counter-cultural role. He is frank in his criticism of the established philosophers, not for being evil but for being *ineffective*: hypocrites, lovers of money, irrelevant logic-choppers, concerned with outward appearance and not reality (for example, 16:14–15; 18:9–14).

Luke's Jesus and his students, by contrast, bring effective teaching, always accompanied by deeds. Jesus is mighty in word *and* deed (Luke 4.31–32; 5.23–24; 7.18–23; 24.19), a combination that preserves them from the philosopher's biggest pitfall: hypocrisy. For Luke, Jesus is a physician in Epictetus' sense: his words and those of his followers pierce the heart of the hearer and bring about a conversion (*metanoia*). Like Socrates in the *Phaedo*, he faces death with perfect equanimity.[60]

In Acts the philosophical themes are even more striking. Like the Pythagoreans and Josephus' Essenes, the early Christians practice communal ownership (Acts 2:44–45). Following Jesus' example, Stephen faces death without fear, even asking forgiveness for his judges (Acts 7:60). In Athens, Luke's Paul has no qualms about ranging Christian teaching alongside Stoicism and Epicureanism. In his appropriation of such a mainstream philosophical apophthegm as Aratus', "We are all God's offspring," he follows the Judean Aristobulus' lead (Eusebius, *Praep. Evang.* 13.12.6) and anticipates Justin's rapprochement with Greek philosophy. Luke's Paul is a model of Christian effectiveness when, by his composure in the face of death (Acts 27:13-38), he saves his shipmates from drowning and casually shakes off a deadly snake (Acts 28:3-6). These are the acid tests of a true philosopher.

Acts not only takes over Josephus' classification of the Pharisees and Sadducees as "philosophical schools" (*haireseis*, 5:17, 15:5; 26:5), interestingly enough, but also speaks of Christianity as "the Path" (*hē hodos*), a term that plainly identifies it as a *bios*, a *disciplina* with a claim to exclusive devotion. Most important, this Path is for Luke another Judean *hairesis* alongside the others (24:5, 14; 28:22). He bases the whole Christian project in Jerusalem, though this requires some manhandling of his sources;[61] he includes in almost every Christian speech a review of Israelite history, which is sometimes so thorough that the "Christian" part looks like an appendix (7.2–53); he makes all of the leaders of the Path, even Paul, devoutly observant of Judean custom;[62] he quotes approving or benign statements from some Judean leaders (Acts 5.33–39); he claims that many thousands of strictly observant Judeans adopted the Path *and* continued enthusiastically in their traditional observance (Acts 15:1, 5; 21:20); and, in general, he makes the Judean–Christian disputes entirely an in-house affair

(Acts 23:6, 10, 29). Admittedly, the designation of the church as a *hairesis* is implicitly rejected by Luke's character Paul (24:15) and elsewhere it appears only on the lips of Judean characters (24:5; 28:22). Yet Luke disdains the title of *hairesis* not because he wants to dissociate Christianity from the established Judean system, but rather because he thinks that this Path would have been accepted by *all* Judeans if they had not been so complacent. The young church, though viewed by established Judaism as merely one of its several *haireseis*, is really but a victim of the Judeans' legendary – to the Romans, after 70 – intransigence.

The standard philosophical theme of the persecuted minority with the truth challenging the complacent majority is worked out in Acts with the word *parrēsia*, which we have already met: fearless, direct speech. The word occurs only five times in Acts, but at strategic places. In his opening address, Peter sets the tone by claiming to confront the Judeans on the issue of Jesus' resurrection, with *parrēsia* (2:29). In the repeated conflicts between the apostles and the Sanhedrin, the word appears three times: first, the judges are amazed at the *parrēsia* of these unlettered (*agrammatoi*) men; then the disciples pray for the ability to continue their bold manner of confrontation (4:29); and finally, their prayer answered, they once again speak with boldness (4:31). The importance of this theme is clear from the fact that Acts closes with the statement that Paul, though under house arrest in Rome, was "preaching the kingdom of God and teaching about the Lord Jesus with all *parrēsia*, unhindered" (28:31).

Admittedly, many of Luke's categories – prophet, Holy Spirit, Messiah, scripture – do not fit the typical language of the Greek philosophical schools. Yet Philo and Josephus are instructive here, for they present Judaism as a philosophical culture while also preserving its biblical connections (cf. Josephus, *Ant.* 1.25). Josephus' portraits of Abraham, Moses, Solomon, Daniel, and other Judean figures as great philosophers does not prevent him from talking at the same time about the priesthood, the temple, prophecy, or other particular Judean items. In the same way, Luke's evocation of philosophical themes does not compromise his much-discussed biblical motifs.[63]

The second century

Whether the self-understanding of some first- and second-generation Christians as a "philosophical school" had much impact on outside observers is unclear. If they knew of such claims, Pliny, Tacitus, and Suetonius – our earliest outside observers – none the less continue to disparage Christianity as another superstition from Judea. The physician Galen, a little later, seems to have understood the pretensions to philosophy of both the "schools of Moses and Christ." At the same time, some Christian teachers began to develop this portrayal more overtly as a way of securing a place for Christians in society.

Galen refers to both Judaism and Christianity as philosophical schools, but he does so casually, while writing on medical subjects, and thus gives no hint that he is making a novel categorization. Committed to the notion of empirical investigation, Galen complains that contemporary philosophy and medicine have capitulated to tradition and blind faith, rather than encouraging original thinking (*On the Natural Faculties* 1.52–53). From this perspective, he polemically compares physicians and philosophers with Judeans and Christians: listening to them is "as if one had come into the school of Moses and Christ and heard talk of undemonstrated laws" (*On the Pulse* 2.4; cf. 3.3). What makes the comparison especially interesting is Galen's observation elsewhere that Christians, though lacking a sufficient theoretical base, were just as capable of *practical virtue* as the philosophers:

> Most people are unable to follow any demonstrative argument consecutively; hence they need parables, and benefit from them just as we now see the people called Christians drawing their faith from parables and miracles, and yet sometimes acting in the same way as those who practice philosophy. . . . For they include not only men but also women who refrain from cohabiting all through their lives; and they also number individuals who, in self-discipline and self-control in matters of food and drink, have attained a pitch not inferior to that of genuine philosophers.[64]

Because philosophy has become preoccupied with practical ethics, Galen can compare the Christians favorably, on matters of behavior, to other schools.

This observation should not, however, be taken to reflect an advance in the social status of Christianity,[65] for Galen's point is quite the opposite: he is using Judaism and Christianity as obvious, extreme examples of uncritical fideism, in order to expose the folly of his contemporaries. Somewhat as James rejected "faith alone" by noting that even the devils believe (2:19), so Galen castigates the philosophers for abdicating critical thinking; for, if their sole merit is practical virtue, then *even* the Judeans and Christians have them beaten.

With Justin and Athenagoras, we see a growing concern to answer critics like Galen; these apologists argue that not only Christian behavior but also its theoretical basis are worthy of the name "philosophy." By the mid-second century CE philosophy seems to have recovered from indignities suffered under the Flavians; it captivates the attention of several successive emperors, and is typically equated with "piety." Lucian's comic attacks on the philosophical schools in his *Philosophies for Sale* presuppose an institution that is secure and comfortable in society.

Justin describes himself as a philosopher: his whole motivation in life, he says, was to find the true philosophy – hence his youthful quest (*Dial.* 2) – and he eventually embraced Christianity. He thus describes his conversion: "I found this philosophy alone to be safe and profitable. Thus, and for this reason, I am a philosopher" (*Dial.* 7). He even continues to wear the simple cloak of the professional philosopher (*Dial.* 1). He finds value in several of the Greek philosophies, especially Platonism, and calls their founders "truly holy men" (*Dial.* 2), even though they have generally missed the point of philosophy.

Like the author of Acts, Justin knows that the credibility of his claim depends heavily on his ability to prove that Christianity is not, as most people think, a *new* teaching. And like the author of Acts, he will base his proof on the relationship of Christianity to both Judaism and Greek philosophy. In the case of Judaism, however, Acts had simply seized the high ground and asserted that, although Christianity was absolutely faithful to the tradition, the majority of Judeans were too stubborn to accept it. In Justin's day, this claim needs a more thorough defense because: (a) Christianity is patently a Gentile religion; (b) its members do not live as the Judeans continue to do (the Judeans did not disappear after 70 or 117 or 135); (c) the Judeans emphatically deny that the Christians belong with them; and (d) within the church itself, at least one strong voice (Marcion) has called for the repudiation of the Judean scriptures. Justin's lengthy *Dialogue with Trypho* is, therefore, an essential ingredient of his apologetic strategy: having asserted that the prophets, "more ancient than all those who are esteemed philosophers" (*Dial.* 7), laid the foundation of Christianity, he must now demonstrate that Christianity is better entitled than Judaism to claim that prophetic heritage.

Justin's emphasis on the Christian right to ancient prophetic tradition over against Trypho might seem to reflect Judean–Christian debates that would have been uninteresting to outsiders. But when we remember that "pagan" philosophers such as Celsus, Porphyry, and Julian will display a keen sensitivity to this question of Christian relations with Judaism, we may still conclude that Justin's *Dialogue* is partly intended for Graeco-Roman observers. Note that the prophets play a prominent role even in the first *Apology*, which is directed to the imperial authorities (*Apol.* 1.47–52).

In his approach to Greek philosophy, Justin employs the conception of the *logos* to baptize, as it were, the worthier insights of the ancients:

> But lest some should, without reason, and for the perversion of what we teach, maintain that we say that Christ was born one hundred and fifty years ago under Cyrenius ... let us anticipate and solve the difficulty. We have been taught that Christ is the first-born of God, and we have declared above that he is the Word (*logos*) of whom every race of men were partakers; and those who lived reasonably (*meta logou*) are Christians, even though they have been thought atheists; as, among the Greeks, Socrates and Heraclitus, and men like them; and among the barbarians, Abraham, and Ananias, and Azarias, and Misael, and Elias, and many others.
>
> (*Apol.* 1.46)

This appropriation of the best in secular philosophy established a strain of Christian thinking that would endure throughout the Middle Ages and into the modern world (cf. Gilson 1938). But in its origin it was only a further development of the Areopagite sermon in Acts 17; both arose from dire apologetic necessity.

Like Justin, Athenagoras deliberately styled himself a "philosopher." One dubious source claims that he founded the Christian philosophical school at Alexandria, but Eusebius omits his name from the succession list there. For our purposes, the crucial point is that, writing for the philosopher–emperor Marcus Aurelius, Athenagoras tries to find a home for Christianity among the established philosophical schools of the empire. He is concerned to refute the charges of atheism, cannibalism, and incest that continued to confront the church; of these, the charge of atheism receives most of his attention.[66] He wants to show that this perceived atheism is really monotheism, which is not essentially different from what the best philosophers and poets have always taught.

Other second-century Christians, whose views are mainly lost to us, seem to have seen themselves as a philosophical school. Eusebius mentions some Christians at Rome who avidly studied Euclid, Aristotle, and Theophrastus, and who regarded Galen as "almost an object of worship" (*Hist. Eccl.* 5.28.30).

It was perhaps inevitable that, once the identification of Christianity as a philosophical school had become secure in some Christians' minds, they would begin to extend the apology into more aggressive literary protreptic, as Josephus had done for Judaism. The early chapters of Justin's *Dialogue* may already fit that description, since he presents in effect an invitation to Christian philosophy, while disparaging all other options.[67] A clear example of the *logos protreptikos* is the *Epistle to Diognetus*, which is variously dated through the latter part of the second century. This document is addressed to one "most excellent (*kratiste*) Diognetus" – a deeply interested outsider who is making active enquiries concerning Christian piety (*eusebeia*) (1.1). After derisively dismissing both pagan and Jewish piety as options (2.4), the author moves to his positive portrayal of Christian piety (5-6). This portrayal parallels Josephus' in striking ways: Christians do not expose their infants and they willingly suffer for their faith, holding death in contempt: "flung to the wild beasts to make them deny their Lord, and yet remaining undefeated" (7, end). Further, "As the soul is diffused through every part of the body, so are Christians through all cities of the world" (6.1). The epistle ends with a forthright appeal to Diognetus to believe and become an "imitator" of God's goodness (10.4), just as Josephus had claimed that Judaism teaches participation in God's virtue (*Ant.* 1.23).

With Clement of Alexandria's *Exhortation to the Greeks* (*Protreptikos*), dating from about 200 CE, we see the complete nativization of philosophical protreptic in Christian circles. Clement knows of Josephus' work (*Stromata* 1.21.147) but relies on other learning here. This rambling, anecdotal treatise is addressed to benevolent Gentile readers, who are willing to tolerate a sustained attack on their native traditions. After a proleptic *sygkrisis* that contrasts popular Greek with Christian views (chapter 1), Clement offers four chapters (2.5) that savagely ridicule common notions of the gods and the gullibility of the masses. Included among his targets are the most popular philosophical positions (chapter 5). Like Josephus, Clement allows that long ago the better philosophers taught the truth, but they derived their knowledge from the Hebrew scriptures (6.60), which are the best source of (Christian) truth (8–9). Having made his theoretical case about the only true source of happiness in the final three chapters (10–12), Clement proposes that his readers convert to Christianity. This section is particularly interesting in social terms because, like Josephus with the story of the Adiabenian royal family, Clement faces head-on the social obstacles to conversion. He must show that the benefits of conversion outweigh the otherwise admirable principle, "It is not proper to overthrow a way of life (*ethos*) passed down to us from our ancestors" (10.72). He closes with repeated appeals to choose life over death.

SUMMARY AND CONCLUSION

In the first two centuries of the empire, the philosophical schools generally retained the honored social position they had won in the Greek and Hellenistic periods. Their role of social criticism and, sometimes, their republican political allegiances, made them potential "enemies of the Roman order," but outside of the Flavian period they seem to have fared well as an institution in society.[68] They were widely seen as instruments for the promulgation of axiomatic social values.

Since the Judeans had often been viewed as a nation of philosophers, it seemed natural to Judean apologists to defend their tradition on precisely this basis. It may well be that the Palestinian religious groups before 70 already saw themselves as philosophical schools; certainly, after the revolt it became necessary to demonstrate that Judaism endorsed the values of piety and justice. Josephus, at least, seems to have gone further by actually encouraging lifecommitment (conversion) to Judaism as the noblest philosophy in existence.

The appropriation of philosophy was not so natural for some strains of earliest Christianity, in view of their eschatological preoccupations. But some early students of Jesus did value their master as a supreme teacher of wisdom. And the young church's emphases on moral exhortation and radical conversion, in the absence of an ethnic base or a sacrificial cult, suggested the social category of philosophical school, both to observers like Galen and to Christian thinkers of the second generation and beyond, who had to find a place for the church in the world. By the end of the second century, some were following Josephus' aggressive lead, writing not only tracts in defense of this philosophy but also positive invitations to conversion.

NOTES

1 A draft of this paper was presented to the Canadian Society of Biblical Studies Annual Meeting, May 1990, in Victoria BC. Intended then as a "state of the question" summary, it has been substantially revised for publication. Still, it retains its programmatic and tentative character. I wish to thank the Social Sciences and Humanities Research Council of Canada for a small grant that facilitated this research.

   In this paper I render *Ioudaios* as "Judean" because to ancient ears it had an ethnic/regional sense, no less than *Babylōnios* or *Aigyptios*. These terms applied to representatives of a whole cultural complex associated with a particular region.

2 For a thorough philological analysis of *philosophia* and its correlatives throughout our period, see Malingrey 1961.

3 So Nock 1933:28 – Pythagoras was the first to found a "sodality with a real feeling of solidarity." Nock (28–31) concedes that the Orphics already had some sort of community; but little is known of them. Cf. Diogenes Laertius 1.12.

4 Diogenes Laertius 6.13, 19, has Antisthenes as predecessor of both Cynicism and Stoicism, especially the former. But Diogenes of Sinope is usually considered the founder of the Cynic school. In somewhat the same way, Socrates had his own disciples; but his work has been subsumed into the school founded by Plato.

5 Cf. Lucian, *Hermotimus* 16; Sandbach 1975:16; Long 1974:107.

6 See the introduction by Hicks in the Loeb edition (1925, 1:xxii–xxxii). Where they are available, I have used the Loeb Classical Library translations.

7 Cf. Diogenes Laertius 1.13–15, introduction by Hicks (1925, 1:xxiv–xxv); also Marrou 1956:207; Bickerman 1980:262; Turner 1918:197–99. Unavailable to me was P. Kienle, "Die Berichte über die Sukzessionen der Philosophie" (Diss., Freie Universität Berlin, 1961).

8 Already Sotion (early second cent. CE) produced a *Diadochē*. See Hicks 1925, 1:xxv.

9 So Seneca, *Epistulae* 40.3, "People speak of 'handing down' precepts to their pupils." Justin observes (*Dial.* 2): "those who first handled it [i.e., philosophy] . . . were succeeded by those who made no investigations concerning truth . . .; and each thought that to be true which he had learned from his teacher: then, moreover, those latter persons handed down to their successors such things, and others similar to them; and this system was called by the name of him who was styled the father of the doctrine." Cf. also Lucian's *Philosophies for Sale* 3, 6, 9, in which the various philosophies are personified.

10 Seneca, *Epistulae* 64.10, writes: "Shall I admit into my soul with less than the highest marks of respect Marcus Cato, the Elder and the Younger, Laelius the Wise, Socrates and Plato, Zeno and Cleanthes? I worship (*veneror*) them in very truth, and always rise to do honour to such noble names."

11 *Nicomachean Ethics* 10.6.1–3. Cf. the discussion in Weiss 1979:427–29.

12 Seneca, *Epistulae* 15.1, says: "Persons like ourselves would do well to say [in letter openings]: 'If you are studying philosophy, it is well.' For this is just what 'being well' means. Without philosophy the mind is sickly. . . ."

13 Cf. the testimonies in the LCL edition of Dio, especially that of Synesius (5:361–423).

14 Already Plato, *Republic* 518D, 521C; Cicero, *De natura deorum* 1.77; Cebes, *Tabula*, chs 3, 6.

15 Cf. the physician imagery in Lucian, *Nigrinus* 35–37; *Philosophies for Sale* 8 (of a Cynic); Plutarch, *On Love of Wealth* 524D.

16 Cf. Plato, *Gorgias* 507b; Polybius 22.10.8; Diodorus of Sicily 1.92.5; Xenophon, *Memorabilia* 4.8.7, 11.

17 Cf. also *Epistulae* 17, esp. 17.3, "Riches have shut off many a man from the attainment of wisdom; poverty is unburdened and free from care."

18 Epictetus says of happiness: "It is not in possessions. If you doubt that, look at Croesus, look at the rich nowadays, the amount of lamentation with which their life is filled" (3.22.27). Cf. Plutarch, *De cupiditate*.

19 Cf. Lucian, *Menippus* 5, which scorns philosophers who fail to live by their own principles, and Epictetus 2.9.17.

20 Cf. the Cynic Teles' work *On Seeming and Being* in O'Neil 1977:2–5; Sextus, *Sentences* 64.

21 Cf. Marrou 1956:206–16.

22 On what follows, see MacMullen 1966. His second chapter (pp. 46–94) is devoted to the philosophers as a disloyal element in Roman society.

23 Dio Cassius 62.24.1 (Seneca); 62.26.1 (Thrasea and Soranus).

24 Dio Cassius 65.12.2 (on Helvidius Priscus).

25 Dio Cassius 67.13.23; cf. 67.12.5, on the sophist Maternus.

26 Cf. Epictetus' statement "Tyranny hates wisdom" (1.29.10–11); this philosopher was

among those exiled by Domitian. On the ideal of *parrhēsia*, see MacMullen 1966:63–69, and the numerous references provided by Malherbe 1970.

27 See MacMullen 1966:1–45. Cato was a Stoic, Brutus an Academic, and Cassius an Epicurean.

28 Seneca also explains that, at that time, abstinence from certain meats might have implicated one in "some foreign rites" that were gaining headway at the time; he seems to be referring to Egyptian and Judean religion, for both Egyptians and Judeans were expelled from Rome by Tiberius in 19 CE. But he insists that his father's motive was merely his hatred of philosophy.

29 Quintilian 11.1.35; 12.2.7.

30 Cf. *Epistulae* 14.14: "The wise man will not upset the customs of the people, nor will he invite the attention of the populace by any novel ways of living."

31 So Nock 1933:185: "there was a general antithesis of philosophic and common ethic [sic] and values."

32 So MacMullen 1966:48: "all was open to choice, and hodge-podge handbooks encouraged everyone to be his own metaphysician."

33 Momigliano 1969:240. Similar things are said of Plutarch and Epictetus; cf. Meredith 1991:290.

34 See Lucian, *Menippus* 4; Tacitus, *Agricola* 4.3; Justin, *Dialogue* 2.

35 See the papers by Kloppenborg and Cotter in this volume. Both papers were originally presented at the Canadian Society of Biblical Studies Annual Meeting, May 1989, Université Laval.

36 On the proscriptions, see Cotter, in this volume.

37 Theophrastus, *On Piety*, cited in Porphyry, *On Abstinence* 2.26 (in Stern 1974:10); Megasthenes, *Indica*, cited in Clement of Alexandria, *Stromata* 1.15.72.5 (Stern 1974:45–46).

38 For example, Whittaker 1984:85–91 and Josephus, *Ag. Apion* 2.209–10.

39 Cf. Acts 13:42–45, according to which "almost the whole city gathered" in the synagogue to hear Paul. I am not suggesting that this particular incident happened, only that the author of Acts generally writes with verisimilitude – one of the requirements of Hellenistic historiography. The author of Acts expects his readers to believe that the scene could have happened.

40 Nock 1933:62. See also Smith 1956:79–81.

41 See Whittaker 1984:85, on Valerius Maximus and the expulsion of 139 BCE, Suetonius (*Tiberius* 36) and Tacitus (*Annales* 2.85) on that of 19 CE. The question of Judean proselytism has become a matter of serious debate in recent years. See, for example, Feldman 1993:177–445; Goodman 1994.

42 For example, Plutarch, *De Superstitione* 8; Strabo 16.2.37.

43 The fragments of Aristobulus are translated, with introduction and notes, in Charlesworth 1985:831–42. On Judaism as philosophy in general, see Hengel 1974:255–67.

44 Cf. Malingrey 1961:77–91.

45 See his *Vita cont.*, esp. 2, 16. In 26 he speaks of their "holy philosophy."

46 Although the LXX lacks a single reference to *eudaimonia*, Josephus includes the word no less than 47 times in his paraphrase of the LXX (*Ant.* 111).

47 On *paradidōmi*: *Ant.* 3.280, 286; 4.295, 302, 304; *Ag. Apion* 2.279. On *diadochē*: especially *Ant.* 20.224–51.

48 See Feldman 1993:594–96, for a convenient bibliographical listing.

49 For example, Moore 1929:283.

50 For example, Neusner 1988–89; 1991.

51 Wilken 1972:274. Cf. 1984:79: "Only a few enterprising individuals, and only after more than one hundred years of Christian history, had begun to take the risk of expressing Christian beliefs within the philosophical ideas current in the Graeco-Roman world."

52 Wilken 1972:277; cf. 1984:72–75.
53 See Malherbe 1970. Malherbe attempts to support Dibelius's view (1937:711), challenged by Schmithals (1972:123–218), that Paul is not responding to any particular charges, but is speaking generally about his ministry. Malherbe's argument, which is based almost entirely on a comparison of Dio's *Orations*, seems to me the less plausible explanation.
54 Cf. Epictetus 3.22.50.
55 The problem with this last claim, of course, is his later remark to the Philippians (Phil. 4:15–16) that, at this very point in his career, while in Thessalonica, his preaching was subsidized by *them*. So even if he did not receive anything from the Thessalonians, he could still justifiably have acquired a reputation for accepting money in return for preaching.
56 Now expanding the work of the old *religionsgeschichtliche Schule* in this respect: Malherbe 1989; 1987, and the works cited by Malherbe.
57 Seneca, *Epistulae* 60.47; Epictetus 3.1.27; 3.23.30–38.
58 See, for example, Kloppenborg, Meyer, Patterson, and Steinhauser 1990:20–25, 93–123; more fully, Kloppenborg 1987.
59 Talbert 1975:89–98; Brawley 1987:56–62.
60 Kloppenborg 1992. I am grateful to Prof. Kloppenborg for allowing me to see this article before publication.
61 Early in his career (Luke 9:51), Jesus is said to "set his face toward Jerusalem," and the gospel continues to point him in that direction (13:22, 33), but it is not until fairly late (17:11) that Jesus actually leaves Galilee! The resurrection appearances, contra Mark and Matthew, are set in Jerusalem and vicinity. And Paul's mission (as the entire church's mission, Acts 1:8) is made to derive from Jerusalem (Acts 9:26–30; 15:2), in marked contrast to his own claims (Gal. 1:11–2:10).
62 Luke 2:22, 24, 41; 4:16; 24:44; Acts 1:12; 2:1; 3:1; 17:2; 21:20–26; 22:3; 28:17, 20, 23.
63 On biblical motifs in Luke–Acts, see now Evans and Sanders 1993.
64 Cited by Wilken 1972:277, from Walzer 1949:15. I have so far been unable to locate either Walzer or the original text, even in the TLG.
65 Here I disagree with Wilken 1972:277: "Yet even this was quite a change. For the first time a non-Christian observer used a socially acceptable category to identify the Christians." Cf. also Wilken 1984:79.
66 Thirty-three chapters out of 37 in total.
67 Aune (1991:279–80) suggests both Justin, *Dial.* 19 and the *Epistle to Diognetus* as examples of Christian protreptic, though he does not discuss them.
68 Tacitus (*Agricola* 3.1) claims that Nerva was able to combine things that were previously thought incompatible: the principate and liberty. Since Nerva, he says, society has become increasingly tranquil. Even though Tacitus and his friends had axes to grind with respect to Domitian's reign, it seems from a variety of indicators that philosophers began to experience better times toward the middle of the second century.

4

EKKLĒSIA AND VOLUNTARY ASSOCIATIONS

Wayne O. McCready

INTRODUCTION

A general working principle for researchers of early Christianity is that by the middle of the third century CE this new religious movement had achieved an effective religious definition. Christianity, by the third century, had established religious practices, as well as a conceptual base, that were comprehensive and of sufficient substance that they accommodated diversity and dissent without compromising normative principles of the religion. However, positioned immediately behind this general principle is a multitude of questions. For example, how was such a self-definition achieved and what factors contributed to the "coming-to-be" of such an effective religious movement? In acquiring and putting into place foundations for a religion of some impact on humanity, what was set in motion that developed religious consciousness and vision for future development? One factor that emerges regularly in dealing with such questions is the importance of the gentile mission which required conscious reflection on what the early Jesus movement was about, and what it represented in its religious rites and rituals.[1] That is, a serious and sustained gentile mission – begun by first-century CE Jewish-Christians – required them to think like gentiles and this resulted in conscious reflection on what it meant to be religious according to emerging Christian principles. The reverse process confronted gentile members of the Jesus movement, because they were required to think (and potentially act) like Jewish-Christians in order to come to terms with the Jewish foundation of early Christianity.

This study takes as a first principle that the gentile mission was an essential component of early Christian eschatology – no doubt largely influenced by Pauline Christianity – and in the endeavor to move deliberately into the gentile world the movement looked to various paradigms that might assist the missionary enterprise.[2] The question posed is: what assisted the gentile mission actually to take place? Early Christian *ekklēsiai* will be examined to determine if they fit within the parameters of voluntary associations of the ancient Mediterranean world and, if they do, then perhaps this is one answer to the "what" and "how" of early Christian missionizing.

In his book *Paul*, E. P. Sanders summarizes the strategy and technique of Paul's missionizing activities (1991:19–21). Sanders observes that religion at the turn of the common era usually fits into one of three possible contexts – civic, ethnic, or personal. Although it is possible that Paul missionized in public discussions and debates, Sanders encourages us to think of other methods and contexts for the spread of the gospel. This study will take up Sanders' invitation by looking at the emerging church, as a concept as well as an organization, within the context of voluntary associations in the Graeco-Roman world at the turn of the common era.[3] Resources for the investigation are primarily literary, and for the sake of controlling the topic matter references will be made mainly to Pauline Christianity. Research indicates there was a significant shift in the Christian understanding of *ekklēsiai* in the mid-second century CE, verified in literary and archaeological resources (cf. Finney 1988).

VARIOUS MEANINGS OF *EKKLĒSIAI*

While there are limitations to a simple word study, it is worthwhile briefly to outline some meanings of *ekklēsiai* in ancient texts. The non-religious use of *ekklēsiai* referred initially to those being called or summoned. Although it may have had reference to an assembled army, its most substantial meaning had to do with the voting legislative assembly of free citizens in Athens and other free cities of Greek constitution.[4] The Greek *ekklēsiai* reached full maturity in the fifth century BCE when they were engaged in decisions on changes to laws, the appointment of officials, and the negotiation of various contracts and treaties. Although *ekklēsiai* opened with prayers and sacrifices to the gods, their character and mandate were principally political and judicial rather than religious.

Ekklēsia occurs over one hundred times in the Septuagint, and typically represents the Hebrew term *qahal* (probably related to *qôl*) having to do with summons to an assembly or the act of assembling. There is a wide range of meaning, frequently determined by the interchange between verb and noun. *Ekklēsia* (translating *qahal*) can refer to an assembly summoned to bear arms, a general assembly of people that included women and children, and a whole congregation in assembly having some significant religious meaning.[5] It should be noted that *synagōgē* occurs more frequently than *ekklēsia* as a translation of *qahal*.

In the New Testament, the overwhelming majority of references are found in Pauline or deutero-Pauline texts, the Acts of the Apostles and in the Apocalypse of John. With the exception of Matthew 16:18 and 18:17, the term is absent from the New Testament gospels, and it is used only occasionally in the non-Pauline epistles.[6] The term is used to refer to Christians living and meeting in a particular place whether it be Jerusalem (Acts 5:11), Antioch (Acts 13:1), Corinth (1 Cor. 1:2) or various assemblies in Asia Minor (Acts 14:23). Thus *ekklēsia* has the basic meaning of people being assembled. However, it is clear in many cases that the term is used to signify an assembly with a particular religious significance. The scholarly consensus on the use of *ekklēsia* in the New Testament is that it has a similar meaning to *qahal* in Hebrew scriptures (cf. Baker 1975). It refers to people who have an ambition to form a new religious and social entity.[7] A formula such as *ekklēsia en theō patri*, "assembly in God the Father" (or some variant) is a regular designation of the community of early Christians that stressed an assembly of people with common ideas of election and destiny.[8] In Ephesians (and perhaps by association with the son – in Colossians), *ekklēsia* is given cosmic consequence. Through the *ekklēsia*, the wisdom of God will be made known to the principalities and powers in heavenly places (Eph. 1:22; 3:10; cf. Col. 1:18–20). The *ekklēsia* is thus part of God's grand design comparable with creation and the raising of Jesus from the dead.

In summary, *ekklēsiai* in both secular and religious texts contains two aspects. Its most primary meaning is a reference to an assembly of people. However, the assembly has a particular consequence and mandate. For the first followers of Jesus, it represents the individual and collective assembly of those who confess Jesus as Lord, and it denotes a common viewpoint of election that motivates assembly.

VOLUNTARY ASSOCIATIONS AND *EKKLĒSIAI*: PARALLEL SOCIAL FACTORS

Voluntary associations were represented by numerous designations including *thiasos, synodos* and *eranos*, and were known to date as early as the fifth century BCE in Greece and a little later in Roman cities.[9] Epigraphical evidence for voluntary associations suggests they involved people gathering and organizing themselves into an extended family for purposes such as athletics, sacrificing to a god, eating a common meal, and regular socializing. In some cases, they may have celebrated the birthday of a patron or founder as well as taking group responsibility for decent burial of members. Typically, membership numbers ranged between thirty and forty but rarely went beyond one hundred.[10] Although trade and professional occupations were common factors for membership in voluntary associations, the primary emphasis was on social rather than business activities.[11] John Kloppenborg, following the lead of Edwin Hatch, makes an important point when he suggests that Christianity did not have "to invent the notion of a religious society distinct from the family and the *polis* or state" since forming associations was a regular activity of ancient Mediterranean societies.[12] From both insider and outsider perspectives, Christian churches might reasonably be understood as a variant on numerous voluntary associations, since they shared many common features.[13]

Connections between voluntary associations and the Christian *ekklēsiai* are most usefully sought in social factors rather than in any specific genealogical relationship. Scholarship in the latter part of the nineteenth century attempted to make direct connections between associations and the early church – and the results were mixed. For example, Georg Heinrici and Edwin Hatch argued that first-century Christians imitated voluntary associations known as *collegia tenuiorum* or burial societies.[14] Part of the problem with making a full assessment of this proposal is that we simply do not have enough evidence for early Christian organizations to match what is known about voluntary associations. Kloppenborg makes an appropriate apology that the research of Hatch and Heinrici on early churches and voluntary associations must be reconsidered – and valued – since their conclusions were frequently given short shrift because scholarship at the beginning of the twentieth century could not accept that a Christian organization had its origins in the "pagan" world. Researchers romanticized the Jewish origins of Christianity as something pure and simple – and standing in contrast to the corrupting paganism that compromised the later church.[15]

Comparisons between *ekklēsiai* and voluntary associations – with reference to social factors – have produced interesting parallels (Meeks 1983:78–80). They include membership by free decision rather than birth and a high degree of democratic internal governance, emphasis on intimacy of membership (likely involving proper burial and commemoration), common meals and other "fraternal" activities, as well as respect for patrons and sponsors (cf. 1 Cor. 16:15–18). In addition to such common features, there were significant differences. The most pronounced contrast between *ekklēsiai* and voluntary associations was the exclusivity of Christian truth claims. Meeks rightly estimated that membership in the Christian *ekklēsiai* supplanted all other potential memberships and resulted in substantial resocialization (1983:78). Voluntary associations were typically more concerned with fellowship and good times than with claims of salvation. There is no evidence that clubs and associations took exclusive epithets such as "holy," "called," or "beloved of God" that characterize references to *ekklēsiai*.[16] Indeed, there is little evidence that voluntary associations or clubs used the word *ekklēsia* as a community designation.[17] One further contrast should be emphasized. Although associations included people from varied social levels and statuses, there was not the inclusive social dimension of early Christian communities. The Pauline letters clearly demonstrate that unity and equality of membership was a major concern of the developing Christian churches (Gal. 3:28; Rom. 12:4–5; 1 Cor. 3:8; 10:17; 12:12–13; Phil. 2:2; cf. Eph. 4:4–6).

The Christian *ekklēsiai* were influenced by at least four contemporary institutions in the first century CE: the "household" (a basic organization of society in antiquity),[18] voluntary associations, synagogues, and philosophical schools. Of these four institutions, scholars regularly estimate synagogues were the most influential. On the one hand, this factor should not be surprising given the substantial interrelationship between the first followers of Jesus and ancient Judaism. Gentiles who were attracted to early Christianity were probably familiar with synagogue organizations.[19] On the other hand, it is surprising that there is minimal evidence in the New Testament showing an effort to imitate synagogue structure and organization. This lack of evidence confirms the estimation that the synagogue is an emerging and developing organization at the turn of the common era.[20] Scholars need to exercise caution in continuing to build a huge superstructure of hypothesis about synagogue and church interdependency given the relatively late evidence for synagogues, especially in pre-70 CE Palestine (cf. Grabbe 1988). In addition, researchers of early Christianity frequently are too easily persuaded by the redactional spin Luke gives in the Acts of the Apostles, when he presents churches as extensions of synagogues in a way that is not so easily supported by the Pauline epistles. Moreover, it may be that the first followers of Jesus deliberately selected the term *ekklēsia* because it was different from a contemporary one generally associated with Judaism.

MEMBERSHIP IN *EKKLĒSIAI*

Some four membership characteristics of the Christian *ekklēsiai* distinguish them from voluntary associations. They give *ekklēsiai* a profile that differentiated and particularized the coming together of Christians.

The first characteristic is the multi-dimensional social status of early Christian assemblies (cf. Hultgren 1994). Malherbe has noted correctly that there is a substantial scholarly consensus that members of the early church came from a cross-section of most of Mediterranean society (1983:86–87). This feature distinguished Christian assemblies from cults and associations that were characterized by a much more homogeneous social membership, often influenced by common trades and crafts (cf. Poland 1909:289–98). Further, the foundational principle for Christian *ekklēsiai* not only crossed social boundaries but it also stressed the equality of members with respect to entrance requirements and membership maintenance within the organization. While this feature clearly gave early Christianity a distinctive look, care must be taken in making a dramatic contrast with associations and clubs, since in some of them membership was also determined by popular vote. The equality issue perhaps contrasted more sharply with entrance and membership in synagogues.[21]

A second distinguishing characteristic of *ekklēsiai* was the degree of intimacy among fellow members. The excessively complimentary language is sometimes discounted as merely formulaic or as a function of the *philophronēsis* typical of ancient epistolography. However, the amount of language emphasizing close personal ties, brotherly and sisterly love, greetings with a holy kiss, concern for the well-being of community members, and so on – not only reinforced a sense of community, but it underscored the internal cohesion that distinguished the assemblies of early Christians. This characteristic is even more important when it is noted that intimacy was applied as a universal principle which transcended local and geographic references and united numerous local communities into a collective whole.[22]

Thomas A. Robinson, among others, has made an important observation about early churches fostering trans-local links in a way that stood in substantial contrast to voluntary associations.[23] Individual associations seem not to have linked up with members of similar associations – such as other professional guilds – located in the same city, even when they worshipped the same deity. Robinson makes the point that churches in one city or location frequently took interest in a church in another city and were aware that the individual church fitted within a larger whole (1990:7–9). The roving apostles moving from church to church, and city to city, would have contributed to this holistic nature of Christianity. The exchange of letters between churches served to solidify the extra-local linkages.[24]

The third characteristic is the familial structure of early Christian communities. A number of scholars have emphasized the significance of "household" as a basic social element of the early church.[25] The term *oikos* can refer to home "quarters," as well as the social network reflected in a family setting. The growth of early Christianity may be related to whole households collectively becoming part of the Christian movement. If this is a correct assessment, it not only forces a reconsideration of the modern understanding of missionizing in antiquity, but also it underscores the "family" dimension of *ekklēsia* membership.[26] Indeed, some would argue that Paul sought to build a socio-religious entity that fostered a familial sense of oneness and that his reference for such a structure was the household factor that linked communities of the Jewish diaspora (Craffert 1993). While examples of voluntary associations being formed in conjunction with households are numerous, the number of references to *oikos* as a dimension of Christian assemblies is rather substantial in New Testament texts and verifies that household contributed to the particularity of church membership. That is, the basic societal unit of household was structured in such a manner as to generate loyalty, group solidarity, and exclusivity, perhaps even with economic benefits, to provide a higher quality of life than was typical in the larger society.[27]

Lastly, membership in the Christian *ekklēsiai* also included involvement in educational activities. Community members were expected to mature intellectually and be enriched with knowledge so they could make sound judgments and reasonable decisions. Initiates were instructed in beliefs and practices of the movement. Members were expected to be able to distinguish between what was good and evil (1 Thess. 5:12–22). The New Testament epistles use terms such as mind, knowledge, wisdom, understanding, discernment, persuasion, and judgment as if they were normal intellectual expectations for early Christians.[28] Meeks has made a worthwhile comparison between early Christian *ekklēsiai* and philosophical schools as well as ancient rhetorical schools.[29] One point to be noted is that philosophical schools promoted not only ideas but also a social model that included community of goods, an ordered daily regimen and a particular dress code.[30] Communities promoted the consolidation of beliefs, development of community consensus and distinctive patterns of behavior, suggesting parallels with *ekklēsiai*.[31] H. Conzelmann made a case that the early Christian church represented a school of thought consciously carrying on wisdom instruction, and E. A. Judge proposed that early Christian missionizing can be compared to the founding of scholastic communities.[32] The educational factor motivated by religious concerns of *ekklēsiai* contrasts with the predominantly social dimensions of voluntary associations.

RITES AND INITIATION

One of the frustrations of researching features of membership for Christian *ekklēsiai* in the first century CE is that we lack an early manual or rule of order stipulating entrance requirements for an initiate. Although the epistles and the Acts of the Apostles deal only indirectly with membership factors, it can be reasonably estimated that followers of Jesus came together on the basis of a common faith in his messiahship. Initiates would have been alerted to the primacy of christology as a first principle for the *raison d'être* of the Christian community. While there likely were a number of community practices and beliefs that an initiate would have encountered such as prayers, liturgies and so on,[33] baptism and involvement in a common meal demonstrate two essential rites of passage for a new community member joining the Jesus movement. In a brief but precise presentation of baptism as an initiation ritual, Meeks proposes that it represented three phases in a process of social reorientation that included separation, transition, and reaggregation. The ritual was particular because the initiate entered a community that did not share the same world view as the larger society. Common Christian motifs of death, burial, resurrection, old, new, "putting on Christ," and "new humanity" are terms and phrases representing a major shift from the social structure a person shared by birth to the new relationships of the Christian *ekklēsiai*.[34] On the topic of this study, Meeks observes that although they sometimes had difficulty living up to theoretical expectations, the *ekklēsiai*, and not just the initiate, were expected to represent sacredness, homogeneity, unity, love, equality, humility, and so on (1983:156–57). Baptism was not a preparatory act. Rather, it was a central transformation rite enacting movement from an outside world that was "unclean" to a community that was "washed," "sanctified," and "justified."[35] Identification with Christ's dying and rising in Christian baptism was the act that moved one inside the boundary of the *ekklēsiai*.[36]

The community meal was not consciously profiled as an initiation rite. However, Gerd Theissen proposed that the community meal included a dimension of eschatological drama where violations of certain norms resulted in disaster. Following the proposals of both Theissen and Meeks, transfer of an individual through the initial rite of baptism resulted in membership in a community where the unity of sisters and brothers in a new humanity was to be demonstrated in the community meal.[37] The community meal not only enhanced internal coherence, unity, and equality – it also set boundaries distinguishing community members from outsiders.

BOUNDARIES

Because we do not possess a first-century manual of membership and initiation, defining the boundaries which demarcated the Christian *ekklēsiai* must be inferred from indirect statements. However, the New Testament epistles do reflect a language of community solidarity, contrasting church members with outsiders.[38]

One of the challenges facing early Christianity was that it inherited from traditional Judaism boundaries distinguishing the community from outsiders that were culturally and religiously specific. Circumcision, dietary observances, and Sabbath observance were some of the factors that contrasted Jews with gentiles, and they effectively separated Jews from the larger gentile society. The Pauline school of early Christianity challenged the appropriateness of these boundaries for a segment of the Jesus movement and by implication for all of the early church.[39] This position in turn raised questions about how Christians would be distinguished from the larger society. The answer suggested by Pauline Christianity was to emphasize a special sense of belonging that generated and reinforced community definition as something distinct from the larger society (Meeks 1983:86).

It was noted above that the Christian *ekklēsiai* emphasized intimacy of membership. Although there were parallels in clubs and associations, as well as in traditional and sectarian Judaism,[40] the "density" of intimate language of community membership[41] – as well as its frequency and conscious application – reflects a deliberate effort to create a sense of belonging that implicitly, if not explicitly, contrasted the group with society at large. Implicit boundaries were reflected in language and phrases that contrasted members to outsiders. Gal. 3:26–29 illustrates this point well. Being baptized into Christ resulted in putting on Christ so that there was neither Jew nor Greek, slave nor free, male nor female. Parallel terms and phrases such as "putting on Christ," being "sons of God," and so on, resulted in the establishment of boundaries which contrasted with past circumstances and reflected an integration into a distinctive community.[42] Natural kinship was replaced by new relationships in the *ekklēsiai*. For example, the metaphor of the "body of Christ" contributed to establishing boundaries for *ekklēsiai*.[43] While it is used to deal with the internal relationships of community members, *sōma* also was used as a term that identified and reinforced group cohesion. The thrust of the metaphor in the Pauline epistles was that different roles and profiles of individual members must not compromise unity of the group (1 Cor. 12:1–31). The concern for fellow members and the idea of belonging to an exclusive and distinctive community was very likely a decisive factor for the growth and success of early Christianity (cf. Gager 1975:140).

Early Christians consciously contrasted themselves with those outside the boundaries of their community and, in consequence, reinforced boundaries as a means of community definition. The language used included a perception of a community whose morality and ethics were pure and sacred, that is, different from the outside world that was impure and profane.[44] Jewish apologetic traditions, like those of pagan moralists, produced lists of vices. For example the Jewish aversion to homosexuality, as well as to sexual practices associated with idolatry, were retained in early Christianity and were thought to distinguish community members from the larger society.[45] Assertions that gentiles indulged in passions of lust, drunkenness, greed, and so on had less to do with objective descriptions of society and more to do with distinguishing outsiders from community members. As Meeks correctly proposed, the essential thrust of contrasting insider and outsider was to establish a qualitative difference. It is also a soteriological contrast. While "once" their life was characterized by vices and insecurity, it is "now" by soteriological consequence a life of virtue and confidence.[46]

One further difference between Christians and the outside society was the claim to be in possession of revelation and hidden wisdom. Indeed, belief in new revelation to their communities was common to Jewish sectarians at the turn of the common era.[47] Meeks observed that such a basic Christian assertion as the resurrection of Christ took the form of claims of fact. Yet it was not open to verification or falsification by an outsider.[48] The claim was cast in metaphoric language only understood through membership and participation in a community that possessed a unique understanding and knowledge of a Christ who rose from the dead (cf. 1 Cor. 15). The exclusive claim to special knowledge went a long way towards confirming group cohesion and distinguishing members from the outsider.

The last element in community boundaries is what Meeks refers to as "gates in the boundaries" (1983:105). While early Christianity promoted a clear sense of community cohesion as well as particular beliefs and norms, it did not withdraw from participation in the larger society like the Qumranites. In fact, early Christians remained in cities and became progressively more urban in the first century CE. The Pauline epistles encouraged freedom of Christians to mix with outsiders and to accept invitations for meals in pagan homes. Although there was a preference for marriages among fellow Christians, the maintenance of existing marriages with pagan spouses was encouraged. The internal life of the Christian *ekklēsiai* was not to operate in isolation from outsider observation and access. Church services and worship forms were to be maintained so that an outsider would see that members conducted themselves in a good and decent manner.[49] A group which claims to be the unique possessor of salvation does not necessarily welcome free interaction with outsiders. However, the missionary drive of early Christianity saw in the outsider a "potential insider" and thus there emerged a creative tension in regard to community boundaries. On the one hand, there is the promotion of a strong internal cohesion establishing clear boundaries that contrasts the *ekklēsiai* with the larger society. On the other hand, there was a conscious and deliberate effort to engage the outsider and continue a normal and acceptable relationship with those outside the boundaries of the *ekklēsiai*. This tension between internal exclusivity and the deliberate attempt to engage the outsider likely distinguished the *ekklēsiai* from voluntary associations.

MEETING PLACES

A review article by Paul C. Finney in the *Harvard Theological Review* (1988) represents a very good estimation of the state of research on places of worship in
early Christianity. Finney reviews previous research of F. W. Deichmann, U. Süssenbach, and H. Turner – and he estimates that a theological polemic of God
not residing in one place was a major directive for their research that makes
their results suspect.[50] The thesis advanced by the three scholars is that earliest
Christianity produced no sacred architecture, and indeed the sacralization of
place and space was understood to be at odds with the spirit of the first generation of the Jesus movement. The *ekklēsia* as assembled believers in Christ was
the true temple of God, and assembly places were intentionally of a secular
nature. Regular homes were the authentic norm of Christian assembly places.
As Christianity developed in the second and third centuries, pagan concepts of
sacred place combined with a developing clerical hierarchy that eventually resulted in *ekklēsia* becoming primarily a reference to a "place" rather than an assembly of believers. In the period of Constantine, place and buildings gained a
new and significant profile in Christian theology that might be viewed as a
deviant development of the early Christian vision. The school of thought represented by Deichmann, Süssenbach, and Turner estimated that Constantine
paganized Christianity (cf. Finney 1988:324). This representation of early Christian meeting places has strikingly similar features to the scholarly reaction to the
Foucart, Hatch, and Heinrici comparisons of the early church with voluntary
associations.[51]

Finney contrasts the positions of Deichmann, Süssenbach, and Turner to research by Richard Krautheimer,[52] who distinguished three periods of early
Christian architecture covering phases from (i) 50 to 150 CE, (ii) 150 to 250 CE,
and (iii) 250 to 313 CE. In the earliest period, there is little archaeological evidence of Christian meeting places, and the fragmentary references are primarily
in theological/literary sources. Krautheimer, along with the vast majority of
other researchers, judged that Christians worshipped in the Jerusalem Temple, in
synagogues, in private apartments, and in private homes. The latter two,
where dining areas allowed participation in the common meal, probably were the
most popular. Contrary to the positions of Deichmann, Süssenbach, and
Turner, Krautheimer estimated that the early Christian view of space for worship was primarily determined by practical concerns (such as the size of the
community, its local organization and finances), and not by a particular theology
about sacred space. In the period from 150 to 250 CE, larger and more complex
buildings for worship and assembly were needed because of community growth,
especially in Asia Minor, North Africa, and in Rome. Eventually, Christians
began to acquire title or control of buildings, and to do renovations to structures
in order to accommodate the needs of assembly and worship. It is likely that
residential buildings had their interiors changed to give secular structures a
religious sanctity.[53] In the time frame of 250 to 313 CE, new structures were built

with specific details included in the planning stages to meet the needs of assembly and worship. Domestic structures were replaced with independent buildings primarily because of growing numbers.

L. M. White's (1990) study of the interrelationship of architecture to the social composition of the church, growth patterns, wealth of members, liturgy, and development of church offices indicates a five-stage development of architecture. The first stage was a period of house churches where private houses served as places of assembly. White estimates that house churches were donated or financed by wealthy community members. In some cases they assumed leadership roles and might be compared to wealthy patrons of clubs and associations. The importance of real and personal property contributed to some of the success of urban Christianity – and was a necessary feature of Christianity acquiring an effective presence in Graeco-Roman society.[54]

CONCLUSION

This study started with two questions: whether the *ekklēsiai* assisted the gentile mission in its formative role in the evolution of Christianity; and whether *ekklēsiai* were structured and organized like voluntary associations. To the first question the answer is unequivocally yes, and to the second – in general terms – the answer is also affirmative.

On the matter of the gentile mission, the *ekklēsiai* provided a focal point for Christian claims of salvation, election, and common destiny for people of God. Membership was inclusive, crossing social boundaries, and religious intimacy was available with fellow believers. When intimacy of membership was matched with a universal vision of salvation it developed a religious consciousness that gave distinctive character to this new religious movement and provided a basis for an emerging Christian self-definition. The point to be emphasized is that the concept of *ekklēsia* as a vehicle for claiming universal salvation was matched with a social institution capable of transcending a local village, town, or city to unite the church into a collective whole.

On the second question, the views of Foucart, Hatch, and Heinrici were more right than wrong. Early churches shared significant common features with voluntary associations, with the consequence that they were viewed as such, certainly by outsiders, and to a degree by insiders. Scholarship needs to continue balancing the consideration of Jewish religious phenomena such as sects, synagogues, and prayer-houses with voluntary associations and philosophical schools as the likely institutions that had impact on early Christian churches. Research by Wilken, Malherbe, and Meeks confirms that voluntary associations are productive resources for investigating what others thought about early Christian assemblies, as well as what Christians believed and how they practiced their religion. It makes eminent sense that voluntary associations offered an initial reference point that placed churches comfortably within the parameters of Graeco-Roman society – especially when the Jesus movement consciously and deliberately wished to appeal to gentiles. Indeed, the diversity of voluntary associations was an attractive feature, for it allowed experimentation and development by the *ekklēsiai* while at the same time providing a special type of belonging that created a form of community definition that was distinct from the larger society.

It is the factor of belonging to something special, as well as personal affirmation by a community, exhibited in such settings as voluntary associations, that functioned as references, as well as points of departure, for Christian churches to move beyond the parameters of a narrow understanding of religion. By "christianizing" personal affirmation as well as the sense of belonging in a larger whole, the followers of Jesus were able to broaden their field of religious vision and eventually produce an effective religious self-definition through the affirmation of these two principles.

NOTES

1 See Meyer 1986 for a refined posing of these questions. There is an overwhelming consensus among researchers on the importance of the gentile mission as a formative factor for the beginnings of Christianity; for example, see Dahl 1941 as well as Dahl 1977; Gaston 1987; Hengel 1971b; Meeks 1983; Sanders 1977, 1983; Stendahl 1978; Wilson 1973.
2 See Donaldson 1993 for an excellent summary of how a paradigm provides a framework of religious meaning for action and belief.
3 White (1988:7–24) makes an important point that the sociology and social history of earliest Christianity indicates that in addition to the Jesus movement being considered as a sect within Second Temple Judaism, it also must be considered within the larger context of the Roman world in order to arrive at an adequate understanding of the beginnings of Christianity. An investigation of *ekklēsiai* and voluntary associations must include a consideration of Meeks 1983. Indeed, Meeks has a chapter entitled "The Formation of the Ekklesia" dealing with the *ekklēsia* as a voluntary association – and Meeks has influenced my study. Also, John Stambaugh and David Balch (1986) have co-authored a volume in the Library of Early Christianity series edited by Meeks. While they do not deal specifically with *ekklēsiai*, their treatment of clubs and cults provides a good complement to Meeks's work. Also, see Fisher 1988a, 1988b; Harrington 1980; Walke 1950.
4 See Hansen 1983; Jones 1957; Staveley 1972.
5 See Hatch and Redpath 1897–1906:433. Cf. Gen. 49:6; Num. 22:4; Jer. 44:15; Deut. 9:10; 10:4. See Berger 1976; Coenen 1975-78; Minear 1962.
6 Cf. Jas. 5:14; Heb. 2:12; 12:23; 3 Jn. 6, 9, 10. See Moulton and Geden 1963:316–17.
7 1 Cor. 1:2 includes not only being called, but it attributes to members of the *ekklēsia* being sanctified as saints, with a wide reference to "all those who in every place call on the name of our Lord Jesus Christ."
8 Cf. 1 Cor. 1:2; 11:22; 15:9; 2 Cor. 1:1; Gal. 1:13; 1 Thess. 1:1–4; 2:14; 2 Thess. 1:1; Eph. 3:10; 1 Tim. 3:15; 5:16; Acts 12:5; 20:28; Heb. 12:23. Meeks 1983:85–86 proposes that there is an interrelationship between the term *ekklēsia* and language of "belonging"; the texts cited in this note verify this observation.
9 Meeks 1983:31–32; Stambaugh and Balch 1986:124–25. For earlier scholarship on this epigraphical evidence see Foucart 1873 as well as Mommsen 1843.
10 Meeks (1983:32) cites Italians at Delos as an example of a large association reflecting an ethnic minority living in a foreign territory who organized themselves into a voluntary association.

11 Malherbe (1983:88–91) emphasizes the importance of trades and crafts for understanding organizational factors of early Christianity. MacMullen (1974:76–77) estimates large trade-craft associations were set up like miniature cities. Both scholars stress that associations were not concerned with improved business but with the social life of their members. Cf. Burford 1972. MacMullen and Burford see parallels between early Christianity and trade/ professional associations. Note Luke presents Paul as a workman in contact with other craftspersons in Acts 18:3; 19:11–12; cf. Hock 1980.

12 Kloppenborg 1993:213. Cf. Hatch 1881.

13 See Foucart 1873:5–12 for comments on involvement of women and slaves in associations that had parallels to church membership; cf. Hatch 1881:30–31. Poland's (1909) evidence suggests that women were frequently associate members dependent upon husbands for membership, and slaves were placed in socially inferior roles to free persons.

14 Hatch 1881; Heinrici 1896. Although there is no direct evidence for identifying early Christianity with a burial society, it should be noted 1 Cor. 15:29 refers to a baptism for the dead and 1 Thess. 4:13–5:11 represents concern for community members who have died. Hatch thought that the offices of bishop and deacon had parallels to the organizational structure of voluntary associations.

15 Kloppenborg 1993:224–28; cf. Weinfeld (1986), who demonstrates that even such separatist Jews as those who wrote the Qumran scrolls shared common features with voluntary associations.

16 Cf. Rom. 12:1; Col. 3:12; 1 Cor. 7:24; Gal. 5:13; Rom. 1:7; 1 John 4:11.

17 Poland (1909:332) cites limited cases of business meetings of clubs being called *ekklēsiai*. Lietzmann (1969:4) could find only three references to *ekklēsia* as a cultic guild or religious fellowship in non-Christian sources.

18 Jewett (1993, 1994) has proposed that in addition to "house churches" researchers should now be paying attention to "tenement churches" that would have been made up of the urban underclass.

19 See Kee 1990 for an estimation that the *synagōgē* and *ekklēsia* emerged concurrently. Maser (1990–91) argues that based on literary sources – such as James, as well as *Didascalia Apostolorum* and *Apostolic Constitutions* – the early church took its organizational structures and interior plans from early Judaism. Also, see Horst 1989 for a profile of godfearers based on inscriptional evidence, as well as Meyers and White 1989 for evidence of religious interplay between Jews and Christians in the diaspora.

20 Cf. Cohen 1987a:111–15; See my article (McCready 1990:160–62) for an estimation that the synagōgē was in an emerging and developmental stage in the first century CE. See also Hoppe 1989 and, for parallels between voluntary associations and Jewish groups, Dombrowski 1966.

21 See Lightstone 1988:51–52 for a discussion of the welcomed participation of gentiles in Jewish religious rituals. Also, see Segal (1993:175) who makes the important point that for rabbinic Judaism – evidenced in the Mishnah – conversion to Judaism by gentiles was not necessary to attain salvation. The rabbis did not hold salvation to be as exclusive a proposition as did early Christians. Kloppenborg (1993:234) notes that under Roman influence voluntary associations in Thrace and Asia Minor had significant equality between slaves and freedpersons.

22 Rom. 16; 1 Thess. 5:26; Phil. 4:21.

23 Robinson made this comparison in an unpublished paper (1990).

24 Robinson (1990:8) makes the telling point that, in the Ignatian letters, schismatics holding separate eucharists and baptisms would have been problematic only if there already existed a sense of membership in a unit larger than the house church.

25 Cf. Gülzow 1974; Banks 1980:33–42; Lührmann 1981; Malherbe 1983:61–66; Lieu 1987; Petersen 1969.

26 See Finger 1994 for the proposal that the early Jesus movement used family structures to create fictive kinship groups that would accommodate all believers.

27 Malherbe (1983:69–70) has made the point that a household included immediate family, slaves, freedmen, servants, laborers and possibly business associates and tenants. Cf. Meeks 1983:222, n. 17. See Rom. 16:5, 14, 15; 1 Thess. 5:27; Col. 4:15. For a discussion of the interplay between the socio-religious unit of household and group responsibility see Blue 1991.

28 See Banks 1980:74–75.

29 Meeks 1983:81–84; Also, see Wilken 1980; and Malherbe 1983:11–20; 1982:46–59.

30 Regrettably, most of this information reflects third-century CE practices that do not make for easy comparison with early Christianity. See DeWitt 1967 for Epicurean communities functioning as a family unit. Blanchetiere 1989 argues that the author of the Epistle to Diognetus was inspired by Philo to present the role of Christianity in cities as similar to that of philosophical schools as detailed by Plato.

31 Malherbe 1990 suggests that Paul used counselling techniques derived from moral philosophers to reform behavior.

32 Judge 1960. Judge suggests Paul's contemporaries would have viewed an *ekklēsia* as a group of sophists with skills in philosophy and rhetoric. See Conzelmann 1966.

33 See Meeks 1983:140–50.

34 See Donaldson 1993:196–98.

35 Cf. 1 Cor. 6:9–11.

36 Meeks 1983:102 refers to early Christian baptism as a "boundary-establishing ritual." Cf. Turner 1969.

37 Cf. 1 Cor. 11:30. Theissen 1982:147–74. Meeks 1983:159–60.

38 1 Cor. 1:20–28; 2:12; 3:19; Gal. 4:3; 6:14; 1 Thess. 4:12; Eph. 2:2; Col. 2:8; 4:5. Cf. Afanassieff 1974.

39 The emphasis being placed here is on membership in an exclusive group rather than on salvation; cf. Segal 1993:188–89.

40 Cf. Lev. 19:17; Deut. 15:7, 12; 22:1–2; Jer. 31:34; 1QS 6:10, 22; CDC 6.20–7.1; also see Nock 1924. See Sanders 1992:349–63.

41 1 Thess. 2:17–3:11; 4:13–5:11; 1 Cor. 4:14; 2 Cor. 6:13; 12:14; Gal. 3:26.

42 Cf. 1 Cor. 12:13; Col. 3:11.

43 See Robinson 1952; also see Conzelmann 1975:210–16, for a discussion of body as a commonplace metaphor in ancient non-Christian sources.

44 Cf. 1 Cor. 5 and 6. 1 Thess. 4:4–5 comments that a Christian man knows how to take a wife in holiness and honor while a pagan is controlled by the passion of lust because he does not know God. Nonbelievers and the unrighteous do not know God and despise the church, 1 Cor. 6:4; 1 Thess. 4:5; Gal. 4:8; 2 Thess. 1:8.

45 1 Cor. 6:9–11; Rom. 1:24–27; Gal. 5:16–25. 1 Thess. 1:9 qualifies the believer as one who turned to God from idols.

46 Meeks 1983:95. Meeks used the phrase "eschatological security" while I have used soteriological consequence. Cf. Gal. 4:8; 3:23; Eph. 2:11–22; Rom. 6:17–22; 7:5; 11:30.

47 See Cohen 1987a:195–213; see also my 1985 article.

48 Meeks 1983:93. Cf. 1 Cor. 2:6–9.

49 Cf. 1 Cor. 7:12–16; 8–10, esp. 10:32–33; 14:23; 1 Thess. 4:11.

50 Deichmann 1983; Süssenbach 1977; Turner 1979.

51 See Kloppenborg 1993:224–25.

52 Cf. Krautheimer 1969, 1975.

53 Cf. Rordorf 1964.

54 White 1990:102–107. Cf. Finney 1988:336. The intermediate stage served as a bridge from house churches to the stage of *domus ecclesiae*, when alterations to domestic

structures accommodated Christian assembly. The third stage was a period when interiors of private homes were altered significantly to meet the needs of worship and assembly. The fourth stage of development is estimated to be another intermediate period when private homes were renovated into large, rectangular, hall-like structures. The last stage of White's scheme is the basilica structure that represented a new phase of development in Christianity that was endorsed and advanced with the sponsorship of Constantine.

5

THE COLLEGIA AND ROMAN LAW

State restrictions on voluntary associations, 64 BCE–200 CE

Wendy Cotter

State restrictions on voluntary or private associations is a subject much more easily investigated with relation to Rome, Ostia, and other cities of the Italian peninsula, where the inscriptional evidence of collegia abounds, than in the western and eastern provinces where the situation must be reconstructed tentatively because the evidence is so slight. Regarding the lack of guilds in the west, Guido Clemente proposes that family-centered crafts made the guild unnecessary in the imperial period. Furthermore, guilds usually boasted benefactors who supplied them with means to arrange for a regular meeting place and for the proper sacrifice and feasting on the days special to the group. In the case of the newly conquered provinces of the west, such a relationship with a prosperous Roman overlord was hardly attractive.[1]

The paucity of evidence in the east is puzzling. Does it mean that indigenous societies were irrevocably dissolved? Does it mean that the guilds that did survive were really off-shoots of respectable Roman collegia spread to the east by emigrating Roman businessmen? Or is it that the voluntary associations cloaked their existence to avoid dissolution? Waltzing's exhaustive analysis of the inscriptions led him to observe the pattern that when the collegia appear they do so in sporadic clusters, as they do in the city of Thyatira (1895–1900, 1:57–58). What does that mean? How did they win approval for their society? These questions far exceed what the evidence allows us to answer with confidence.

In this chapter, I will present a first step, namely the evidence that is available concerning Roman legislation on and practical control over the voluntary associations, the private collegia, both in Rome and in the provinces. Because I proceed chronologically, a certain amount of repetition occurs as one emperor reinstates a ruling first made in Augustus' time. Nevertheless, it seems to me that even this repetition is important since it is a practical illustration of the Roman dependence on jurisprudence as the main system for determining new policies for Rome and the provinces of the empire.

THE PUBLIC STATUS OF PRIVATE COLLEGIA UNDER ROMAN LAW[2]

The earliest law recognizing the rights of the collegia occurs in Table VIII of the Twelve Tables:

> His (sodalibus) potestatem facit lex pactionem quam uelint sibi ferre, dum ne quid ex publica lege corrumpant.[3]

> Guild members shall have the power . . . to make for themselves any rule they wish provided that they impair no part of the public law.
>
> (Johnson 1961:12)

The difference between public and private law had been well defined by the late republic. In the early empire the distinction was even more intricately elaborated. The collegia were situated under *private* law since they were formed of and by private persons for private ends. The large state corporations, organized for and by the state, were located under *public* law, of course. Once a group was granted its identity as a public corporation, it took on the identity of a "juristic person." That is, the corporation was perceived as a single entity, not as a group of individuals. As such, the public corporations had the rights of an individual. For example, the public corporation could hold private property in its own corporate name. On the other hand, these privileges also carried responsibilities to the state. Taxation and public services were expected commensurate with the resources of the group. And, of course, the corporation served state interests according to its own specialty. Such corporations would include shipbuilders, goldworkers, bankers, and the like.

In contrast, a private guild was never awarded the status of a "juristic person." It was always regarded as a group of individuals. Such associations were also expected to be available for public service commensurate with their resources but, practically speaking, their attention was absorbed with the activities associated with their own common interest, that is, their trade or their particular deity's proper adoration.

THE ROMAN REPUBLIC: THE BEGINNING OF LEGAL RESTRICTIONS ON COLLEGIA

During the republic the collegia had organized rather freely. Waltzing concludes from his study, "[j]amais on ne le voit intervenir dans la création d'un collège industriel ni d'un collège religieux privé."[4] These societies convened meetings, collected funds, and held celebratory banquets in honor of their patron deities – all without intervention of the state. Naturally, as Roman conquests spread across the Mediterranean, the Roman population swelled, as did the membership and types of guilds. This situation reached a climax with the political upheaval of the civil war in Rome. The collegia took their stand now with this leader, now with that. It became clear, furthermore, that some guilds had only masked

75

revolutionary activities. The frequent meetings of the guilds had been a cloak for their seditious plans to take over the city.[5] For this reason, in 64 BCE the Senate dissolved all suspect collegia: "senatus consulto collegia sublata sunt, quae adversus rem publicam videbantur esse." (By decree of the Senate, all guilds which appeared to conflict with public interest were abolished.)[6]

The shadow that had fallen on collegia was never really to lift. Furthermore, the scars were only deepened when, after six years, Clodius reopened the barely healed wound. Manipulating himself into the position of elected tribune of the people, Clodius removed the ban on the collegia. Cicero was among his major denouncers, charging that this was a ruse to fill the city with Clodius' supporters, motley groups of dangerous, ignorant, and low-status persons, veterans who had fought for Catalina, ex-convicts from recently opened prisons, freedmen and slaves.[7] Cicero was proved right when Clodius took his place right inside the Forum where he rallied the prospective new "members" as their patron. These armed forces became Clodius' warriors, terrorizing the Roman populace in a vendetta against his opponents, Pompey, Cato the Younger, and of course Cicero. Although Clodius was not successful, his use of the collegia for purposes of insurrection only reaffirmed the strict Roman legislation against the formation of guilds. From that time onward, all collegia, "professional" or "religious,"[8] were subject to strict regulation.[9]

Between 58 BCE and the beginning of Julius Caesar's dictatorship in 49 BCE two further decrees forbade the formation of societies. In 56 BCE the Senate ordered the dissolution of all political clubs.[10] The following year Crassus passed a law against the illegal activities of certain political *sodalitates* that were responsible for organized bribery. The danger of these societies meant that all the collegia were subject to the same restrictions. It was obvious to all that it was possible to mask a politically seditious party under the guise of a professional or religious club.

Julius Caesar, 49–44 BCE

Julius Caesar took immediate measures against the guilds his one-time friend Clodius had initiated. Only the most ancient were permitted to continue.[11] The precise wording of this proscription, the *Lex Julia*, is no longer extant; we must rely on historians and inscriptions for the evidence of its content and application.[12] The ruling applied to all but the most ancient collegia. In this category, Caesar recognized Jewish communities. This would seem the appropriate place for an excursus on the implications of Caesar's concessions to the Jewish collegia or synagogues.

Jewish synagogues in Rome [13]

The first reference to a Jewish community in Rome occurs in the writings of Valerius Maximus who reports the expulsion of Jews in 139 BCE by order of Cn.

Cornelius Hispanus, the *praeter peregrinus* (or city magistrate for foreign visitors) on the grounds that "they had tried to infect Roman morals with the cult of Jupiter Sabazius" ("Sabazi Iovis cultu Romanos inficere mores conati erant").[14] Jews were allowed to practice their own cult but were not to proselytize.

Josephus is the next author to treat the question of Jewish presence in Rome. In estimating the relative population of Jews in the city he describes two influxes of Jewish prisoners. First, Pompey returned from his conquests in 62 BCE with hundreds of Jewish captives. Then in 32 BCE the champion Sosius arrived in Rome fresh from his victory over Herod's half-son Alexander with a large number of Judean prisoners. Josephus concludes that about eight thousand Jews resided at Rome at the beginning of the principate.[15]

To the Romans, Jewish synagogues would have appeared very much like other religious collegia, with their weekly meetings, community prayer to their patronal deity, and the regular collection of funds from the members.[16] However, it is important to observe that even when the Senate abolished the collegia in 64 BCE, Jewish synagogues were exempt. This special treatment cannot be assigned to Roman ignorance of Jewish gatherings. Cicero's *Pro Flacco* 66 attests that Jewish collegia in Rome had already received legal approbation. Waltzing suggests that Jews were allowed to continue unhampered because they were "indifférents à la politique romaine" (1895–1900, 1:110, n. 4).

Smallwood holds that Romans would have noted that Jewish collegia were distinct from others in four ways. First, their religious meeting was more of a community event than a meeting of disparate members. Second, the various Jewish synagogues were not separate, unconnected assemblies but were similar in organization, suggesting homogeneity and stability. Third, membership was more predictable since the community usually accepted only other Jews, either by birth or conversion. Fourth, the exclusivity of Jewish worship already set the community apart from free involvement in the larger religious rallying of other city collegia (Smallwood 1976:133–34). Here, one could argue that Smallwood presumes too much on such little evidence and that she seems unwittingly to retroject the greater uniformity of post–70 CE rabbinic Judaism into an earlier era. But even if Smallwood is correct in her description, the four distinct characteristics she notes could be read in a different light. They could present a threatening, unified force that embraced a non-Roman deity, and whose membership was steadily growing within the city walls. In my own view, Jewish assemblies must have achieved a reputation for stability and loyalty. Without these virtues, no other factors would have saved them from dissolution.

Synagogues received their most important ratification from Julius Caesar. His public approbation of their rights as a *religio licita* was proclaimed in letters he wrote to the major cities around the Mediterranean. Josephus records one of these letters written to the peoples of Parium where Jews were given the right to observe "their national customs and sacred rites . . . to collect contributions of money . . . [and] to hold common meals" (*Ant.* 14.214–15). These concessions stand out when they are contrasted with the regular policy of dissolution which Caesar also reiterates here:

> Similarly do I forbid other religious societies but permit these people alone to assemble and feast in accordance with their native customs and ordinances. And if you have made any statutes against our friends and allies, you will do well to revoke them because of their worthy deeds on our behalf and their goodwill towards us.[17]

The importance of this approval becomes clear as soon as it is recalled that Roman law of the republican and imperial period relied on the system of jurisprudence since no system or code of law had yet been organized. Thus, Caesar established a precedent which obliged all future emperors to recognize the legitimacy of Jewish religious practice. Even when the suppression of collegia included Jews, as was the case with Claudius' dissolution of the clubs, Jewish communities were eventually reinstated.

RESTRICTIONS ON COLLEGIA DURING THE PRINCIPATE

Augustus (28–14 BCE)

Suetonius notes that one of Augustus' first acts was the abolition of the guilds that had sprung up during the civil wars of Rome, allowing only the venerable ones to remain ("collegio praeter antiqua et legitima dissoluit"; *Augustus* 32.1). Notice that the act is ascribed to Augustus' initiative and not reported as a revival of Julius Caesar's *Lex Julia*.[18] Perhaps this is because Augustus was the first to stipulate two requisites of all recognized collegia. These are expressed in an inscription from his principate:

> Dis manibus. Collegio symphoniacorum qui sacris publicis praestu sunt, quibus senatus c(oire) c(ogi) c(onvocari) permisit e lege Iulia ex auctoritate Aug(usti) ludorum causa.
>
> (CIL VI 2193 = ILS 4966)

The collegia are required to receive approval for their convocation from Augustus via the Senate ("senatus coire cogi convocari permisit"). Second, they must accept responsibility for providing public service ("ludorum causa"). The total of three requisites – venerable age, approval by Augustus through the Senate, and the obligation for public service – ensured that the voluntary/private societies were conservative in character and *publicly* loyal to Augustus' administration.

Augustus' policy to Jewish communities was sustained in accordance with the approbation bestowed by Julius Caesar. Moreover, Augustus demonstrated his beneficence to the Jewish community by ordering that whenever gifts to the population of Rome were to be distributed on a day that coincided with the sabbath, the portion for the Jews should be set aside and given to them later (see Philo, *Legat.* 156–58).

During the republic, the introduction of any foreign cult required an authorization from the *quindecemviri*,[19] but Augustus took this prerogative to himself when the Senate bestowed upon him the title of *Pontifex Maximus*. Thus state and all religion were joined in the emperor's person.[20]

As the empire spread, the number and kind of foreign cults coming to Rome increased dramatically.[21] Therefore, the introduction of any foreign cult presupposed that a large contingent of foreign devotees had taken up residence in the city.[22] Since religion was integrated with social and political tradition, it is little wonder that the Roman administration was suspicious of such new cults. This explains the advice of Maecenas to Augustus that he deny authorization to any of the foreign cults because

> such persons by bringing in new divinities in place of the old, persuade many to adopt foreign practices, from which spring up conspiracies, factions and cabals, which are far from profitable to a monarch.
>
> (Dio Cassius 6.52.36)

Augustus did not adopt so stringent a policy but as Suetonius notes, "he treated with great respect such foreign rites as were ancient, and well established, but held the rest in contempt" (*Augustus* 93). Again, we see this idea that the ancient guilds are the ones to be trusted.

Policies in the Empire

The overall scarcity of literary evidence from the Roman provincial administrations does not allow much to be said about the impact of Augustus' restrictions on the larger empire. However, in Roman Egypt, papyri survive which cast some light on this question. Inscriptions that survive from the second and third centuries mention the approval the guilds received from Augustus. For example, a document from Oxyrhynchus reaffirms the permissions and privileges granted by Augustus to a guild of "victors in music competitions."[23] It is fair to say, even with such little evidence as this, that scrutiny of voluntary associations extended well beyond Rome's gates during Augustus' administration.

Tiberius (14–37 CE)

It is clear that Tiberius was ruthless with foreign cults in Rome. Suetonius reports that five years into Tiberius' principate, he

> abolished foreign cults at Rome, particularly the Egyptian and Jewish, forcing all citizens who had embraced these superstitious faiths to burn their religious vestments and other accessories.
>
> (*Tiberius* 36)

Moreover, the Emperor exiled 4,000 adult ex-slaves from these foreign religions from Rome to Sardinia (Tacitus, *Annales* 2.85).

We possess no law of Tiberius concerning the restrictions of collegia in the provinces but the strict control of them in Egypt under Tiberius' appointed governor, Flaccus, suggests that Tiberius' distrust of guilds had become imperial policy for the empire. This is more easily seen in the case of Egypt because formerly Egypt's own system of collegia had been well supported by the governors. The members had been co-operative in paying taxes and fulfilling government requisitions.[24] But a change occurs during Flaccus' administration and the phenomenon of clubs is seen as a political danger. Philo notes that Flaccus justified his suppression of the collegia on moral and political grounds:

> The sodalities and clubs, which were constantly holding feasts under pretext of sacrifice in which drunkenness vented itself in political intrigue, he dissolved and dealt sternly and vigorously with the refractory.[25]

To be sure, the province of Egypt was of special concern to the imperial government since its corn fed the Roman populace and the corn ships could not be halted for any reason. But it would seem overly rigorous to conclude that Tiberius' exceptionally strict measures with foreign cults and Flaccus' adamant censure of any guilds meant that Egypt alone aroused the suspicion of the emperor about the formation of guilds.

Claudius: 41–54 CE

We hear of no restrictions on clubs at all during the reign of Gaius (Caligula) Caesar (36–41). This comes as no surprise, since for the most part, Gaius did not focus his attention on administration. When Claudius took office in 41 CE he faced the need for restoration of order at every level of the empire's organization. We know that Gaius had allowed the clubs to proliferate without supervision because Dio Cassius reports that Claudius "disbanded the clubs which had been reintroduced by Gaius" (60.6.6). But the Jewish communities, for all their antiquity, also received Claudius' censure. Although they were permitted their religious practices, they were forbidden to assemble (ibid.).

Many of the clubs had a reputation for drunken behavior, which was one reason why Flaccus closed down Egyptian guilds. Often clubs had no rich benefactor to supply them with funds to acquire a meeting room and therefore they met in local taverns. This might explain Claudius' orders to close taverns in Rome and Ostia. Again, the justification given could simply uphold virtue in the city. But it also was effective in eliminating a place for meetings on a regular basis (Dio Cassius 60.6.6). Certainly, Philo considers the guilds a place of drunkenness and he uses this reputation to contrast the upright and serious character of Jewish assemblies: Jewish gatherings "are not based on drunkenness and carousing, but were schools of temperance and justice."[26]

The fear of a revolutionary group meeting under the guise of a social club might also explain Claudius' ban on the sale of boiled meat and hot water in the street (Dio Cassius 60.6.6). It was odd behavior to eat in the street in any case, as Hermansen (1982:200) observes:

> [It was] next to indecent for a respected Roman – and who cared about others (?) – to be seen eating in public. Since travelers in antiquity procured their own food . . . it well might be that meals could not be bought in Ostia (Rome) during times of restriction.

These measures would have made it almost impossible for any group to meet publicly for any length of time and escape notice.

Nero: 54–68 CE

In 59 CE, fighting broke out in the theatre at Pompeii between the residents of Nuceria and Pompeii during a gladiatorial exposition. Many of the spectators were wounded and some actually mutilated. Nero demanded a Senate investigation. The consuls were instructed to make their report on the matter. As a result of their findings, Nero ordered three punitive measures: the city of Pompeii was forbidden any similar gatherings for ten years; the sponsors of the games and the co-planners were exiled; and "illegal associations in the town were dissolved" (Tacitus, *Annales* 14.17). This injunction demonstrates the immediate response of Roman authorities to any social unrest: the "illegal" associations are closed. A question that arises naturally is how the local authorities could locate such associations with what appears to be relative ease. It would seem that they were well aware of their existence, but had chosen to turn a blind eye, perhaps because of some benefit derived from their presence in the city.

The Christians

While Christian groups are not designated by the Romans as guilds or collegia, Suetonius categorizes them as *"genus hominum superstitionis novae ac maleficae"* (a group of people belonging to a new and malevolent fanaticism) (*Nero* 16). Christians are thus designated as members of an unhealthy cult. We have already noted Roman suspicions of such unauthorized sects.

Nero counted on the public acceptance of imperial propaganda about dangerous illegal sects to support his assignation of blame for the fire in Rome to the Christians. When Tacitus characterizes the Christians by an *odio humani generis* (*Annales* 15.44), it is difficult to say whether he is representing only his own view, or a rather common perception even in Nero's day. We must note that he condemns the Jews in similar fashion for *omnis alios hostile odium* (*Historiae* 5.4.5). What Tacitus does tell us, despite his own aversion to the group, is that the populace viewed the torture of Christians with pity. He notes that despite Nero's justification of the deaths on the grounds of the "welfare of the state," the people knew that these deaths were really only to satisfy "the ferocity of one man" (*Annales* 15.44).

The important issue about Nero's grounds for condemnation arises with this incident. Roman law held persons liable for actions and not for any name they professed. Yet it appears that Nero had Christians arrested and killed on the basis of their membership, that is, their "name." We have good reason to suppose that he did institute that precedent. As will be seen below, the lawyer Pliny wrote to the Emperor Trajan about trials of Christians which he conducted. Do the Christians have to be arrested for a deed, or is the name sufficient? Since much of Roman law was based on jurisprudence, Pliny's question would be quite in order if Nero's precedent allowed the arrest of Christians by name alone.

Christians are very conscious of such a breach in Roman law, but one wonders how other unknown collegia fared in Neronian times. Nero's treatment of Christians shows the power of Imperial dictates and the precarious character of any collegium.

Trajan: 98–117 CE

Trajan's policies about voluntary associations are known to us through the emperor's replies to the enquiries of his newly appointed governor to Bithynia, Pliny the Younger.[27]

Three pairs of letters are of particular importance to our investigation. The first (*Epistulae* 10.33, 34) addresses the petition for a fireman's guild by the people of Nicaea. Pliny offers the Emperor three assurances about the plan: (a) that only professional firemen (that is, only known firemen and no impostors capable of "infecting" the group with seditious ideas) will be allowed as members; (b) that their privileges will not go beyond the guild; and (c) that their numbers will be maintained at a modest and manageable 150. This information is extremely important because it points out those elements that separated acceptable from unacceptable societies in the aristocrat Pliny's eyes: strictly controlled membership based on serious professional training, confined privileges, and small numbers.

In a telling reply, Trajan reminds the governor that it was precisely guilds such as this which have been responsible for so much disturbance in the province, especially in the cities. And he concludes his refusal with this conviction: "Whatever title we give them, and whatever our object in giving it, men who are banded together for a common end will all the same become a political association before long." This is the premise that articulates Roman resistance to the formation of any voluntary society.

The second pair of letters (*Epistulae* 10.92, 93) serves to reinforce the point. The free city of Amisus in Pontus pleads to form *erani*, clubs devoted to charity. Here, the emperor knows that the constitution of a free city is approved by Rome and therefore he instructs Pliny to allow what their constitution permits.

But even here he cautions the governor that the clubs must not be used *ad turbas et illicitos coetus*. And he closes the letters with his ruling on those cities that fall under Roman law: "I would have all such societies of this nature prohibited."

The third and final pair of letters (*Epistulae* 10.96, 97) is the famous correspondence about Christian arrests and prosecution. The fact is that Pliny has condemned Christians on the basis of name alone. Now he writes to ask about the continued employment of these "grounds." Should actions rather than the "name" alone be required? As stated above, such a question would be strange for someone as well prepared in law as Pliny were it not for the possible precedent set by Nero. As a matter of fact, Tertullian refers to an *"institutum Neronianum"* (*Ad Nationes* 1.7.9). While it is true that an *instituto* (a type of instruction) does not have the weight of a statutory law, Roman reliance on jurisprudence may be responsible for Pliny's recourse to it. However, the governor now sees that the prosecution of Christians on the basis of the name alone would have far-reaching effects on the province, since the Christians are "persons of all ranks and ages, and of both sexes . . . in the villages and rural districts."

Pliny's report of his examination of them provides evidence of the main concerns over the more particular features of an "illicit" religious group. The Christians admit that they did disobey the law by meeting at night, something they no longer do. And Pliny judges them harmless because in their meetings, (a) they do not sing a *carmen* (i.e., an incantation) but "a hymn to Christ as to a god"; (b) they gather to eat food which is "good and innocent"; (c) their behavior is guided by an oath "to avoid all evil behavior, respect the property of others, renounce adultery, lying and to keep their word."

Trajan's answer does not clarify whatever precept Pliny has followed on the issue of "name alone." Furthermore, he refuses to state "any general rule which can be applied as a fixed standard in all cases of this nature." However, as we know, he counsels Pliny to adopt a policy of prudence and moderation. He is to ignore the unsigned lists denouncing the presence of specific Christians in his province. When Christians are tried, they should be required to burn incense before the images of the gods, a test sufficient to prove where their loyalty lay.

Evidence from Egypt confirms Trajan's close scrutiny of guilds. A guild of hieroglyph writers from Oxyrhynchus sends a report concerning their membership, swearing by the Emperor Trajan that their statement is true:

To Claudius Menandrus, basilico-grammateus, from Teos, younger son of Onnophris son of Teos, his mother being Taseis, and Asclas son of Onnophris son of Osmolchis, his mother being Tesauris, both of the city of Oxyrhynchus, hieroglyphic carvers, who have been delegated by their fellow carvers: the list of ourselves and the said fellow carvers of hieroglyphics for the present 11th year of Trajanus Caesar the Lord [108 CE], as follows:

In the quarter of the Tenth, Teos son of Onnophris, the aforesaid,

Onnophris his brother, Asclas son of Onnophris, the aforesaid, Osmolchis his brother, who is also a hieroglyphic carver of Osiris the most great
god.

In the quarter of the square of Theoris, Ptolemaeus, son of Petosorapis,
son of Petosorapis.

Total 5 men. And we swear by the Emperor Caesar Nerva Trajanus
Augustus Germanicus Dacicus that we have honestly and truthfully presented the foregoing list, and that there are no more than these, and that
we have no apprentices or strangers carrying the art down to the present
day; otherwise may we be liable to the consequences of the oath."[28]

One may fairly surmise that all societies would have had to be prepared for
similar declarations concerning their gatherings, disclosing fully their
membership.

The evidence that survives from the provinces of Bithynia, Pontus, and Egypt
suggests that Trajan's prohibition of voluntary societies was a policy he enacted
throughout the empire.

Hadrian: 117–138 CE

The codification of edicts

Hadrian commissioned the African jurist, Salvius Julianus, to gather and codify
all former edicts. Up until that time, the laws for the governance of the city were
drawn up each year by the governor and the two Roman praetors, one representing the city, the other representing the foreign "visitors." While many of the laws
in these edicts were predictable, some were specific to particular situations. With
time, the mass of these edicts proved burdensome rather than helpful since
there was no organization to their injunctions and ad hoc legislation stood beside
foundational precepts. It required ten years for Salvius Julianus to complete the
codification of these laws. They were ratified by the Senate in Hadrian's principate and became statutory law. This code held ground for 400 years until the
principate of Justinian (527–65 CE).[29]

In this chapter we have not appealed to any of the formulations found in the
codifications and digests, even though many of them probably represent usual
state policy from the late republic. Since the codes do not come into effect until
Hadrian's administration, I have chosen to rely for evidence on epigraphical and
literary evidence from the actual reign of each emperor. With the reign of
Hadrian, however, the existence of codified laws authorized by the emperor
himself provides the best testimony of his interest in stability and consolidation
of social/political practice. To reach the codes from Hadrian's day, however, we
must turn to the Justinian *Digest* (527–65 CE).

The evidence of second-century collegia law in the Digest

In 550 CE the minister of justice, Tribonianus, five professors and eleven lawyers carried out a three-year task of reorganizing all past codes of Roman jurists. While the origins of the material are meticulously noted, the precise method by which the *Digest* was composed is still unknown (Scott 1932, 1:8-9). Included under the laws for the collegia are those ascribed to Gaius, a famous jurist from the reign of Trajan and Hadrian. He composed the textbook, *The Institutes*, for his own law students. It is generally assumed that later jurists such as Ulpianus (early 3rd cent.) used Gaius even though they did not cite him. The *Institutes* is the only legal treatise to have survived in its original form. The following two records of laws concerning collegia are attributed to Gaius' *The Institutes* and therefore would reflect the policies during the administrations of Trajan and Hadrian:

Digest 47.22.4 (Gaius, *Institutes* [On the Law of the Twelve Tables] 4)
Members are those who belong to the same association which the Greeks call *hetairia*. They are legally authorized to make whatever contracts they may desire with one another, provided they do nothing in violation of the public law. The enactment appears to have been taken from that of Solon, which is as follows: "If the people, or brothers, or those who are associated together for the purposes of sacrifice, or sailors, or those who are buried in the same tomb, or members of the same society who generally live together, should have entered, or do enter into any contract with one another, whatever they agree upon shall stand, if the public laws do not forbid it."

Digest 3.4.1 (Gaius, *Institutes* [On the Provincial Edict] 3)
All persons are not permitted indiscriminately to form corporations, associations, or similar bodies, for this is regulated by laws, Decrees of the Senate, and constitutions of the Emperors. Associations of this description are authorized in very few instances; as, for example, the right to form corporations is permitted to those engaged as partners in the collection of public taxes, or associated together in the working of gold, silver, and salt mines. There are also certain guilds at Rome whose organization has been confirmed by Decrees of the Senate, and Edicts of the Emperors; as, for instance, those of bakers, and some others, as well as that of ship-owners, which also exists in the provinces.

1 When persons are allowed to form associations under the title of a corporation, guild, or any other body of this kind, they are, like a municipality, entitled to have common property, a common treasure chest, and an agent or syndic, and as in the case of a municipality, whatever is transacted and done by him is considered to be transacted and done by all.
2 Where an association has no one to defend it, the proconsul says that he will order its common property to be taken into possession, and if, having been warned, they do not take measures to defend themselves,

he will order the property to be sold. We understand that an association has no agent, or syndic, when he is absent, or prevented by illness, or is otherwise incapable of transacting business.

3 Where a stranger appears to defend a society, the proconsul permits him to do so, as it happens in the case of the defense of private persons; because in this way the condition of the society is improved.

These laws demonstrate the seriousness with which the formation and conduct of *all* associations were taken under the empire, and particularly in Hadrian's day.

Policies in the provinces

Signs of imperial restrictions on the guilds can be seen in the surviving evidence from Roman Egypt. In the following example a diploma to victors of public competitions, recognized throughout the empire, is awarded to a new member of that guild. Notice that the guild had received its initial approbation from Augustus. At the conclusion, a list of rights proclaimed by Hadrian itemizes the privileges of the members:

> Tiberius Claudius Caesar Augustus Germanicus, *pontifex maximus*, holding the tribunician power for the second time and the consulship for the third time, saluted as emperor for the fourth time, *pater patriae*, greets the crowned victors of the cult of Dionysus and their fellow contestants. [. . .] but the privileges granted to you by the divine Augustus, I join in preserving as legal and philanthropic. The delegates were Claudius Pho[.]us, Claudius Epagathus, Claudius Dionysius, Claudius Thamyris. Written at Rome in the third consulship of Tiberius Claudius Caesar Augustus and the second consulship of Vitellius.
>
> Summary from a proclamation of the divine Hadrian concerning privileges granted to the guild: among which are the right of asylum, right of *proedria* [?] [-] and to judge, freedom from appointment as sureties, exemption from taxation, right of assembly as a guild, immunity from the liturgy of entertainment of public guests, immunity from imprisonment in any other prison.
>
> (*BGU* 1074; Johnson 1936:400)

The summary of Hadrian's exemptions for this guild emphasizes the expectation of *ludorum causa* that Augustus prescribed for those guilds authorized by the Senate. Here, the group appears to be relieved of this burden, probably because the membership does not have the resources to offer the state.

Collegia Tenuiorum[30]

Trajan employs *tenuiores* – society's poor – in (Pliny's) *Epistulae* 10.93 when he stipulates that the *erani* are "*ad sustinendam tenuiorum inopiam.*" That sense of the term also occurs in Justinian's *Digest* (47.22.1). There, a law recorded in Emperor Septimius Severus' principate by Marcianus, a jurist from the early third century, states:

> By the Decrees of the Emperors, the governors of the provinces are directed to forbid the organization of corporate associations, and are not even to permit soldiers to form them in camps. The more indigent soldiers, however, are allowed to put their pay every month into a common fund, provided they assemble only once during that time, for fear that under a pretext of this kind they may organize an unlawful society, which the Divine Severus stated in a Rescript should not be tolerated, not only at Rome, but also in Italy and in the provinces.
>
> (Institutiones Regulae, Book 3)

Notice that despite the ban on collegia, the poorer soldiers are allowed to assemble to pool their pay, but only once a month. And the reasons given for these restrictions are precisely those articulated by Trajan to Pliny (10.34) in denying permission for the establishment of a fireman's guild. The fear is that the group will become "unlawful," that is, politically seditious.

Another example of legal recognition of the needy concerns the membership of slaves. Again, it is Marcianus who records the law:

> It is also lawful for slaves to be admitted into associations of indigent persons, with the consent of their masters; and those who have charge of such societies are hereby notified that they cannot receive a slave into an association of indigent persons without the knowledge or consent of his master, and if they do, that they will be liable to a penalty of a hundred *aurei* for every slave admitted.[31]

These laws are in place during the reign of Septimius Severus, hence by the early third century CE. A famous inscription from Lanuvium predates these formulations by almost a century. Dated 136 CE, the document contains the statutes of a group of *tenuiores*.[32] It states there that the members meet once a month in order to sustain a fund for the burial of the members.

This inscription influenced Mommsen to conceive of these groups as *collegia funeraticia*. He further proposed that these associations were of two kinds. The first were organized for charitable works, such as the *erani* who petitioned for recognition by Pliny (*Epistulae* 10.93). The second type of *tenuiores* would be those whose members pooled their dues for the burial of members. For his part, Waltzing noted that Mommsen's suggestion of two kinds of club for the *tenuiores* lacked any inscriptional evidence in the west (1895–1900, 2:143). But there was good evidence for the existence of clubs of poor people and the provenance of these inscriptions was the west, that is, mostly the Italian Peninsula.[33] Here, we should note that there was a need for the poor to take practical measures for a proper and dignified burial. But what is not clear is that a monthly assembly of *tenuiores* really was a burial society. It is sufficient here to reiterate that Roman administration was acutely aware of the threat such groups could hold for the stability of the government.

CONCLUSION

This evidence illustrates that from the time of the late republic, the prohibition against and dissolution of voluntary societies was an unquestioned right and frequently employed policy of the Romans. Yet these measures do not seem to have been uniformly enforced. If Claudius, Nero, and Trajan are seen to suppress the collegia, it is because these clubs continued to spring up and grow whenever the political climate allowed them to do so. Thus the examination of the suppression of these clubs shows how important they were to the people of the Mediterranean world. Modern scholarship needs to address more closely the reasons for the continuing interest in collegia, despite their politically illicit character.

Second, the Roman restrictions on voluntary associations must be seen as part of the backdrop of early Christian communities. Did Christians pass "informal" scrutiny by city officials because their Jewish hero and their appeal to Jewish tradition cloaked them as a Jewish society? Is it due to these restrictions that Paul gathers the "church" in homes?

In the Q source, the cluster of sayings usually called "The Mission Speech" (Q 10:3–12) uses the image of the community as "lambs in the midst of wolves" (10:3). The ones being sent should be as discreet as possible. No signs of a long trip should be visible (sandals, staff, money bag). They should greet no one on the way (10:4). Do these exhortations arise out of a consciousness of the censure that could fall on these "missionaries"? Are the injunctions to stay where one is received, and to leave definitively when rejected (10:7–11) all part of the protection of this movement from public prosecution?

The very real dangers in belonging to an unrecognized society during the imperial period are usually ignored in any reconstruction of the first-generation Christian reality, as it is in the exegesis of the Christian texts themselves. Yet the clear evidence of Roman prohibition of such societies and the constant threat of their sudden investigation and dissolution must become incorporated into both aspects of our exegetical enterprise.

NOTES

1 Clemente 1972: esp. 156. See also Collingwood 1933–40, 3:90–93. Collingwood notes that when Roman armies traveled they brought their own craftsmen to ensure as complete an independence as possible.
2 See Gierke 1977: esp 95–142; Sohm 1907.
3 Latin text from Riccobono, Baviera, Ferrini, Furlani, and Arangio-Ruiz 1940–43, 1:63.
4 The scandal of 186 BCE about Bacchanalian groups led to the banishing of Dionysiac societies in Rome. But the legislation was directed to a particular society and not collegia in general. See Waltzing 1895–1900, 1:97.

5 Asconius, *In Senatu contra L. Pisonem* 8 (in Clark ed. 1918).

6 ibid. 7; De Robertis 1934, 1:83–108.

7 Cicero, *In L. Calpurnium Pisonem* 9: "conlegia non ea solum quae senatus sustulerat restituta, sed innumerabilia quaedam nova ex omni faece urbis ac servito concitata." Cf. Cicero, *Post Reditum in Senatu* 13.33; *Post Reditum ad Quirites* 5.13.

8 Of course, it is obvious that *all* collegia were "religious" as Waltzing (1895–1900, 1:75) observes ("à l'époque lointaine dont nous parlons, une corporation sans culte ne se conçoit pas"). The distinction would give special attention to the primary reason for the group's particular organization, which in the case of religious collegia would be common devotion to a deity.

9 See Sohm 1907:198–99.

10 Cicero, *Epistulae ad Quintum fratrem* 2.3.5.

11 Suetonius, *Divus Julius* 42.3: "cuncta collegia praeter antiquitus constituta distraxit." On this, see De Robertis 1934, 1:195–96. For a survey of imperial perspectives on the *collegia* see ibid., 1:244–45; 1938:216–17.

12 See, for example, the titulus of the *Collegium symphoniacorum* from the first century BCE (*CIL* VI 2193 = *ILS* 4966; Waltzing 1895–1900, 1:116): "Dis Manibus. Collegio symphoniacorum qui sacris publicis praestu sunt, quibus senatus c(oire) c(ogi) c(onvocari) permisit e *lege Iulia ex auctoritate Aug(usti) ludorum causa*" (emphasis added).

13 See Smallwood 1976. In large measure, this section is dependent on her excellent treatment.

14 Valerius Maximus, *Factorum dictorumque memorabilium* 1.3.3 (Stern 1974: no. 147b); Smallwood 1976:128–29, n. 27.

15 Josephus, *Ant.* 17.300; *War* 2.80.

16 LaPiana 1927:348–51; Guterman 1951:130–50; Smallwood 1976:133–36.

17 Josephus, *Ant.* 14.216. The gratitude that Caesar expresses refers to the support he received from the Jewish forces under Antipater in Caesar's war against Antony. Caesar had a good relationship with Hyrcanus II and Palestinian Jews were agreeably disposed towards Caesar.

18 Waltzing 1895–1900, 1:117.

19 See Nock 1933:68; 1972:757–58.

20 *Resgestae divi Augusti* 23; Greene 1933:321.

21 See Cumont 1911:179; Willoughby 1929; Hadas 1959:182–97, esp. 183.

22 Against Cumont, Ramsay MacMullen holds that it is the foreign immigrants and not enthralled Roman devotees who are responsible for the spread of a foreign cult in the city (1981:112–17).

23 P. Lond. 1178. See Johnson 1936:400. The text of this inscription will be recorded under the treatment of Hadrian.

24 "Code of Regulations of an Idiologus" in Johnson 1961:256 (*BGU* 5 R 469) 108 and n. 24.

25 Philo, *Flacc.* 4; De Robertis 1934, 1:266–67.

26 Hermansen 1982:199–200; Philo, *Legat.* 311–12. See the essay by Seland, in this volume.

27 Legally, Bithynia had been a senatorial province but it appears that the unrest had escalated in Trajan's time so that he intervened and named his own governor. See Pliny the Younger, *Epistulae* 10.58.

28 P. Oxy. 1029. See Johnson 1936:397.

29 See Perowne 1961: esp. 75–79.

30 On this type of collegium, see the treatment of Mommsen 1843:87–106; Waltzing 1895–1900, 1:141–53; De Robertis 1934, 2:275–340; Schiess 1888.

31 Marcianus, *Public Prosecutions* 2.2; *Digesta* 47.22.3.

32 See *CIL* XIV 2112; Waltzing 1895–1900: no. 2311 for the Latin text; for the English see Lewis and Reinhold 1966b: 273–75.

33 Waltzing 1895–1900, 2:146.

6

EARLY SYNAGOGUES AS COLLEGIA IN THE DIASPORA AND PALESTINE

Peter Richardson

Some years ago Simeon Guterman argued that "on the basis of Josephus's specific evidence and the general similarity in the organization of synagogues and the collegia we may feel justified in regarding the Jewish communities as *collegia licita*."[1] More recently, Mary Smallwood has affirmed that view.[2] This paper aims to carry their views on one aspect of the matter somewhat further.

It is surprising that the view that synagogues were collegia has never caught on; most writers on synagogues ignore the claim. In the extensive – often intensive – debate, for example, on the *origin* of synagogue buildings, the various disputants do not list voluntary associations as one of the possibilities.[3] Instead we get such divergent and improbable views of synagogal origins as basilicas, *ekklēsiastēria, triclinia, naoi* and the like. In the equally vigorous debate over the various functions of the synagogue and the roles that synagogues play there are few mentions of voluntary associations. The general sense of these debates is that the development of synagogues was *sui generis*, when in fact it was part of a larger movement.

I shall argue that synagogues functioned as – and were perceived as – collegia in the diaspora, that the earliest evidence for synagogues is from the Mediterranean (not Mesopotamian or Babylonian) diaspora, that this coincidence suggests that synagogues actually began life as collegia in a diaspora setting, that when they came into Palestine they continued to show signs of being collegia though that terminology was no longer appropriate, and that only gradually did they take on (especially in the Holy Land) a new set of characteristics deriving from the loss of the Temple. This last point is beyond the main point of this paper but an important adjunct. The earlier points fly against the opinions of most scholars, especially Israelis, who are key players. This is still a hotly debated topic, on which opinions are strongly held. To present those views I will begin with an analysis and critique of the most recent and important major work on synagogues. This contribution to a study of voluntary associations will take the following shape:

1   The state of the question
2   The legal situation in the Diaspora

THE STATE OF THE QUESTION

The first volume of the most recent full-scale study of synagogues has just appeared. It contains an important selection of individual studies, many translated from the Hebrew for the first time, with a heavy emphasis on Israeli participation (Urman and Flesher 1995). I have three overall reactions: first, there are important methodological issues at stake, with Israeli scholars tending to one side of the debate and American scholars on the other side.[4] Second, and related to this, there is no agreement on what role the later literary evidence of Talmud and Mishnah is to play. Third, there is still a strong attachment to a typology of synagogue development that according to many scholars is outdated and no longer viable. Put summarily, the fundamental question is whether the evidence from the earliest period – the focus of this paper – is to be heard and followed.

J. Gwyn Griffiths complains, correctly, that only a minority of scholars have recognized that the synagogue had its origins in Egypt. By most, the "possibility of an Egyptian influence is not even considered" (1995:8). He is tolerant of the idea of the influence of "Hellenistic associations," but in the end he draws back from agreeing with a substantial influence. Aryeh Kasher also rehearses Egyptian evidence, arguing that while synagogues were for torah reading and prayer, "they should resemble the Jerusalem Temple in their functions . . . not involved with the sacrificial worship" (1995:200, cf. 209); with this is linked his repeated insistence that Leontopolis (and Elephantine) were insignificant in Egyptian Judaism.[5] Lester L. Grabbe claims that Judean synagogues were not Pharisaic, and that there is only the slenderest of evidence before the first century CE, while Paul V. M. Flesher comments, in an important footnote (1995:29 n. 8) that "none of the rabbinic texts published prior to about 250 refers to synagogues prior to 70 . . . [including] the Mishnah." He assesses pre-70 synagogues helpfully, though he gives too much weight to such matters as orientation and not enough to such matters as the presence of *mikvaoth* at Gamla (which is *not* in Galilee, p. 35) and Herodium (p. 37). He is too concerned to distinguish between Galilee and Judea, and not sufficiently interested in the party affiliations of those building the structures.

Dennis Groh provides an extremely important fresh analysis of datable archaeological evidence for synagogues. His view is absolutely clear: "stratigraphic excavation has flat-footedly destroyed the sequential development" of (1) a basilical type; (2) the fourth-century broadhouse type; (3) a Byzantine synagogue with apse toward Jerusalem. This is a model of care, precision, and accurate analysis.[6] His main conclusions for my present purpose: "The first-century Galilean synagogue. . . is essentially a room to gather the community" (1995:60); the first basilical synagogues were mid-third century and orientation towards Jerusalem appeared first in the second century (69). Yoram Tsafrir fights a rearguard action against the newer views, not only with respect to the typology against which Groh argues, but even in favor of the view that "prior to the third century synagogues did not exist as special structures, with external identifying signs" (1995:79); "the Galilean synagogue is a third-century Jewish invention"; "there are no architectural connections between the third-century synagogues in Galilee and the synagogue structures of the Temple period" (80). It is a model of special pleading! Similarly Gideon Foerster seems still to support a typological schema, though he avoids doing so explicitly.

On Diaspora synagogues, Kraabel's views are represented by reprinting his *ANRW* article (1979). His unrevised conclusions, relevant to what follows, are: we must abandon the basilica model, there is no one pattern, Rabbinic statements are irrelevant, and Diaspora synagogues were often deliberately inconspicuous community buildings for various functions.

Several contributions deal with one or several synagogues: David Amit with southern Judean synagogues (making an interesting case for specific halakic influences); Shimon Dar and Yohanan Mintzker on the synagogue at Horvat Sumaqa; Zvi Gal on the eastern Lower Galilee synagogues; Zvi Ilan on Meroth. But none of these sheds light on my limited set of questions; nor does the contribution of Zeev Safrai, important as it is, on Rabbinic communal synagogue functions (for example, he argues that the *bet ha-Mishnah* was not attached to the synagogue), though he acknowledges that "in the early synagogue, the role of community center was of greater importance; this was a major daily function of the building" (1995:200). Aharon Oppenheimer stresses that the Babylonian community had traditions about the origins of some of their synagogues in the early days of the Exile, though he does not offer a view on the correctness of their views. Isaiah Gafni also deals with Babylonian synagogues.

Dan Urman, in addition to commenting on nineteenth-century photographs, argues that the house of assembly (that is, synagogue) was "first and foremost . . . a community center"; only later did it become a house of prayer in the land of Israel. Further, the *bet ha-Midrash* of the second Temple was a real building; he concludes that "a good part of the structures uncovered thus far and identified as houses of assembly were, in fact, houses of study" (1995:255), an unusual and unconvincing suggestion. Ronny Reich presents the evidence cogently for a link between synagogues and *mikvaoth* in the second Temple period (1995:295), though not in the later period when there is a "drastic decrease in the construction and use of *miqwaot* in general" (296).

In summary, the book is a mixed bag, though it is the best book on synagogues available. It shows that helpful insights can still emerge from continued archaeological work and analysis, but efforts to construct a typological development of synagogues have almost run their course;[7] there is still no consensus on synagogue origins, though there is a growing inclination to look to the Mediterranean Diaspora. Finally, there is still a good bit of misinformation, even from Israeli scholars who should know the sites at first hand.

THE LEGAL SITUATION IN THE DIASPORA

Synagogues were viewed as collegia by Roman authorities in the first century BCE, yet their status was special.[8] Two figures dominate the interpretation of such evidence as there is: Julius Caesar and Caesar Augustus. Elsewhere, Wendy Cotter has summarized briefly the main outlines of the legal position, drawing on Mary Smallwood's earlier analysis.[9] Here all that is needed is a reminder or two, and filling in a few blanks.

In 64 BCE the Senate prohibited all collegia on principle because of their danger to the state as private institutions.[10] In the political and social turbulence of the period it was appropriate that in 58 BCE collegia were permitted again (during the First Triumvirate),[11] and that in 56 BCE the Senate again dissolved one specific class of collegia, political clubs. A few years later (the date is not certain but sometime between 49 and 44 BCE), Julius Caesar prohibited all collegia empire-wide, except for the most ancient ones. One exception – it conformed to the notion "ancient" – was Judaism,[12] and this exception was also empire-wide. By this action Caesar made Judaism a *religio licita*; Jewish gratitude for this status was demonstrated by Jewish attendance at Caesar's funeral (Suetonius, *Divus Julius* 84.5).

During the chaos of the civil wars the law against collegia again fell into abeyance. At some unknown date Octavian/Augustus re-enacted it, and under his law against collegia synagogues were again exempted. Philo, for example, though not an exact contemporary, provides good evidence for Augustus' generosity:

> [H]e did not expel them from Rome or deprive them of their Roman citizenship because they remembered their Jewish nationality also. He introduced no changes into their synagogues, he did not prevent them from meeting for the exposition of the Law, and he raised no objection to the offering of first fruits. . . . Moreover . . . if the distribution [of money or food in Rome] happened to be made on the Sabbath . . . he instructed the distributors to reserve the Jews' share . . . until the next day.[13]

The pattern is this: in times of factionalism and strife collegia tended to be permitted, but in times when reconstruction and consolidation were important, collegia were restricted: in 64 BCE, in the 40s under Julius Caesar, and in the 30s or 20s under Augustus. In the latter two cases, but perhaps not the first, synagogues were exempted from the laws against collegia; in the Augustan legislation in particular Judaism held its "preferred" status.

EPIGRAPHIC AND QUASI-EPIGRAPHIC SOURCES FOR THE DIASPORA

The earliest datable evidence for synagogues is an important group of inscriptions from Egypt that refers in almost all cases to *proseuchai*. Let me say straightaway that I believe terminology is not crucial to the decision about what is and is not a synagogue. Buildings for cultic and community purposes, whether *proseuchai*, *synodoi*, *sabbateia* or *synagōgai* all qualify. Most of the inscriptional evidence from Egypt is either described or reproduced in Schürer, and in what follows I largely follow the pattern of his analysis.[14] Of the nine inscriptions he lists from Egypt, eight are from the Delta region, exactly the same region in which both Leontopolis and the Therapeutae were to be found.[15] The main point to observe is that all eight presuppose a building, not just the worshipping community.[16] The ninth inscription, from Arsinoe-Crocodilopolis in the Fayum, is matched by two important papyri from the same region and period, in which again a building is presupposed.[17] One piece of evidence from Egypt uses the term *synagōgē*, linked with the more common word *proseuchē*.[18] In this case the word *proseuchē* refers to the building and *synagoge* appears to refer simply to the "gathering."[19] In sum, this evidence speaks strongly of a set of buildings from the third to the first centuries BCE serving the needs of the Jewish communities, mostly in Lower Egypt.[20] The favored terminology in Egypt is *proseuchai*, but I have no doubt that these buildings – despite the absence of archaeological evidence about their precise size, shape, or form – were what in other places were called synagogues.

There is also literary evidence from Egypt, the most important of which is Philo. Generally Philo, writing in the early first century CE, follows Egyptian usage and employs *proseuchē* when he wishes to refer to buildings for the Jewish community. This is especially frequent in both *Legatio ad Gaium* and *In Flaccum*, where most of the time the reference is to the buildings in Alexandria that were vandalized, burned, or desecrated by the mobs in the violence surrounding the year 38 CE.[21] In two cases in *Legatio* he refers to Rome and the *proseuchai* there: they meet on the sabbaths, collect money for the Temple in Jerusalem and so on, all of which, he says, Augustus knew but did nothing about (*Legat.* 156, 157). In *De Vita Mosis* 2.216, he has a variant on this, referring to Jews every seventh day occupying themselves with the philosophy of their fathers: "for what are our places of prayer (*proseuktēria*) throughout the cities but schools of prudence and courage and temperance and justice, and also of piety and holiness and every virtue."[22] A very similar sense is given in *Spec. Leg.* 2.62, though he uses *didaskaleia* in that case.[23] Further, still speaking of seventh-day worship, Philo says of the Essenes (*Quod omnis* 81) that "they proceed to the sacred places (*topous*), which they call synagogues (*synagōgai*), where the young sit ranked in rows below the elders . . . ." And in like fashion he says of the Therapeutae (*Vita cont.* 30) that "they meet together as for a general assembly (*koinon syllogon*) and they sit according to their ages . . . ." Speaking of a Palestinian group he uses *synagōgē*, speaking of an Egyptian group that is different from the norm he uses *syllogon*, and speaking of urban groups in the cities of Egypt he uses, as the inscriptions themselves do, *proseuchē*. But in almost all cases, except the Therapeutae, he appears to mean the same thing, a building serving various community needs.[24]

Elsewhere in the Diaspora there is somewhat similar evidence. At Rome, for example, inscriptions from catacombs refer to eleven synagogues. Since these are informal grave inscriptions they cannot be dated securely, though most of the inscriptions and some of the synagogues to which reference is made are undoubtedly later than the period with which this chapter is concerned. Some of the synagogue references, however, refer to earlier communities of Jews in Rome: probably the earliest is the "synagogue of the Hebrews," followed by a "synagogue of the Augustesians/Augustans,"[25] a synagogue of the Agrippesians/Agrippans,"[26] and a "synagogue of the Volumnians,"[27] together with a "synagogue of the Herodians."[28] It cannot be certain whether *synagōgē* in these cases refers to the community itself or to a building, though a building seems likely. On the north shore of the Black Sea there were first-century CE synagogues,[29] indicating a strong presence of Jews there and a wide distribution of Jewish community buildings. The epigraphic evidence could be expanded, but the point is perhaps sufficiently made that the evidence is rather good for synagogues at an early period in a range of places, and for a range of terminology to describe them.

Josephus quotes decrees that we might have found as inscriptions, had we been so lucky (I think of these as "quasi-epigraphic"). These few paragraphs must be highly selective since a considerable body of data is available. I begin with Josephus, *Ant.* 16.160–73, because it ties in neatly with the preceding, then go back to *Ant.* 14.190–264.[30] *Antiquities* 16 contains a series of decrees all from the reign of Augustus.[31] In general, these Augustan decrees describe lenient treatment of Jews in the Asian Diaspora, specifically with respect to the collection and transmission of the Temple tax (probably including additional free-will gifts) and exemption from attendance at court. Both these protections went beyond what was usual in collegia: the transmission of money to Jerusalem hinted at a high degree of foreign allegiance, and the exemption from court attendance was unusual. In at least these two respects Judaism's status went beyond that of the other collegia that were exempted from the anti-collegia decree of Augustus. One explicitly refers to thefts from a building and from an "ark" (16.164: *ek te sabbateiou ek te aarōnos*), the building being named a *sabbateion*, the functions of which were related to the functions of a synagogue, containing the inviolable "sacred books" (*tas hieras biblous*) and "sacred monies."[32]

Regarding the decrees in *Ant.* 14.190–264, the following general comments can be made on the twenty-three pieces of "archival" material.[33] Their main theme was exemption from military service, an important issue during the civil war; this appeared first in a decree of Lucius Lentulus to Asia and Ephesus (19 September 49 BCE; 14.228–29), was repeated by him in two other decrees, and his decision was cited in three more decrees. The exemption from military service was also dealt with by Dolabella in another decree to Asia and Ephesus, probably in 44 (14.223–27). Among the other rights noted in this collection were making offerings in Jerusalem, deferring appearances in court on the Sabbath, managing produce, celebrating festivals, keeping the Sabbath. For our purposes, the two most important decrees were those by Lucius Antonius, son of Mark Antony, to Sardis (14.235) and one by the people of Sardis (14. 259–61). The latter allowed Jews to build their own place of prayer and confirmed the right to adjudicate suits among themselves as well as the right to approved food. The former confirmed Jews' right to a place of their own, together with the rights of association and of civil judicial authority. Both confirmed a range of rights, both were set in Sardis, one of the places that has remarkable archaeological evidence of a synagogue.[34]

Josephus alludes to another early synagogue in *War* 7.44; describing the Jewish community at Antioch (which he claims was specially large) he implies that at some indeterminate point after Antiochus IV Epiphanes and before 64 BCE, the synagogue in Antioch was again treated leniently. This information, if correct, may suggest a synagogue building in Antioch during this period, not otherwise attested.

Sometimes in the face of the opposition of local authorities, the Jewish community was sustained in its status, able to run its own affairs in the same way others were able to do. Judaism in the Diaspora was surprisingly protected by the actions of Julius Caesar, the Senate of Rome, and Augustus; this protection went beyond that of other collegia.[35] The group was visible; even though a collegium was not a legal person, Jewish communities could collect the half-shekel Temple tax and send it to Jerusalem; they could also send larger voluntary gifts (an arrangement that was resented, resulting in delegations being attacked); they could collect and transmit produce as fulfillment of the requirement for tithing first-fruits.[36] The decrees underscore the varied group life a Jewish community could have: common meals, observance of festivals (especially the seventh day), carrying out of religious ritual (prayer and reading of torah particularly), special gatherings, educational opportunities, special food; in short, the communities had the opportunity to carry out their traditional rites and customs. Other rights could be exercised individually: exemption from military service, freedom to observe the Sabbath, opportunity to adjudicate their own civil suits. Local communities of the Diaspora were able to preserve their way of life against the weight of opinion in many of the cities in which they settled, and they had official sanction for this preservation. They were both like and unlike other *thiasoi* and collegia, but in their group life they were seen by the officials, by their neighbors, and probably by themselves as voluntary associations.[37]

OTHER COLLEGIA, *THIASOI*, AND *SYNODOI* IN THE DIASPORA

Synagogues were like, but in a better position than, most other associations in the eastern Mediterranean (for more details on some of these other groups, see other essays in this volume). Much of the authorities' concern in the case of voluntary associations was whether other illegal societies were meeting under the pretext of a licit one: "permission cannot be given for the existence of societies, and . . . soldiers may not have clubs in the camps. However it is permitted [by decree of the Senate] for poor people to make a monthly contribution, provided they meet only once a month and that no illegal society meets under a pretext of this nature."[38] Some of these worries come through vividly, just after our period of concern, in Pliny's correspondence with Trajan (for example, *Epistulae* 10.33–34, 92–93).

Few buildings have survived (or have been identified) belonging to guilds and societies. There are, therefore, few studies of the buildings of voluntary associations generally, and not many of individual structures, though there are rich investigations into Mithraea, for example (see Roger Beck's essay in this volume).[39] The Bakcheion for the Iobacchoi in Athens (between the Areopagus and the Pnyx) is one that can be traced.[40] There was a large hall with a decorated altar built for worship of Dionysos, probably in the second century. A good bit can be known of the activities of the association from a stele,[41] and these can be connected with the architecture in limited ways.

THE EARLIEST DIASPORA SYNAGOGUES

The earliest archaeological evidence for synagogues comes from Egypt[42] (where they are often referred to as "Houses of Prayer"), the Aegean islands, especially Delos and Aegina, where the remains are rather slim and have led to considerable debate, and Ostia, the port of Rome.[43] Despite the large number of Diaspora communities in which synagogues were to be found, most of the Diaspora building evidence is later than the first century.[44] The two most helpful sites from the Diaspora are Delos[45] and Ostia[46] (see Figure 6.1).

Delos. The earliest Diaspora synagogue sites of which we have evidence were remodeled houses adapted to the needs of the worshipping community.[47] The synagogue at Delos (which McLean, in this volume, argues was one of two Samaritan synagogues) was renovated in the late second century BCE and again in the mid-first century BCE, and continued on into the second century CE. It had inscriptions to *theos hypsistos*; architecturally there were benches, a *thronos*, ancillary rooms, all fronted by a stoa; in many respects it was like other "collegial halls" on Delos.[48]

Ostia. Here the renovations run from the first century CE to the fourth.[49] In the earliest renovation as a synagogue a dining hall was added; it too had other ancillary areas. (Other later renovations do not concern us.) Stobi, Priene, and Dura Europus (possibly Sardis), were first adapted to synagogue use in the second century CE or later, so I leave them to one side.

Assessment. White's view is clear and correct: "From a public perspective many of the synagogue communities were organized after the fashion of a collegium, as merchant guilds or ethnic trading agencies"; it was an "ethnic *thiasos* . . . often

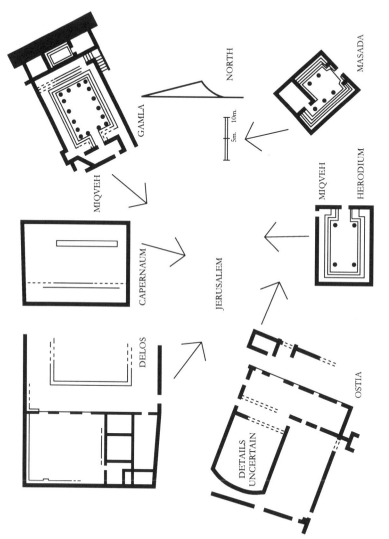

GAMLA

MIQVEH

NORTH

MASADA

CAPERNAUM

MIQVEH

HERODIUM

JERUSALEM

DELOS

OSTIA

DETAILS
UNCERTAIN

5m. 10m.

Figure 6.1 Pre-70 CE synagogues

98

designated by . . . *synodos* or *koinos*."[50] He argues that "Before 70 the synagogue was not an institution in the later talmudic sense. It originated, rather, as a place of Jewish assembly, of ethnic and religious identity, especially in the alien environment of the Diaspora. Here the *proseuchē* as 'house of prayer' served both as place of assembly and as social center to the congregation (*synagōgē*)." This is correct and well said; the practices influenced, as White hints, synagogues in the Holy Land. It is important to stress, however, that "the later talmudic" sense does not refer to a different institution but to one that has been further refined and developed in the light of the changes called for by the destruction of the Temple, as I shall suggest below.

EPIGRAPHIC AND LITERARY SOURCES FOR PALESTINE

The well-known Theodotos inscription undoubtedly dates from the period before the destruction of the Temple, though how long before cannot be said;[51] the text is well known:

> Theodotos, son of Vettenus, priest and *archisynagōgos*, son of an *archisynagōgos*, grandson of an *archisynagōgos*, built the synagogue for the reading of Torah and the study of the commandments, and the guest-house and the rooms and the water installations, for the needy travelers from abroad. The foundations of the synagogue were laid by his fathers and the elders and Simonides.[52]

The inscription confirms that the building was a synagogue and it described its functions: reading of Torah and study of commandments for residents of Jerusalem who attended the synagogue and, for occasional Diaspora visitors, beds and washing facilities and other rooms.[53] Regrettably we have no indication of how these functions were given architectural form, though the inscription broadens the evidence gained from other building remains, for it provides a description of the areas that might be included in a larger-than-average synagogue. The extra facilities were needed for visitors, of course, in Jerusalem for a festival. Regrettably we cannot say how such a synagogue might have been recognized by visitors, or was oriented or decorated.

There is also literary evidence, foremost of which is Josephus. In his fullest reference he describes a prayer house in Tiberias, "a huge building" (*tēn proseuchēn, megiston oikēma*; *Life* 272). This building must be dated roughly between 18 CE (when Tiberias was founded) and 65 CE. The town assembly that became a military council met there (cf. 279, 280, 293), but it was primarily intended for prayer within the ordinary service (295), though obviously matters of public business were addressed there (295–98). Josephus uses the term *synagōgē* in *Ant.* 19.300–11, describing events in Dora (Tell Dor) when some youths tried to introduce an image of Claudius into the building. Agrippa I was angered by this attempt to overthrow the laws of his fathers, says Josephus, and referred the matter to Petronius, governor of Syria. Josephus quotes Petronius' letter to the community leaders at Dora, which describes the building as a "synagogue," insisting that the emperor had decreed that Jews could follow their own customs. While it is impossible to date the building, the events described presuppose that it was standing in the late 30s. A somewhat similar situation obtains with *War* 2.285–92, describing a synagogue in Caesarea Maritima just prior to the outbreak of the revolt in 66 CE, using *synagōgē*;[54] he describes an argument over a neighboring Greek landowner's workshop that left Jews using the synagogue with only a narrow and awkward passage. When faced with an offensive sacrifice on a Sabbath the Jews went to see Florus at Sebaste.

What is especially significant in this evidence from Josephus, limited as it is, is that he does not say – or even imply – that synagogues in Palestine had other earlier forebears than the instances he uses.[55] His evidence bears on the first century CE. That is not to say that there were no earlier synagogues, only that Josephus' evidence for Diaspora synagogues is a good bit earlier than his evidence for Palestinian synagogues.

THE EARLIEST PALESTINIAN SYNAGOGUES

There are four pieces of primary evidence to consider:[56] Gamla, Masada, Herodium and the Theodotos inscription[57] (see sketch-plans – to the same scale – of the various buildings; figure 6.1).

Gamla. Despite some scholars' reservations, the community building at Gamla was the earliest synagogue we have, probably from the first century BCE. Located on the high side of town, adjacent to the casemate wall (in this respect not unlike Masada), it had a simple meeting room with an additional room within the wall and a ritual pool (*mikveh*) a few steps away outside the front entrance. The building was constructed of black basalt ashlar masonry, with columns supporting the roof, the corner ones being heart-shaped; the capitals were carved in relatively plain style. The interior was plain. Around the walls were benches, the main portion of the floor was packed dirt. There were two entrances, the main door (with an unusual indirect entrance) on the axis of the large room faced approximately south-west, and a side entrance faced approximately south-east, dropping down by stairs to the street that ran along the south wall. Jerusalem was to the south-west.

The building was a simple community hall, able to be used for a variety of functions. There was little to differentiate functions in the building. Did it provide for liturgical functions in any way? The evidence is not so clear. There was a cupboard or niche in the north-west corner of the building, possibly suitable as a torah-niche, though that is unclear; if it was it was an early and unique solution. A row of stone pavers across the middle of the dirt floor has been proposed as the location of a reading desk – possible but not certain. The *mikveh* outside the door was connected with the building, since the water channel cuts through the floor plan. The room to the north-east within the casemate wall was probably a *bet ha-Midrash*.

Masada. Any assessment of Masada must now react to the recently published technical reports of the excavations (Netzer 1993). Yadin concluded that a synagogue from the time of the First Revolt (Masada II) was underlain by an earlier building (Masada I), also probably a synagogue, within the same walls but with a different configuration of the space. If Masada I were used as a synagogue, and this is not certain, it could have been an even earlier one than Gamla. This too was a plain structure. It lacked the benches almost uniformly found in Palestinian synagogues, but had an entrance and a pattern of columns somewhat similar to the Gamla synagogue. Like Gamla, Masada I was backed up against the casemate wall, but in this case there was no separate room within the width of the wall itself – the outside defensive wall was the wall of the synagogue.[58] There was no evidence of provision for liturgical functions in Masada I: no niche or reading desk. There was one door, facing roughly south-east; Jerusalem was west of north. This part of the Masada complex was late Herodian.[59] If Masada I was a synagogue, it was the only synagogue in any of the extant remains from Herod's building activities.[60]

In the renovation of the space – Masada II – to suit the Sicarii defenders of Masada in the First Revolt certain changes were made. A genizah was created with an underfloor compartment in which to store biblical scrolls no longer used; the renovators compensated for the loss of space by removing the entrance area and incorporating it into the main hall, re-using columns from the Northern Palace. Benches were added around the now awkwardly shaped room. Though no *mikveh* was provided adjacent to the synagogue, there was one not far away.[61] Masada II was a synagogue of the late first century CE.[62] There was no provision for liturgical functions, and no effort was made to alter the orientation of the seating or the location of the door. When Yadin says "it was wholly oriented towards Jerusalem as required . . ." (1966:184), he obscures the issue by using later requirements for orientation and by ignoring the fact that its door faced *away* from Jerusalem.

Herodion. Exactly contemporaneous with Masada II was the synagogue in the Upper Palace of Herodion adapted by its defenders during the First Revolt from the *triclinium* of the palace.[63] It accommodated the religious needs of the defenders by adding benches around the walls, with relatively few other alterations. The main door faced due east;[64] Jerusalem was almost due north. There is little evidence to tell how it was decorated or what other fittings were provided, but there seems no torah niche and no reading desk, though a *mikveh* was built outside the door. The room was a simple community hall with no decoration or artistic elaboration.

Assessment. There was no consistency in orientation of the pre-70 synagogues: at Gamla the door was oriented more or less to Jerusalem, though this may have been purely accidental since the location would hardly admit of any other arrangement. In Masada I and II the wall *opposite* the door was closest to lining up with Jerusalem; if Masada I was purpose-built, the builders could have chosen another location with a different orientation. Even Masada II, the revolutionaries' synagogue, could have been located elsewhere within the overall complex had orientation been a factor. Herodion offered its renovators little choice in location or orientation, once it was decided to squeeze the synagogue into the *triclinium*. A long side wall was oriented to Jerusalem and the door faced east.[65] In early Palestinian synagogues orientation to Jerusalem was irrelevant; it mattered little to the builders how the building faced.[66]

Neither Masada I, Masada II, nor Herodion provided for liturgical functions.[67] Gamla may have had some minor provisions: the line of stone pavers across the middle may, but need not, have been intended as a location for a movable desk; there may have been a cupboard; there was a *mikveh*. There was no reflection of Jerusalem, no visual sense of attachment to Temple, no symbolic decoration: none of the synagogues was decorated with symbols reminiscent of the Temple in Jerusalem. Such symbols – found profusely in later synagogues in mosaic floors, capitals, lintels, and other architectural features – were completely absent in pre-70 buildings. The menorah, lulab and ethrog, all calling to mind Temple services, came into synagogue art only after 70, it would seem.[68]

Also absent from early synagogues was a separation between men and women.[69] None had a gallery, which might have been a "women's gallery," nor a horizontal division between men and women, for example, through the middle of the benches. When the space was so obviously designed to high-light the communal – almost democratic – character of the space, it was unlikely that the builders would have subdivided it so as to destroy that sense of oneness.[70]

It should be underlined that all the Palestinian synagogues of which we have remains from this earliest period were purpose-built. There are no remains analogous to the adapted buildings of the Diaspora, whose importance White stresses so effectively. One element of the buildings remodeled from private houses is the important role of patrons. Though patrons may have been in-volved in purpose-built Palestinian structures as well, of course, as inscriptions in later buildings attest so clearly, there seems no clear evidence of patronal activ-ity in the early synagogues in the Holy Land. These structures were community buildings, both in the sense of for and by the community.[71]

SYNAGOGUES AS VOLUNTARY ASSOCIATIONS

Buildings have social meaning, expressing the goals, aspirations, and values of a community or society. These early synagogues were strikingly consistent. All ex-press a high sense of community, especially in the arrangements of the benches[72] so that members – presumably male and female – were equally in-volved in the activities of the community. Good analogies are found in the "pur-itan" and left-wing streams of reformed Christianity, with their rejection of ex-plicit liturgy, visual symbolism, reminders of other traditions.[73] The synagogues were plain, uncomplicated structures, with a primary emphasis on a "demo-cratic" communal experience – the meeting space focused not on some function or office or liturgical feature but on the community itself. They were relatively unsophisticated.[74]

Provision for worship at this stage of the synagogue's development in the first century was not highly refined. They were flexible – differing markedly from later ones – and space was not constrained by fixtures or holy functions or different statuses that required architectural definition. No elements in pre-70 synagogues directed attention to the Temple in Jerusalem, not even orientation, for the synagogue had not yet replaced the centre of worship in Jerusalem, and none of its features needed to call the Temple to mind. Quite the contrary, synagogues had an architectural character radically different from the Temple. They provided spaces intended for multiple community functions, not for functions modeled on the Temple's highly articulated functions and notions of holiness.

These early synagogues were community-oriented collegia, in which people gathered together (*synagein*) for multiple purposes as portrayed in the inscriptions and the documents of Josephus and Philo and reflected in the archaeological remains. These small communities ate meals together, observed Sabbaths and festivals, organized the collection of Temple tax dues, taught their children, arranged for the transmission of first-fruits, heard civil law cases and so on. When they had a building for these purposes – and not all did – the buildings were called *synagōgai*.

It is possible, of course, that there were other more liturgically developed synagogues co-existing with these early buildings; we simply have no evidence of them. Until we have such evidence, it is incumbent on us to base reconstructions on what is known.

CONCLUSIONS

Synagogues as collegia had a special place in the early Roman Empire; privileges, going beyond what other collegia could claim, were carefully defined. Roman interest in these questions peaked in the late first century BCE, a period during which several of the earliest synagogues of which we have helpful remains were built. The range of functions that our earliest sources ascribed to these synagogues was fairly broad, and the physical remains matched the descriptions. No feature of early synagogues was modeled on the Jerusalem Temple, its character, divisions, or motifs.[75]

It is striking that the Palestinian evidence – written, epigraphic, and archaeological – is consistently to be dated in the first century CE, with the possible exceptions of Gamla and Masada I. On the other hand, the evidence from the Diaspora goes back hundreds of years earlier, to the late third century BCE. Political, social, and religious conditions for building such structures existed in the Diaspora; it is not so clear that the requisite conditions existed in Palestine while the Temple still stood, though they might have. If we are to follow the evidence we have, however, setting to one side arbitrary arguments from later conditions, later buildings and later literature, we can only conclude that synagogues were first found in Egypt and Greece, where they were seen as buildings for ethnic communities, collegial structures analogous to and probably indistinguishable from other such structures.[76]

The synagogues of the Holy Land were like those of the Diaspora, serving as "places of their own" for the Jewish community. The architectural model for synagogues was the collegium,[77] though a more cautious way of putting it is that the development of synagogue buildings before 70 CE cohered with their social character and legal definition in the same period. Early synagogues, both in the Diaspora and Palestine, were collegia.

When synagogues began to appear in the Holy Land, before the trauma of 70 CE, they were purpose-built buildings, yet they still replicated the general approach to synagogues as collegia in the Diaspora: multi-purpose community buildings serving the disparate needs of the local worshipping community. Views that impose a limited set of descriptive "markers" on early synagogues are almost certain to be wrong.[78] Just because the community met, ate, studied, debated, and received visitors together, it was no less a worshipping community of Jews gathered in one place, devoted to the God of Israel, whose main cult centre stood in Jerusalem.

The one commonality among them all[79] is that outsiders, and perhaps even insiders, will have thought of them as voluntary religious associations, though they will have been unsure whether to call them *synagōgai, proseuchai, sabbateia, collegia, thiasoi, synodoi, eranoi, syllogoi* or simply a "holy place."[80]

NOTES

1 Guterman 1951:150. His prime concern was the legal question, which is not a special concern in this paper.
2 Smallwood 1976, especially pp. 133–43.
3 No doubt a part of the reason for this is that buildings of collegia are not well known, while synagogues as a building type are visible and dramatic.
4 Among methodological issues: What constitutes a synagogue? Are there other public buildings with which a synagogue could be confused? What role should the presence or absence of "defining" elements (for example, niche, bema, reading desk, *mikveh*, gallery, orientation, symbolism, benches, architectural decoration) play in deciding whether a building is a synagogue or not? Should an inscription or lack of an inscription settle the issue? And so on.
5 See Richardson and Heuchan, in this volume.
6 He includes Magdala (Migdal), which I shall largely exclude; he excludes Capernaum and Chorazin. Netzer 1987 (in Hebrew) has argued that Magdala was a nymphaeum, not a synagogue; this suggestion seems unlikely.
7 See also, recently, Seager 1989, an excellent article making many of the same points as I should wish to. Also useful is Gutmann 1981, especially the articles by Seager, Kraabel, Marilyn J. Chiat, and Eric Myers.
8 In earlier years the point was disputed, especially in the competing views of Mommsen and Juster. The point now is more readily accepted. Guterman's assessment (1951:150) cited above, though idiosyncratic, summarizes it adequately.
9 Cotter 1989 (see also in this volume); Smallwood 1976.

10 *Senatus consulto collegia sublata sunt, quae adversus rem publicam videbantur esse.* See Cotter in this volume. The phrase used is reminiscent of the later coin of Nerva when he suppressed the Jewish tax (or the offensive way it was being collected): *Fisci iudaici calumnia sublata.*

11 The character of the period is visible in Cicero's defense of Flaccus: "There follows that ill-will stemming from Jewish gold . . . . Although it is the practice annually to send gold in the name of Jews to Jerusalem from Italy and all the provinces, Flaccus ordered by an edict that it was forbidden to export it from the province of Asia. . . . 'But,' you will say, 'Gnaeus Pompey, when he captured Jerusalem, although a victor, touched not a thing in that shrine.' In this especially, as in many other matters, he acted wisely, for, in the case of such a suspicious and abusive state, he left no occasion for gossip on the part of his opponents. For I do not think that it was the religion of the Jews and of his enemies that acted as an obstacle to this very distinguished general, but rather his sense of honor" (*In Flaccum* 66–69).

12 Smallwood argues that Caesar's favorable view of Judaism depends upon (i) the help gained from Antipater, (ii) the fact that Caesar's enemy was Pompey, the desecrator of the Temple, and (iii) that he had friendly relations with Hyrcanus II. These may all be factors – indeed the evidence adduced from Josephus, noted below, supports some of them – but our curiosity is still left unsatisfied by this minimal explanation.

13 Philo, *Legat.* 156–58; cf. 311–17. See further below re Josephus.

14 Schürer 1973–87, 2:425–26, n. 5. I have adjusted the translations, which he has taken from their publication in *CIJ*, in the direction of a more literal reading. I have taken dates from Ferguson 1993:15–17.

15 See Valerie Heuchan and Peter Richardson in this volume. See also Richardson 1993.

16 i   Schedia, *CIJ* 1440, 246–221 BCE ("On behalf of King Ptolemy and Queen Berenice, his sister and wife, and their children, the Jews [dedicated] this prayer house");

   ii   somewhere in lower Egypt, *CIJ* 1449, 246–221 BCE (the older inscription, included in a later one, reads "King Ptolemy Euergetēs [bestowed the right of asylum] on the prayer house");

  iii   Athribis, *CIJ* 1443, 180–145 (?) BCE ("On behalf of King Ptolemy and Queen Cleopatra, Ptolemy son of Epicydus, the commander of the guard, and the Jews in Athribis [dedicated] the prayer house to the Highest God");

  iv   Athribis, *CIJ* 1444, 180–145 (?) BCE ("On behalf of King Ptolemy and Queen Cleopatra and their children, Hermias and his wife Philotera and their children [dedicated] this *exedra* for the prayer house");

   v   Nitriai, *CIJ* 1442 (not 1422 as Schürer says), 144–116 BCE ("On behalf of King Ptolemy and Queen Cleopatra his sister and Queen Cleopatra his wife, benefactors [*euergetai*], the Jews in Nitriai [dedicated] the prayer house and appurtenances");

  vi   Xenephyris, *CIJ* 1441, 144–116 BCE (similar to (v) but " . . . the Jews of Xenephyris [dedicated] the gateway of the prayer house when Theodoros and Achillion were benefactors" [*prostatai*]);

 vii   Alexandria, *CIJ* 1433, second century BCE ("To the Highest God [who hears prayer] the holy [precinct (*peribolos*) and] the prayer [house and the app]urtenances [were dedicated]");

viii   Alexandria, *CIJ* 1432, 36 (?) BCE ("On behalf of the Qu[een] and K[ing], Alypus made the prayer ho[use] for the Highest God who hears prayer, in the fifteenth year in the month Mecheir").

17i   Arsinoe-Crocodilopolis in the Fayum, *CPJ* III 1532A, 246–221 BCE ("On behalf of King Ptolemy son of Ptolemy and Queen Berenice his wife and sister and their children, the Jews in the city of the Crocodiles [dedicated] the prayer house");

   ii   Fayum, a papyrus *CPJ* I 129, 11 May 218 BCE (referring to the thief of a cloak who deposited it "in the prayer house of the Jews");

iii   Arsinoe in the Fayum, a papyrus *CPJ* I 134, late second century BCE (a list of properties with two references to "a prayer house of Jews" that owned a "holy orchard" (or "holy garden," *hiera paradeisos*)).

18   The reference is found in a fragmentary papyrus, *CPJ* I 138, whose provenance is unknown, dating from the second half of the first century BCE: *epi tēs genētheisēs synagōgēs en tēi proseuchēi*, "at the gathering which was held in the prayer house." The papyrus is suggestive in its linking of *synagōgē* with *proseuchē*, in its retention of *synagōgē* for the actual gathering, and for the date at which this distinction was still retained in Middle Egypt. This sole allusion ought not to be used to argue either that *synagōgē* is not used of the building by this date in other areas or that a *proseuchē* is in some way different from a building referred to as a *synagōgē*. The distinction is a cultural and geographical preference.

A second inscriptional reference, location not identified, *CIJ* 1447, occurs on a statue base: *Artemōn Nikōnos pr[ostatēsas] to IA [etos] tēi synagōgēi [. . .]nēteki*, "Artemon son of Nikon, having been *prostatēs* for the eleventh year, in (or to) the synagogue [dedicated] [. . . .] " The allusion could be either to the gathering or the building; the fact that it appears on a statue base favors a building, in which case there would be repercussions with respect to synagogal accommodation to external iconic norms. *CPJ* says, incorrectly, that "*synagōgē* is not otherwise found in Egypt"; see the papyrus just referred to and Philo occasionally (see below).

19   An unusual inscription from Berenice in Cyrenaica (42 CE) uses *synagōgē* twice, two lines apart, once to refer to the community and once to refer to the building: "Year two of Nero Claudius Caesar Drusus Germanicus Autokratōr, 6th day of Choiach. It seemed good to the gathering (*synagōgē*) of the Jews in Berenice to inscribe the names of the contributors to the repair of the synagogue (*synagōgē*) . . . ." See Lifshitz 1967:81. I take the name to be a mistaken form of Tiberius Claudius Drusus Nero Germanicus.

20   Three inscriptions refer to "the holy place" – in one case certainly, in one case probably, and in one case maybe as a part of the clause, "I give thanks to God and to the holy place . . . ." This usage could refer to a synagogue, but seems to me not to do so; it is more likely to refer to a Temple, probably the Temple in Jerusalem as *the* holy place *par excellence*, possibly to the Temple at Leontopolis. See *CIJ* 1435, 1436, 1437.

21   For example, *Legat.* 132, 134, 137, 138, 148, 152, 165, 191; *Flacc.* 41, 45, 47–49, 53, 122. Some references are explicitly or implicitly to *proseuchai* in other cities in Egypt as well: *Legat.* 346, 371; cf. *Flacc.* 47–49, 41, 45. See also 3 Macc. 7:20, set in the reign of Ptolemy IV (221–205 BCE), perhaps written in the early second century BCE.

22   His use of *phronēsis, andreia, sōphrosynē, dikaiosynē* echoes exactly the Stoic virtues, while his addition of piety and holiness is intended to make their virtue more Jewish. He clearly imagines in this text that other Egyptian cities also had similar places of prayer fostering such virtues.

23   I take the shift in language as indicative of Philo's understanding of the range of functions: not just prayer but also teaching, as in a school.

24   Observe also that the Temple at Leontopolis was built *after* synagogues were already a fact of life in Egypt. This may suggest both that there was conflict between the two forms of Jewish piety (thus explaining differently from Kasher the absence of references to Leontopolis in the Alexandrian Jewish literature) and that there was "room" in the range of Jewish activities for two different types of structures.

25   *CIJ* 284, 301, 338, 368, 416, 496.

26   *CIJ* 365, 425, 503.

27   *CIJ* 343, 402, 417, 523.

28   *CIJ* 173; see Peter Richardson (forthcoming, 1996). The case of the Herodians is debated; but the other three named after public figures – Augustus, M. Agrippa and Volumnius – all of whom were active in the late first century BCE, probably implies that they were founded or refounded at the same time. See also discussion in Leon 1960.

29 *CIRB* 70 (Panticapaeum; 81 CE) and 71, both referring to *synagōgai*, perhaps buildings, in one case linked with a *proseuchē*. CIRB 985 and 1128 also refer to *proseuchai* in the context of manumission. Andrew Overman is attempting to find a first-century synagogue below a Byzantine church.

30 Though his record of decrees and letters has sometimes been considered inauthentic, historians now tend to view them as generally trustworthy (though not always accurate translations). See the discussion in Moehring 1975; Saulnier 1981. Moehring contends that they are apologetically cast.

31 There are six in all, two from Augustus (to Asia, probably from 2–3 CE, and to Norbanus Flaccus, probably 31–27 BCE), two from Marcus Agrippa (to Ephesus, perhaps 14 BCE, and to Cyrene, before 12 BCE), one from Norbanus Flaccus (to Sardis, 31–27 BCE) and one from Julius Antonius (to Ephesus, 4 BCE).

32 The decree was to be set up in the Temple of Roma and Augustus at Ankara (16.165).

33 Those attributed to Julius Caesar (i.e., the first six in 14.190–212, dating from 49 to 44 BCE) deal with Judea, not with the Diaspora; they refer in every instance to Hyrcanus II and shed little light on the question of synagogues as collegia. (Among the other topics treated are Hyrcanus' loyalty and bravery in Caesar's causes, his right to sit among senators at the gladiatorial games and to enter the Senate, Jews as "allies and friends," refortification of Jerusalem, reduction of tribute payable in Sabbatical years, prohibition against quartering of Roman troops among Jews.) Two other decrees confirm those of Julius Caesar, one by Julius Gaius to Parium and the other by Mark Antony and Publius Dolabella (11 April 44 BCE; *Ant.* 14.213–22). Another refers to the decrees of the Senate (Gaius Fannius to Cos; 14.233). Three decrees are earlier and refer to Hyrcanus I (14. 241–43, 247–54). Hyrcanus II was High Priest from 76–67, re-appointed High Priest and Ethnarch in 64 in Pompey's settlement, holding this position more or less continuously until 40 BCE. Josephus gives the impression that he was a weak and ineffective ruler, but this judgment needs re-assessment in the light of the indication of Caesar's high regard for him. See Peter Richardson (forthcoming, 1996). His sons could hold the same offices.

34 In 14.261, the decree of the people of Sardis instructed the magistrates to set apart a place for Jews to build and inhabit, vaguely suggestive of the much later incorporation of the synagogue in the gymnasium–bath–imperial cult site in Sardis. There is no archaeological evidence of a late first-century BCE building.

35 This is not to deny that occasionally there were actions against Jewish communities, as in the Edict of Claudius, but these were infrequent.

36 How widespread sending of tithes in kind was is not clear from the records; some of the evidence comes from Tyre and Sidon, so it may be that it was unusual except from areas close to the Holy Land.

37 See especially for exactly this contrast, Julius Gaius to Parium (*Ant.* 14.213–16), sometime before 44 BCE; Caesar "forbade religious societies (*thiasoi*) to assemble in the city [i.e., Rome], but these people alone he did not forbid to do so . . . or to hold common meals . . . ." Cf. also Dolabella to Ephesus (14.225–27; 24 Jan. 43 BCE); Lentulus to Ephesus (14.228, 234, 236–40; both 49 BCE); Laodicea to Gaius Rabirius (14.241–43; 45 BCE ?); P. Servilius Galba to Miletus (14.24–46); Ephesus re Brutus (14.262–64; possibly 42 BCE ?).

38 *Digest* 47.22.1; cited in Sherk 1988:234. See some of the other inscriptions he cites.

39 See Poland 1909; Waltzing 1895–1900; Barton and Horsley 1981. See further John Kloppenborg's and B. H. McLean's essays in this volume.

40 See Dörpfeld 1892, 1894.

41 See Wide 1894. I am indebted to Philip Harland for his assistance with the Iobacchoi.

42 See the various inscriptions and papyri cited above.

43 Dion 1977; Mazur 1935; Kraabel 1979; on Delos, B. H. McLean in this volume; on Ostia, White 1990:60–101, esp. 69–70.

44 For example, the lintel from Corinth which provides good evidence of the name *Synagōgē Hebraiōn* is dated to the second century.

45 Kraabel claims that it may well be the earliest one yet excavated. The first-century building is a very simple structure, "the sort one would expect from this early period: a converted residence, little more than an assembly hall, with no permanent Torah shrine and no Jewish symbols" (1979:493). The marks distinguishing this building as Jewish are epigraphic references to *proseuchē* and *theos hypsistos* (*CIJ* 725, 726, 769). Concerning Aegina, see Kraabel's updating of Mazur (1979:480, n. 9).

46 Kraabel also discusses the Ostia synagogue of the fourth century CE, which likewise has a first-century CE building below it (1979:497–500). For an updating see White 1990.

47 See White 1990, a lucid comparative study making the point forcefully about "architectural adaptation."

48 See also White 1990:64–67.

49 White runs against the consensus and assigns its origins to a private building (1990:69).

50 White (1990:82); see the inscriptions he refers to in notes 59–61 (p. 180).

51 I am persuaded of its pre-70 date by the reference to "needy travelers from abroad," presupposing pilgrims from the Diaspora on their way to fulfill Temple obligations, a part of Jewish life that must have ceased with the disastrous conclusion to the Revolt. Contra Kee 1990.

52 *CIJ* 1404. Note how this early epigraphic reference ties the Diaspora to the practice of the Holy Land.

53 A somewhat similar inscription from the second century comes from Stobi in Macedonia (*CIJ* 694): "[Claudius] Tiberius Polycharmus also called Achyrius, father of the synagogue in Stobi . . . built the building for the holy place and the dining room, together with the colonnaded hall, from his own funds, without touching in any way the funds of the sanctuary. But the complete right to and ownership of the upper story I . . . reserve for myself . . . ."

54 It is just possible that stratum II of the synagogue excavations at Caesarea provides evidence of this synagogue; see Avi-Yonah 1993:278–79.

55 Curiously, this seems to be regularly overlooked.

56 See Strange 1979.

57 The presumed first-century synagogues at Capernaum (underlying the present large structure) and at Magdala might have been included. The level of speculation would rise significantly and no great gain would result.

58 Netzer now argues that Masada I was a stable, as shown by a layer of horse dung between the floor levels. He does not deal with the problem this must have created for the Sicarii defenders who remodeled Masada I as a synagogue in Masada II.

59 So Netzer.

60 See Peter Richardson (forthcoming, 1996).

61 In the north-east corner of the administrative building; a fine *mikveh* was found at the diametrically opposite side of the site.

62 A case has been made that it was rebuilt simply to accommodate the needs of the defenders for a council chamber or war-room; see Flesher 1995:137.

63 This fact has led Netzer (1981) to argue, unpersuasively, that the origins of the synagogue lay in Herodian *triclinia*.

64 This fits the later Mishnah with respect to orientation.

65 If the published reports of a first-century synagogue at Capernaum are trustworthy, there were two doors, one on the west and one on the east wall – an unusual arrangement. At Magdala the door may have been on the north-west, more or less away from Jerusalem. In the latter case there is no particular orientation to Jerusalem.

66 Wilkinson 1984 tends to interpret wide-ranging archaeological data in the light of literary evidence from a later period, though he correctly emphasizes the variety of orientations.

67 See the summary statements in Strange 1979:656–61.
68 See Kee 1990 and the literature cited there, especially Zeitlin 1930–31. Kee is misleading, however, when he claims that synagogues even in this period were indistinguishable from private houses; there was a discernible group of community buildings with distinctive features. He is correct that third-century features are missing, but he goes too far in denying the similarity of features in pre-70 synagogues.
69 The seminal study of Brooten 1982 is still unrivalled.
70 See, however, my remarks in Richardson 1993 concerning a dividing wall in one of the Therapeutae's buildings.
71 The evidence of Egypt is not clear enough to let us determine exactly what the situation was there.
72 At Magdala the benches were against one of the *short* walls; in the hypothesized first-century Capernaum synagogue there were benches along one *long* wall, though this is not certain.
73 A Mennonite or Quaker meeting house, Plymouth Brethren assembly, Orange Order hall, or Women's Auxiliary.
74 See Turner 1979; J. G. Davies 1987.
75 See Kee 1990:18: "there emerge no hints of liturgical formulae, of institutional organization, of formal programs or patterns of instruction, just as from the architectural side there is no evidence of stylized architectural settings for group worship. Instead from both perspectives we can discern informal gatherings for fresh appropriation of the Torah, for the strengthening of group identity, and for heightening devotion to the God of Israel." On some features of the process of developing a Temple imagery, see Rosenau 1979.
76 Their earliest form in the Diaspora was often remodeled houses, though this seems not to have been true in Egypt, where few inscriptions refer to donors and most give honor to the reigning monarchs.
77 Not the *naos, pronaos, basilikē, ekklēsiastērion, bouleutērion, triclinium*, etc.
78 No synagogue known to me has all the usually claimed "markers": orientation, benches, torah niche, bema, *mikveh*, Temple imagery, gallery or other separation, highest point of land, door to the east, adjacent to the sea, and so on. These later attempts to formulate "rules" summarize some aspects of previous practice; they are not first principles, formulated at an early stage, to which later buildings must conform – without which they are not synagogues.
79 There was variety: there were renovated houses and purpose-built buildings, a range in size, synagogues associated with various groups or opinions (Sicarii, Samaritans, Galileans, Egyptians, Idumeans, Greeks and Romans, Pharisees, and Essenes). This variety needs much more attention than it receives.
80 I gratefully acknowledge the assistance of L. Michael White in preparing the synagogue plan of Ostia.

7

PHILO AND THE CLUBS AND ASSOCIATIONS OF ALEXANDRIA

Torrey Seland

> In the city there are clubs (*thiasoi*) with a large membership, whose fellowship is founded on no sound principle but on strong liquor and drunkenness and sottish carousing and their offspring, wantonness. "Synods" (*synodoi*) and "divans" (*klinai*) are the particular names given to them by the people of the country.

This quotation from one of the works of Philo of Alexandria (*In Flaccum* 136) is one among several that mention the Graeco-Roman clubs and associations in Alexandria. But most of his comments have been noted only in passing by modern scholars. In fact, we have been unable to find any comprehensive study that deals with Philo's remarks on, and his attitudes concerning this particular part of the Graeco-Roman culture.[1]

This is an astonishing circumstance, and that by reason of two facts: first, the Graeco-Roman clubs and associations were to be found in almost every town of the Roman Empire in the first century CE, Alexandria being no exception.[2] Second, there are several passages in Philo's works dealing with clubs and associations.

It is the purpose of this article to deal with the passages in the works of Philo related to the phenomenon of Graeco-Roman clubs and associations and to try to get a picture of how he conceives of these institutions. It is argued here that Philo had a fairly good knowledge of various clubs and associations in Alexandria. But he uses this knowledge in a very specific way. He does not strictly and totally forbid participation, but he is very critical of the associations, and skeptical of joining them. Though they may be frequented if the purpose is to acquire virtue, to Philo they represented dangerous settings that might very easily lead to idolatry and apostasy. Philo's arguments may therefore be said to have specific social functions: they are set forth to warn his fellow Jews, to keep them together, to discourage them from mingling with the "many," and thereby to function as inducements to preserve their identity as Jews.

Philo's remarks on these societies in his own home town Alexandria can be studied and presented in several ways, but we shall here concentrate on two related sets of questions. First, what does Philo tell us about these clubs and associations compared to what we know from other sources? What does he tell us about their existence, their structures, and activities? Second, we ask: How does he perceive the various aspects of these clubs and associations? What are his evaluations of them? While this distinction may be difficult to substantiate consistently, it may be functional as a heuristic device in studying his works.

We present the relevant material found in Philo subsumed under three headings: (1) Various aspects of the associations according to Philo. (2) Philo's comparison of the Jewish gatherings and feasts with those of the associations. (3) Philo's discussion of contributions and participation in the associations. In order, however, to set this study in the perspective of other research on the Graeco-Roman associations, we first outline some trends in earlier research.

Research on Graeco-Roman clubs and associations flourished at the end of the nineteenth and in the first decades of the twentieth centuries. One of the main reasons for such great interest in the associations at that time was the many papyrological and epigraphical finds that brought "Light from the Ancient East" as Adolf Deissmann called one of his famous books (1908, ET 1927). Some of the important studies from this period are still indispensable reference works.[3] In fact, most of the more recent studies on the associations confirm the basic picture we get in the older studies, even though there may be some variations or changes in emphasis.[4] The time for all-encompassing works, like those of Waltzing and Poland, seems to have passed. More recent scholars have concentrated on various aspects of or types of associations, or have tried to relate them to other social settings in the first-century world.[5] Mention could here also be made of the older studies that have tried to relate features of emerging Christian groups to those of the associations,[6] and some more recent, relating features of the associations to the Qumran community.[7]

When social and sociological studies of the early churches gained popularity in the 1960s and 1970s, comparisons with the associations were renewed.[8] Today further study of the various clubs and associations holds great potential for enriching our understanding of the social life and structures of both Jewish and the early Christian groups.[9]

But in spite of the renewed interest in the social aspects of the associations and Christian groups, we have no comprehensive study dealing with the attitudes of diaspora Jews toward the Graeco-Roman associations. At the beginning of the first century CE there were Jews living over almost all the Graeco-Roman world[10] and they could not have overlooked the many clubs and associations that were also to be found in nearly every city of that world. It seems quite natural, therefore, to ask how these Jews related to such societies. The present study endeavors to take us one step in this direction by concentrating on Philo's attitude toward the clubs and associations of his home town, Alexandria.

CENTRAL ASPECTS OF THE ASSOCIATIONS

Sociologically speaking, the clubs and associations may be characterized as corporate groups, that is, as groups with fixed rules for admission and exclusion, and with a fixed purpose for their existence (cf. Boissevain 1978). A set of rules was sometimes inscribed on steles erected in their localities. Furthermore, with regard to financial matters, sometimes extending to leadership, associations were deeply involved in the patron–client structures so typical of this world.[11] Rich men – or women – could serve as benefactors and patrons of several clubs. They in turn could draw upon the loyalty of the members if needed. The membership was diversified: on the one hand club members could be drawn primarily from specific occupations, for example, weavers, bakers, artists; on the other hand they could consist of people from various age groups. An association could also consist of people from various segments of society, occupations, sex, and of people of various levels of influence and status. Women, freedmen, and slaves are found in several, though not in all. Hence membership could be characterized as based on fictive kinship: members were fictive brothers and sisters.

The internal organization of the clubs and associations, especially in the Greek cities, had the polis as its structural model; they had a structured leadership and laws regulating activities, duties, and responsibilities. In this way, people who had little influence in their polis could find a setting where they were acknowledged. Club membership gave a feeling of belonging. Hence, whether the ostensible purposes of the clubs were convivial, political, or economic, most often these features were intertwined. Clubs also had a social function; and they represented a part of the general *paideia*. This aspect is most evident in the clubs of the young people that were associated with their educational and gymnasial settings (cf. Forbes 1933), but is probably to be considered as inherent in the others too.[12]

Scholars have also tried to group and characterize the associations according to various types. This may be an artificial way of looking at the associations;[13] and no consensus has evolved with regard to the kinds or number of types.[14] Efforts have also been made to associate some of the most current terms with specific types of associations: most common is the opinion that *thiasos* signifies "cultic association"; and *hetairia* is viewed as a term typical of the convivial clubs and associations, especially the more politically active associations.[15] But as most of the clubs and associations known to us had both "cultic" and "convivial" aspects, such efforts at classification would now appear fruitless. At least it is not possible to see any consistent groupings in the ways Philo uses these terms. Furthermore, the danger of anachronistic characterizations is near at hand: for example, when dealing with the aspect of religion in ancient societies, one should take account of the fact that religion is not something which can be isolated from the general social life. "[T]he Greek city knows no separation between sacred and profane. Religion is present in all the different levels of social life, and all collective practices have a religious dimension."[16] Participation in symposia and associations was a central part of the collective life, but there were also other group formations. The typology of group formations offered by Schmitt-Pantel (1990:205) may here be useful:

(i) groups with more or less official roles as administrative and political divisions (in Athens, deme, tribe, phratry);
(ii) cult associations, groups whose principal function is the cult of a divinity, a hero, or a dead man (*genos*, *thiasos*, *eranos*, *orgeon*, and various types of *koinon*);
(iii) age-classes, particularly the group of young men;
(iv) groups of friends (*philoi*) and companions.

The various terms used for clubs and associations in the Greek and Latin sources have been intensively studied by several scholars.[17] Philo uses three of the better-known terms from the other Greek sources: *synodos*, *hetairia* and *thiasos*. And he adds a fourth, the somewhat rare term *klinē*. All of these terms can be found in several of Philo's texts but in relatively few cases do the contexts unambiguously relate to the field of clubs and associations.[18] Most regularly *synodos* refers only to "assembly," "gathering" or "union."[19] The term *hetairia* is frequently used in its more general sense of "friendly connection," "friendship," and "comradeship."[20] In *Flacc.* 136 *thiasos* is used in a way that suggests that Philo himself considered this word to be the most common, typical designation for "association." But even this term most frequently seems to demand the more general meaning of "company," "gathering," or "group" without any connotations of "association."[21] In this way, all of these terms turn out to be polysemous. "Association" or "club" is only one possible meaning and in Philo it is not even one of the most frequent.

In *Flacc.* 136, however, Philo characterizes the terms *synodos* and *klinē* as terms being "given to them by the people of the country." *Synodos* is well known from other sources. This might suggest that the other term, *klinē*, which is rarely used for "club" or "association" in the other Greek sources (Poland 1909:358), in fact was also a much-used term in Egypt. Poland calls "die Ägyptische *klinē*," a "Spezialname" and "merkwürdigste Erscheinung."[22] The term is not, however, used often by Philo. With the sole exception of *Flacc.* 136, he always uses it in a more general way, signifying "that on which one lies," "couch."[23] But Philo also uses the compound word *klinarchēs* to name the function of Isidorus at the banquets (*Flacc.* 137). This might strengthen the interpretation that *klinē* really was a common term for association in Egypt (cf. Westermann 1932:24–25).

Several details known to us from other sources of the activities in various clubs and associations can also be found in Philo's works.[24] In *Flacc.* 136, cited in the beginning of this study, Philo uses two well-known terms for associations – *thiasos* and *synodos*. He also states that they had many members. In the same passage he also mentions one of their leaders (the leader?), Isidorus. Philo here shows that he was familiar with the fact that the leaders or patrons could be at the heads of more than one association. In *Flacc.* 136–38, further, we have one of the most vivid accounts from the first century CE of the kind of dependency members could be bound up with in the relation to their patron. According to *Flacc.* 137–38, "when he [Isidorus] wished to get some worthless project carried out, a single call brought them together in a body, and they said and did what they were bidden." Further on in the same treatise Philo states that Isidorus once bade some of them to launch accusations and slanders against Flaccus. Then, when some of them were arrested, it was revealed that they had been promised both money and wine as payment (*Flacc.* 140, 142).

In spite of the evident coloring of the story by Philo, there is no compelling reason to doubt such a relationship between a patron and his association(s), for we have other evidence witnessing similar kinds of relationship. In the ruins of Pompeii there have been found placards telling whom various associations were supporting in the elections (Liebenam 1890:135), and it is well known that patrons not infrequently supported their associations with wine, food, or money.[25] That poor people also could be members of the associations is substantiated in other sources.[26] The story of Philo is thus an admirable presentation of the patron–client relationship so well known from the time of the Roman empire, and of its practice of "do ut des."[27]

But Philo also knew that members themselves had to pay dues, whether as entrance fees or as monthly contributions: *eranous* or *symbolas pherein* are his expressions for these (*Ebr.* 14–15, 20–21, 35). In *Ebr.* 20–26 he discusses contributions; and since this obviously is an important issue to him, we shall later return to it. Philo was also familiar with the fact that contributions might be necessary in order to make the gatherings and feasts financially possible (*Vita cont.* 46).

Such feasts and gatherings were typical traits of the Graeco-Roman clubs and associations, according to other sources.[28] In *Flacc.* 4 Philo mentions their sacrifices and their conviviality. But it is in his descriptions of these aspects that he is most expressive and negative. He emphasizes eating and drinking (*Spec. Leg.* 2.193; *Legat.* 312) and he mentions intrigues and even poisonings that occurred in these associations (*Spec. Leg.* 3.96, cf. *Vita cont.* 40–41, perhaps also *Cher.* 91–92 and *Plant.* 100).[29] Philo's emphasis is especially notable when we study his comparisons of Jewish gatherings and feasts with those of the Graeco-Roman associations.

PHILO'S COMPARISON OF THE JEWISH GATHERINGS AND FEASTS WITH THOSE OF THE CLUBS AND ASSOCIATIONS

To the Romans, who watched Jews coming together in their synagogues, these gatherings might resemble those of the associations. In fact, we have evidence to substantiate such a supposition. In *Ant.* 14, Josephus refers to letters and edicts that either compare the Jewish synagogal gatherings to the clubs (*thiasoi*) or designate them as *synodoi* (*Ant.* 14.215–16, 235–36, 259–60).[30]

A similar use of these terms can also be found in *Legat.* 312 and 316. Here Philo argues against Gaius that his predecessors had not forbidden the gatherings of the Jews. In 312–13, which he says renders "the substance if not the actual words" of a letter from the emperor, Philo states:

> He ordered that the Jews alone should be permitted by them to assemble in synagogues. These gatherings, he said, were not based on drunkenness and carousing to promote conspiracy and so to do grave injury to the cause of peace, but were schools of temperance and justice where men while practicing virtue subscribed the annual first-fruits to pay for the sacrifices which they offer and commissioned sacred envoys to Jerusalem according to their ancestral practice.

In *Legat.* 316 he then cites from a letter of Gaius Norbanus Flaccus to the Ephesians declaring what the emperor had written to him. From this Philo concludes: "He did not think that the form generally adopted about meetings (*tōi koinō typōi tōn synodōn*) should be applied to do away with the assemblages of the Jews." These passages are fairly informative. They disclose Philo's knowledge of both the tendency toward political unrest in some of the associations (cf. *Flacc.* 4 and *Spec. Leg.* 4.46–47), and the fact that the Roman authorities were critical of such "collegia," sometimes prohibiting their existence. This restrictive attitude of the Roman authorities is also witnessed in Pliny's letters.[31]

Philo further plays on the aspect of "drunkenness and carousing" of the associations in his defense of the Jewish synagogal gatherings. In this comparison the synagogues are described as "schools of temperance and justice," that is, places where the virtues are nourished and practiced[32] and thus of no danger to the Pax Romana.

We here get a glimpse of the Jews' insecure position in the Diaspora. While some emperors might be of a favorable mind toward the Jews, others were certainly not; and the standing of the Jews varied from place to place, from city to city (cf. Rajak 1985). To place the Jewish synagogues in the same category as the associations was not without danger, and Philo is concerned with showing the differences, in order to secure the peace of the synagogues. What is of special importance to our present topic is his pinpointing of the issue of political unrest and drunkenness as a feature of the associations. We shall see below that this latter aspect is one of Philo's favorite themes in his descriptions of such gatherings.

In *Vita contemplativa* Philo describes a Jewish group of which we might know almost nothing if we lacked his account. This group, the Therapeutae, lived near Alexandria and Philo seems to have had a fairly good knowledge of them.

In *Vita cont.* 40–47, he contrasts their gatherings (*tas koinas synodous*) and meals (*symposiois*) with the Greek symposia (*tōn allōn symposia*). In this comparative account the other symposia are described almost as orgies in wine-drinking, drunkenness, and strife. The gatherings of the Therapeutae, however, are sober – in fact of quite another kind and quality. They are not disturbed by drunkenness and intrigues; no slaves are serving at the tables (71–72), and no drinking of wine occurs (73–74), but the participants listen in silence to the expositions of holy Scriptures, sing hymns and offer prayers (see 80, 83–84, 89–90).

It must be admitted that Philo here most probably gives a somewhat exaggerated description both of the excesses of the Greek symposia and of the sobriety of the Therapeutae. There is also criticism of the symposia in Greek, non-Jewish literature; to some degree Philo is applying a literary topos (cf. Collins 1983:143). But he is most expressive and articulate in *Vita cont.* Hence, his tendency is obvious: his attitude toward the Greek symposia is one of contempt and rejection.

This description of the symposia would not have been so valuable to the present study had it not been for the fact that the symposia activities were similar to those of the associations – even though they were not necessarily identical – and for the fact that the term *symposion* plays a considerable role in other passages dealing more explicitly with the activities of wine-drinking and drunkenness so closely associated with the gatherings of the clubs and the associations.

The word *symposion* is not a common word signifying "association" in our sources from this period, but some compound forms, especially *symposiarchos* and *symposiastai* are found not infrequently.[33] The term *symposion* itself has a long history as a term signifying "drinking party" (Mühll 1976). Usually it refers to the second half of a gathering. First came the meal; then, when this was finished and the women and the children had left, the symposium began. Such a symposium contained some cultic traits too, especially in connection with the three first drinking cups which were for the gods and the heroes. Then hymns were sung. These cultic aspects have led P. von der Mühll to go so far as to say that "[j]ener kultische Character besagt ferner, dass die Symposiasten keine 'Gesellschaft' in unserem Sinne, sondern eine Gemeinde sind, ein Thiasos, der so wenig wie jeder andere sakraler Bindung entbehren kann" (1976:489).

In this way, these symposia closely resemble the gatherings of the clubs and associations, indeed represent one aspect of their gatherings. Philo probably does not use the word *symposion* in the meaning of "association," but he makes use of it to emphasize one aspect of them: the wine-drinking. This enables us to draw into our consideration the text of *Vita cont.* 40–47 (cf. above) as being important for his understanding of this aspect, as well as the texts presented in the following section.

The excesses of food and wine-drinking in non-Jewish gatherings is also dealt with in Philo's presentations of various Jewish feasts as he contrasts them with Graeco-Roman feasts and associations.

In *Spec. Leg.* 2.145–46 he is considering Passover and in 2.148 he describes the actual gatherings in Jewish homes. Here he makes it explicit that they "are not as in other festive gatherings (*ta alla symposia*) to indulge the belly with wine and viands, but to fulfill with prayers and hymns the custom handed down by their fathers" (2.148).

The word used by Philo for "feast" is *heortē*, and in *Spec. Leg.* 2.193 the great Day of Atonement is described as a feast:

> Perhaps some of the perversely minded who are not ashamed to censure things excellent will say, What sort of a feast is this in which there are no gatherings to eat and drink, no company of entertainers or entertained, no copious supply of strong drink nor tables sumptuously furnished, nor a generous display of all the accompaniments of a public banquet . . . ?

Philo then adduces three arguments in favor of the ascetic features of this feast: first, the self-restraint (*egkrateia*) which it entails (2.195); second, the holy day is entirely devoted to prayers and supplications (2.196); third, the season at which the celebration occurs, namely when all the fruits of the earth have been gathered in (2.197).

The first argument is the most interesting for us here. Philo points to the self-restraint this feast entails, namely "in controlling the tongue and the belly and the organs below the belly" (2.195). This is something the Jews are exhorted to do every day, but especially on the occasion of the fast. But his emphasis on this aspect is more important, since it represents one of the more outstanding duties ignored in the other symposia. To Philo, those who liked to participate in the symposia were persons who could not control their tongues, their belly, or their sexual behavior (*Spec. Leg.* 1.192; *Vita cont.* 52, 55; *Somn.* 2.167–68). Such lack of self-restraint could very easily lead into apostasy from the Law. In *Virt.* 182 he is in fact pointing to the observation that among persons who become apostates are those "ministering to the delights of the belly and the organs below it." Participation in the symposia, whether that be in an association or not, could, according to Philo, easily end up in apostasy.

Thus, his comparisons of Jewish gatherings with the symposia and his praise of the former could certainly function as warnings to his fellow Jews. The "other gatherings" represented dangerous milieux and as such they could easily lead into situations of apostasy.

THE PAYMENT OF CONTRIBUTIONS: *DE EBRIETATE* 20–26

The context

Since in most of his references to clubs and associations Philo concentrates especially on wine-drinking and drunkenness one might naturally ask if there is further discussion of the clubs in his treatises on drunkenness and sobriety. And that proves to be the case!

Philo uses the figure of Noah from Gen. 9:20–29 in four treatises to present his discussions of wine and drunkenness.[34] In *Plant.* 140–41 he states other philosophers' views expressed on drunkenness, and in *De ebrietate* he purports to "consider what the great law-giver in his never failing wisdom holds on this subject" (*Ebr.* 1). And it is in this work that we find his discussion of the payment of dues.

In this work, however, Philo soon breaks away from the text of Gen. 9:20–21 and concentrates on Deut. 21:18–21: the case of the disobedient son. In *Ebr.* 14–95 he then discusses the four accusations launched against the son by his parents. These Philo finds to be disobedience, contentiousness, payment of contributions, and drunkenness (*Ebr.* 15). But before we proceed further into his presentation of this issue, we must take a closer look at its context in *De ebrietate*.

At the beginning of this treatise Philo states that Moses uses wine as a symbol for five things: foolishness or foolish talking, complete insensibility, greediness, cheerfulness and gladness, and nakedness (*Ebr.* 1–5). Having given a short introductory explanation of each of these (*Ebr.* 6–10), he proceeds to a more detailed consideration. But there is only a discussion of the first three in what has come down to us as *De ebrietate*.

The first, "folly" or "foolish talking," is treated in *Ebr.* 11–153. The chief cause of folly is *apaideusia*, and this leads Philo to consider the text of Deut. 21:18–21 as an example. This topic is then developed in §§13–98, and it is this part of his discussion we shall consider here.[35]

The four charges brought against the rebellious son are set forth in *Ebr.* 13–14, and of these drunkenness is the chief.

Ebr. 20–26 discusses the payment of contributions.
Ebr. 27–28 treats drunkenness.
Ebr. 30 then introduces a consideration of the terms "father" and "mother." Several meanings are mentioned, but Philo goes on in *Ebr.* 33–34 to the suggestion that "father" is "reason, masculine, perfect, right reason" (*phamen ton arrena kai teleion kai orthon logon*). "Mother" is "the lower learning of the schools" (*tēn mesēn kai egkyklion choreian te kai paideian*).

This understanding is then developed in a rather lengthy allegory extending from *Ebr.* 35–92. In this part Philo also shows that there are four ways in which one can relate to one's parents:

Ebr. 36–37: obedient to the mother, but not to the father.
Ebr. 65–66: obedient to the father, but not to the mother.
Ebr. 77–78: disobedient to both.
Ebr. 80–81: obedient to both.

In *Ebr.* 93–94 Philo then points out that the pronoun *houtos* in the OT text shows that the parents had sons that were not disobedient, and in *Ebr.* 95–96 he returns to the payment of contributions and adds his final arguments for the punishment of death.

The rest of the treatise is of minor importance with regard to our main subject since Philo here changes the subject.

The text

The text of Deut. 21:18–21 figures in the discussion in *Ebr.* 14. Then Philo states his preliminary conclusion that "we have it as a clear and admitted fact that submission and obedience to virtue are noble and profitable (*kalon kai sympheron*) and the converse follows, that disobedience is disgraceful and highly unprofitable" (*Ebr.* 16).

Then in *Ebr.* 20–23 comes the more extensive treatment of the payment of contributions. The passage deserves to be cited in full, since it is crucial to our argumentation:

(20) As for contributions or club subscriptions, when the subject is to share in the best of possessions, prudence, such payments are praiseworthy and profitable (*symbolas ge mēn kai eranous pherein epi men tēi tou aristou ktēmatos metousiai, phronēseōs, epaineton kai sympheron*). But when they are paid to obtain that supreme evil, folly (*aphrosynēn*) the practice is unprofitable and blameworthy.

(21) We contribute to the former object by desire for virtue, by zeal for things noble, by continuous study therein, by persistent self-training, by unwearied and unflagging labor.

We contribute to the opposite by slackness, indolence, luxury, effeminacy, and by complete irregularity of life.

(22) We can see indeed people preparing themselves to compete in the arena of wine bibbing and every day exercising themselves and contending in the contests of gluttony. The contributions they make are supposed to be for a profitable purpose, but they are actually mulcting themselves in everything, in money, body and soul. Their substance they diminish by the actual payments, their bodily powers they shatter and enfeeble by the delicate living, and by excessive indulgence in food they deluge their souls as with a winter torrent and submerge them perforce in the depths.

(23) In just the same way those who pay their contributions only to destroy training and education are mulcting their most vital element, the understanding (*dianoian*), and cut away therefrom its safeguards, prudence and self-control, and indeed courage and justice to boot. It was for this reason, I think, that Moses himself used a compound word, "contribution cutting" (*symbolokopōn*), to bring out more clearly the nature of the thing he was describing, because when men bring their efforts like contributions or club-money, so to speak (*hōsper tinas symbolas kai eranous eispherontes*) to bear against virtue, they wound and divide and cut in pieces docile and knowledge-loving souls, till they bring them to utter destruction.

After having presented the four ways of how to relate to one's parents, Philo then returns to the payers of contributions in this way:

(95) It is with good reason, then, that the disobedient and contentious man who "brings contributions," that is, contributes and adds sins to sins (*symbolas eispheronta, tout' esti symballonta kai synarptonta hamartēmata hamartēmasi*), new to old, voluntary to involuntary, and as though inflamed by wine drowns the whole of life in ceaseless and unending drunkenness, sodden with drinking deep of the unmixed cup of folly, is judged by the holy word to be worthy of stoning. Yes, for he has made away with the commands of right reason (*orthou logou*), his father and the observances enjoined by instruction (*tas paideias nomimous*), his mother, and though he had before him the example of true nobility in his brothers whom the parents honored, he did not imitate their virtue, but contrariwise determined to be the aggressor in wickedness. And thus he made a god of the body, a god of the vanity most honored among the Egyptians, whose symbol is the image of the golden bull.

Reading the text

From a first cursory reading of the text, one might surmise that Philo is here just taking the payment of dues as a point of departure for an allegorical exposition of how one may destroy one's education. The context, as we have already pointed out, is surely one of education. Philo here sets forth his view of how to relate to the *egkyklia paideia* and his understanding of *orthos logos*: right reason. The best attitude is to give due honor to both education and right reason (*Ebr.* 80–92). It is only in *De congressu* that Philo discusses education at comparable length.[36]

The allegorical character of the text segments may necessitate some heuristic comments: Philo may sometimes indulge in rather elaborate allegorizations of the Pentateuchal texts. He does not, however, follow those who abolish the literary meaning in preference to the allegorical (cf. *Migr.* 89–93). Furthermore, when he, as in this text segment, uses the social reality of contributions as a foil for the sin of the disobedient son, we should not ignore this social reality. His allegorical expositions often refer to and tell us something about his stand on social phenomena of his time.

Hence, a cursory reading should not lead us into "spiritualizing" interpretations of this text. Such exegesis would set us immediately counter to Philo's own arguments in *Ebr.* 22: here he is talking about payments which actually result in the diminution of the contributor's substance. A reading should consider both the issue of the payment of contributions as a historical problem in the diaspora, and the ways Philo deals with this problem. There are certainly several allegorical elements in the texts of *Ebr.* 20–26, but these do not necessarily diminish the historical value of the treatise for our topic.

Ebr. 20 has been taken by Peder Borgen as evidence for the existence of differ-ing attitudes and practices with regard to participation in pagan cult. He argues that some Jews "limited the question of idolatry strictly to the direct participa-tion in libations and sacrificial acts," and that "Philo seems to have followed this approach."[37] Thus participation in the associations could be accepted by some. Borgen's interpretation coheres with his general view of Philo's attitude to the Graeco-Roman culture: "Philo's intention is to conquer the surrounding culture ideologically by claiming that whatever good there is has its source in Scripture and thus belonged to the Jewish nation and its heritage."[38] This view of Philo as an "infiltrator," trying to conquer is a stimulating perspective which we will try to test in *Ebr.* 20–26.[39]

On the one hand we must take into consideration the integral place and function of cultic activities in the gatherings of the associations. On the other hand, *Ebr.* 20–26 must also be interpreted in the light of Philo's attitude toward the associations as manifested in other portions of his writings.

The integral place of cultic activities in the associations and comparable gath-erings has been pointed out by several scholars.[40] In most of such gatherings it would have been very difficult, if not impossible to participate without at the same time being a participant in the libations and other cultic ceremonies. The other references presented in in the first two sections of this chapter, moreover, point to a fairly strict attitude on the part of Philo.

Yet *Ebr.* 20–26 seems to indicate that Philo nevertheless accepts the payment of contributions when one is driven by right intention, that is, when the purpose is to gain prudence. What does Philo mean by this statement? What is the mean-ing of prudence to Philo? Where or how does one attain prudence? The answers to these questions inhere in his conception of prudence as a principal virtue and in his view of education as the means of acquiring it.

Philo is familiar with the Platonic–Stoic view of the four cardinal virtues: *hē dikaiosynē kai hē phronēsis kai hē andreia kai hē sōphrosynē.* Several times he makes use of this traditional enumeration of the four virtues,[41] but he can also use a shorter list of three, and he may change the order of the virtues or ex-change some of them with others. The ways he does this seem to be influenced by his specific purposes in the various contexts.

Both in Plato and among the Stoics there are statements to the effect that prudence or wisdom is the leader among the virtues, and similar statements can also be found in Philo.[42] But more often in Philo *eusebeia* is the queen: "it ap-proaches the role of philosophy and wisdom and thus *phronēsis*" (Mott 1978:esp. 25–26). This is probably a consequence of his work with the Scriptures, and of his view of theology as an integrated and central part of his own philosophy, the ordinary philosophy being regarded as a handmaid of Scripture (Wolfson 1947, 2:214–15). Thus if Philo agrees to the payment of contributions when the object is to gain prudence, we may ask: How and whereby does one gain such prudence?

Philo's answer to the first part of this question must be conceived in accordance with his philosophical heritage: *aretē*, virtue, is firmly associated with *paideia*, education. The goal of *paideia* is to help one gain virtue (Mott 1978:25). This firm connection of *paideia* and virtue is obviously the main reason for Philo's complaint in *Ebr.* 23 against those who pay contributions: "they are mulcting their most vital element, the understanding, and cut away therefrom its safeguards, prudence and self-control, and indeed courage and justice to boot." This linkage is also the key to an understanding of *Ebr.* 21 where he delineates how one may contribute to "prudence." The attitudes here enumerated are used several times in contexts of virtue and education.[43] Thus, the acquisition of prudence, of virtue, is also associated with *paideia* in Philo's writings.

The second part of our question, also the part most difficult to answer, remains to be considered: whence comes such education that promotes acquisition of the virtues?

That Philo here speaks about Jewish educational settings is rather implausible, and that for the following reasons. First, the Jewish synagogues are repeatedly described by Philo as educational settings in which prudence is sought and taught. The synagogues are not only characterized as schools, but as schools of prudence (*Vita Mosis* 2.216; cf. *Spec. Leg.* 2.62; *Praem.* 60; *Legat.* 312). Hence, a suggestion that *Ebr.* 20 relates to Jewish synagogal education would comprise a kind of tautology: whereas the synagogues are schools of prudence one then says that contributions are praiseworthy if their intention is to gain prudence. Second, evidence for other Jewish associations outside, or even in connection with, the synagogues is both scarce and ambiguous.[44] Accordingly, it might be more natural to relate the sayings of *Ebr.* 20–26 to Philo's attitude respecting non-Jewish clubs and associations.

According to the evidence presented in the first two sections above, Philo tends to be critical of the activities of gatherings for symposia and associations. On the other hand, several scholars have pointed out that Philo shows an excellent knowledge of Graeco-Roman culture and many of its institutions. He appears to be well informed about the encyclical education (*Congr.* 74–76), he himself had participated in banquets, frequented the theatre, heard concerts and watched competitions of boxing, wrestling, and horse-racing (*Ebr.* 177; *Prov.* 58; *Prob.* 26, 141, cf. *Migr.* 116).[45] Thus he might have held the opinion that these "settings" were not to be avoided by any means, but that they could be used and frequented by Jews. We shall next present some material substantiating the interpretation that Philo did not strictly *forbid* participation, but that the clue to an accurate understanding of *Ebr.* 20 lies in his disclaimer of *misusing* such institutions.

According to Philo, education may be misused in two ways: if one uses it for personal political gain, and to achieve folly. Philo deals with the first misuse of education in *Leg. All.* 3.162–68; *Flacc.* 130–45.[46] The second way is dealt with in *Congr.* 73–74; *Spec. Leg.* 1.333–45 (Mendelson 1982:42–44). This observation leads us directly to *Ebr.* 20–26.

The decisive support for such an interpretation lies in the text of *Ebr.* 20 itself. Here Philo says that contributions are praiseworthy if they are to gain prudence, and in 21 he states what purposes and activities make such participation blameworthy. In this section he points to "slackness, indolence, luxury, effeminacy and by complete irregularity of life" (cf. 22–23). Philo blames such gatherings as being those of pleasure lovers. This stance is further substantiated by *Ebr.* 95–96. Here Philo states that the disobedient son has in fact been disobedient to both his mother and his father: that is, to both the encyclia and right reason. Accordingly it is not participation "per se" that is blameworthy, but the use of such gatherings for unworthy profit. Such participation is described as that of one who "drowns the whole of life in ceaseless and unending drunkenness," comparable to *Ebr.* 22 where such behavior is described as "excessive indulgence in food." The summation of such an attitude accordingly is formulated thus by Philo: "And thus he made a god of the body, a god of vanity most honored among the Egyptians, whose symbol is the golden bull" (*Ebr.* 95).

This last characterization does not differ very much from that of *Ebr.* 21b. When Philo in the last-mentioned passage writes of "complete irregularity of life" (*pantelēs ekdiaitēsis*) he employs a description which in other contexts he invariably uses to denote idolatry or apostasy. In four of its occurrences it is used of unspecified apostasy,[47] and in *Vita Mosis* 2.167; 2.270 and *Spec. Leg.* 3.126 it is invoked in descriptions of idolatry of the golden calf in the desert. The term *ekdiaitēsis* is thus very strong, as is the description in *Ebr.* 25–26 where the contributor is characterized as one who purposes to do a wrongful act "in spite of the direct injunction of the Law, not to go with the many to do evil" (Exod. 23:2).

Hence the settings where one may enter if the purpose is to gain prudence, are the educational settings in Alexandria as represented particularly by the gymnasial clubs and associations. But this statement should immediately be further qualified. The educational settings should not be limited to such settings alone; education is not only to be sought in the gymnasial settings. To Philo, education has a theoretical aspect and a practical part. In the idiom of *De ebrietate*, one should be obedient to both the mother and the father. These are described by Philo in *Ebr.* 80–81 as secular, lower education, and right reason:

> This fourth class are valiant guardians of the laws which their father, right reason, has laid down, and faithful stewards of the customs which their mother, instruction, has introduced. Their father, right reason (*ho orthos logos*), has taught them to honor the Father of the all; their mother, instruction (*hē paideia*), has taught them not to make light of those principles which are laid down by convention and accepted everywhere [cf. *Ebr.* 33].

Hence the educational settings of Alexandria are many and diverse. But one should not forget that the "right reason," that which "bids us follow in the steps of nature and pursue truth in her naked and undisguised form" (*Ebr.* 34), points to the study of philosophy as represented by the Jewish Law, the Torah. In fact, obedience to *orthos logos* means obedience to the Law of Moses. "Apparently 'right reason' is identical with the divine Word, a central idea in the thought of Philo" (Sandelin 1991:138). The norm for considering the use of education is to be considered in light of the Law, having the study of the Law as its goal. Philo admits that the lower education should come first, but then philosophy is the higher (*Congr.* 74–80).[48] This aspect of education, according to Philo, which also is the practical one (cf. *Ebr.* 82–83), the progression from the lower to the higher education, is also to be carried out in the settings of daily life, including the right use of the clubs and associations (*Ebr.* 20–21).

The purpose of *Ebr.* 20–21 is thus not totally to forbid participation and payments of contributions to non-Jewish institutions, but to be deliberate in the use of such institutions and to strive for the acquisition of virtues, rather than for their ruin. And to strive for the virtues, is to live with the Torah as one's guide. The virtues are promoted by the Torah (*Spec. Leg.* 1.299; 2.224; 4.134; *Praem.* 162), and they cannot in fact be gained save through the service of God (*Sacr.* 37).

This attitude may be further illuminated by pointing to a passage in which Philo discloses his own participation in banquets: *Leg. All.* 3.155–56. The context here is how to overrule the passion by reason, and the argument from his own experiences runs thus:

> When we are present at entertainments (*synousiais*) and are about to take and enjoy the viands provided, if we take our places at table with reason (*syn logōi*) like some weapon to parry blows, we shall neither gorge ourselves with food beyond measure like cormorants, nor, overdosed with unlimited strong drink, shall we succumb to intoxication with its resultant foolish talk: for reason will curb and bridle the impetuous rush of the passion.
>
> I, to mention myself in proof of what I say, know by frequent experience (*pollakis pathōn oida*) how true it is. Many a time have I been present at a gathering with little that was sociable about it or at costly suppers. When I did not arrive with reason for my companion, I found myself the slave of the enjoyments provided, at the mercy of harsh masters, entertainments for eye and ear and all that brings pleasure by way of taste or smell. But whenever I arrive with convincing reason at my side, I find myself a master not a slave, and, putting forth all my strength, win the noble victory of endurance and self-mastery, in a vigorous and pertinacious encounter with everything that incites the unruly desires.

Though this may seem only an example of how to manage through a party without getting too drunk and satiated, read in the light of *Ebr.* 95 and Philo's view of the pleasure-lover as comparable to an idolater, the passage brings us closer to his intention as set forth in *Ebr.* 20–21. Those who intend to participate only to drink and to live according to their pleasures are in fact indulging in worship of the created instead of the creator and as such are to be blamed and avoided (cf. *Spec. Leg.* 1.176). But with reason as one's companion, one will succeed, and make progress in one's education. Hence, as described in our sociological characterizations of the clubs and associations, they also had socializing aspects, even when read in the light of Philo's view of education.

SUMMARY AND CONCLUSIONS

The purpose of this study has been to investigate Philo's attitude respecting a part of the social life of Alexandria. The part studied, the phenomenon of various clubs and associations, has been a neglected subject in previous research on Philo.

Philo describes various aspects of the activities of Graeco-Roman associations: he employs several terms known from other sources, and he describes such features as the payment of dues, sacrifices, symposia, the tendency to cultivate political unrest, the consequent anxiety of Roman officials and their limited tolerance of associations.

In his comparisons of Jewish feasts and gatherings with those of the Greeks and Romans Philo emphasizes wine-drinking and drunkenness in the latter. In *Ebr.* 20–26 he discusses the payment of dues, a discussion which shows that he does not totally forbid participation. Hence, he is in a way an "infiltrator" in these Graeco-Roman settings. But he nevertheless is cautious about joining such associations. In fact, he seems to be of the opinion that participation could easily lead to idolatry and apostasy by fostering the love of pleasure. His restrictive attitude can thus be summed up by quoting his remarks on symposia in *Spec. Leg.* 1.176:

> All these things should be held in little account by those who are minded to live with God for their standard and for the service of Him that truly *is* – men who, trained to disregard the pleasures of the flesh and practiced in the study of nature's verities, pursue the joys and sweet comforts of the intellect.

NOTES

1 In working out this paper, I have profited greatly from the discussion of an earlier version presented in the Research Seminar at the Department of Religion, University of Trondheim, and especially from suggestions offered by Peder Borgen. I am also very grateful for a bibliography on the associations offered by John Kloppenborg in the later stages of my work. The article has been laid out for some time on the *IOUDAIOS* listserver (formerly) at York University, Toronto, Canada, now at Lehigh University, and I have also profited from interesting suggestions offered by, among others, Gildas Hamel, University of California.

2 Cf. for example, San Nicolò 1913–15; Muszynski 1977.

3 Cf. especially Liebenam 1890; Waltzing 1895–1900; Ziebarth 1896; Poland 1909; San Nicolò 1913–15; see also Kornemann 1901.

4 These "more recent studies" seems in fact to be rather few, but cf. Herrmann 1978 and

Waszink 1978. See also De Robertis 1955; Forbes 1933; Burford 1972. The work of Graeber (1983) treats only associations of the fourth century. See also the two articles by Fisher (1988a, 1988b).

5 Cf. Nock, Roberts, and Skeat, 1936. Worth mentioning also is Reicke 1951:320–38.

6 For example, Heinrici 1876.

7 For example, Bardtke 1961; Dombrowski 1966.

8 See especially Judge 1960. Judge 1980 gives some of his reactions to the more sociologically oriented studies published in the period 1960–80. See also Wilken 1972; 1984:15–25, 31–47; Malherbe 1977:60–91.

9 Cf. Barton and Horsley 1981; Klauck 1986; Meeks 1983. See also Seland 1984.

10 Cf. Harnack 1906:5–13; Smallwood 1976:120–22, cf. Philo, *Legat.* 281–82.

11 Cf. Eisenstadt and Roniger 1984; Moxnes 1991.

12 Cf. Schmitt-Pantel 1990:esp. 206.

13 Cf. Tod 1932:77: "a satisfactory classification is well-nigh impossible ... ". See now, however, the article by Kloppenborg in the present volume.

14 The following classifications may be found in the older standard works: Handels und Kaufmannsgilden, Verschiedene Vereine unter Industriellen, Krämern und Handwerker, Vereine unter Gladiatoren und Schauspielern (Liebenam 1890); Kultvereine, Wissenschaftliche Vereine, Künstler Vereine, Politische Vereine, Berufsverbände, Vereine für Leibesübung, Gesellige Vereine verschiedener Art (Ziebarth 1896); Kultvereine, Vereine unter Altersgenossen, Agonistische Vereine, Berufsvereine, Private und sonstige Vereine (San Nicolò 1913–15); le associazioni religiose, le associazioni conviviale, le associazioni politiche, le associazioni funerarie, le associazioni professionale (De Robertis 1955).

15 Poland 1909:16–28; San Nicolò 1913–15, 1:11–29; Ziebarth 1896:92–95; cf. Liebenam 1890:19–20, 165–66.

16 Schmitt-Pantel 1990:200. The model worked out by Malina (1986b) may here be illuminating in order to understand the role of religion.

17 Cf. Liebenam 1890:63–158; Kornemann 1901:380–81; Ziebarth 1896:133–90, esp. 133–40; Poland 1909:8–172.

18 See especially *Flacc.* 4; 136–37; *Vita cont.* 40–47; *Legat.* 312, 316; *Spec. Leg.* 2.193; 3.96.

19 See for example, *Opf.* 161; *Cher.* 29, 50, 124; *Ebr.* 24; *Congr.* 12, 62; *Agric.* 145; *Abr.* 137; *Jos.* 43 (in Loeb edition, these are translated as "assembly"); *Spec. Leg.* 1.178; 3.170, 172, 187; 4.239; *Vita cont.* 124; *Migr.* 26, 30, 63; *Fuga* 140; *Mutat.* 38 (translated "gathering"); *Agric.* 49; *Immut.* 56; *Confus.* 40, 188; *Spec. Leg.* 2.40, 140; *et. al.* (translated "union"). Cf. LSJ 1720, which gives the following possibilities: 1. assembly, meeting, 2. national gathering, 3. company, guild, 4. in hostile terms, meeting of two armies, 5. = *synousia*, sexual intercourse, II. of things, coming together, constriction, 2. astron., conjunction. Most of these are relevant for Philo's texts.

20 Cf. *Agric* 104; *Confus.* 97; *Migr.* 158; *Abr.* 126; *Dec.* 89; *Spec. Leg.* 2.95; *Vita cont.* 18. In *Spec. Leg* 3.96 and *Flacc.* 4, however, the contexts demonstrate that clubs/associations are denoted.

21 For example, *Post.* 101; *Plant.* 14, 58; *Ebr.* 70, 94; *Fuga* 32, 198, 205; *Somn.* 1.196; 2.10, 127, 139, 277; *Vita Mosis* 2.185, *et al.*

22 Poland 1909:152. He refers further to Ziebarth 1896, who refers to Philo's *Flacc.* 136. Cf. Poland 1909:358.

23 Cf. *Spec. Leg.* 2.20; *Somn.* 1.123, 125; 2.57.

24 On the organization of the clubs in Graeco-Roman Egypt, see Boak 1937.

25 Cf. Nock, Roberts, and Skeat 1936, where such a practice is codified in the laws of an association. See also Danker 1982:152–53.

26 Kornemann 1901:402, 410, 414; Liebenam 1890:41, 260, 264; Wilken 1984:35–40.

27 Cf. Reicke 1951:327; cf. Eisenstadt and Roniger 1984:43–63.

28 MacMullen 1974:77; Poland 1909:502.

29 Cf. here the prohibition of sorcery given in the law of the association of Philadelphia in Lydia (Barton and Horsley 1981:8–10).

30 See further on this issue, Smallwood 1976:133–38. [See also the article by Richardson, in this volume – Ed.]

31 Cf. Liebenam 1890:29; Ziebarth 1896:95; Reicke 1951:325; Wilken 1984:12–15.

32 Cf. his descriptions of the synagogues in *Vita Mosis* 2.216; *Spec. Leg.* 2.62 and *Praem.* 60.

33 Cf. Poland 1909: see index. On wine-drinking, see especially pp. 262–64. Cf. further Henrichs 1982, here esp. 140–42.

34 See *De agricultura; De plantatione; De ebrietate,* and *De sobrietate.*

35 Philo deals with Deut. 21:18–21 in two other passages in his writings: in *Spec. Leg.* 2.232 and *Mutat.* 206.

    The context of *Spec. Leg.* 2.232 is Philo's explanation of the fourth commandment (the fifth according to his way of counting). Philo here restates that the authority of the parents extends to punishments of death, but he does not comment on the possible crimes of the disobedient son.

    The other text is somewhat closer to *Ebr.* 14–15. Philo here elaborates on the pronoun *houtos,* and states that it is not used carelessly, but that it points to the fact that the parents had other sons too. Cf. *Ebr.* 93–94.

36 It has been pointed out that there seems to be a certain dissimilarity or change of emphasis in Philo's view of the encyclia, i.e., secular education, in *De ebrietate* compared to his presentation in other writings, especially in *De congressu.* In *De ebrietate* the encyclia is presented as representing the conventional side of things, the conventional customs and rules laid down by human ordinance (*Ebr.* 34b, 36). In *De congressu* the encyclia is more presented as preparation for philosophy. See Colson 1917:158–60. Mendelson (1982), however, finds no great conflict, but only two divergent emphases.

37 Borgen 1983a:73 (repr. in 1983b:74); 1987:227.

38 Borgen 1984a:151. Borgen also states that "in this endeavor, Philo goes so far as to be a conqueror on the verge of being conquered" (150).

39 Borgen supports his suggestion by pointing to Tertullian *De Idolatria* 2, and *m. Sanh.* 7.6. See further the discussion in Baer 1961:79–145.

40 Poland 1909:173; Bell 1953.

41 *QG* 1,13; *Leg. All.* 1.63; *Spec. Leg.* 2.62; *Agric.* 18.

42 Wolfson 1947, 1:215. Cf. *Leg. All.* 1.70–71.

43 Ad *pothos aretēs,* see *Spec. Leg.* 2.230; *Congr.* 112, 166; *Prob.* 22; ad *kalōn zēlos,* see *Vita cont.* 68; *Somn.* 2.235; *Praem.* 11; ad *meletai synecheis, Gig.* 26; *Agric.* 160; ad. *askēseis epimonoi, Leg. All.* 1,89; *Sacr.* 63.

44 Mendelson (1982:33) says that "since there is no evidence that synagogue schools were open on weekdays, we may conclude that if the Jews encountered secular studies in an institutional setting, it would have been in the Greek gymnasium."

    The evidence for Jewish associations is scarce. It is not obvious that the traditions in *t. Sukkah* 4.6 and *b. Sukkah* 51b; *y. Sukkah* 5,1.55a about the seats in the great synagogue of Alexandria being arranged according to the professions point to the existence of Jewish associations or guilds. See Ziebarth 1896:101. Meeks (1983:39) and Applebaum (1976b:703) interpret them as witnessing Jewish associations. See further Seland 1984:54–55.

45 Cf. Borgen 1984b:252–56. See also Mendelson 1982:31–33.

46 Borgen 1965:122–46; Mendelson 1982:42–46.

47 See *Praem.* 98; *Vita Mosis* 1.31, 278; *Somn.* 2.123, cf. 4 Macc. 4:19; 18:5 and Josephus, *War* 7.264.

48 Mendelson 1982:35–38; Borgen 1965:108–15.

8

GRAECO-ROMAN VOLUNTARY ASSOCIATIONS AND THE DAMASCUS DOCUMENT

A Sociological Analysis

Sandra Walker-Ramisch

The focus of this chapter is twofold. First, as the title indicates, it is an attempt at an interpretive analysis of the social relations and organizational patterns suggested by a document commonly associated with the Dead Sea Scrolls and a comparison of that pattern with that of Graeco-Roman voluntary associations in general. But second, and perhaps more importantly, it is an attempt to identify some of the methodological problems in undertaking such a study, and to suggest tentatively wherein we may find some solid methodological ground.

In dealing with the Dead Sea literature itself, scholars have tended to pursue one of two methods: either they have tried to synthesize a picture of an historical community (identified with Khirbet Qumran) by a conflation of the documents, suppressing important differences in those documents; or they have focused on the exegesis of one document, assumed on various grounds to best represent the Qumran community, and then made judgments about the "historical accuracy" of the other documents on the basis of that document. In both, explicitly or implicitly, the goal is a reconstruction of the history of the social group which produced the "library" of the Dead Sea caves. Conflicting or renegade bits of data (such as the enigmatic "390 days" of CDC (the Damascus Document), or the geographic designation of Damascus, or halakah regulating observance of the Temple cult) are ignored, dismissed as inaccurate, or labelled "symbolic."

These reconstructions often rest upon questionable assumptions, for the most part implicit, about the nature of the Dead Sea texts. The most pervasive of these assumptions is that the documents found in the caves were together because they belonged together; that is, that they represent (more or less completely) the literary output of a unified and definable social group ("*the* Qumran community"), and that this literature reliably reflects the life of that community, providing a window (albeit cloudy) on to its social practices and institutions. Further, it is assumed that the cryptic allusions in the documents (or some selected allusions) refer to actual historical events. Thus one need only identify those historical events to know the origins and identity of the sect which produced the texts. That sect is most commonly identified as "*the* Essenes," a social group itself conceptualized by a harmonization of the works of Josephus, Pliny, and Philo. A generic type of historical reconstruction which emerges is that the Essenes (=the Qumran community) were an offshoot of the Hasidim (1 Macc. 2:42) who scurried off into the desert when Jonathan (or Menelaus) declared himself High Priest. Here they shut out the outside world and established a "monastic" (closed, male celibate) style of life and social organization which the Graeco-Roman world had not seen before and would not see again until it blossomed within certain wings of the Christian movement 400 years later!

Granting a connection of some sort between the archaeological and literary remains, the nature of that connection, and the nature of the relationship of text to extra-textual reality in general, remain highly problematic. As W. S. Green warned over a decade ago:

> the presence of a document in a particular group does not attest to the role of the group in its production, nor does it reveal how members of the community regarded the status or content of the text. The relations between literature and society are complex and frequently obscure; to assume that the former always reflects the latter is naive, facile, and unwarranted.[1]

Further, a text is already a schematized model, giving representation to some social elements and suppressing others. No matter how careful one's exegesis of that text is, it is never equivalent to the "field work" upon which one can base a Geertzian "thick description." The existence of the remains of the hindquarters of animals buried in jars, and burial grounds for men, women, and children nearby, both totally unaccounted for by the literature, is a good case in point. The assumptions that have guided much of Qumran scholarship regarding the relationship of the manuscripts to Khirbet Qumran and the degree to which the literature reflects the beliefs of its owners, remain for the most part implicit, and quite possibly misleading if not altogether erroneous.

Further, if we allow that the Qumran manuscripts may reflect with some degree of fidelity the life of a definable social group or groups, to attempt to synthesize a picture of that group from the diverse manuscripts found in the caves is to create a Weberian ideal type, which while methodologically useful, has no historical existence. The advantage of the ideal type is that, as an invariable reference point for comparison, it serves as a tool to bring into focus the uniqueness of empirical cases, exposing essential differences. One may then construct theories to account for those differences and test them against other empirical cases. But the synthesized or harmonized picture itself (the ideal type) must suppress differences. For example, the Damascus Document (CDC) known originally from two differing and incomplete medieval manuscripts found in the Cairo Genizah, has been integrated on the basis of fragments of these documents found in the caves, with the Qumran documents, in spite of the fact that CDC regulates for life in 'camps', for family life, private property,

temple participation, and relations (business and social) with Gentiles, things in-
imical to *Serek Hayyahad* (1QS). To harmonize CDC with 1QS one must do violence to both texts. Yet these differences in organization and social relations
have been consistently devalued in the service of an historical reconstruction of
"the Qumran community," and explained away by positing that each document
represents the community at a different stage of historical development. Deciding which came first then becomes the *crux criticorum*. It is notable that although
fragments of Jubilees have been found among the Qumran manuscripts, and although there are significant affinities between Jubilees and the other Qumran
manuscripts, it is not assumed that Jubilees belongs in "the Qumran library."[2]

Another preoccupation of Qumran scholarship has been the drawing of parallels between this reconstruction of the so-called Qumran community and
other groups of the ancient near east – notably Christian communities. The theories about the connection between "the Qumran Essenes" and Christianity
follow the full range, from those who posit direct modelling or influence, to
those who see in Qumran a "general pattern" of organization which was pervasive in the ancient world. Moshe Weinfeld's book on the Qumran literature is a
thorough and scholarly example of the latter.[3] Methodologically, his broadening
of the interpretive context for the Qumran manuscripts to the whole ancient
Graeco-Roman world is a decided advance over interpreting the texts in the context of an anachronistic concept of "normative Judaism" and focusing on the
group's "sectarian" consciousness. Instead, Weinfeld highlights a number of
parallels in the organizational patterns and procedures of Graeco-Roman and
Egyptian collegia and guilds and those of Qumran, "the primitive Christian
sect," the *haburah*, and the *yeshiva*. Unfortunately though, he, as other notable
Qumran scholars before him (Vermes, Jeremias, Stegemann, Cross, and to an
extent, Murphy O'Connor) assumes a monolithically unified historical community in the case of both Qumran (a harmonization of the Dead Sea scrolls)
and Christianity, (a harmonization of the New Testament documents).[4] Although Weinfeld purports to focus on 1QS, specifically columns V–VII which
he identifies as the "legal constitution of the sect" (1986:8), he consistently
draws on a number of other Qumran manuscripts to "round out" his Essene
"pattern." Further, to proceed as he does on the presupposition that "the organizational rules of the Qumran sect have nothing to do with specific Jewish
ideals" (1986:71), but are "congruent" with "the universal character of sectarian
organizational procedure" (1986:72), is, as I will argue, questionable. Apart from
the debatable use of "sect" terminology here, a "universal," or even a cross-
cultural pattern may be more difficult to establish than Weinfeld allows. Without
taking into account the systemic context of a "constitution," one's supposed
congruences may be no more than surface similarities which can obscure profound and crucial differences. Scholars are becoming increasingly sensitive to the
idea that "social facts" are only understandable within entire systems of thought.
As Sarason writes, "the same detail or ruling can take on entirely different
meanings in the context of different systems" (1980:83).

This rather lengthy excursus into the general character of Qumran scholarship (with apologies to particular and often creative endeavors which do not fit the mold) is by way of making a waiver at the outset to any comprehensive critical analysis of this vast scholarly field and its various and conflicting theories. Rather, methodologically, I decided to analyze the Damascus Document without any *a priori* assumptions as to its connection with other documents, with the Qumran excavations, or indeed with any historical community. My question was a simple one: Do the organizational patterns and social relationships suggested by the Damascus Document correspond to the model of Graeco-Roman voluntary associations? The findings turned out to be rather interesting.

VOLUNTARY ASSOCIATIONS

At the outset some nominal definition of 'voluntary association' would be methodologically useful. Based upon modern sociological and anthropological data,[5] a voluntary association might be defined as *an organized association of persons who come together on a voluntary, contractual basis* (rather than kinship, caste, national, or geographic association) *in the pursuit of common interests, both manifest and latent. To the association each member contributes, by contractual agreement, a part of his/her time and resources.*

Four points in this definition are to be noted. First, the distinction between 'voluntary' and 'involuntary' is seldom as clear-cut as the definition suggests. For example, one may become a member of a church group by family affiliation, or of a trade union as a condition of employment. Second, membership is part-time; members of such associations remain autonomous individuals with separate interests, occupations, and property. Third, voluntary associations are private organizations and as such operate independently of the state's governing apparatus. This makes it possible for them to serve a mediatory function between the individual and the state. The voluntary association's relationship to the state can take a number of forms. For definitional purposes, I have distinguished three kinds of voluntary association along this relational parameter:

1   Those which are fully integrated within the state and hold values and goals consonant with it; the emphasis would be on affirmation of the existing order.
2   Those which are integrated within the state, yet hold some opposing values or goals; the emphasis would be on reform of the existing order.
3   Those which promote a radical rejection of cultural values and goals; emphasis would be on separation from the existing order and strict regulation of socio-economic exchange with that order; at the extreme it may result in physical withdrawal or revolutionary activity.

Fourth, although usually requiring by constitution the active and equal participation of all members, a voluntary association has some kind of formal (structured) organization, with a "council" with judicial and deliberative powers (sometimes salaried). In spite of their democratic ethos, voluntary associations tend to take on an oligarchic organization, a division of the membership into "a minority of directors and a majority of directed."[6] Membership is often hierarchical, with positions designated by a plethora of honorific titles, and initiation, advancement and achievements of members, as well as special days of significance to the group celebrated with elaborate ceremony.

The manifest interests of membership served by voluntary associations are many. They may be recreative, social, military, economic, political, ceremonial/ritual, religious, educational, and so on, or a combination of two or more such interests. Some associations may take on a mandate to serve the interest (as they see it) of society at large and therefore direct their activities to non-members. Among the latent functions of voluntary associations are the provision of solidarity or of social mobility, the conferring of status/prestige, the enabling of social integration, the affirmation or expression of values, and so on.

Voluntary associations tend to proliferate in times of rapid cultural change and institutional disintegration, providing innovative forms of organization, roles, and social relationships. However, they also appear to provide, in societies with a strong corporate structure, the counterbalancing force of a federative type of organization. In either case, where the traditional political, economic, and social institutions of a society fail to provide for the needs of individuals, voluntary associations will arise to fill those needs: to provide loans to help the small business get started, to improve water supplies to a village, to provide scholarships for the promising but economically deprived student, to enable a more efficient hunt, to build needed parks, to ensure proper burial for the deceased, to supply support for the bereaved and soup kitchens for the hungry. In short, where government and kinship fail, voluntary associations provide fictive polities and fictive families.

GRAECO-ROMAN COLLEGIA

In order to compare the organizational patterns and procedures suggested by CDC with those of Graeco-Roman collegia, I generated a homomorphic model[7] or "ideal type" (not a historical reconstruction) of a Graeco-Roman voluntary association to serve as a speculative instrument and reference point for the comparison. As noted above, such a comparison serves not only to indicate similarities but, more importantly, to throw into relief differences between CDC and the collegia. Because of temporal and geographical cultural proximity one would expect many similarities. It is the differences then which demand attention, and which must be assessed within the interpretive context of ancient Mediterranean cultural systems and discourses as a whole.

The imperial period of Roman history saw an extraordinary proliferation of voluntary associations as evidenced by the profusion of inscriptions from this period throughout the Greek cities of Asia Minor.[8] Within the empire the *polis* was the essential form of social organization. However, in spite of varying degrees of regulation and at times suppression of collegia, Roman citizens and residents alike were afforded, by Athenian law, the right of private association "provided they do nothing in violation of the public law."[9] Thus any group could assemble, draw up a constitution and regulations, declare themselves a collegium (*thiasos, synodos, eranos, orgeōnes*) and acquire a permanent structure in which to meet. Because they were formed by private persons for private ends, the collegia came under private law, and thus their internal organization and government was, as the modern voluntary association, independent of the state.[10] Within the collegium, members were free to elect their own officials, collect dues, own common property, regulate their own social relations, honor their own gods, and celebrate their 'special days' such as the birthday of their patron, the feast day of their god, or the anniversary of the death of a former member. To these ends, members of the collegia gathered to share in cultic rites, conviviality, a common meal, and good wine. Social relationships within the society were strictly regulated, and internal disputes were settled within the community, not in public courts. Abusive, slanderous, disruptive, or dishonest behavior was strictly prohibited, and offending members punished by the imposition of fines or by expulsion.[11]

In a society which was barely literate it was often necessary to enlist or hire a clerk (*grammateus*) to take care of financial records – tax receipts, dues, license fees, expenses – and hence the preponderance of financial records from the remains of these societies. However, as Ramsay MacMullen warns, one should not be misled by the economic focus of the records; collegia were not constituted for economic purposes. Although there could be an economic advantage to the incorporation of herders or weavers or longshoremen, even the professional guilds assembled for social purposes. It was primarily the experience of conviviality and *communio* provided by the collegia which drew people together, and this is reflected in the names they gave to their societies – "Mates and Marble Workers," "Brother Builders," "The Comrade Smiths" (MacMullen 1974:75), "The Late Drinkers" (*CIL* IV 575). As MacMullen cautions, "any analogy with a medieval guild or modern trade union is wholly mistaken" (1974:19).

Collegia members customarily sought a patron from among their municipal government officials, not primarily as a defender of their economic interests, but as someone who would add status to their association – a status not possible for individual members. In turn, the association would often lend political support to its patron (which could be substantial)[12] and honor her or him with grand titles and inscriptions.

As did the mystery cults, some associations prided themselves on closely guarded secret knowledge to which only the fully initiated members of the society could be privy. This secrecy was particularly characteristic of medical or healing societies,[13] but is found also in the professional guilds. For example, the "charter" in the mosaic floor of the 'Ein Gedi synagogue prohibits its members from revealing the "secret of the city" (involving the growing of spices) to anyone outside their professional guild.

Although the collegia were functionally independent of the state, their autonomous government in no way absolved the citizen member from participating in public worship, sacrifices, and festivals, and in general honoring (*eusebeia/pietas*) the state gods and ancestral customs; nor did it exempt her or him from showing honor and respect for the council and people (*philotimia*). *Pietas* and *philotimia* were considered the sacred duty of every citizen and their observance an act of loyalty to the empire and an affirmation of the social order. To fail in this duty was *asebeia* (*impietas*) and this could mean exile, or even death. But if *pietas* and *philotimia* were the 'glue' of the empire, the collegia too, were an integral[14] and integrating part of the socio-political life of the city-states. For the most part, the third type of modern voluntary association suggested above would not be found in the Graeco-Roman World. Collegia did not represent an opposing or 'sectarian' way of life which rejected the dominant social order. They may have used the language of secrecy but they did not use the language of separation. No condemnation of the power structures regulated or restricted their interaction with the macrosociety, no "conversion" in the sense of a radical resocialization of members was required to join a collegium; only the promise, on oath, to uphold the society"s 'constitution".[15] Nor were the collegia characterized by innovative restructuring. On the contrary, their social relations and organization tended to mirror the municipal organization and public cult of the *polis*. For example, a collegium would normally have a formally enrolled "citizenry" which would be termed a *populus*, or *dēmos*; a governing council (*boulē* or *gerousia*); the division of members into voting groups called *curiae*, or *centuriae*; plus an enormous variety of titles such as *curator, tamias, logistai, epistatai, archontes*, etc.[16] Collegia would also have priests and priestesses – the guarantors of tradition – to officiate, along with their ruling body of *magistri* and an impressive variety of other titled posts. A rigid class system in which class was legally defined and hereditary meant that upward social movement was a virtual impossibility for the lower classes. The upper-class ephebes received their gymnasium education and went on to become members of the *gerousia* or to take prestigious municipal posts. The lower classes joined a collegium. Within it they structured a microcosm, a society with prestigious positions and grand titles which were attainable by all members. In short, they took over the "nomenclature of officialdom" and in their social relations and organization "constituted in every detail miniature cities" (MacMullen 1974:76). As Wayne Meeks writes: "Evidently, besides conviviality, the clubs offered the chance for people who had no chance to participate in the politics of the city itself to feel important in their own miniature republics" (1983:31).

Within the collegium, members found status, community, and security. And at the end of their lives, not only burial, but a proper burial was guaranteed them.[17] In sum, apart from the many and varied manifest purposes of the collegia, they appeared also to serve the latent functions of providing "fictive kinship" for those who, for whatever reasons, were uprooted from family and clan, and "fictive polities"[18] for those who were denied political voice and social mobility within the state structures.

A "UNIVERSAL PATTERN?"

Much of what is said of modern voluntary associations seems applicable to the collegia of the Graeco-Roman world. The associative principle of both is voluntary/contractual; both, although organized along "democratic" lines tend, because of their hierarchical organization, to be a "minority of directors and a majority of directed"; both organize their own internal financial structures; both own common property, elect their own officials (to whom they give honorific titles), deal with their own internal discipline, and so on. In both, even where group consciousness is intense, membership is part-time; the *populus* of the collegia is still the *populus* of the city, of the empire. And besides their varied manifest purposes, both appear to function as fictive families and fictive polities. But it is the differences thrown into relief by this comparison which are, I suggest, more significant, and which indicate that the positing of "universal" patterns of human organization and social behavior is extremely problematic.

First, the associative principle of modern associations might be religious, economic, political, educational, or social. But in the ancient world, which did not know this type of institutional differentiation, voluntary associations such as the church or trade union would have been impossible. As Bruce Malina points out,

> At the concrete level there were only two significant and discernible social institutions in the first century world . . . : kinship or family and politics or government. The other social institutions so clearly and distinctly discernible by us, namely, religion, economics, and education, simply did not exist as separate, differentiated, and distinct social institutions. Rather, these "modern" distinct institutions were embedded in either the kinship or the political institution of the societies of [this] . . . period.
>
> (1986a:85)

To speak of a religious association in the ancient world is to speak anachronistically. "Religion" was embedded in institutions of the ancient world, and all associations, public and private, were "religious."

Second, the concept of voluntary association in the modern world does not preclude a trans-local organization; that is, a group of individual associations with varying degrees of autonomy united under one executive governing body. Again, the church is a good example. The Congregational Church would represent a loose federation of semi-autonomous groups, while the Episcopalian Church would represent a strongly centralized federation. In Graeco-Roman political organization, the autonomous nature of the city-states precluded the formation of an inter-city federative structure among the collegia which modelled their organization on the city-state; thus voluntary associations were for the most part local phenomena – autonomous bodies without any kind of trans-local organization. While they may have offered *isopoliteia* (reciprocity of rights) between similar organizations (as between city-states), membership, like citizenship, was not transferable.[19] Any groups which did begin to develop a trans-city organization would have been perceived as a threat to the sovereignty of the imperial government, and such were often brutally suppressed. As long as collegia were "families" (albeit organized as "miniature city-states") they would not appear to pose a threat to the political order of the empire; in fact they would constitute, in Aristotle's words, the very building blocks of empire. But should a local association become a movement[20] which transcended the jurisdictional boundaries of the *polis* to achieve a inter-city organization with a centralized authority, it would no longer be "familial" but "political," not the building blocks of empire but an independent public institution vying for political dominance.[21]

Finally, as the tentative typology suggested above indicates, the modern data on voluntary associations include sectarian groups. Sects are characterized by reformist or rejectionist attitudes to the dominant culture and by innovation and experimentation in an attempt to develop new structures, new forms of grouping, and new role relationships. The Graeco-Roman collegia on the other hand, as noted above, not only mirror the organization of the *polis*, but are instrumental in the perpetuation of the dominant social order.

THE COLLEGIA AND THE DAMASCUS DOCUMENT

H. Bardtke (1961) was the first to draw attention to the similarities in organization between collegia and "the Qumran sect," and Weinfeld, as noted above, extended the work of Bardtke into a detailed comparison of the organizational pattern and penal code of "the Qumran sect" with that of both Egyptian and Graeco-Roman associations. The weight of Weinfeld's argument rests upon a detailed etymological analysis of the terminology of "the Qumran sect," much of which he says is not found in any other second Temple literature. His conclusion is that much of this specialized terminology was "coined intentionally to serve as a substitute for common Hellenistic terms for association" (1986:15–16). Thus for example, *serekh* = *taxis*, both meaning a set of rules, a military unit and/or a political or religious [sic] association; *yahad* = *koinōnia*; *rabim* = *plēthos* or *hoi polloi* (an organized public); *mebeker* = *tamias* or *quaestor*, etc.

Weinfeld also identifies a number of role and procedural parallels between "the Qumran sect" and the collegia. Like the collegia, the Qumran manuscripts suggest a hierarchically ordered ruling council consisting of laymen and priests with juridical and deliberative powers over the "many" (*rabim*). The roles and functions of this council, argues Weinfeld, are congruent with Hellenistic associations. The priest holds first place and functions as a president or magister. He presides over meetings and meals, and has the final word on the acceptance or rejection of candidates. Next comes the "official at the head of the many" (PK'D BR'SH HRB'M = *epimelētēs*) who was an administrative overseer. There would also be an "overseer of the possessions of the many" (MBKR 'L ML'KT HRB'M = *tamias* or *quaestor*) in charge of the economy and finances of the group, and so on. As with the collegia, new members had first to be registered with the priest who would examine them as to their worthiness. The candidates would then be approved (or rejected) by the vote of "the many." In both there is also evidence of a graded entry, with candidates undergoing a probationary period. For example, Weinfeld points to a second-century inscription from Rome of a Bacchanalian association (with a *populus* of 400 members!) whose members are listed according to their rank. At the end of the list one finds the *sigetai* (silent ones) – those who do not as yet have the right to speak or to vote. Weinfeld says that this parallels precisely the presence of those in 1QS who "when two years have elapsed the Many (HRBM) shall be asked concerning his affairs. If they admit him, he shall be asked concerning judgment" (1QS 7:21). Again, according to 1QS (5:8–10) every new candidate must swear to uphold the Torah of the community, an entrance procedure also found in Hellenistic collegia.

Weinfeld also notes the importance attributed to a society's founder (*ktistēs*) in Hellenistic associations (1986:45), and draws attention to the prominent position in CDC, and in the Commentary on Psalm 37 (1QpPs37), of the Teacher of Righteousness "whom God commanded to arise and [whom] he established to build for him a congregation. . . ." Weinfeld's investigation of the Qumran penal code, the procedure for judging violations of discipline and the punishments inflicted upon offending members also reveals a number of parallels with the statutes of Hellenistic associations.

Throughout his analysis, Weinfeld also draws attention to some interesting differences between the Qumran manuscripts and Graeco-Roman collegia and attempts to account for those differences. For example, while the Hellenistic associations collected monthly dues and required new members to pay an entrance fee, "the Qumran sect" did not because it was based on joint participation in property, making this practice "inappropriate." Likewise, while the most frequent penalty among the collegia is a monetary fine, this practice is "out of place in the Qumran sect, which is based on joint capital" (1986:41). For "the Qumran sect" penalties included instead a reduction of food allowance, or temporary (or permanent) expulsion. However, I would suggest that the evidence of the manuscripts is much more ambiguous than Weinfeld's descriptions and explanations suggest, particularly when they are examined separately rather than "harmonized." CDC certainly assumes the presence of private funds and property as well as the collection of monthly dues, and even 1QS once indicates the existence of private property (1QS 7:6–8). Likewise, based on his harmonized text, and steered by his presupposition of a sectarian monastic sect voluntarily cut off from social intercourse with the community of Israel and from the cult of the Temple in Jerusalem, Weinfeld finds "ordinances concerning sacrifice and oblations . . . completely absent from scrolls of the Sect" (1986:46) in spite of evidence in CDC to the contrary. And ordinances regulating burial and mourners' rites he finds absent in the Qumran manuscripts because "the normal rite was observed without difficulty since all the members were present in place and did not venture far one from another" (1986:46). This latter explanation suppresses the evidence in CDC of a multitude of rural "camps." Finally, Weinfeld notes the intrusion of hymns and poetry into the statutes of 1QS, an occurrence which he puts down to "the peculiar religious fervor which the Judean desert sect exhibits" (1986:47). As has been argued, all collegia were economic and religious institutions. In spite of the economic focus of many of the extant Graeco-Roman records, the collegia were hardly lacking in "religious fervor."

THE DAMASCUS DOCUMENT

This last section will focus specifically on the Damascus Document in order to compare its organizational procedures and social relations "on their own terms" with Graeco-Roman collegia. Again, in that the comparison is between two social groups (or a social group and an "ideal type" or model) which are close temporally and geographically, it is the differences which will be the focus of interest. Taking up the typology suggested in the definitional section on voluntary associations above, I will look specifically at the way in which the Damascus Document conceives of its membership's relationship to the macrosociety of which it is a part. Finally, I will attempt to move beyond surface parallels by placing social data within the cultural discourses which give them meaning.

Although there are two differing and incomplete manuscripts of the Damascus Document, as Sidnie Ann White (1987) concludes from her textual analysis of the overlapping portions of the A and B manuscripts, both stem from the same original document. The two manuscripts therefore have been treated as one document, with, following Vermes, the variations in the overlapping portions noted.[22] These variations appear relatively insignificant.

As one would expect, the organizational patterns and procedures of CDC appear for the most part "congruent," to borrow Weinfeld's term, with those of Hellenistic associations. CDC suggests a hierarchical structure in which the priests hold first place, followed by Levites, Israelites, and proselytes in that order (14:3–12). There is also an administrative overseer (*MBKR*) who records cases of litigation, collects dues, and examines and registers new members. Each "camp" (rural community) has its own overseer, who watches over the camp "as a shepherd over his sheep" (13). There is also an administrative overseer, apparently required to be adept at social relations, who is placed over all the camps. He must be one "who has mastered all the secrets of men and the languages of all their clans" (14). This is suggestive of a *federation of communities* under a central executive body (*gerousia?*).[23] The clearest evidence for this type of Jewish federative organization is to be found in the literary and epigraphical sources for the large Jewish populations of Alexandria and Syrian Antioch. In these cities, an executive council (*gerousia*) performed some kind of administrative function over the city's Jewish *politeumata*, including all its synagogues and professional guilds. It would appear too, that the jurisdiction of the *gerousia* extended also to surrounding rural communities.[24] Similarly, CDC points to an "executive" council composed of ten judges (*shoftim*), four of whom are priests, and six Israelites.

The members of this council are "elected from the congregation for a definite time" and are "learned in the Book of Meditation (Hagu) and in the constitutions of the Covenant" (10). The centre of authority appears to reside in these *shoftim* who are responsible for legal and constitutional decisions (10) and the distribution of common funds (14), but it is not clear whether they constitute a local council or are part of the central executive body.

In CDC all members are inscribed in the roll of the community (the *populus?*) according to their rank, and are seated according to this order in meetings. New candidates must undergo a probationary period, during which they cannot give testimony in a capital case (10.1). CDC provides a code of conduct regulating the interpersonal relations of its members. However this code diverges somewhat from the typical collegia pattern in that it also regulates the conduct of its members with those outside the community. Thus one may not commission a Gentile to do business for him on the Sabbath (11.2) nor sell clean beasts or birds or servants to Gentiles (12.6–11), or cause bodily harm to a Gentile "for the sake of riches and gain" (12.6–11). In short, the statutes of the community regulate the member's "commerce with all the living," and strictly control his/her commerce with non-members.

The Damascus Document specifies some particular rulings regarding interpersonal relationships, for example,

> each must seek his brother's well being (6.21) and not sin against his near kin (7.1); one should not bear grudges from one day to the next (7.2–3), or in anger bring false charges against a brother (9.2–8); one must not rob the poor or take advantage of the widow or orphan (7.16–17); and one must take only one wife (4.21).

For the most part, however, its code for interpersonal relations is subsumed under "the ordinances of God's covenant" or the "commandments of God" (Mosaic Law). The elaborate code of conduct found in 1QS stipulating penalties for such offenses as lying to, insulting, deceiving, slandering or interrupting a brother, speaking in anger, or exposing one's nakedness to a brother, etc., is absent in CDC. Likewise, in CDC the punishment to be meted out to those who "despise God's commandments" is basically eschatological. Those who "breach the bound of the Law" (b.2) "will be rewarded with the retribution of the wicked when God shall visit the Land" (7.9). However, there is some legislation for disciplinary measures to be taken against members. One who fails to observe the rules of the community may be expelled from the congregation or excluded from the pure Meal (9) until s/he repents. During the offender's time of expulsion no "man" may have commercial or professional dealings with "him" (b.2). Note that the ostracization extends to "his" public life. To be reinstated, "he" must "confess and make restitution" (b.15) and may be liable for a guilt-offering (15). Column 14, although badly fragmented, mentions that one who deliberately lies regarding matters of property, or utters [. . .] unjustly shall be "mulcted"[25] (a fine or forfeiture of property?) for a certain period of time. The "possessed" who preach apostasy seem not to be held culpable, and are merely kept "in custody" (12).

The congregation of CDC, as the collegia, also has its own economic system with common funds and property to which members contribute. However, there is no evidence of members turning over all their property to the community when they become full members as indicated by 1QS. On the contrary, although they belong to the assembly, they live and work independently of it in both rural and urban settings.[26] Each member contributes "the earnings of at least two days out of every month" (14), which is collected by the guardian and handed over to the judges. From these common funds, the poor and needy of the congregation are provided for. This is very similar to the practice of the collegia.

The regulations of CDC also cover its own cultic practices. There are a number of statutes dealing with participation in the Temple cult (9.10–15; 10.14–12.2). There are references to ram- and guilt-offerings and burnt-offerings, and offerings of cereal, incense, and wood. Offerings which are "sent" to "the altar" must be carried by "clean hands." There is also an interesting Sabbath law prohibiting the offering of "anything on the altar except the Sabbath burnt-offering." This may indicate the use of the solar calendar within the community, according to which festivals would always fall upon the same day, and thus never on the Sabbath. The observance of this law would clearly distinguish the members of the community from those following the lunar calendar. Further, the members of the Damascus community seem to have considered "outsiders" (who observed a different calendar?) to "enter the Temple to light His altar in vain" (6.12). The only efficacious Temple cult was that practiced by the Damascus congregation. There is no suggestion that the group did not participate in the (or a) Temple cult, but its claim to practice the "one true way" suggests an exclusivism not found in the collegia.

As with some of the Hellenistic associations, the community of CDC also speaks of its secret or "hidden things." To the members of the community alone, God has revealed

> the hidden things in which all Israel had gone astray – His holy sabbaths and His glorious festivals, His righteous testimonies and His true ways, and the desires of His will, which a man should do and live by.
>
> (3.14–16)

As with the collegia, new members were required to swear an oath of "allegiance" and then were "registered" by name and rank in the community and examined by the "overseer." At this point too, CDC diverges somewhat from the practice of the collegia. It is not clear whether "the many" cast votes regarding the candidate, but it is clear that the overseer has the power of veto over admissions:

He shall examine every man entering his Congregation with regard to his deeds, understanding . . . and shall inscribe him in his place according to his rank in the lot of Light. No member of the camp shall have authority to admit a man to the Congregation against the decision of the Guardian [Overseer] of the camp.

(8.7–19)

And again at 14.3–12:

Whoever enters the Congregation shall do so according to his [the Overseer's] word, each in his rank.

The Damascus Document opens with a homiletic recitation of the group's history, a practice common in Hellenistic associations. However, here we have no *ktistēs*. According to CDC, the community's founder was not the Teacher of Righteousness whom God raised up for them "to guide them in the way of His heart" (1.11), but rather the community was founded by the "returnees of Israel" (*shubi yishrael*) "who went out from the land of Judah" (4.3). To these "who adhered to the commandments of God" (3.12), God has revealed his "hidden things" and "confirmed His covenant with Israel" (3.13–16).

From a sociological perspective, what is most significant about this account of the group's history is that, unlike the collegia, it is characterized throughout by the language of separation. The members are admonished to "separate from the sons of the Pit" (6.15), the "turners from the way" (1.13), the "'builders of the wall' who have 'followed after Zaw'" (4.19). The eschatological lot of these outsiders is "destruction by the hand of Belial" (b.19.14), and he who associates with them "will not be held innocent" (5.15). As suggested above, the belief that the "way" of the community is the only true way, and the concomitant condemnation of and separation from the way of life of non-members, reflects a sectarian ideology[27] uncharacteristic of the collegia. Even a member of a mystery cult with its emphasis on "secrecy," was free to join as many cults as s/he wanted, and still honored the gods and council of the *polis*. The member of a collegium was always at the same time a loyal participant in the *polis*.

CONCLUSIONS

Can we appropriately label the organizational patterns and social relations suggested by CDC a "voluntary association" as that term is understood within the cultural context of the ancient Mediterranean world? Examined on their own terms, the organizational patterns and social relations suggested by CDC certainly seem to bear many "congruences" with the typical Hellenistic collegium. However, to return to the opening argument of this paper, "congruences" are constituted of social facts, and social facts have meaning only within specific historical discourses or symbol systems. Jewish communities may have adopted some of the "nomenclature" of the empire but their appropriation and application of that terminology was informed and shaped by Jewish historical experience and cultural traditions. In short, contrary to Weinfeld's statement, the organ-izational conduct of CDC has everything to do with "specific Jewish ideals." I think this is in part what Safrai is getting at when he comments on the Sanhedrin:

> The Sanhedrin . . . applied to itself part of the terminology then in use in the Hellenistic-Roman East with regard to civic administration, but there is no justification for regarding the administration of Jerusalem as similar to that of a *polis*. In the main, it was administered in the traditional Jewish way.
>
> (1976:390)

Regardless of what Safrai might mean by "the traditional Jewish way," the point I take from his statement is that social and symbolic forms may remain more or less constant, but their meanings are in constant transformation in response to socio-historical experience. The organizational pattern of CDC may be hier-archical; it may indicate an executive council of judges and priests and an ad-ministrative overseer who rules the *populus*; it may provide a strict code of con-duct for members; it may claim to conduct its own internal economic system, and to care for its poor. But it is its sectarian ideology – with its language of sep-aration and of exclusivity, of the righteousness of insiders and the eschatological destruction of outsiders – which renders it incongruent with the collegia. This sectarian ideology places CDC in an oppositional, indeed antagonistic, relation to the larger system of which it is a part, and thus the structured social group (or the literary ideal of a social group) represented by CDC has a social function and exhibits social behavior fundamentally different from those of the collegia.

A final word on "universal patterns": as anthropologist Clifford Geertz argues, before we can begin to posit general patterns of social organization or behavior, we must concentrate on microsociological analyses of particular social groups[28] – what Geertz calls "local truths." And we must attempt to interpret our local truths within the dynamics of the macrosociety of which they are a part. Obviously Jewish historical experience under Greek and Roman rule was not monolithic. The Jewish populations forced into settlements in Ptolemaic Egypt, the Jewish military settlements (*katoikiai*) established in Cyrene, Phrygia, Lydia to secure the Ptolemaic empire, the densely populated Jewish *politeumata* of Roman Alexandria and Antioch, the sparsely populated rural villages, subject to the institutions and leadership of Greek cities . . . in short, the constant drawing and redrawing of political and social boundaries and the Roman reorganization of Jewish settlement patterns, appointment of Jewish officials and definition of Jewish privileges all create a complex grid in which Jewish populations in various ways negotiated temporary patterns of coexistence with the dominant power. These negotiated patterns in all their variety, and the systematic relationships be-tween them, must be the prior subject of our analyses, even if the general theor-ies are forever deferred. In the words of Clifford Geertz, who always manages to put things so succinctly, "we need to look for systematic relationships among di-verse phenomena not for substantive identities among similar ones" (1973a:44).

NOTES

1 Green 1983:195. Referring to the Qumran manuscripts, Morton Smith (1960–61:347) nearly thirty years ago cautioned against drawing conclusions about a basically esoteric sect from its extant exoteric literature. We have no way of knowing, he argued, what proportion of their literature is represented by the cave manuscripts, or what the status of that literature was within the community. Unfortunately, Smith's warning has for the most part gone unheeded.

2 Noted by Davies 1983:14–15.

3 Weinfeld 1986. A similar method is followed by Sanders 1977.

4 In the case of the early Christian movement, to harmonize the New Testament documents not only suppresses significant differences in those texts, but ignores the greater volume of non-canonical literature belonging to that movement.

5 The literature is extensive. For a helpful introduction and bibliography see the articles on voluntary associations by Sills (1968) and Banton (1968). See also Sills 1959; and Robertson 1966.

6 Michels 1959:32, quoted in Sills 1968:369.

7 See Carney's distinction between isomorphic and homomorphic models in Carney 1975:9–11. The homomorphic model is an abstraction which, unlike the isomorphic model, reproduces only selected gross features from what is often, itself, an abstraction. The isomorphic model replicates to scale all features of the original. My model of Graeco-Roman collegia necessarily glosses over the sometimes substantial historical variations in the constitution, function, and official acceptance of private associations from pre-classical Greece to imperial Rome.

8 From the thirty-odd *CIL* volumes, Waltzing (1895–1900) has selected a good body of those dealing specifically with aspects of Graeco-Roman guilds and associations. For Greek inscriptions, see Dittenberger *Syll*³ (1915–24). For a selection of Greek inscriptions dealing specifically with voluntary associations, see Foucart 1873. Cenival 1972 contains relevant demotic texts.

9 Cited by Gaius, *Dig.* 47.22.4. In 64 BCE the Senate, recognizing the possible anti-social nature and potential political power of collegia, rescinded the right of association. From this time on, under changing emperors, the right of association was variously allowed and restricted, until in the early third century CE collegia lost their "private" status altogether and became institutions of the state.

10 At least until the third century CE (above, n. 9).

11 Many of these points are well illustrated by the lengthy inscription on marble columns of the Code of the Iobacchoi, from 178 CE (*Syll*³ 1109) and the Code of the Labyads in Delphi from the third century BCE (*RIG* 995 = *Syll*² 434).

12 In the period of the Late Republic the political recruitment of occupational collegia became commonplace and was attended, not infrequently, by political riots. In 55 BCE Consul Crassus outlawed *sodalitates* – those private associations overtly attempting to influence elections.

13 Note the *Oath of Asaph the Physician*: "You shall not speak of the herbs. You shall not hand them over to any man, and you shall not talk about any matter [connected] with this" (ll. 49–50); and the *Hippocratic Oath*: the science of healing can be taught only to those "who have taken an oath according to the medical law, and to no one else" (ll. 9–10). "Things . . . that are holy are revealed only to men who are holy. The profane may not learn them until they have been initiated into the mysteries of science" (cited from Weinfeld 1986:60–61).

14 As Aristotle observed, "All these associations then appear to be parts of the association of the state" (*Nicomachean Ethics* 1160a, 28).

15 Again, these are general contours of collegia, and historical cases obviously offer differences which must, for the purposes of the homomorphic model, be suppressed. A notable exception to the model are the *hetaireiai*, aristocratic groups of political activists in

143

pre-classical Greece, who sought political power or social advantage by violent challenge and overthrow of existing regimes. However, by the classical period, even members of the *hetaireiai* conspired mainly within the political system for personal advantage, though they remained an object of officialdom's suspicion. The emperor Trajan, for example, warned Pliny the Younger to be wary of collegia which all too often became *hetaeriai*.

Another interesting historical case is that of the Bacchic *thiasoi* in the middle Republic period. In 186 BCE the Roman state brutally suppressed the Bacchic *thiasoi*. Although the then fashionable charges of sexual orgy and child sacrifice were levied against them, I think it more likely that the society's unusual promotion of separation from family and local community, as well as its formation of what may well have been inter-city "cells" put it well beyond the definition of local and loyal collegia.

16 See MacMullen 1974:178 n. 70; Meeks 1983:31.

17 Resident aliens, too, were permitted collegia within their *politeumata* in which they were able to assemble according to their own ancestral customs (*kata tous patrious nomus*), and to own communal property, elect officials, and collect revenue from members. But they too, (with the notable exception in some cases of the Jewish *politeumata*) were required to take part in the imperial cult and honor the state gods.

18 Malina (1986a:87) speaks of "fictive political groups" in which "members hold office and look for limited collective effectiveness, for example, burial societies."

19 For example, the members of a marble-workers' union or a Bacchic society in one city could seek out the marble-workers or Iobacchoi of another city and receive from them the same conviviality offered by his/her own society. But just as citizenship was not transferable from one city to another (when one moved to a new city, one adopted the public cult of that city), so membership in a collegium was not transferable. Someone initiated into a society in one city would have to be initiated again if s/he sought membership in a similar society in another city.

20 A modern sociological concept, "movement" suggests some kind of trans-local organization (a number of geographically dispersed communities joined under a common rubric, ideology, purpose, structure, leadership, economy, etc.). "Movement" might also suggest pervasive shifts in world view and ethos – a shift in cultural consciousness as in the modern liberation and feminist movements. This latter, of course, also has institutional repercussions.

21 It may be this trans-local type of organization that the zealot movement achieved by infiltrating the synagogues (Jewish collegia?) throughout the empire, and perhaps it was just this type of "political" organization which transformed Christianity from a diverse group of *collegia licita* (synagogues?) within the constitution of the city to a political movement with a centralized leadership. The synagogues, at least those of Alexandria and Antioch, appear to have had some kind of intra-city organization. Applebaum (1976a:475) records the action of the Alexandrian "federation" of synagogues in calling a general meeting, exposing its revolutionary members, and turning them over to the Roman authorities.

22 For the most part, I have followed Geza Vermes' (1962) translation of the document. However, where critical passages are concerned, his translation has been checked against Philip Davies' (1983) publication of the Hebrew manuscript which follows the critical edition of Rabin (1958).

23 The Alexandrian *gerousia* was composed of a number of *archonte*, headed by a *gerousiarches*. This executive body was responsible for the administration of the Jewish *politeuma*'s numerous synagogues and craft guilds (Applebaum 1976a:475; 485–86). In 213 CE Caracalla referred to the Jewish federation of communities in Antioch as a *universitas* (*Cod. Iustiniani* 1.9.1).

24 For a review of the evidence supporting these points see Applebaum 1976a.

25 The word is Gaster's (1956:92). Vermes' translation of "do penance" has overtones of Christian monasticism.

26 There are a number of references to the labor and business of members in the statutes regarding Sabbath observance.

27 I use the word "sectarian" in a very general way to indicate an ethos and action in conflict with the macrosociety. There are many problems in transporting modern concepts of sects into the ancient world. For example, Wilson (1970) lists among characteristics of sects a sense of mission to the macrosociety. There is no evidence of this in CDC, which instead awaits the "destruction" of all "outsiders."

28 This is the method which Elliott (1981) argues for and applies.

9

VOLUNTARY ASSOCIATION AND NETWORKS

Aelius Aristides at the Asclepieion in Pergamum

Harold Remus

"The world is composed of networks . . ."
(Wellman 1988:37).

In the second century CE Asclepius sanctuaries were thriving when many others were in decline (Edelstein and Edelstein 1945, 2:101–25). Even as many today turn to faith healers or alternative medicine, so the ill – both rich and poor – turned for help to Asclepius, present and accessible in his many sanctuaries. There, through "incubations" in which he revealed himself to the sick as they slept in one of his temples, they obtained the healings reported in inscriptions and ancient literature.[1]

Archaeological data[2] supplement the literary sources on the Asclepieion at Pergamum, including the most extensive one, Aelius Aristides' *Sacred Tales.*[3] Taken together, they offer revealing glimpses of life in the precincts of the most notable of the Asclepius sanctuaries in the empire in the second century (see Habicht 1969:6–7) and raise questions of social relations among persons drawn to Asclepieia in the second century CE. How did the incubants relate to one another socially, especially if their incubancy was lengthy, as was true of Aristides? Did acquaintanceships ripen into friendships, and can one discern reasons for transitions from one to the other? How did acquaintanceships or friendships relate to ties of kinship? Where do persons in professional capacities such as physicians and Temple personnel fit into the picture? How fixed or flexible or shifting are the lines connecting individuals or groupings to one another? Do any groupings discerned fit common sociological categories such as "voluntary association" or "network"?

In what follows, Aristides (117 CE–180 CE)[4] is the focal person: it is his account of the relation of various persons and groupings to himself that offers glimpses of social relations at the Asclepieion at Pergamum from the summer of 145 CE to September 147 CE, the period of his extended incubancy there, and again in the early part of 148 CE when he returned to Pergamum for a time.[5] The first part of this chapter examines some of the conceptual and terminological similarities and differences between collections or groupings of individuals and relates these in a general way to the picture in Pergamum and to various terms

146

that Aristides employs. The second part relates these general considerations to the individuals and groupings mentioned in the *Sacred Tales*. It is the contention of this chapter that, with one possible exception, no voluntary associations in the usual sense of the term are evident among Aristides and others at the Asclepieion in Pergamum; nonetheless, there was much voluntary association that in various ways fits the category of network. The third part seeks to show that these networks played a significant role in whatever healing Aristides experienced at the Pergamum Asclepieion and in his return to the practice of rhetoric and, moreover, contributed to the continuance and "plausibility" of the Asclepius cult in Pergamum.

1   VOLUNTARY ASSOCIATIONS AND NETWORKS

Voluntary social relations cover a spectrum from temporary collections of individuals to long-lasting associations such as clubs and friendships. Robert MacIver, one of the major earlier theorists of voluntary associations, cites the example of a crowd gathered to watch a fire, drawn by a common interest that dissipates once the fire is out or the police move them away: the individuals constitute an aggregation but not an association. However, if they were to organize to fight the fire, then they would be "transformed into an association," the individuals falling into "social relations with one another," and "the order attendant on social purpose" permeating the group for the time it took to put out the fire (1970:32).[6] An instance of what MacIver postulates is seen in the often-cited exchange between Pliny the Younger and the emperor Trajan in 109 CE in which Pliny requests permission of the emperor to form just such an aggregation into a volunteer fire company (*collegium fabrorum*), so that the passive spectators at a ruinous fire in Nicomedia, the capital of Bithynia, would be organized to avert future such disasters (*Epistulae* 10.33, 34).

Would this imperial judgment have applied in Pergamum in the Province of Asia three decades later during the reign of Antoninus Pius (138–61) when Aristides was an incubant in Pergamum? Several variables deserve attention.

One is the nature of the voluntary association. *Collegia tenuiorum* (Greek equivalent: *eranoi*), societies organized by persons of the lower social strata (*tenues*) around a particular cult for the mutual benefit of the members, had been permitted by Rome since the mid-first century CE;[7] Trajan's negation of Pliny's request (*Epistulae* 10.34) changed that in Bithynia.

Another factor is place: Was the locality difficult to govern, as was Bithynia where rival factions made life difficult for Roman proconsuls?[8] There Trajan's ruling made imperial sense. Was the locality under imperial jurisdiction, in which case the emperor paid it closer attention, or did it enjoy some autonomy, in which case it concerned him less?

How these variables might function in a particular case is seen in another exchange between Pliny and Trajan a while after the one about the fire company (110 CE). Pliny asks (*Epistulae* 10.92) whether Trajan thinks an *eranos* would be

147

permissible in Amisus, a "free and federated city [*civitas libera et foedera*]"[9] in Pontus. The emperor replies (10.93) that if the Amisenians' laws, granted them through federation, allow such an *eranum*, he sees no reason to interfere, especially if any collections gathered benefit the needy and do not result in disturbances and illegal assembly; in cities subject to his own jurisdiction, however, "this sort of thing is forbidden."[10]

Under Antoninus Pius imperial reaction to social disturbances was similar. Labour unrest, in Pergamum as in several other Asianic cities, resulted in intervention by the proconsul; in Ephesus a strike of a bakers' association evoked an edict (probably by the proconsul) regulating future conduct of the organization (Magie 1950, 1:635). However, inscriptions recording permissions granted by Antoninus Pius to associations of youths and of athletes (Hammond 1959:153 n. 59) indicate that Trajan's policy of tolerating what were evidently considered non-seditious associations persisted into Antoninus' reign (see further Magie 1950, 1:635). Non-seditious voluntary associations among Aristides and persons with whom he came into contact at the Asclepieion at Pergamum would thus not be out of the question. However, it was not persons of Aristides' class (see section 3 below) who were inclined to form them. By virtue of their birth, means, and education they had little need to resort to such organization to attain the ends – social and professional – that motivated persons beneath them in the social scale to form voluntary associations (see Wilken's remarks, 1984:35–36). Beginning with Augustus and continuing into Antoninus' reign, imperial policy in the Roman Province of Asia granted the cities greater autonomy but also placed more power in the hands of the wealthy (Magie 1950, 1:600, 640) – persons like Aristides and individuals such as those he identifies as in social relationships with himself. For males of the social elite the ties of friendship established in their youth and cultivated on into adult life, sometimes coalescing into ad hoc associations or conspiracies, functioned to achieve shared goals (cf. Hutter 1978: chap. 2).[11] The modern sociological category that corresponds closely to such informal relationships, and to what one observes among Aristides and his associates, is "network," that is, "a set of elements connected by relations" (Flap 1988:2), or, more specifically, "a set of ties linking social system members across social categories and bounded groups" (Wellman 1988:21).

Common to "network" and "voluntary association" is some element of choice in the social relationship,[12] but the latter term as used in the literature entails in addition a basic modicum of organization essential to the pursuit of the members' common interests (cf. MacIver and Page 1949:12).[13] Individuals in a network also have common interests, and they may move to constitute an organization to achieve them, but that does not necessarily replace the informal ties they have with one another. These informal links set network apart from association.[14] They relate the individuals in a network to one another in a way that is not necessarily congruent with, and indeed may be quite distinct from, the manner intended by the rules that constitute and regulate organizations to which they may belong. Indeed, these links may be more important in the functioning of an association – voluntary (club, church, political party, corporation) or involuntary (school, the military, prison) – than the regulations that supposedly govern and guide it.

As a schoolboy C. S. Lewis perceived this to be the case, and later he came to see "inner rings" as permeating human association generally (Lewis 1955: chap. 6; 1949; cf. further Carpenter 1978:161–64).[15] For Lewis, the most important and least problematic of inner rings was friendship, which (along with Aristotle)[16] he situated among the virtues (Lewis 1949:65). Friendship is one of the terms Aristides uses, alongside others, to designate what I am calling his networks of social relationships. The next section examines the terms that Aristides uses to designate his relationships with various individuals he identifies by name or occupation. As was stated earlier, Aristides is the "focal individual" (Wellman 1988:27), the "point of anchorage" (Mitchell 1969a:13). Such egocentric or personal networks "provide Ptolemaic views of networks as they may be perceived by the individuals at their centers" rather than "the universe as it is perceived by an outside observer" (Wellman 1988:27).

Fundamental to networks are commonalities, whether of kinship, social status, needs, interests, or presuppositions and beliefs – any or all of these that link persons in a network with one another. Geographical propinquity is also important,[17] especially in the ancient world, as is some frequency and/or regularity of encounter over a period of time sufficient to sustain and foster significant association. All of these are true of Aristides and the persons he mentions by name or generically.

2 ARISTIDES' NETWORKS

"Co-incubants/co-pilgrims" (*symphoitētēs*, or *symmoriai* [2.75] and *agelai* [2.68]) in the barest sense denote simply persons who have come for help to the Pergamum Asclepieion, which does not necessarily entail association with one another. Most of Aristides' references to them, however, indicate more than casual relationships among at least some of them. His co-incubants, he tells an audience, are in a position to describe his behavior to them in the Pergamum Asclepius Temple (28.133). In a dream he sees himself distributing to them portions of a sacrifice he has made to the god (48.27). Sedatius comes to the fore as an incubant (50.16, 43) with whom Aristides develops a mutually supportive relationship (see pp. 152, 156, 157–8, 168 below). Another incubant teaches him an epigram (28.88; see further n. 46 below). In his oration on concord (*homonoia*) Aristides asserts that belonging to a chorus, being together on a sea voyage, or having the same teacher cannot compare with having been incubants together at the Asclepius Temple in Pergamum (23.16).

Sharing incubancy did not necessarily entail intimacy, however, as becomes evident when considering the next term designating persons Aristides calls "acquaintances" (*gnōrimoi*[18] or *eiōthotēs*, sometimes *synētheis*). This would seem to be a loose grouping. For example, in one passage dated to Smyrna in 149 CE, he labels certain physicians *synētheis*, distinguishing them from friends (*philoi*) (48.20). In the same passage Aristides refers to a physician, "a certain Heracleon," as "an acquaintance of ours."[19] In one of the Pergamum passages (146 CE) he pairs (and distinguishes) "friends [*tōn philōn*] and acquaintances [*tōn eiōthotōn*]" (49.2). In another (Pergamum, 145 CE), he pairs, and seems to equate, "acquaintance" (*gnōrimos*) and "companion" or "comrade" (*synētheis*) (50.23). He is referring to Euarestus of Crete, whom he had met during a stay in Egypt and who had come to Pergamum to learn more about Asclepius. In Pergamum the two men resume their association, sufficiently that Euarestus, like others in Aristides' writings, recounts to Aristides a dream he has had, in this case commanding Aristides to resume the practice of oratory (50.23). This suggests that while Aristides does not specifically call Euarestus a friend, he none the less associates with him enough to think of him as more than a mere acquaintance (see pp. 158, 160 below). That Aristides uses "acquaintance" with some care – and perhaps "an element of snobbery" (Behr 1968:42 n. 5) – is suggested by his distancing himself from a man who reports a dream pertaining to Aristides: he is a co-incubant (*symphoitētēs*, 50.42) at the Asclepius Temple, but, more specifically, he is an associate (*eichēn synēthos emoi*) – *not* of himself, Aristides points out – but of the physician Theodotus (see pp. 151, 153, 160–1, 162 below), who reports the dream to Aristides, who refers to the incubant as "a Macedonian man" (50.42) or, even more distantly, as "the Thasian stranger, or Macedonian" (40.21). Though he and Aristides are once removed from each other, the two are nonetheless linked, through Theodotus, thus illustrating the observation that "ties are important not only in themselves but also as part of the social networks in which they are embedded. Each tie gives network members indirect access to all those with whom their alters are connected" (Wellman 1988:37). However, incubancy and dreams also connect Aristides and the Macedonian; as Horatio comments in explaining the "Theory of our Friends" in Paul Goodman's *The Empire City* (1959:67), "if two of us find we have one acquaintance in common, we will prove to have three hundred in common," for the many activities the friends in the novel have in common draw them together.

In a number of passages Aristides speaks of companions/comrades (*hetairoi* or *synētheis*). In one case, he seems to be using the term in a professional sense: Quadratus, a fellow orator (50.63), is termed a *hetairos* (50.71).[20] In other instances, however, these are persons close to Aristides at Pergamum or elsewhere. In his eulogy for his one-time teacher, Alexander of Cotiaeum, he describes him as not only a teacher but also as foster-father (*tropheus* [on this term see pp. 162–3 below]) and father to him, as "companion [*hetairon*], everything" (32.2 [Smyrna, *c.* 150 CE]). A *hetairos* at Pergamum instructs him (28.88 [147 CE]) and some *hetairoi* give him advice and explain his dreams (48.72 [146 CE]). *Hetairoi* participate in one of the risky ventures the god commands of him (48.76 [146 CE]). The ancient writers whom Asclepius instructs Aristides to study while in Pergamum seem to him to become virtual comrades (*hetairoi schedon*; 50.24 [145 CE]). A *hetairos* named Dion for whom Aristides expresses great respect relates to him an experience he had while sailing to Egypt (36.10 [Smyrna, 147–49 CE]. In another passage Aristides speaks in the same breath of a man he knew in Egypt as both "a friend and a companion [*philon kai hetairon*]" (36.33), indicating a degree of synonymy in his use of the two terms. Similarly in his mention of Pryallianus, a Platonist with whom Aristides has a relationship significant enough to place him in the category of friends (see pp. 159–60 below), he appears in one of Aristides' dreams as a *hetairos* guiding Aristides to perceive the relation between Platonic teaching and Asclepius (50.55 [147 CE]). The synonymy accords with much Greek usage,[21] and distinguishing sharply in Aristides between companions and friends seems unwarranted.

The references to "friends" (*philoi* or *epitēdeioi*) are numerous. Although many of these refer to persons situated outside Pergamum, these passages give some idea of what friendship meant for Aristides and his friends. They behave as one might expect of friends, modern or ancient.[22] A notable example is Socrates' friends who (in Plato's telling) offer to arrange his escape from prison; for his part, if he rejects their offer, he expects them to look after his children (*Crito* 45a–46b, 54b). When Aristides is afflicted with a (seeming) tumor (see Behr 1981–86, 2:428 n. 89) while staying in Smyrna in 147–48 CE, some of his friends (*philoi*) are amazed by the way he, at the command of Asclepius, so patiently endures the affliction; others of them criticize him for paying too much heed to dreams, and others accuse him of cowardice for refusing surgery or cauterization (47.63). When, in response to Asclepius' instructions, Aristides applies a drug to the growth and it virtually disappears, his friends (*epitēdeioi*) rejoice and express incredulity (47.66). The next year, again in Smyrna, friends (*philoi*) concerned about his health or survival if he follows the god's command to bathe in a river in mid-winter escort him to the site (48.20; 149 CE). A few months later we see Aristides and friends (*philoi*) in the Temple of Isis in Smyrna observing and discussing an omen (49.49–50). Living in Smyrna many years later (167 CE), he says he gets together with friends (*philoi*) at his home whither he summons the most "important" ones (*epikairous*) to tell them Asclepius has commanded him in a dream to declaim (51.30, 32). He and his friends go on sea voyages together (*epitēdeioi*, 48.12 [170/71 CE]), once at his own expense (*philoi*, 50.36 [144 CE]). It is friends (*epitēdeioi*) who ask him to record, orally and in writing, "such great deeds [*tosoutois ergois*]" on the god's behalf (48.1), and when he finally undertakes to do so in 170/71 CE he notes the unsuccessful efforts of friends (*philoi*) to persuade him to do so (47.2).

The references to "friends" at the Asclepieion in Pergamum in the years 145–47 CE are similar, presenting a picture of persons with much in common and in frequent association.

Two of these passages are accounts of dreams recounting what must have been typical scenes in the Asclepieion. In one dream, recorded in the first *Sacred Tale* (47.55), Aristides is lying on a couch in the Temple, fasting; the physician Theodotus (see pp. 160–1, 162 below) and "certain friends" (*tinōn philōn*) approach and sit down beside him; he and Theodotus engage in conversation regarding Aristides' illness. When Aristides wakens from his dream, friends (*philoi*) do in fact come to visit him where he is now (171 CE) living on his Laneion estate north of Pergamum. In another dream one of his friends (*epitēdeioi*), whom Aristides has not seen for some time, encounters him at the entrance to the Temple and embraces him, and they engage in conversation (47.10).

Other passages depict a circle of friends at Pergamum larger than that evident in these dreams. In the winter of 145–46 CE, when Asclepius commands Aristides to bathe in the river Selenus that flows through Pergamum and was then rising because of rains (48.51), the most concerned of his friends (*philoi*), worried about what might happen and also to observe it first-hand, accompany him (48.51). They can't bring themselves to encourage him, and (he reports) are anxious about the outcome (48.52). In the narrative of the healing of the tumor (47.61–68; see above), Aristides mentions that his friends – "first among the Greeks of that day" – come to see him and hear his speeches (47.64). The setting is Smyrna in October 147 CE to January 148 CE, but the description of these friends and of their behavior tallies well with what he and other sources reveal about those persons who emerge from the generic obscurity of "friends" at the Pergamum Asclepieion and are discussed below in the analysis of the networks (pp. 156–61).

Some of the same persons may be included in another important category mentioned by Aristides: *therapeutae*, "[temple] worshipers" or "servants." Aristides names Sedatius (50.16; see p. 156) and himself (47.23; 50.104) as among the *therapeutae*. Rhosander (see p. 156 below), says Aristides, is especially devoted to service/worship (*therapeian*) of Asclepius (50.19). In other passages Aristides speaks of the *therapeutae* collectively. In an oration on one of the three wells in the Temple complex he says that "we Asclepius *therapeutae*" must agree with the god that Pergamum is the best of all his sanctuaries (39.5). When in 145 CE Asclepius commands that Aristides undergo numerous phlebotomies, all the god's *therapeutae* agree he had never before required so many of anyone (48.47). In a vision (*phantazomai*) set in the Asclepius Temple before Aristides' ancestral home but seen in Pergamum, one glimpses a typical ritual action of Asclepius *therapeutae*: they stand by the god's statue as they do "when the paean is sung" (50.50). Of all the terms Aristides employs this one may designate a voluntary association more than a network. Frequent mention (Aristides, Galen, inscriptions) of Asclepius *therapeutae*, among whom native Pergamenes as well as others are numbered, leads Habicht (1969:114) to postulate a *Kultverein* at the Pergamum Asclepieion. Behr, likewise, speaks of the *therapeutae* as "an association" (1981–86, 2:413 n. 7) but, in a more cautious phrasing, says they "seem to have formed a special group at the temple" (ibid. 2:392 n. 33).[23] That *therapeutēs* was a recognized designation – whether denoting a member of a *Kultverein*[24] or simply persons enjoying special status – is evident from Galen's use of the designation to secure from Marcus Aurelius exemption from military service (Habicht 1969:114) and from one of Aristides' dreams in which he presents himself to the emperor as a *therapeutēs* (47.23).[25] For our purposes, whether or not the *therapeutae* constituted a *Kultverein* is not as important as how various *therapeutae* functioned for Aristides as a network (see section 3 below).

These are not the only persons or groupings of persons Aristides mentions or names as associated with himself. There are others who are related to him through office or profession or through family ties and whose association with him might or might not be voluntary, depending on circumstances.

Physicians, understandably, occupy an important place in the life of a person so plagued by illness as Aristides. His relation to two he names – Porphyrio (51.12 [Cyzicus, 166 CE]; 51.19 [?], 24 [Mysian plain, 166 CE]; perhaps 47.57 [Laneion estate, 171 CE]; see further Behr 1968:100), but especially Theodotus in Pergamum – would seem to go beyond that of doctor–patient.[26] In the case of Theodotus, at least, the closeness correlates with his positive attitude to the Asclepius cult and the god's prescriptions (pp. 160–1, 162 below). By contrast other physicians are doubtful about them (47.73 [Mysia, 148 CE]) or prescribe differently than he (47.62, 63 [Smyrna, 148 CE]);[27] 49.8–9 [Pergamum, 147 CE];[28] 49.19 [Aristides' ancestral estate, 148 CE]), though they may be won over if healing ensues upon carrying out the god's instructions (47.67 [Smyrna, 148 CE]; 48.20 [Smyrna, 149 CE]).

Incubants in the Pergamum Asclepieion would have had much to do with the priest (*hiereus*), the person responsible for the oversight of the sanctuary, and with the two (48.30) sacristans (*neokoroi*), ostensibly the supervisory "hands-on" personnel (i.e., "management"). If *neokoros* was a (purely?) honorary title in Asia Minor at this time (see Hanell 1935; Edelstein and Edelstein 1945, 2:193 n. 6), there is no indication of that in the *Sacred Tales*, where the two sacristans are portrayed as actively involved in life at the Asclepieion. In an extended incubancy, such as Aristides', that would be especially true. The Pergamum priesthood was hereditary among the descendants of Asclepiades, the son of Archias, the man credited with bringing the cult to Pergamum (Edelstein and Edelstein 1945, 1: nos 491, 801; Habicht 1969:7, 93). The priest received a portion of all the offerings (Edelstein and Edelstein 1945, 1: no. 491) and may also have received a salary (ibid. 2:192 n. 5). Given Aristides' devotion to Asclepius, one would expect the god's priest to be an important figure during his incubancy. Whether the priest's relations with Aristides extended beyond what one would expect of a person in that office is not clear from the *Sacred Tales* (see section 3 below).

As to sacristans, in the Asclepieion on the island of Cos the person thus designated received a portion of the offerings, according to Herondas *c.* 250 BCE (Edelstein and Edelstein 1945, 1: no. 482.88–90). That was likely the case at Pergamum as well where the priest received portions of the offerings, according to an inscription from the second century BCE (?) (ibid. 1: no. 491); but from the extant sources it is impossible to say for sure. Whether or no, it is evident from Aristides' accounts of Asclepiacus and Philadelphus, the two sacristans during his time there, that they took their responsibilities seriously and with Aristides, at least, developed a significant relationship (p. 161 below).

Family is another category of persons designated by name or by various terms in the *Tales*. "Family" has a distinctive signification, however. Aristides' birth parents figure hardly at all in his writings.[29] Indeed, it is his oratory, he says, that he has made his parents as well as his children and work and recreation (33.20). What Behr (1968:8) characterizes as "an almost total disregard for his parents" contrasts sharply with his close attachment to his *trophos* and his *tropheis*, the family retainers entrusted with his rearing (see pp. 162–4 below).

There are various ways of characterizing personal networks and of representing them, visually and mathematically, in order to delineate the ties between individuals (whether single, multiple, strong, or weak), the density of the ties (the relation of actual to possible ties), the clustering of individuals and cross-linkages between clusters as well as between individuals, symmetry and asymmetry in the various relations, content (what draws the persons together and what significance they attach to their relations with one another), durability, and so forth.[30] As network theory has developed and grown more complex, so too have the ways of characterizing and depicting networks.[31] How one proceeds depends on the data available, their complexity, and the purpose of the analysis. In the case of Aristides' networks, the data are insufficient to construct matrices of much significance (for examples of such see Breiger 1988:84–85, 91; Clark 1992:98–99) or to characterize in much detail the ties linking Aristides and the individuals and groupings identified in the preceding, or the ties linking these to one another. The data do, however, lend themselves to network analysis pertinent to the purposes of this essay as delineated in the next section.

3   TIES THAT BIND: STRUCTURAL AND INTERACTIONAL CHARACTERISTICS

Several different schemes of network analysis and graphic presentation are necessary in order to depict the various ways in which Aristides relates to individuals and groups and their linkages with one another and how these figure in his healing and return to rhetoric and the fostering of the Asclepius cult in Pergamum.[32] One of these is social circles, a concept espoused by Georg Simmel, who along with Emile Durkheim is claimed for "network tradition."[33] In developing the distinctions between *Gemeinschaft* (community) and *Gesellschaft* (association) and the nature of group formation (*Vergesellschaftung*), Simmel devoted a long essay to "Die Kreuzung sozialer Kreise,"[34] that is, the interaction between social groups, specifically the way these may intersect in a particular individual.[35] The terminology or categories employed by Aristides denote not only social relations, however, but taxa as well. "Acquaintances," "companions," and "friends" are social-relations categories, designating the individuals' relations to Aristides but leaving open their relation to one another. Temple personnel, sacristans, priest, co-incubants, *therapeutae*, physicians, philosophers, family (that is, foster-family) are functional designations, with identity apart from Aristides but important for him in so far as they relate to him, so that some will be acquaintances, some companions, some friends. These various configurations are represented in Figures 9.1–4 (pp. 163, 165–7), which gives some idea of the relative size of the various circles and their closeness to Aristides but also indicates that, while the circles and individuals within them may not relate directly to one another, through Aristides they stand in an indirect relation with one another (cf. the Wellman and Goodman quotations above, p. 150).

The picture is more complex, however. What Figure 1 does not show is the links between persons in one circle with one another, or with persons in one or more of the other circles. The Temple personnel interact with one another but also have daily contacts with Aristides' co-incubants; so, too, presumably do some of the physicians. Some of the co-incubants would have or develop ties with one another and perhaps with some of Aristides' various friends. And so forth. Such relations are suggested in Figure 9.2.

The ties between persons, and linking networks, are thus many and diverse among those connected with Aristides in some way. How do these ties and networks function in relation to him? Persons linked socially and professionally are not necessarily cordial or helpful to one another – they may even dislike one another or engage in conflict because of conflicting loyalties (see Flap 1988) or to establish distance from one another. In what Aristides relates of his networks, however, such does not seem to be the case. They function for him, rather, to "structure resource flows" (Wellman 1988:45), that is, they contribute to his healing and return to rhetoric. The association of these various individuals with Aristides and with one another is not by chance: tying the friends to one another and to Aristides is their upper-class status, and interests and concerns that attend it such as a common interest in literature, philosophy, and dreams. Beyond that, they are all devoted to Asclepius and his Pergamum sanctuary, whether because of need – illness, their own or that of others – or piety or local patriotism. So, too, for members of the other networks linked to Aristides. These commonalities "thicken" the following analysis of Aristides' networks.[36]

In Aristides' circles of acquaintances – persons he "just knows" (Wheeldon 1969:178) – the connecting ties would be somewhat tenuous, a characteristic represented in the examples in Figure 9.3 by linkages of few strands. These are probably the most socially heterogeneous of Aristides' networks, marked by asymmetry in the relationships (Figure 9.3: the arrows tend to be unidirectional). Though acquainted with Aristides, the individuals do not necessarily know one another, that is, these are not "dense" networks (Figure 9.3: not all the persons are connected with one another). Their encounters with Aristides, and at least for some of them with one another, would be infrequent, that is, these are not "compact" networks. Nor would they be high in "reachability": Aristides would know some of the individuals in each better than others, and (as is indicated by the dotted lines in Figure 9.3) in order to contact the latter he might need to go through the former, or through persons in other networks. Aristides would interact with the acquaintances in various ways, depending on what it was that would have brought about the acquaintanceship.[37] With physicians the most significant bond would be health and healing. With others he is linked by a common devotion to Asclepius and an attendant interest in dreams. Despite the social heterogeneity of the circle, a certain "floor" of social status may be assumed and along with it the Hellenistic education and culture that were common denominators in Aristides' day (see Marrou 1956: Part 2, chap. 1; Part 3, chap. 2); in the interactions between individuals, however, these linking strands may be more latent than manifest.

The number of *therapeutae* is uncertain.[38] They would be fewer than the co-incubants, a certain social standing evidently requisite to the designation (see n. 24); but for Aristides (our point of anchorage) the "effective" network of *therapeutae* – friends or acquaintances – would not be that large.[39] Everyone he knows knows everyone else, that is, it is a dense network. It is also a compact network, the members encountering one another frequently, perhaps daily, in the Asclepieion, so that the network rates high in reachability: Aristides has direct contact with the others in his *therapeutae* network, and they with him; they do not need to go through other persons. The data are insufficient to allow for more than speculation about how socially heterogeneous the network is. Asclepius was accessible to sufferers regardless of social status or means, as the Epidaurus inscriptions and other evidence make clear (Edelstein and Edelstein 1945, 1: no. 423, 2:113–18, 120, 189–90). Had persons of lower social status or means been admitted to a select group such as the *therapeutae*, it seems unlikely that Aristides would have had much to do with them.[40] If he had, his relation with them would have been asymmetrical. A fair degree of symmetry, and reciprocity, seems more likely, however. Such would be true of his relation with the *therapeutae* he mentions by name, Sedatius and Rhosander (see pp. 157–8 below). The ties linking the *therapeutae* are many-stranded: similarity in social status and education but especially devotion to Asclepius; interest in health, healing, and dreams; the day-to-day contact in the Pergamum Asclepieion which (says Aristides) the *therapeutae* agree is the best of Asclepius sanctuaries (39.5), and participation in its rituals.

The larger group of co-incubants at Pergamum would presumably have been more socially heterogeneous, though again it seems doubtful Aristides would have numbered persons much removed from his own social status among those he speaks of as his own co-incubants. The two circles of co-incubants – friends and acquaintances – are therefore represented in Figures 1 and 2 as, for him (our point of anchorage), effectively not much larger than those of the *therapeutae*.[41] The ties in this network would be fewer and sometimes unidirectional, that is, it is characterized by lower density and lower compactness and reachability but greater asymmetry than the *therapeutae* network. On the other hand, the ties would none the less have several strands: health, healing, devotion to Asclepius and the Pergamum Asclepieion where they share incubancy, that is, the things that brought them to the Asclepieion in the first place.

Though the companions would not necessarily have ties with one another (low density), through Aristides they are indirectly linked and through him could conceivably make contact with others whom Aristides considers his companions (low reachability). However, as we have seen earlier, the dividing line between companions and friends is not sharply drawn; they are thus represented in Figures 1 and 2 as overlapping. The friends' circles would constitute dense networks, high in reachability, with multidirectional ties but restricted in range, that is, these are Aristides' peers, though some rank higher in the social scale than do others. None the less these networks would approximate Aristotle's characterization of genuine friendship as that between persons of like goodness and virtue,[42] that is, relationships would tend to be symmetrical.

A prosopographical "roll call" of persons Aristides names provides some warrant for including these individuals in the circles of friends and offers insights on the "content" of his ties with them, that is, what significance he attached to his relations with them.

Aristides' writings as well as contemporary literary and inscriptional evidence about him make clear that he shares with these persons similar social status, means, and education. Born into a wealthy family that possessed various farms and estates to the north of Pergumum and enjoyed Roman citizenship and other honours (Behr 1968:1–8), Aristides prided himself on never having accepted the fees tendered to orators (28.127, 33.19; further, Behr 1968:8 and n. 12). His education was commensurate with his family's social status and means (ibid:9–14). Wealth, rank, education, and rhetorical repute won him access to those similarly situated in Pergamum and at the Asclepieion.

One of the most prominent of these, L. Salvius Junius, the famous Roman jurist and holder of many high offices (*OCD*, s.v.), was an incubant with Aristides (48.9). His significance for Aristides is indicated by Asclepius' appearance, as Salvius, in a dream to Aristides' foster-father Zosimus in which the title "Sacred Tales" was imparted (48.9).[43] Even more significant is L. Sedatius Theophilus,[44] a Nicaean (50.16) whom, along with himself, Aristides describes as "two of the distinguished [*gnōrimoterōn*] *therapeutaé*" (50.16): a member of the Roman Senate (*ek tēs Rhōmaiōn boulēs*, 48.18), he also held the rank of a Roman praetor (*tōn estratēgekotōn Rhōmaiois*, 50.16). In two vignettes set in the summer and fall of 145 CE one sees clearly the close, reciprocal relation of Sedatius, "the best of men" (48.48),[45] and Aristides, and the important role Sedatius played in Aristides' therapy and return to rhetoric. In the first, presumably set in the Asclepieion, Aristides learns from Sedatius that both of them have received identical prescriptions from Asclepius. In the second account, set some months later in the Temple of Hygieia, which everyone else has deserted in favor of some public show (*theōria*) in the city, the two men, as was their wont (*hōsper eiōthemon*, 50.16), are comparing prescriptions from Asclepius imparted in dreams (50.17) since there was some similarity in their sickness (50.16). Aristides objects he does not know how he can possibly carry out what the god had commanded – to resume his oratory (50.17) – except, as he explains to Sedatius, with a pro forma performance (50.17). Not so, replies Sedatius: offering himself as a listener, he tells Aristides to do his utmost, leaving the supplying of strength to Asclepius, and that Aristides' dream may portend more than the delivery of a single oration (50.17). He adduces as an example "a wondrous deed of the god [*ergon tou theou thaumaston*]": another incubant given the same command followed it, and the perspiration resulting from his effort cured him (50.17).

At this point the two men are joined by another co-incubant (*symphoiton*, 4.2) and friend, Q. Tullius Maximus, also a Roman senator and later the holder of various high imperial offices (Behr 1968:48 n. 26; 1981–86, 2:479 n. 4).[46] Aristides describes him as a lover of the arts, a foremost Roman orator and admirer of Aristides' own efforts (4.2), which Aristides had reciprocated by composing and delivering a (now lost) oration to him (4.3), and as "a worshiper of the ancients [*therapeutēs tōn palaiōn*]" and enthusiastic "after a fashion [*tina tropon*]"[47] about oratory (50.18). Maximus proposes the theme of the oration commanded by the god, and in delivering it Aristides finds strength such as the god would provide (50.18). This, he says, was the beginning of his return to oratory (50.19).

Aristides and Salvius are linked with one another also through a common friend, Euarestus,[48] whom he had come to know in Egypt (50.23; see p. 150 above) and who reports to Aristides that Asclepius has commanded Aristides to resume oratory (50.23). Despite a counter-communication of the god to Hermocrates of Rhodes, a lyric poet (50.23),[49] Aristides in response to encouragement from all sides continues to declaim, with Asclepius continuing to strengthen him (50.24).

In another vignette Sedatius appears with another mutual friend, L. Cuspius Pactumeius Rufinus, "probably the foremost person in Pergamum in his day" (Behr 1968:48), consul in 142 CE and a priest of Olympian Zeus who had endowed "the great votive offerings" at the Asclepieion and the Temple (50.28), that is, the imposing round Temple of Zeus Asclepius Soter in the Asclepieion.[50] Aristides mentions that he himself endowed ten choral performances in the Asclepieion (50.43), and at one Sedatius and Rufinus are present – Rufinus at the god's invitation – and the two stand by him to assist him (*symparestexomen*) (50.43).

Rufinus and another mutual friend, Bassus – "Perhaps C. Julius Bassus Claudianus" (Behr 1981–86, 2:426 n. 35), a Pergamene *strategus* (see Behr 1968: 48–49 and n. 30, 84 n. 84) – figure in a dream in which Aristides interprets for Bassus what Rufinus has said to Aristides as a message from Asclepius (50.28). In this dream and in another, much longer one (47.19–21) set at the statue of Asclepius (mentioned also in 50.48, 50), Bassus and Aristides appear on friendly terms.

Another strong supporter of Aristides is L. Claudius Pardalas, whom Aristides refers to as "our companion [*tou hēmeterou men hetairou*]" (50.87). So well known is he that Aristides introduces him simply as "that [*ekeinos*] Pardalas" (50.27), hence Behr's rendering: "that famous Pardalas," a fame resting on his expert knowledge of rhetoric (50.27), the prominence of his family in Sardis (Habicht 1969:142), and his own position, attested on coins from the time of

Antoninus Pius, as *strategus* and *neōkoros* (sacristan) in Pergamum (ibid.). Aristides nowhere identifies Pardalas as one of the two *neōkoroi* during his incubancy there, suggesting that in his case it was an honorary title (bestowed later), rather than the hands-on kind that appears in Aristides (see p. 152 above). An inscription from Pergamum names Pardalas as the offerer of a sacrifice (*perithytikon/Pardalas/perithytēs*) (Habicht 1969:141 no. 140).[51] The pairing of *perithytēs* (attested in only three inscriptions in Pergamum [ibid:141]) with *therapeutēs* in one (perhaps two) of these tends to confirm the view that the *therapeutae* constituted a *Kultverein* and suggests that Pardalas was also a *therapeutēs*. A believer he certainly is: Aristides (50.27) remembers him as telling him that he thought it was "by some divine providence [*tychē tini theia*]" that Aristides had become afflicted so that with the god's assistance he might improve his oratory, which Pardalas was in the habit of praising.

That praise plays a crucial role in a protracted account from the year 153 CE that illustrates the high reachability of the friends networks functioning to assist Aristides in a situation marked by low reachability.[52] Aristides, recovered sufficiently to deliver occasional orations, has not yet resumed his career. A new governor, C. Julius Severus, appoints Aristides as police commissioner in Hadriani. Aristides, averse to holding any public office no matter how honorific, successfully appeals what is a technically non-appealable decision with a little help from his friends and an acquaintance. At the command of Asclepius, Aristides had gone to Pergamum, where he saw his friends Rufinus and Pardalas; Rufinus writes an official letter to Severus on Aristides' behalf, and Pardalas writes praising Aristides' oratory. In addition, from Aristides' appeal in another, earlier case there arrives, fortuitously, a letter from Heliodorus, former prefect of Egypt and a fellow orator whom Aristides had met during his stay in Egypt, along with letters, evidently solicited by Heliodorus, from the emperor Antoninus Pius and his adopted son Marcus Aurelius. Aristides sees the successful resolution of his case as fullfilment of a communication from Asclepius (50.75, 80–82, 94), but the god worked through a network of persons sufficiently highly placed to influence the governor.[53]

A narrative that concludes the fourth of the *Sacred Tales* (50.105–8) shows there was precedent for this sort of proceeding and the interpretation Aristides placed on it. In 146 CE, while Aristides is in Pergamum, some persons lay claim to, and then occupy by force, the Laneion estate he has purchased in Mysia. Aristides, severely affected by the news, is at a loss what to do, but, following upon a dream/vision, manages to make his way to the Temple where the governor at the time[54] and Rufinus happen to make an appearance. Aristides tells his tale to Rufinus and then to the governor, who subsequently settles the matter in Aristides' favor in court. Aristides credits Asclepius with gaining him access to the governor, but again a human intermediary from the friends circle plays a significant role as well.

In addition to these older (50.27; cf. 50.15) friends, Aristides encounters at the Asclepieion members of a school of Platonists[55] who also figure importantly in

159

his healing and return to rhetoric. Rhosander, a philosopher unknown except for Aristides' mention of him, seems to have been a member of the school[56] as well as one of the *therapeutae* (see p. 152 above). In a significant dream Rhosander comments that Aristides' speeches have improved and that he now compares favorably with Demosthenes (50.19). "This comment inflamed all my subsequent ambition," says Aristides (50.20). The next day Aristides takes up oratory again, to the applause of friends (50.20). Rhosander figures also in a later dream in which his name is revealed to be equivalent to that of Aristides' favorite physician, Theodotus, and of Asclepius himself (50.21). In another dream Aristides jokes and banters with another Platonist, Pryallianus "from the Temple" and "a companion [*hetairon*]," who reveals to him a significant connection between Plato and Asclepius (50.55–56; p. 151 above). Euarestus of Crete, whose importance has been indicated above, may also have been a member of the school (50.23).[57]

It is clear that the ties linking Aristides to these friends, whom he characterizes as "the best and most distinguished persons [*hoi beltistoi kai gnōrimotatoi*] of those times" (50.27),[58] and them to one another, are many-stranded, reciprocal, and strong, as is indicated in Figure 9.4 (p. 167). One of the strongest ties is the friends' shared devotion to Asclepius and his Pergamum sanctuary, a devotion rooting not only in the god's healing powers but also in his inspiration and protection of literati like themselves (see Edelstein and Edelstein 1945, 2:206–8). Habicht's description (1969:15, 17) of the Asclepieion as the "Zentrum des geistigen Lebens" in the city, indeed in the province of Asia, is justified by literary evidence as well as by Asclepieion inscriptions that name various sophists, including Aristides[59] and others mentioned in the *Orations* (Habicht 1969:16). The sanctuary had its own theatre and library (ibid.:x, 17), that is, cultural foci that comport well with Aristides' mention of discussions, declamations, lectures, poetry, epigrams, and choral performances produced or patronized by Aristides and the sophists, poets, and philosophers who appear in his pages. Asclepius is, one might say, the key networker in the friends' circle, communicating through them to one another as they recount and discuss with one another their ailments and dreams.

Although various physicians distance themselves from some of the god's instructions to Aristides (p. 153 above), Asclepius figures importantly in the medical tradition generally (Edelstein and Edelstein 1945, 2:139–41), and at least in the case of Theodotus, Aristides' physician during the incubancy, a friendship develops between him and Theodotus who, despite any professional misgivings, is none the less amenable to the god's prescriptions as imparted to him by Aristides. He is the physician who reports to Aristides the dream of the Thasian or Macedonian incubant mentioned earlier (50.42; p. 150 above). When Aristides summons Theodotus one morning at dawn to recount to him dreams granted both to himself and the Temple sacristan Asclepiacus, the doctor marvels at their divine character but as a physician wonders about divine instructions that seem to be incongruous with his patient's weakened condition (48.29–34

[Pergamum, 146 CE]). Aristides' ties to Theodotus are suggested by the dream recounted earlier in which Theodotus and some friends come to him in the Pergamum Temple and sit down beside him, and he and Theodotus discuss his condition (47.55–56), and by another in which Aristides is living in Theodotus' house (51.57 [Laneion estate, 170–71 CE]).[60] Theodotus would not have served Aristides gratis, but their association goes beyond that of doctor–patient. Behr's summary (1968:44) is just: Aristides was "deeply fond of him."

The other physicians who appear in the *Sacred Tales* during the incubancy would fall in the category of acquaintances. This would be a fairly dense network – the physicians all know one another – with high reachability, but presumably of restricted social range since physicians serving, and associating with, persons of Aristides' social status would likely enjoy at least status by association.[61] Similarly, the sacristans and the priest. All of these would have contact, regular and frequent in the case of the sacristans and priest, with some or all of the *therapeutae* and the co-incubants and to some degree with one another. Again, devotion to Asclepius and his Pergamum sanctuary would be an essential strand in the ties linking these various persons to Aristides and to one another.[62]

With the two sacristans, Asclepiacus and Philadelphus, his ties are close enough to locate Asclepiacus and perhaps Philadelphus as well in the category of friends. Aristides does not say if he is living in Asclepiacus' house gratis or as a paying guest (48.35 [Pergamum, 145 CE]), but in various passages the sacristan's concern for his guest becomes evident. Aristides tells him many of his dreams (48.35 [Pergamum, 145 CE]), the sacristan's customary response being to listen and marvel (49.21–22 [Pergamum, 148 CE]). Asclepiacus supplies an ointment Aristides has dreamt of and later informs him of the ingredients (49.22, 23). Not surprisingly, in one dream Asclepiacus appears as a physician, prescribing a poultice (which Aristides uses on awaking) and then in a subsequent dream removing it (49.25 [Pergamum, 148 CE]). In another, Asclepius himself appears in the form of Asclepiacus, offering a remedy and instructions to Aristides (47.58 [Laneion estate, 166 CE]). It is Asclepiacus who, in a "vision-dream [*opsis oneiratos*]," imparts to him a communication regarding Aristides' *tropheus* Zosimus (47.76 [Pergamum?, 148 CE). Asclepiacus appears in another, predictive dream that then comes true (48.48–49 [Pergamum, 145 CE]). On one occasion Asclepiacus, knowing nothing beforehand of certain of Aristides' ailments, reports to him a communication from the god that turns out to confirm the healing Aristides has experienced (49.14 [Pergamum, 148 CE]). When Aristides undertakes the risky venture mentioned earlier (p. 152 above), the sacristan – either Asclepiacus or Philadelphus – is present along with other concerned persons (48.52 [Pergamum, 145–46 CE]). The ties in the sacristan network are seen functioning when Asclepiacus reports to Aristides one of Philadelphus' dreams in which the god indicates a certain remedy for Aristides, which Aristides then verifies first-hand with Philadelphus the next day (48.30–31, 35 [Pergamum, 146 CE]). It is clear that these two older (48.47) servants of Asclepius became significant others for Aristides.

In recounting one of his dreams Aristides praises the present priest's grand-father[63] as "the most eminent [*endoxotatos*] of those to date" during whose incumbency Asclepius "performed many and great surgical feats" (50.64). In the dream the grandfather and grandson are seen to be on cordial terms with Aristides and praise him and his speeches (50.64–66). In another dream Aristides is himself clothed as a priest when he sees the Pergamum priest (47.11). In what seems his official capacity, the priest along with the sacristans decide, with Aristides, where Aristides should dedicate an epigram Asclepius has imparted to him (50.46). Judged simply by these infrequent mentions of the priest, Aristides and he do not seem to have been close enough to be considered friends.

How much voluntary association there was between Aristides and other Temple personnel is also unclear. Such relationships would be asymmetrical in so far as these are functionaries either employed as servants or owned by the Temple as slaves, on whom Aristides held common views.[64] A second-century BCE(?) inscription from Pergamum mentions such personnel generically – *tōn hierōn paidōn* – as under the oversight of the priest (Edelstein and Edelstein 1945, 1: no. 491), a generality echoed in Aristides: "one of the Temple servants [*hypēr-etōn*]" (47.11). A number of specific personnel are attested from Asclepieia in various times and places.[65] These sorts of personnel and others would be essential to the operation of an establishment as large and busy as the Pergamum Asclepieion and may be assumed to have been present there. Aristides mentions specifically a doorkeeper (*thyrōros*, 47.32), a "sacred herald [*ton keryka ton hieron*]" (50.48), and especially choirs, necessitated by the frequent singing of hymns to the god. These perform either standard pieces (47.30) or ones Aristides himself had composed (50.38, 43–44), for which he had hired them in accordance with a command from Asclepius imparted in dreams (50.38). Thus they do not stand in a voluntary relation with Aristides, being in the employ either of the Temple or himself (50.38, 43). However, through certain of his voluntary associates the choirs he hires come to play an important role in his therapy and return to oratory. His wise physician, Theodotus, recalling his patient's dreams in which Asclepius issued the command to hire a chorus of children/boys (*paides*),[66] was accustomed to order (*ekeleue*) them to sing some of Aristides' verses, whereupon any troublesome symptoms ease or cease (50.38). Aristides' friends Rufinus and Sedatius, as mentioned earlier, assist him at the first performance of the choirs of *paides* and men he has hired (50.43), which Aristides sees as a significant step in his return to oratory (50.44–47).

Aristides' (foster)-family is the densest of his Pergamum networks and the most durable: the ties antedate and persist beyond the Pergamum incubancy. Formally, his ties with these surrogate parents, Philumenē his foster-mother (*trophos*) and his various foster-fathers (*tropheis*),[67] and with their offspring are asymmetrical – they are family retainers[68] – but the mutual affection, solicitude, and assistance that characterize their ties to one another point to a reciprocity that transcends the official status of those ties. The high regard in which Aristides held these surrogate parents is indicated by the many references to

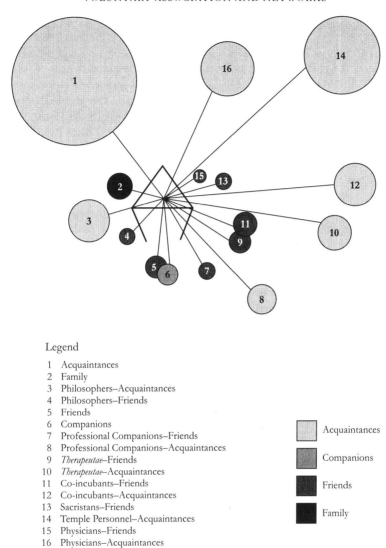

Legend

1 Acquaintances
2 Family
3 Philosophers–Acquaintances
4 Philosophers–Friends
5 Friends
6 Companions
7 Professional Companions–Friends
8 Professional Companions–Acquaintances
9 *Therapeutae*–Friends
10 *Therapeutae*–Acquaintances
11 Co-incubants–Friends
12 Co-incubants–Acquaintances
13 Sacristans–Friends
14 Temple Personnel–Acquaintances
15 Physicians–Friends
16 Physicians–Acquaintances

☐ Acquaintances

▨ Companions

■ Friends

■ Family

Figure 9.1 Intersection of Aristides' circles through Aristides

them[69] and to their children and grandchildren, his surrogate siblings and children, and by his designating Homer as the *tropheus* of the Greeks (17.15), and the Romans as caring for the Greeks as though they were their *tropheis* (26.96) – even as we see him caring for Zosimus, his beloved *tropheus* (47.69–77 [Mysia, 148 CE]), and his foster-mother, Philumenē, "than whom nothing was more dear to me" (47.78 [ancestral estate, 148 CE]). Both are readily accessible to him, and he

163

to them (high reachability), during the Pergamum incubancy and thereafter. Zosimus is present when Aristides begins his incubancy at the Pergamum Asclepieion, and it is to Zosimus that the god appears on that first night (48.9 [145 CE]). Later, the god imparts to both men the prescription that heals Aristides' tumor (47.66 [Smyrna, 148–49 CE]). Zosimus, sent to enquire of Apollo, is told Asclepius will heal Aristides (49.12 [Lebedus, 147 CE]). On another occasion Asclepius communicates to Aristides the prescription that heals Zosimus, and the two men celebrate together (47.69–74 [Mysia, 148 CE]). Both Zosimus and Philumenē are present when Aristides is taken severely ill (49.16 [ancestral estate, 148 CE]). He in turn, sent by Asclepius, goes to Philumenē's bedside, whereupon she recovers from her illness (47.78 [ancestral estate, 148 CE]). Another time a visit from him also revives her (50.10 [ancestral estate, 153 CE]). These surrogate parents figure repeatedly in his dreams,[70] as do his foster-siblings or their children.[71] Zosimus' death sends Aristides into an extended period of grieving (49.47 [Smyrna, 149 CE]), and when, two decades after the Pergamum incubation, two of his foster-sister's children die, he sees their lives as given for his, a divinely wrought exchange (48.44 [Smyrna, 165 CE]; 51.21–24 [Laneion estate, 166 CE]). Although these are family retainers in Aristides' service,[72] it is clear from the mutual affection and care that more than duty is present. In addition to the long-standing bonds between them, devotion to Asclepius is another, which grows stronger during the incubancy and subsequently.

It is perhaps not without significance that Asclepius himself was part of a large but close family (Nilsson 1967:808). The various networks Aristides established during his incubancy functioned for him, one might say, as an extended Asclepius family, with the Asclepieion where he spent so much time as its dwelling. Within and through this family the god – for Aristides the key figure in the various networks[73] – effected Aristides' therapy and his return to the practice of oratory.

CONCLUSION

Various studies of modern networks have shown how they influence individuals' actions; "even their chances of getting sick and of recovering or their chances of dying seem to depend on their social networks" (Flap 1988:2, citing Pilisuk and Froland 1978, Berkman and Syme 1979). The nature of their networks "may significantly affect focal individuals' health, longevity, and well-being" (Wellman 1988:28).[74] The *Sacred Tales* were written to record all that Asclepius had done for Aristides, but those pages are replete with named and unnamed individuals to whom he also gives credit, explicit and implicit, for his healing and return to oratory. Behr (1968:47) has aptly summarized the role Aristides' friends played, 'a role only slightly less significant than that of Asclepius himself. If at first the god's enjoinders and approval seemed little more than emanations from a world without substance, the vigorous support and encouragement of the ever-growing circle of Aristides' friends provided a real confirmation of what was

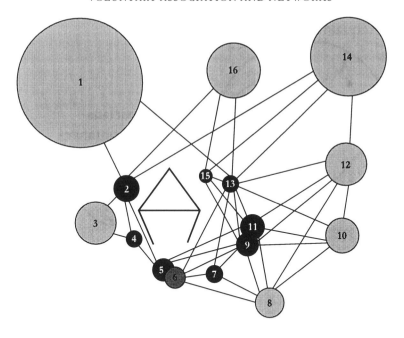

Legend

1   Acquaintances
2   Family
3   Philosophers–Acquaintances
4   Philosophers–Friends
5   Friends
6   Companions
7   Professional Companions–Friends
8   Professional Companions–Acquaintances
9   *Therapeutae*–Friends
10 *Therapeutae*–Acquaintances
11 Co-incubants–Friends
12 Co-incubants–Acquaintances
13 Sacristans–Friends
14 Temple Personnel–Acquaintances
15 Physicians–Friends
16 Physicians–Acquaintances

Acquaintances

Companions

Friends

Family

Figure 9.2 Intersection of Aristides' circles with one another

taking place, until faith in the god grew robust enough to stand alone and Ascle-pius invaded the world of reality.'

Elsewhere (Remus 1983:99) I have suggested how the whole Asclepieion – people and edifices, ceremony and song, dreams and temple medicine – fits well Berger and Luckman's designation "plausibility structure" (1966:92, 154–58) within which the god, his healings, and the devotion of his adherents were credible.

165

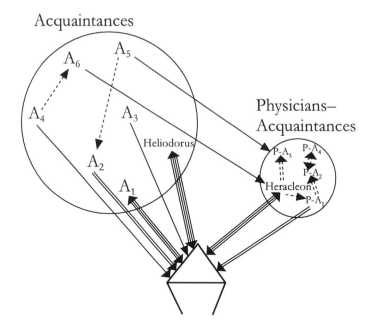

Legend

≡ Number of strands in a tie

— Direct tie

----- Indirect tie

→ Asymmetry

◄► Symmetry

The designations (names and ciphers, A_1, A_2, etc)
and the number of strands connecting them are merely
suggestive of the actual numbers.

Figure 9.3 Circles of acquaintances, illustrating interactions with Aristides and with one another

Networks such as those glimpsed in Aristides' *Orations* were part of the lively intellectual and religious life of Pergamum in the second century CE and subsequently, and help to account for the persistence of the Asclepius cult and the slow growth of Christianity there despite the early presence of a Christian community (Rev. 2:12–17).[75] Ultimately, however, Asclepius *ho sōtēr* yields to Jesus *ho sōtēr*,[76] and the site of the Pergamum Asclepieion eventually accom-

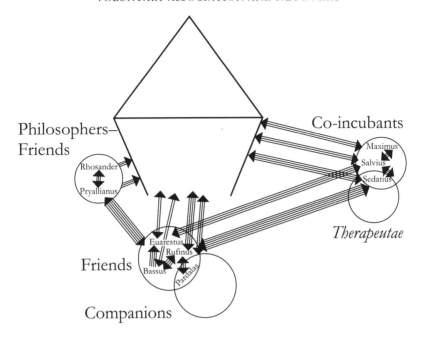

Legend

≡ Number of strands in a tie

▭ Direct tie

◀▶ Symmetry

The names and the number of strands connecting
them are merely suggestive of the actual numbers
of individuals.

Figure 9.4 Friends' circles, illustrating interactions with Aristides and with one another

modates a Christian sanctuary (Habicht 1969:20).[77] What role was played in that
development by Christian voluntary associations and networks, or by networks
among pagan social strata other than those discernible in Aristides, is another
story.[78]

APPENDIX

Persons named and identified/categorized by Aristides
(Keyed to Figures 9.1–9.4; some names fall in more than one category)

1 **Acquaintances**
   Priest

2 **Family**
   Trophos: Philumenē
   Tropheis: Zosimus, Neritus,
      Epagathus
   Suntrophos (male): name
      unknown
   Suntrophos (female):
      Callitychē
      Her son: Hermias
      Her daughter: Philumenē

3 **Philosophers–Acquaintances**

4 **Philosophers–Friends**
   Rhosander
   Pryallianus
   Euarestus?
   Capito?

5 **Friends**
   Bassus
   Euarestus
   Maximus
   Rufinus
   Salvius
   Sedatius

6 **Companions**
   Pardalas
   Pryallianus

7 **Professional Companions–
   Friends**
   Alexander (Aristides'
      teacher)
   Dion
   Quadratus

8 **Professional Companions–
   Acquaintances**

9 ***Therapeutae*–Acquaintances**

10 ***Therapeutae*–Friends**
    Rhosander
    Sedatius

11 **Co-incubants–Friends**
    Maximus
    Salvius

12 **Co-incubants–Acquaintances**
    Thasian or Macedonian
       stranger

13 **Sacristans–Friends**
    Asclepiacus
    Philadelphus

14 **Temple Personnel–
    Acquaintances**
    Heliodorus

15 **Physicians–Friends**
    Theodotus
    (Later: Porphyrio)

16 **Physicians–Acquaintances**
    Heracleon
    Satyrus

NOTES

1 The procedure is outlined in Edelstein and Edelstein 1945, 2:148–52, 186–89. In place of the Greek term *egkoimēsis*, Aristides refers – "whimsically," says Behr (1968:26 n. 20) – to his incubancy as his *kathedra* (*Sacred Tales* 48.70, 49.44; also 50.14: *kathēmenō de moi*).

2 Behr 1968:27–30 (plan of the Temple complex at pp. 28–29); Habicht 1969:1–20 (detailed plan, p. x).

3 Volume one of Lenz and Behr's edition of the Greek text of Aristides (1976–80) covers *Orations* 1–16 plus fragments and inscriptions; the second volume, promised by Behr (in Lenz and Behr 1976–80:vi; Behr 1981:vii) and covering the remaining *Orations* (17–53), has, to my knowledge, not yet appeared and I have therefore used Keil's edition (1898). The *Sacred Tales* are numbered 47–52; I cite the *Sacred Tales* and the *Orations* simply by number and section (for example, 47.3).

    Behr's translation (1981–86) of the Aristides corpus and his earlier study of Aristides (1968) provide invaluable expositions, annotations, and indexes of the *Orations*. Aristides' text and other sources on the Pergamum Asclepieion are conveniently collected in Edelstein and Edelstein 1945, 1: nos 425, 433–37, 569–71, 800–11 and *passim*.

    The six *Sacred Tales* (numbers 47–52 in Lenz–Behr) were composed in 170/171 CE on Aristides' Laneion estate where he was living in retirement. In composing them he drew on his memory as well as on the 300,000 or so lines he says he devoted to recording his dreams at the command of Asclepius (48.3–4); the title, *Sacred Tales* (*Hieroi Logoi*), was communicated by the god to Aristides' foster-father (48.9). See further Behr 1968:41 n. 2, 116–20; 1981: 425 n. 1.

    Translations of Aristides in my text are my own.

4 117 CE: Behr 1981–6, 2:1 and Behr 1973:vii, where Behr corrects his earlier date, 118 CE (1968, 1 and n. 2, with a detailed rejection of 129 CE). 180 CE: Behr 1973:xiii and 1981–86, 2:4. *OCD*, s.v. Aristides (5): "A.D. 117 or 129–81 or later."

5 In dating the events recorded by Aristides and in placing them geographically I draw on the chronology in Behr 1968:121–30 and the dates given in the margins of his Brill translation (1981–86).

6 Cf. the terms *turba* and *grex*: though both designate collections of animals or humans, *grex* when applied to humans connotes "not a crowd, but a group of people with interests and characteristics which unite them," with "the unifying element" commonly indicated "by a substantive in the genitive (for example, *grex amicorum*, *grex Epicuri*) or by an adjective" (Kirsopp Michaels 1953:40); other examples in *Thesaurus Linguae Latinae*, s.v. *grex*: IIA,B (vol. 6.2:2332–33).

7 See Sherwin-White 1966:600; the long inscription from Lanuvium, Italy (136 CE) setting down the by-laws of a burial society gives a good idea of how such a collegium might function (*ILS* 7212; trans. in Lewis and Reinhold 1966b:272–75).

8 Sherwin-White 1966:609–10 calls attention to orations of Dio Chrysostom that mention these rivalries.

9 On these terms see Sherwin-White 1966:687.

10 As Jean Bodin remarks (*Les six livres de la république* [1576]), it appears that tyrants always "have hated the corporations and communities of the people, and by all means endeavored to have them utterly extinguished" (cited in Nisbet 1970:128); so too in the state envisaged in Hobbes' *Leviathan* (Nisbet 1970:134) and in various modern states (Cohen 1969:3).

11 The important role played by three close friends of the emperor Julian in both his personal life and public career offers an instructive example (see Bowersock 1975: *passim*).

12 I say some element of choice, for person A may choose a social relationship with B but not necessarily with C with whom B chooses to associate and whom A may in fact dislike but is none the less connected to through B. Or A may not like C and D and yet associate

169

with them because it serves her/his individual interests or what she/he sees as wider interests. "Such ties are involuntary in that they come as part of the network membership packages" (Wellman 1988:41).

13 The general focus of the voluminous sociological literature on voluntary associations has been on modern Western democracies, a setting in which they flourish (for example, Pennock and Chapman 1969), or at most on the Reformation and post-Reformation period (for example, Robertson 1966; Nisbet 1970: chap. 6 offers interesting treatments of "Sovereignty and Association" according to Bodin, Hobbes, and Rousseau). On the other hand, social anthropologists have been examining the role of voluntary associations and, increasingly, networks within and between them, in "rural pre-industrial societies in the non-Western world" (Wheeldon 1969:128) and the effect of industrialization on social relations in such societies (Flap 1988:6). Earlier, classical scholars had examined the nature and role of voluntary associations in the ancient Mediterranean, a line of study continuing to the present (see the studies cited in Kloppenborg 1989 [and in this volume]). Recently students of early Christianity have begun to draw on network theory in seeking to understand the social history of early Christianity (see White 1991b; Clark 1992; Maier 1995).

14 As Kadushin (1966:792) characterizes the particular social circle he studied, the members "do not have a listing in the telephone book, but only in that sense are they a non-existent social unit." That is, networks have "a relatively low degree of institutionalization" (791). Kadushin (799) cites the example of the Vienna Psycho-Analytical Society formed by Freud from the informal group that gathered once a week in his waiting room. Other terminologies expressing the distinction between voluntary associations and networks include "formal" and "informal" "interest groups" (Cohen 1969:3) and "membership" and "social relations" (Breiger 1988:86, following Goffman 1971:188).

15 So, too, Flap (1988:3), calling attention to everyday expressions such as "pulling strings," "good connections," "through the grapevine," "not what you know but who you know." Anderson 1974 demonstrates how "networks of contact" – "who you know" – function among Portuguese immigrants to Toronto both on entry to Canada and then in finding of jobs. David Freeman ("A Hollywood Lexicon." *The New Yorker* [15 Feb. 1993] 108), commenting on Hollywood lingo and mores:

> *Buff*: People in the movie business believe deeply in the power of personal alliances. Each day, all over Hollywood, telephone calls are made apparently to exchange information and gossip. The true purpose, however, is to establish relationships and keep them in good order: to buff them up, just as car retailers continually buff up the BMWs, Mercedeses, and Jaguars of Hollywood's ruling class. These calls are made within status lines. A junior agent at William Morris might call a senior agent across town at I.C.M., but only if there was a specific purpose, easily stated to the senior agent's assistant. . . .

16 *Nicomachean Ethics* 8.1.1 (1155a.4): "a kind of virtue, or associated with virtue" (*aretētis, met' aretēs*); cf. Cicero, *Laelius de amicitia* 6.20: "*sine virtute amicitia esse nullo pacto potest.*"

17 Though not absolutely essential, as was noted by Malinowski of ceremonial exchanges over long distances among Trobianders (Flap 1988:4), by Cohen (1969:6–9, chap. 4) of Hausa trading networks in West Africa, and by others of societies with modern means of communication (Adams 1968:169).

18 *Gnōrimos* at times means "distinguished person," i.e., *clarissimus* (for example, 50.12; see n. 45 below), also in the comparative (50.16) and superlative (50.27, 51.29). Some have taken *gnōrimos* in connection with the Diophanes mentioned in 47.49 to mean *clarissimus*, but since nothing more is known of him, this seems unwarranted; cf. Behr 1981–86, 2:427 n. 78.

19 Behr 1981–86 translates *gnōrimos* here as "companion"; however, Aristides' introduction of the man as "a certain [*tis*] Heracleon" suggests that "acquaintance" would be a more faithful rendering.

20 This is assuming (with Behr 1981–86, 2:438 n.109) that the Quadratus termed a *rhētōr* in 50.63 is the same Quadratus named as *hetairos* in 50.71. On *hetairos* as colleague cf. 2.76–77: the writings of Aeschines (Socrates' devoted follower) are so Socratic that some have taken them to be by Socrates himself, and it is quite proper to call the two men *hetairoi*.

21 See the examples in BAG, s.v. *hetairos*, and cf. Philo, *Leg. all.* 2.10: in friendships (*en tais philiais*) flatterers are enemies rather than *hetairoi* (similarly, 3.182). Cf. also LSJ 1940 s.v. *hetaireia*, II: "*friendly connexion, friendship, comradeship.*" On the other hand, the various denotations of *hetairos* (LSJ, s.v.) show the term is not simply synonymous with *philos*; the designation of pupils as *hetairos* (LSJ, s.v. 3), for example, does not obliterate the distinction and distance between teacher and pupil; that Jesus' disciples are never called *hetairoi* in the New Testament gospels implies distance in the relation they have with him. The casual designation of hearers (disciples?) as *philoi* in Luke 12:4 (the only such occurrence in the synoptic gospels) contrasts with John 15:14, which expresses both closeness and distance: the disciples may attain the status of Jesus' *philoi* if they do what he, their teacher and Lord (13:13), commands.

    Behr 1968:42 n. 5 provides no warrants for his view that *hetairos* denotes "persons connected with the Temple but not necessarily incubants," in contrast with "an incubant proper"; Aristides' phrasing in 28.88 could support either denotation: "a man, a *hetairos* – thus [*houtōsi*] he sits very close [Behr: as an incubant]."

22 Cf. Aristotle, *Nic. Eth.* 8–9; Cicero, *Laelius de amiticia*; Plutarch, *Peri polyphilias* (*Moralia* 93A–97B); Hutter 1978: chaps. 3–5; Rader 1983: chap. 2; Wadell 1989: chap. 3.

23 But see Behr's earlier, even more specific identification (1973:xi n. a) of *therapeutae* as "a class of officials at the temple" (citing 30.15, where Aristides refers to the young man whom his speech is honoring as a *theraponta* [sic] in succession to his grandfather). In Behr's translation (1981–86) of *pantes hoi peri tōn theōn therapeutai kai taxeis echontes* (48.47) – "all who were worshipers of the god and who held office in the Temple" – the second "who" could either identify *therapeutae* with Temple officeholders (on which see Behr 1968:30–31) or distinguish them from one another. If the words preceding and following the *kai* are read as denoting the same persons (cf. Smyth 1956 §1143), then *taxeis* might refer to holders of office (if that is what *taxeis* means here) in a *Kultverein* of *therapeutae* rather than officeholders "in the Temple" (a qualifier supplied by Behr).

24 In which social status played an important role: Habicht 1969:141 speaks of "einer exklusiven Vereinigung von Asklepiosverehrern" and (114) characterizes it as "einen Kultverein prominenter Personen"; the *therapeutae* Aristides names fall in this category.

25 If the *therapeutae* constituted a *Kultverein*, they might then be compared with the *therapeutae* described in Philo's *De vita contemplativa* (see Richardson and Heuchan 1992, and in this volume), a significant difference being that no women – *therapeutrides* – are mentioned by Aristides.

26 For the third one named, Heracleon, see n. 19 above.

27 Cf. Aristides' observation that physicians cannot but shudder when they hear of many of the god's deeds (2.70).

28 Satyrus, the physician in the passage, described by Aristides as "a sophist not of lowly birth (it was said)" (49.8), was one of Galen's medical teachers (Bowersock 1969:60).

29 Father, 48.40; in 49.16 his mother is mentioned in the same breath with Philumenē, his *trophos*, and Zosimus, his dearest *tropheus* (on these terms see n. 67 below), and other servants.

30 See, for example, Mitchell 1969a; Wheeldon 1969; Breiger 1988; Wellman 1988.

31 See the overviews in Mitchell 1969b, Wellman and Berkowitz 1988; Flap 1988; for recent applications of network theory to ancient situations see Elizabeth Clark's analysis (1992) of the Origenist controversy and Harry Maier's examination (1995) of how social contacts and networks were used to win legitimacy for proscribed movements in late fourth-century Rome.

32 See Wellman 1988:26 on the use of "a variety of network analytic concepts and

techniques" in doing "whole network" analysis in order to see "how the structure of a system affects the behavior and attitude of its members." For one example in early Christian studies see Clark, especially her detailed matrices and graphic representation of social relations in the complex case of the Origenist controversy (1992).

33 See Flap 1988:3–4; in their case one might speak (in Merton's terms [1967:9–26]) of "anticipations" or "adumbrations" of later network theory.

34 In Simmel 1923; ET in 1955.

35 Cooley (1922:148) speaks in strikingly similar terms but does not develop the thought: "A man [sic] may be regarded as the point of intersection of an indefinite number of circles representing social groups, having as many arcs passing through them as there are groups."

36 And thus diminish the reductionism implicit in depicting complex social relationships in diagrams and persons as nodes and lines on a page. (I take this to be the import of Firth's warning [1954:4–5, cited by Mitchell 1969a:2] against taking networks, graphically represented, as something more than metaphor.) On "thick" and "thin" see Geertz 1973b. For the various terms employed in section 3 see the works cited in nn. 30 and 31 above.

37 Some of these details are given in the paragraph on acquaintances on pp. 149–50.

38 Habicht 1969:114: their number "*kann nicht ganz gering gewesen sein*"; citing 50.16 (on which see the discussion of Sedatius below), he evidently takes *gnōrimoteron* as comparative – i.e., "two of the more notable therapeutae" – rather than as equivalent to *clarissimus* (n. 18 above).

39 Cf. Mitchell's distinction (1969a:40) between "potential links" and "effective links" in a network, the latter "those that are actually being used in social interaction." So also Epstein 1969:111–13, who distinguishes between "effective" and "extended" networks. Mitchell (1969a:20 and n. 1) reports as a "general impression" that the number of persons with whom one "might be in direct and regular contact" in an urban setting, i.e., one's effective network, to be about 30. The number of persons Aristides names as *therapeutae*, or as co-incubants, is not large; for example, Galen (on whom see n. 62 below) is not named.

40 See the discussion of acquaintances in pp. 149–50 above, and of friends on pp. 151–2 below, the observance of status lines in the Freeman quotation in n. 15 above, and Aristides' views on slaves in n. 64 below.

41 See n. 39 above. Technically, all the *therapeutae* would fall in the circle of co-incubants; they are kept separate in Figures 1 and 2 to accord with Aristides' usage, but where friends are concerned there is overlapping of the circles.

42 *Nic. Eth.* 8.3.6 (1156b.7–8): *Teleia d'estin hē tōn agathōn philia kai kat'aretēn homoiōn.*

43 On the problems connected with identifying Aristides' *Salbios* with L. Salvius Junius see Behr 1968:41 n. 1, retracted in Behr 1973:x n. b and 1981–86, 2:429 n. 18; Bowersock 1969:76–80.

44 On the identification of Aristides' "*Sedatos*" (48.18; cf. 50.16: he was originally called *Theophilos*) with L. Sedatius Theophilus see Behr 1968:47 n. 25 and 1981–6, 2:431 n. 81, contra Bowersock 1969:86–87, who identifies him with the Severianus ridiculed by Lucian of Samosata in his *Alexander the False Prophet*.

45 *beltistos andrōn*, which Behr 1981–86, 2:431 n. 81 suggests may in fact be an indication of rank (i.e., *vir clarissimus*; see Lewis and Short, s.v. *clarus* IIB), though (comments Behr) one would then expect, instead, *lamprotatos*.

46 I follow Behr (1981–86, 2:469 *ad* 50.18) in emending *Biblos* in 50.18 to *Libus*, i.e., Maximus, who was African in origin (4.2). In favor of the emendation is the congruity in description, seen in our text, of Maximus in 4.2–5 and of the *Bublos/Libus* in 50.18. The mention of Demosthenes, in 4.2–4 in connection with the speech delivered to Maximus, and in 50.18, in the theme proposed by the *Bublos/Libus*, is another point of contact. Behr 1981–86, 2:385 n. 128 suggests that the co-incubant who teaches him an epigram (28.88; see above, p. 149) may "just possibly" be the same Maximus.

47 The *tina tropon* would accord with Aristides' deprecation of orators other than himself (Behr 1968:55, 106–7).

48 Behr 1973:x n. b, citing *ILS* 7776 as establishing the connection.

49 Nothing more is known of him.

50 On the identification of Rufinus see Behr 1968:48 and n. 29; Bowersock 1969:60–61; Habicht 1969:24 and n. 2; for his building of the Temple, Edelstein and Edelstein 1945, 1: no. 803 (Galen); for its renown, Habicht 1969:x, 24.

51 LSJ s.v. *perithytēs, perithytikon*: "dub sens."; the context postulated by Habicht 1969:141–42 makes clear, it seems to me, the meanings I have indicated; see also LSJ s.v. *prothytēs*.

52 Aristides recounts the story in 50.71–94; Behr's summary and commentary in 1968:77–84.

53 Given the character of the governor (50.71, 77; Behr 1968:80 and n. 64), the trouble the appointment and appeal cost him, and the distance between himself and Aristides evident in the judgment handed down (50.87), Aristides' designation of him in 50.12 as *gnōrimos* would best be construed as "distinguished man" (Behr 1981–86) rather than "acquaintance."

54 On his identity see Behr 1968:56 n. 55.

55 On the school see Behr 1968:48 and n. 50; Habicht 1969:162 and sources cited there.

56 Aristides describes him as simply "of/among the philosophers [*tōn philosophōn*]" (50.19); see further Behr 1968:54 n. 50.

57 Another Platonist, Capito, perhaps Sextus Julius Capito, a Pergamum priest (Behr 1981–86, 1:479 n. 1), figures, at least negatively, in Aristides' return to oratory: in his *Or.* 4 (Pergamum, 147 CE), Aristides defended his oration in defense of oratory (*Or.* 2 [Pergamum, 145–47 CE]) against Capito's criticism of it.

58 Another such person (whose connection with the incubancy is not clear), "Antoninus, son of Pythadorus," who appears in one of Aristides' dreams discussing with him the praises of the nymphs (47.35), has been identified as the son of Sextus Julius Major Antoninus Pythodorus, noted (Pausanias and inscriptions) for his rich benefactions to the Asclepius sanctuary of Epidauros and, evidently, to the Pergamum Asclepieion where a statue honored him (Habicht 1969:64–65).

59 Despite the high regard in which the *sophistai* of the second century CE were held (Behr 1968:106 and n. 39; Bowersock 1969:1), Aristides disdained the term (references in Behr 1968:106 n. 39)

60 The dream places the house in Athens, but Theodotus lived in Pergamum, not Athens: "a dream transference from Aristides' doctor to the contemporary sophist Julius Theodotus" (Behr 1968:14 n. 34), who did live in Athens (Philostratus, *Vit. Soph.* 566) where Aristides had studied?

61 As did slaves (Bartchy 1973:75–77).

62 Galen, the philosopher–physician and the Pergamene of most enduring fame, would be linked to Aristides through a shared devotion to Asclepius (Edelstein and Edelstein 1945, 1: nos. 436, 458, 459) and through Satyrus, one of Galen's medical teachers who once offered Aristides medical advice (49.8–9; cf. n. 28 above). According to a fragment preserved in Arabic, the only eyewitness account of Aristides (see Bowersock 1969:61–62), Galen mentions symptoms he observed in Aristides and the cause of his death (a diagnosis Behr suggests Galen may in fact have got from Satyrus [1973:xiii n. a; 1981–86, 2:427 n. 28]). Whatever direct contact the two men may have had, it receives no mention by Aristides.

63 On whom see Habicht 1969:7.

64 Cf. 3.672, when the enemies of the Greek order whom Aristides is attacking (on their offenses and their disputed identity see Remus 1983:101 and 259 nn. 21–23) speak ill of oratory, they are behaving like slaves (*tous doulous*), the worst sort, who curse their masters;

24.58, it is better to be a slave (*douleuein*) than to employ freedom in the service of evil (cf. Plato, *Crito* 52d: those who disregard a city's *nomoi* are behaving like the worst kind of *douloi*; on the relation between *nomos* and *eleutheros* see Pohlenz 1953:428–29); 26.80, a master (*despotēs*) who fears his own slaves (*tous heautou doulous*) displays behavior unworthy of his privileged birth (*agennēs*).

65 Temple servant (*propolos*) (Edelstein and Edelstein 1945, 1: no. 421.670 [Aristophanes, *Plutus*, Athens, 388 BCE]); guards (*phrouroi*) and *hieromnēmones*, distributors of portions of sacrifices to Asclepius, to themselves, to members of the choir, and to the guards (no. 562 [Epidaurus, inscription *c.* 400 BCE]; no. 562 [idem.]: distribution of sacrifice to Apollo and to the same personnel as in no. 562); fire-bearer (*ho pais ho tōi theōi pyrphorōn* (no. 423.5 [Epidaurus, inscription *c.* second half of fourth century BCE; cf. Aristides 47.11, sacred lamps [*lychnous* . . . *tous hierous*] are to be lit; 47.32, in Aristides' dream a *thyrōros* brings lamps into the Temple); custodian of the key(s) (*kleidouchos*) (no. 553 [Place? inscription 138–37 BCE]; in Aristides' dream in 47.11, it is one of the sacristans who carries the keys to open the Temple); bath attendant (*balaneus*) (no. 432 [Epidaurus, inscription *c.* 160 CE]).

66 *Paides* could mean "servants" or "slaves" (as in 36.1); the Edelsteins (1945, 2:194 n. 10) suggest that Asclepieia servants may have sung in the temple choirs alongside their other duties; however, in Aristides the pairing of *paides* and *andres* (50.43) and his dream of *paides* in a school (*didaskalia paidōn*) singing his verses (49.4) indicate that children/boys are intended rather than slaves or servants.

67 *Tropheus.* "An impossible term to translate" (Behr 1968:9 n. 15); Behr paraphrases (1968:8–9) as "those who raised [i.e., *ethrepsan*] him, his foster-fathers." *Trophos*, the term designating Philumenē, the woman who raised Aristides, is commonly translated as "nurse" (thus LSJ and Behr); but considering the important role she played in his life from infancy to her death, and that LSJ and Behr translate *tropheus* as "foster-father," "foster-mother" would be a corresponding rendering.

68 But Aristides distinguishes them from the servants and slaves mentioned in various passages (cited in Behr 1968:8 n. 14); his *tropheis* had their own house about 200 yards/metres from the main residence on his ancestral estate (49.20).

69 In addition to Zosimus and Philumenē (on whom see below), Aristides mentions Neritus, a *tropheus* (49.15 [Pergamum, 147 CE]) and Epagathus, the *tropheus* "who first reared me" and whose recounting of oracular dreams to the child left a deep impression on the man (50.54 [Pergamum, 147 CE]).

70 Zosimus: 47.27.40 (Laneion estate, 171 CE); 47.71, 76 (Mysia, 148 CE); 48.9 (Pergamum, 145 CE); 49.3 (Aliani, 146 CE); 49.37 (Smyrna, 148 CE); 50.41 (Pergamum, 146 CE); 50.69 (Laneion estate, 171 CE). Philumenē: 47.45 (Laneion estate, 166 CE).

71 Foster-brother (*syntrophos*), name unknown: 51.64 (Cyzicus, winter 170/171 CE) reveals that he and Aristides had spent time together in Athens (studying, says Behr 1968:9 n. 18). Foster-sister (*syntrophos*), Callitychē: 47.45 (Laneion estate, 166 CE; she appears with Aristides' foster-mother Philumenē); 48.41 (Smyrna, 165 CE; Aristides identifies her with the Athena whom he has just seen in a dream).

72 For example, Aristides sends Zosimus to consult Apollo on his behalf (49.12 [Lebedus, 147 CE]), or to represent him in a civic matter (50.103 [Pergamum, 148 CE]).

73 For some of which a present-day modern term might be "support groups."

74 Cf. also Kadushin's study of the New York City network, Friends and Supporters of Psychotherapy, which found "how important the circle of Friends is to the development and continuation of the psychoanalytic movement as well as to the personal well-being of members of the Friends" (1966, 801).

75 Details in Potter 1992:230.

76 On the absolute use of *sōtēr* referring to Asclepius and Jesus see Dölger 1929–50, 6:257–63 (Latin equivalents 264–66).

77 So also other Asclepieia (Fox 1987:676–77; Thrams 1992:105–6), with Christian incubation ultimately replacing the pagan model (Hamilton 1906: Part 2).
78 I want to express my gratitude to Pamela Schaus, Department of Geography, Wilfrid
Laurier University, for her skillful preparation of the network graphs.

10

THE MYSTERIES OF MITHRAS

Roger Beck

Of all the mystery religions, Mithraism is the most opaque in its myth and theology but the most transparent and accessible in its structure and activity as an association. The reason for this accessibility to modern research is twofold. First, Mithraism's initiates met in distinctive, uniform, and thus easily recognizable chambers. These *mithraea*, as we term them (their original users, for ideological reasons to be explained below, called them "caves"), reveal much both about their functioning as meeting places and about their symbolic intent as sacred space. Second, Mithraism's chosen medium of expression was visual art. Hence there survives a mass of sculpture, many pieces still carrying dedicatory inscriptions which, in the habit of the times, are as garrulous about the worldly standing of the dedicators as about the power of the god. Accordingly, we have been able to recover – what we have not for any of the other cults – widely distributed and fairly representative samples of Mithraism's actual membership. To these two primary factors we may add Mithraism's practice of keeping its cells small and of expanding by cloning new communities nearby, each with its own mithraeum and cult apparatus. As a result, the volume of recovered data, structural, iconographic, and epigraphic, is out of all proportion to the actual size and strength of the cult.[1] While the import of much of the iconography remains quite enigmatic, that of the physical structures and (even more) of the epigraphy is to a large extent self-revealing.

Another factor making for straightforwardness of interpretation is the relative uniformity of Mithraic cells across the empire and throughout the cult's time-span (roughly, late first to late fourth centuries CE). For all we know to the contrary, not only were all mithraea broadly similar and similarly furnished, but also the groups which met there were organized on the same principles, performed the same activities, and believed themselves in the same relationship to their saviour god. One does not, then, encounter widely varying patterns of organization, as one does, for example, in Dionysiac cult, where the *thiasos* of Agrippinilla is manifestly different in organization (and probably in function too) from the Athenian Iobacchoi and both again from the maenadic *thiasoi* of earlier Greece. Furthermore, there does not appear to have been any activity of Mithraism which was not an activity of the standard Mithraic community meeting in its mithraeum. The cult consisted solely of its *mysteries*, that is, of *initiations* into fellowship with the god in bands of fellow-initiates. There is thus no problem of disentangling the initiates in their associations from other manifestations of the religion – for example, from a professional priesthood and temple apparatus as in the Isis cult. Entirely missing is any public, let alone official, form of Mithras worship: no temples of the classic style, no open-air pomp and pageantry, not even (with one local exception at Tarsus – V27) an issue of coinage in Mithras' honor. The lack of a public face to Mithraism is indeed remarkable – and unique. Not a single piece of all that elaborate artwork was meant for display to the world at large.

In broad terms, then, it is relatively easy to determine from the extant epigraphy what sort of people became Mithraists. The profile of the typical cult member has indeed long been known. Recently, however, the picture has been greatly sharpened by Manfred Clauss' collation, quantification, and analysis of all the data on individuals recorded on the monuments of the cult (1992). Clauss' *cultores Mithrae* (the phrase is the title of his study) comprise 997 persons. Who were they? First, they were all male. Though striking in comparison with the other mystery cults (and Christianity), this fact becomes less so if one thinks of Mithraism in its aspect of association, that is, as a type of collegium or network of collegia, rather than in its aspect of religion of salvation. As a norm, the collegia were exclusively male. The Mithraists, however, took their maleness a stage further, from the functional to the ideological. Not only were women excluded in practice, but the female was also a suspect category in theory.[2]

Second, cult members, like the mithraea to which they belonged, were quite unevenly represented across the different regions of the Roman empire. At the most general level, the Latin-speaking west is over-represented, the Greek-speaking east under-represented. In the west, the two areas of strength are, first, the city of Rome and its port town Ostia, and, second, the empire's European frontier zone, from Hadrian's Wall in Britain via the Rhine and Danube to the latter's mouth on the Black Sea. This second area suggests, of course, a certain type of member, namely the military, an inference which, as we shall see, is amply borne out by the epigraphy, not to mention the location of several mithraea close to camps. Even here, however, Mithraism was not exclusively a soldiers' society, and it was certainly not so in any normative or official sense. Soldiers happened to have been the agents of the cult's arrival in these regions and its principal recruits, but once established it spread into the civilian populations, though always with a certain bias to minor officialdom or those related to the empire's organizational structures. It was particularly strong, for example, among the employees, mostly servile, of the *publicum portorii Illyrici*, the customs syndicate controlling the Danubian provinces (Beskow 1980). Mithraism, indeed, can be seen as one of those instruments of Romanization in the raw western provinces, a function that accounts for its relative absence from the east, where the process was neither needed nor wanted in the entrenched Hellenic cultures. This Romanizing function sets Mithraism somewhat apart from the other mysteries. It probably also explains why the cult, although promoting its supposed derivation from the empire's most serious historic rival, was so universally tolerated and encouraged. Everyone knew that behind these make-belief "Persians" stood aggressively loyal Romans, just as everyone knows, for example, that there is no more conformist North American than a Shriner playing at being an "Egyptian".

This paradoxical Romanness of the so-called "Mysteries of the Persians" may be related to the cult's presence in strength in the capital city and its port.[3] Although a typical Roman or Ostian Mithraist is more difficult to characterize, members do frequently seem to belong to those organizational structures of public service and imperial or private familiae which were the fabric of the empire. Dangerous though it is to do so, one might take as the quintessential city mithraeum that in – and of – the police barracks for seconded detachments (the Castra Peregrinorum),[4] and as the quintessential city Mithraist the imperial freedman and *father and priest of the unconquered Mithras of the imperial household* (*domus Augustanae*) L. Septimius Archelaus,[5] or the dedicant of the earliest known icon of the bull-killing Mithras, Alcimus, the slave *vilicus* (bailiff) of Trajan's Praetorian Prefect Ti. Claudius Livianus.[6] Though respectively a mere freedman and a slave, such persons were in fact successful careerists within the public and private administrative structures of the empire. It has been rightly argued that Mithraism was a cult of and for loyalists and conformists that replicated within the sacred sphere the systems and values of the secular.[7] It was not a religion for failures, the disaffected, social outsiders or the unworldly. A pleasing image of Mithraism's conformism is presented by the recently excavated Caesarea mithraeum. Set, as often, in a cellar, this mithraeum lay beneath and was connected by its light scuttle to a structure dubbed by the excavators the Honorific Portico, a sort of garden cloister in which were displayed monuments and plaques honoring past notables of the province and city.[8] The two integrated structures nicely encapsulate Mithraism's relationship to its secular context.

Of the 997 Mithraists catalogued by Clauss (1992:262), elements of status, rank, and occupation are known with certainty for about one third – as follows: senators 11, equestrians 37 (28 in public service, 9 not), municipal decurions 18, military personnel 123 (25 centurions, 52 *principales*, 28 common soldiers, 18 veterans), imperial freedmen 15, imperial slaves 23, other freedmen 32, other slaves 64. The majority of the remainder display the *tria nomina* (416 certainly, 59 probably), the distinctive mark of Roman citizenship. One hundred and twenty-nine have a single name (slaves, non-citizens?), while 24 are definitely *peregrini*. About the standing of the remaining 46 nothing at all can be conjectured.

The first qualification to be made about this data is that the individuals concerned are for the most part dedicators, thus persons of some means and the success stories of their groups.[9] Our data, then, probably locates Mithraism too high on the social scale. The many anonymous Mithraists will typically have been more humble folk. Second, and militating towards the same result, Clauss has included several persons on whose behalf dedications were made (1992:10–11).

Some of these may not have been Mithraists at all, but all of them lie toward the upper end of the scale, since in ancient society one dedicates on behalf of a superior, not an inferior. Third, and again to the same effect, it is not certain even that all of the dedicators should properly be classed as Mithraists. Some may well have been patrons rather than active members. Indeed, the records of the recently discovered fifth Aquincum mithraeum virtually confirm that this was so. Dedications were there made by no fewer than six *tribuni laticlavii* (Clauss 1992:183–84). These legionary officers were of senatorial rank, so this single mithraeum accounts for a good half of Clauss' total for the *ordo*. What explains this concentration? A unique custom of local military patronage is a far more likely hypothesis than a succession of practicing Mithraists of senatorial rank here and here only. These tribunes, then, were formally *cultores Mithrae* in that they paid cult to Mithras, but they were not necessarily cult members in the real sense of initiates. Active cult membership can safely be assumed for the elite only when there is explicit evidence for it, as, for example, for A. Caedicius Priscianus at the Mithraeum of the Castra Peregrinorum, who is described both as an *eques* and as the *antistes* and *Pater* of the cell.[10]

To the opposite effect, Clauss' data exclude all Mithraists of the fourth-century pagan revival. This exclusion is justifiable, since Mithraism of this era, although the same in form, was arguably a very different social phenomenon from the classic Mithraism of the two preceding centuries. It was an artificial construct and very much the creature of the aristocracy. It is here, then, that we find the elite, who are under-represented even in the unrefined earlier data, both as practitioners and as dedicants.

How were Mithraists recruited? The character of the cult and its membership should make us think in terms of joining a club rather than of religious conversion. Here, the argument from silence is compelling. As we have seen, there is no trace of the sort of external promotion and self-advertisement through exotic public display in which the Isis cult or the cult of the Magna Mater so effectively engaged. And it is surely not merely a loss of texts that has deprived us of records of proselytizing by such charismatic figures as a Paul of Tarsus, a Peregrinus, or an Apollonius of Tyana. This is not to say that there was no individual *prophētēs* who first cast Mithraism in the form known to us and launched it on the Roman world, or that there was no doctrine of salvation to turn to. Quite the contrary, the former is entirely possible,[11] the latter certain.[12] Once formed, however, the cult gives every indication of growth, not by the proclamation of a gospel, but by the quiet recruitment of comrade by comrade within local social groupings, especially the military. The movement of personnel within the empire rather than deliberate evangelism is sufficient reason for its spread.

By the same token, there appears to have been no overarching authority controlling multiple Mithraic cells or defining Mithraic orthodoxy.[13] Each mithraeum and its congregation seems to have been self-sufficient. This autonomy, remarkable perhaps in a "religion," is altogether less surprising if we think of

Mithraism instead as a congeries of collegia focused on a common purpose. Nevertheless, and by whatever means, an impressive degree of uniformity, especially iconographic, was maintained empire-wide over the centuries.

As often in such enterprises, the Mithraic cell existed in a tension of hierarchy and egalitarianism. All Mithraists were "brothers" (*fratres*), "handshakers" (*syndexioi*), and "initiates" (*mystai*). Yet there were of course leaders. In the generally accepted model of the cult, these were typically the "Fathers" (*Patres*), those who had achieved the highest rank in a cursus of seven grades. This cursus was peculiarly Mithraic, and indubitably of great significance in the economy of the cult. Recently, however, there has been some question of it pervasiveness. Manfred Clauss has pointed out that only some 15 per cent of the epigraphically recorded Mithraists carry explicit ranks. The conclusion he draws is that only those initiates who specified a rank actually entered the cursus, which he sees accordingly as a voluntary option. He views it, moreover, as a type of priesthood, to be contrasted with the generality of lay initiates.[14]

Even if the grade-holders constituted only a small minority of the membership, it seems unhelpful to construe them as priests in default of explicit testimony to that effect. The usual words for priest (*sacerdos, antistes*) do occur in Mithraic contexts, which would surely be otiose, were the grade-holders themselves the priests of the cult. Unfortunately, we have no clue to the function of the explicitly styled "priests," though the rarity of the titles suggests that it was not a central one. It is not difficult to see why that should be so. The primary function of a priest in antiquity was to offer sacrifice. But paradoxically, although an apparent act of sacrifice, namely Mithras' bull-killing, was at the heart of its mysteries, Mithraism was not in practice a sacrificing cult.[15] Its sacred space, the "cave," set as often as not in an interior room of a large complex, was incompatible with the killing of any but the smallest animals and fowl. Though Mithraists may have sacrificed, where appropriate, outside their mithraea,[16] the absence of external altars is telling evidence against it as a normal practice. Priests, then, were marginal to the functioning of the cult. That, it can be shown, was not the case for the grade-holders, especially the Fathers. Thus, priests, not grade-holders, were the real exception.

Before demonstrating its centrality, let us first review the cursus of the grades.[17] Each grade was under the protection of one of the seven planets, allotted as follows (in descending order of seniority):

Father	Pater	Saturn
Sun-Runner	Heliodromus	Sun
Persian	Perses	Moon
Lion	Leo	Jupiter
Soldier	Miles	Mars
Nymphus	Nymphus	Venus
Raven	Corax	Mercury

Immediately notable is the novelty and strangeness of this hierarchy. The titles themselves suggest no simple organizing principle, and while some of the ranks seem trite in both nomenclature and implied function (for example, Father, Soldier), others are strikingly original. "Heliodromus," for example, occurs outside Mithraism only as the name of a race-horse and of a species of fabulous bird,[18] while "Nymphus" is the cult's very own coinage and quite untranslatable, signalling, if anything, the paradox of a "male bride."[19] Equally idiosyncratic is the sequence of the planets. It does not correspond to any of the known orders in contemporary astronomy or astrology (though, arguably, it draws on them) and must accordingly be deemed Mithraism's own ordering of cosmic reality.[20]

Opaque and subtle though it is, some picture of the logic and economy of the cursus may be pieced together from various scraps of information concerning both the structure as a whole and the individual grades. We know, at least, that the cursus was divided into two stages. Those in the lower three ranks were "underlings" or "servitors" (*hypēretountes*), those who had reached the median grade of Lion were the true "participants" (*metechontes*).[21] That the Lions were indeed the pivotal grade fits well with the archaeological evidence. After the Fathers, they are by far the best attested epigraphically and their presence is pre-dominant in the all-important grade frescoes of the Sa. Prisca Mithraeum.[22] Of the individual grades, we may say, somewhat tentatively in some instances, that they carried the following functions and associations:[23]

Father	authority; Mithras' counterpart[24]
Sun-Runner	astronomical knowledge; Sol's counterpart[25]
Persian	growth and fruition (lunar matters)[26]
Lion	fire; purification[27]
Soldier	warfare; self-abnegation[28]
Nymphus	the female; renewal; "new light"[29]
Raven	service[30]

Some intimation of the ideology of this hierarchy as a whole is given by two individual monuments. The first is the Sa. Prisca Mithraeum: in addition to the processions of Lions, already mentioned, these show on opposite sides (1) another procession, this one of representatives of each of the grades bearing offerings to an enthroned Father,[31] and (2) a banquet scene in which the feasting Mithras and Sol are waited upon by servitors, at least one of whom is a representative of a junior grade, i.e. a theriomorphic Raven.[32] The latter scene is badly damaged, but its subject matter and the identity of its figures are confirmed by our second monument, a relief from Konjic in Dalmatia (V1896). Like a few other important reliefs, this one is two-sided, showing the banquet scene on the reverse of the bull-killing. Here too the feasting Sol and Mithras are attended by servitors, of whom there are four. One is damaged beyond recognition, but the other three are indisputably a Raven, a Lion, and a Persian. From this we may conclude that the grades are linked centrally to the myth of the cult, to its life, and to its theology. The feast of the initiates replicates the feast of Mithras and

Sol, and within the mithraeum the cult's two highest officers, the Father and the Sun-Runner, are the gods' earthly surrogates. Finally, one may add the evidence of the Felicissimus Mithraeum in Ostia (V299). The mosaic pavement of this mithraeum presents the cursus in a series of panels, one for each grade, running ladder-like up the aisle. The panels display appropriate symbols not only for the grades but also for their tutelary planets. The grades are thus linked to the passage of souls through the celestial spheres, which we know, from independent literary sources, was an element in Mithraic teaching and cult experience.[33]

It may well be that in many mithraea, perhaps even in the majority, the full sevenfold cursus was not in use. That is not to say, however, that it was some sort of special optional priesthood. It is too well and too widely attested, too ideologically central for that to be credible. In particular, the grade of Father is too pervasive to warrant any conclusion but that that officer was the normal ruler of the Mithraic cell within its mithraeum. And if Fathers, then presumably the other ranks of a cursus of which Father was the culmination: chiefs imply indians or, if one prefers, generals imply colonels, sergeants and privates.

What, finally, did Mithraists do in mithraea? What forms did the life and activities of the cult take? Clearly, there will have been rituals of initiation. From the frescoes on the side-benches of the Capua Mithraeum we have an evocative picture of what these were like.[34] In the best preserved scenes, a naked initiand, small and vulnerable, undergoes a ritual at the hands of two of his fellows, a mystagogue clothed in white stationed behind him and an actor in front who manipulates the props and symbols of the ritual. The damaged state of the frescoes prevents us from recovering the precise details of each action, but their ethos is clear: the passivity, helplessness, and confusion – no doubt terror too – that must precede admission and enlightenment.

Initiations apart, we know of two activities that were part of the ongoing life of the mithraeum. Both have already been touched on in the context of the grades. They are the cult meal and the celestial journey. To juxtapose them in this way is to highlight their dissimilarities as activities of an ancient association. The former is utterly predictable. Associations assemble for fellowship, and an obvious expression of fellowship is a common meal.[35] In Mithraism, as we have seen, that shared meal is emphasized by the construction of the meeting place as a dining room with a pair of facing benches on which the initiates reclined to eat in the Roman manner. The ubiquity of the structure guarantees the ubiquity of the practice. Fortunately, the meal's theological warrant, its charter myth, is accessible to us in the iconography of its monuments. The banquet celebrated by Mithras and Sol on the hide of the slaughtered bull is an important and frequently represented episode in the cycle of the cult's myth. Indeed, it is the most important event after the bull-killing itself, to which it stands as salvific effect to salvific cause.[36] That it is replicated in this world in the cult meal has already been demonstrated. We can conclude, then, that the Mithraic cult meal was sacrament as well as fellowship.

The second activity, participation in celestial soul-travel, is as unexpected as

182

the first is trite. And yet it is the one Mithraic activity which a literary source of any credibility describes with any specificity. Porphyry, in his allegorical essay explicating the "cave of the nymphs" in Homer's *Odyssey* (13.103–12), gives the following functional description of the Mithraic "cave":

> Similarly, the Persians call the place a cave where they introduce an initiate to the mysteries, revealing to him the path by which souls descend and go back again. For Eubulus tells us that Zoroaster was the first to dedicate a natural cave in honour of Mithras, the creator and father of all . . . This cave bore for him the image of the cosmos which Mithras had created, and the things which the cave contained, by their proportionate arrangement, provided him with symbols of the elements and climates of the cosmos.
>
> (*De antro nympharum* 6, trans. Arethusa edn.)

This passage tells us not only that induction into a mystery of the soul's descent and return was an activity of the cult but also that mithraea were designed and equipped for that very purpose. They function as "cosmic models" for the accomplishment, no doubt both by ritual and instruction, of a celestial journey.[37] Porphyry is right about the mithraeum as cave, for that is what the Mithraists called them, using natural caves or crypts when available and making them cave-like in decor. We may suppose him right too about the cosmic symbolism of the cave, for certain extant mithraea and much Mithraic artwork is indeed furnished with cosmic symbols such as zodiacs and images of the planets.[38] We should not, then, lightly disbelieve him – or his sources and their ultimate Mithraist informants – when he tells us that instruction and rituals of soul-travel were the purpose of these arrangements, even though such activities do not square with our preconceptions of the appropriate behavior of sergeants and customs officers. The actual mimesis of the celestial voyage is probably lost to us for ever, as most certainly is the experiential consciousness of those who undertook it. But that it was undertaken in the mithraeum – in some if not in all – should not be doubted.

NOTES

1 All data discovered before 1960, which still comprise a preponderant majority, are catalogued in Vermaseren 1956–60. Monuments from this corpus are here cited by number with a prefix "V."

2 Gordon 1980:42–64. In cult language women were called "hyenas" (Porphyry, *De abstinentia* 4.16).

3 On the approximate numbers of mithraea and Mithraists in Rome and Ostia, see Beck 1992:11.

4 Described in Lissi-Caronna 1986.

5 V511; Clauss 1992:20.

6 V593/4; Gordon 1978.

7 Gordon 1972; Merkelbach 1984:153–88; Liebeschuetz 1994.

8 Painter 1994:150–57.

9 Until quite recently, only three membership lists (*alba*) with significant numbers of names had been recovered: V325 (Clauss 1992:32–34) from Ostia, V688 (Clauss 1992:56–58) from Sentinum, and V2296 (Clauss 1992:222) from Histria in Moesia Inferior. A fourth, in bronze, has now come to light in Virunum (Noricum) which, unlike the others, is intact and complete. It records 98 names. What is extraordinarily interesting is that only the first 34 names were engraved at the time of dedication (183 CE). The others were added in batches in different hands until the plaque was full. Almost certainly, then, we have the record of recruitment over a number of years (183–201?). The plaque has been published by Piccottini (1994).

10 Clauss 1992:24–25; Panciera 1979:88.

11 The profile of Mithraism's hypothetical founder is best drawn by Merkelbach 1984:77.

12 One of the liturgical lines painted on the walls of the Sa. Prisca Mithraeum reads: "You saved us by the blood . . . shed" (Panciera 1979:103–5).

13 As far as we can tell, the "Father of Fathers" (*Pater patrum*) was the senior Father in a mithraeum, not a Father with jurisdiction over several mithraea and certainly not a Mithraic Pope. On the rank and title of Father, see below.

14 Clauss 1990b; 1992:275–76; contra, Merkelbach 1990.

15 On Mithraic sacrifice, see Turcan 1981.

16 A recently discovered mithraeum at Novae in Moesia Inferior has revealed numerous bovine as well as other bones in a ditch outside (Naydenova 1994:227).

17 By far the best and most penetrating study of the grades is Gordon 1980. General works on the cult of course all carry full descriptions: for example, Vermaseren 1963:138–53; Clauss 1990a:138–47; see also Beck 1992:8–10. Merkelbach (1984:77–133) has an interesting, if ultimately unpersuasive, hypothesis that the scenes in the myth cycle relate to the grades and to promotion through them.

18 Gordon 1994:110–12.

19 Gordon 1980:48–49.

20 Beck 1988:1–11.

21 Porphyry, *De abstinentia* 4.16.

22 Two of the processional scenes are composed entirely of Lions (V482–83).

23 In addition to the Sa. Prisca Mithraeum, most of the archaeological data on the grades is conveyed by (i) the mosaics of the Felicissimus Mithraeum in Ostia (V299 – see below) and (ii) the graffiti of the Dura Mithraeum in Syria (Cumont 1975:194–205; Francis 1975).

24 Among the Father's symbols in the Felicissimus mosaics are the sceptre and Mithras' Phrygian cap; see below on the Father and Sun-Runner as the earthly proxies of Mithras and the Sun.

25 At Dura the term for Sun-Runner appears to have been *sophistēs*, signifying that he is the repository of intellectual knowledge and theoretical wisdom (Cumont 1975:202–3). The Heliodromus commands, in particular, esoteric and exoteric knowledge of the solar journey, its stages (*dromos* is a technical term for a planet's arc of longitude), the temporal and seasonal cycles which that journey defines, and the entire system of planetary motion which it was deemed to orchestrate.

26 The Persian is the "guardian of fruits" (Porphyry, *De antro* 16); his planet, Luna, links him with agriculture.

27 Both aspects are alluded to in the Sa. Prisca text, "Receive, holy Father, receive the incense-burning Lions, through whom we offer incense and through whom we ourselves [that is, fellow-initiates] are consumed." In ancient animal lore the lion is a fiery, solar beast, naturally continent and moral (Gordon 1980:32–37, 46–47); Leo, the zodiacal sign, is the Sun's astrological "house" where it spends the hottest season of the year (July–August) (Beck 1994:45).

28 Warfare, presumably a *sacra militia*: obvious from the title and the tutelary planet, Mars.

Self-denial: Tertullian, *De corona* 15, that the Mithraic Soldier declines the crown offered him, with the words "Mithras is my crown."

29 On the female implications of the Nymphus, see esp. Gordon 1980:42–64. Venus is the grade's tutelary planet and its Felicissimus symbol the bridal diadem. The other symbol is a lamp, alluding to the planet's identity as Phosphorus, the Light-Bringer, and the grade's function as the community's "new light": cf. the Mithraic *symbolon* in Firmicus Maternus, *De errore* 19.1: "Behold, Nymphus, welcome, Nymphus, welcome, new light!"

30 On this liminal grade, see esp. Gordon 1980:25–32, 43–46. The Raven's tutelary planet is the messenger Mercury. Raven-headed servitors attend the banquet scene at Sa. Prisca and on the Konjic relief (see below); also on V397.

31 Vermaseren and vanEssen 1965:155–58.

32 Best seen in Bianchi 1979:Appendix I, Tav. X.

33 Porphyry, *De antro* 6, 24; Origen, *Contra Celsum* 6.22. See Beck 1988:73–100.

34 Vermaseren 1971:esp. Plates XXI–XXIII, XXV–XXVIII.

35 Best on the Mithraic cult meal is Kane 1975.

36 This causal relationship is clearly emphasized in the important two-sided reliefs which carry both scenes (see above). Some of these could be rotated (e.g. V1083), presumably at a key moment in the liturgy.

37 Beck 1992:4–7; also my "Cosmic Models: Some Uses of Hellenistic Science in Roman Religion," forthcoming in *Apeiron* 27 no. 4.

38 Most notably the Ostian "Seven Spheres" Mithraeum (V239ff.). See Gordon 1976; 1988:50–60; Beck 1979; also, on the Ponza Mithraeum, Beck 1976; 1978; and in general, Beck 1988; 1994.

11

THE PLACE OF CULT IN
VOLUNTARY ASSOCIATIONS AND
CHRISTIAN CHURCHES ON
DELOS

B. Hudson McLean

Situated in the center of the Cyclades, Delos is one of the smallest of the Greek islands measuring scarcely 5 km by 1.3 km.[1] Despite its size, Delos' renown as the birthplace of Apollo and Artemis has resulted in the founding of more than fifteen temples dedicated to various deities. Alongside the groups attached to these many cults were numerous voluntary associations. They were comprised of many nationalities, of free men, freedmen, and slaves, both men and women. In short, the island of Delos manifests in a microcosm the social pluralism of Graeco-Roman Antiquity.

THE ESTABLISHMENT OF VOLUNTARY ASSOCIATIONS ON DELOS: AN HISTORICAL OUTLINE

Delos was a protectorate of Naxos until the Athenians recognized its importance for trade. They then seized control of the island and governed it for the next three centuries (540–314 BCE). In 540 BCE the tyrant Peisistratus erected the archaic temple of Apollo and purified the sanctuary by the removal of all graves around the sanctuary of Apollo. At this time Delos became the center of the Ionic amphictyony. A second and more extensive purification was performed in 426 BCE; all tombs were removed and Delos was declared a consecrated island no longer to be defiled by human birth or death. Those in danger of dying and women nearing childbirth were ferried to nearby Rheneia so as not to have to repeat the elaborate purification ceremonies (Diodorus 12.58). Administration of the Delian temple finances was given over to Athenian officials called Amphictyons. The island's prosperity rapidly increased during the Persian wars. Its strategic position in the Aegean was such that Delian commerce began to overshadow that of Piraeus. Perhaps in a move to protect the commerce of Piraeus, Athens forcefully removed the Delians from the isand in 422 BCE.

Voluntary associations were not to be founded on Delos until this first period of Athenian rule came to an end and Delian independence was established. The history of voluntary associations which follows can be considered in three successive periods: Delian independence (314–166 BCE), the second period of Athenian rule (166–88 BCE), and finally, Delos after the destruction of 88 BCE.

Delian independence (314–166 BCE)

When the Athenians were defeated in the Peloponnesian war, the Delians successfully appealed to the Spartans for independent status. The eponymous official of this new Delian state was the *archōn*. Second in importance were the *hieropoioi* who were charged with oversight of the temple accounts. The wealth and reputation of Delos steadily increased during this period. The third and greatest of the temples of Apollo was erected, attracting costly gifts from kings and princes.[2]

The political independence of Delos was limited in the first half of the third century BCE by its membership in a league of islands under the control of the Ptolemaic dynasty. Delos became the religious centre of this federation. When the league dissolved (mid-third century BCE), the independence of Delos continued, though the Macedonians exercised influence in the form of new festivals and the erection of monuments.

The growing importance of Delos as a centre of trade and commerce continued through this period. Public and private banks were established. Corresponding to this trend, the sacred character of the island gradually dissipated.

A steady stream of foreigners arrived from all over the Mediterranean and settled on the island. Egyptians brought with them the worship of their native gods Sarapis, Isis, Anubis, and Harpokrates, and constructed two Sarapeia.[3] By 200 BCE, Italian merchants and bankers also began to arrive from southern Italy. Decrees from Delos at this time also mention men from Tyre and other wealthy trading cities of the east.

Second period of Athenian rule (166–88 BCE)

In 168 BCE, the Romans defeated Perseus, the last king of the Macedonians, at Pydna. Having remained faithful to Rome during the Third Macedonian War, Athens appealed in 197 BCE for the return of some of her former territory including Delos. As a reward for twenty-five years of loyalty, the Romans granted this request and Delos was returned to Athenian control in 166 BCE. Delos became a cleruchy of Athens and an *epimelētēs* sent annually from Athens replaced the *archōn* as head of state.

The course of events which followed upon this change of government would have a profound impact on Delos for years to come. First, those Delians who remained were exiled, their land confiscated, and much of it redistributed to the newly arriving Athenian colonists. Second, Rome declared Delos a free port in order to enhance the commercial position of the Italian businessmen established on Delos, and to deprive Rhodes of its commercial supremacy. When Delos achieved its free-port status, the influx of merchants, importers, shippers, warehousemen, and bankers increased dramatically. Italians and Greeks immigrated from Italy and Sicily. Other nationals, most notably Phoenicians, Egyptians, and Asians – including Jews and Samaritans – also arrived and set up business. The influx of Italians to Delos was accelerated by the destruction of Corinth (146 BCE). Italian businessmen resident in Corinth fled in search of sanctuary and a location suitable to continue their businesses.[4] Most of the Italians who emigrated to Delos were bankers, merchants, and artisans. The fact that all known bankers on Delos are from Italy strongly suggests that banking was a monopoly held by the Italian population. The large number of inscriptions by Italian bankers (*ID* 1715–29) testify to the great profits made from the second century BCE onwards from the large-scale movement of merchandise and capital in and out of Delos. Associations of Greek and Italian oil-merchants (*olearii*) and wine-merchants, under the patronage of their gods, imported olive oil and wine from Italy both for local consumption and especially for resale to buyers and shippers from Laodicea, Tyre, Berytos, and Alexandria.[5]

Delos had become the emporium of the Aegean, two of the most important commodities being grain and slaves. Strabo records that Delos "could both admit and send away ten thousand slaves on the same day" (14.5.2). This tremendous commercial activity attracted ever larger numbers of foreigners from all over the Mediterranean. Like the Egyptians who had arrived before them, these foreigners established their ancestral cults and the voluntary associations of their homelands. Many of these associations grew into strong and influential economic powers. For example, two Phoenician associations of merchants are known to have existed: the Heraclesiastai of Tyre Merchants and Shippers was a merchant association dedicated to their ancestral god Heracles–Melkart; another commercial association, the Poseidoniastai of Berytos, Merchants, Shippers, and Warehousemen, originated from Berytos (Beirut) and was under the patronage of Poseidon.

Delos after the destruction of 88 BCE

In 88 BCE, Delos was sacked by Menophaneses, the general of Mithridates Eupator, for siding with Rome in the Mithridatic war. According to Pausanias and Appian, 20,000 of the island's inhabitants were slaughtered.[6] Following its victory over Mithridates, Rome reasserted its control, marked by Sulla's victorious visit to the island. Rome returned the Athenians to govern the island and the islanders began to repair the damage. The population had only just begun to recover from this attack when a second attack was wrought in 69 BCE by pirates of Athenodoros, an ally of Mithridates. Many of the remaining inhabitants were led away as slaves.

Hasty repair work, under the direction of the Roman general Triarius, was carried out on the damaged buildings. A protective wall was constructed around the buildings in the area of the sanctuary of Apollo and the theater quarter. Many of the stately houses lay abandoned and were taken over as workshops for artisans. The former prosperity of Delos had departed, never to return. The trade routes had altered, shifting to ports in Italy and the eastern Mediterranean. Before long, Athens lost interest in the island and ceased to appoint a governor. Even the priest of Apollo vacated the island and resided in Athens, returning but once a year with twelve animals for sacrifice. Hadrian, the great philhellene, was unsuccessful in his attempt to revive the old Delian festivals which had ceased in 316 BCE.

By the late third century CE, Christians had arrived and soon began to convert abandoned buildings to Christian use and erect new churches, often employing the abundant building material resulting from the previous years of destruction. Delos was designated as the bishopric for Mykonos, Syros, Seriphos, Kythnos, and Kea. In 451, Sabinus, a bishop from Delos, attended the Council of Chalcedon. The Christian habitation of Delos could not have lasted more than 200 years, for there are no signs of life on Delos from the sixth century CE onward. The bishopric was moved to the island of Syros, and Delos ceased to be named on episcopal lists thereafter. Its final desolation was stressed by the new name it was given on navigation maps, *Adelos*, that is, "unseen/unknown."

VOLUNTARY ASSOCIATIONS AS CONGREGATIONS AND CULTS

The epigraphical evidence on Delos documents over twenty-four voluntary associations. These associations customarily grouped individuals under the patronage of an ethnic deity according to nationality and/or profession. Voluntary associations had both congregational and cultic dimensions. As congregations, they reinforced a sense of kinship and national identity on an island where disparate nationalities and languages abounded. Such solidarity also helped to protect the commercial interests of particular groups. As cults, voluntary associations provided the opportunity to worship the gods of their homeland, and seek their protection and patronage by offering sacrifice.

Various kinds of spaces were required for these two spheres of activity. As congregations, they required a meeting space, sometimes in a building constructed especially for the purpose. Such buildings were utilitarian in function. They were primarily intended to provide a space protected from the sun, wind, and rain, in which many – if not all – could have a bench to sit upon. Though prayers and rituals might be performed in such a space, this was not a cultic space nor was it a sacred space, properly speaking. For this reason, individual purity was not required of those who entered the space as would be required of those entering a sanctuary.[7] Moreover, the functionaries for this space were not cultic officials; rather than a priest or priestess, a president (for example, *archithiasitēs*, *episkopos*) or board of magistrates (*magistreis*) would preside. Associations also had a cultic dimension to their life which *did* require cultic ministers (especially a priest or priestess) and cultic space, normally a sanctuary with an altar and temple.

189

The purpose of this chapter is twofold: first, to describe how the congregational and cultic domains of voluntary associations were expressed functionally in architectural forms (pp. 190–213), and second, to consider the role of cultic worship in the emergent Christian churches on Delos (pp. 213–18). Discussion of the first point will require that the reader has some acquaintance with the use of the altar and temple, and so to this subject we shall now turn our attention.

ASSOCIATIONS WITH CULTIC SPACE EXTERNAL TO THE PLACE OF ASSEMBLY

Many associations performed their cultic acts at an altar and temple that were external to their place of assembly. Either they made use of an existing public altar and temple dedicated to their patron god, or they constructed a new altar and temple in a sanctuary that was proximate, but external to, the building in which the association assembled. Two examples of this will be discussed, the Heraclesiastai of Tyre, and the Italian Hermaïstai. Moreover, other associations, notably those of Jews and Samaritans, related to a remote cult in a different country.

The cult external and proximate: the Italian Hermaïstai

Three of the best-known Italian colleges were those under the patronage of Mercury, Neptune, and Apollo. Of these, the most important was the association dedicated to Mercury (Hermes) known in Greek as the *Hermaïstai*. The Latin name of its magistrates was *magistri Mercurii*.[8] The Hermaïstai erected statues, altars, two temples, and a monument in the agora of the Competaliastai (also named the agora of the Hermaïstai). This agora is thought to be the place where the Italian merchants were located prior to the construction of the Agora of the Italians.[9]

Though it is not known which building the Hermaïstai used for their assemblies, their cultic life was exterior to their meeting place, centered around the altars and two temples which they had erected in the agora of the Competaliastai. A small rectangular Doric temple with a façade of four Doric columns was constructed in the centre of the agora (146/5 or 145/4 BCE).[10] An inscription engraved on three blocks of the architrave of its façade announces that "the Hermaïstai dedicated (this) temple to Hermes and to Maia,"[11] the principal gods of their cult. On the north side of the agora, next to the Portico of Philip V, are the remains of an Ionic temple with a façade of four columns.[12] In front of the Ionic temple was set up an offertory treasury, its lid decorated with two snakes.[13] Altars dedicated to the gods of the Hermaïstai have been discovered in the agora and were probably used by these two temples.[14]

Cult external and proximate: the Heraclesiastai of Tyre Merchants and Shippers

As their name would suggest, the Heraclesiastai of Tyre Merchants and Shippers was a merchant association (*koinon*) from Tyre under the patronage of their ancestral god Heracles–Melkart. The meetings of this *koinon* were led by a non-cultic official entitled an *archithiasitēs*.[15]

In 153/2 BCE they sent an embassy to Athens to seek "to build a temenos of Heracles who is the author of many benefits for people and the founder of the native land" (*ID* 1519). The Athenians granted their request. In all probability their sacred enclosure was external to their place of meeting. The *koinon*'s sacrifice, offered at the altar in the newly constructed temenos, was presided over by their own priest, named Patron (*ID* 1521.57).

Cult external and remote: the Samaritan synagogue

According to literary evidence, a community of Jews was established on Delos by the mid-second century BCE.[16] Of particular interest is a Roman edict of Julius Caius (44 BCE), praetor of Rome, quoted by Josephus, which divides the Jewish population on Delos into two classifications, namely the "Jews in Delos" and "some other Jews who sojourn" on Delos.[17] The former seems to refer to those Jews who had official status as resident foreigners; the *sojourners* were aliens with non-resident status. This evidence leads Michael White to conclude that there were "several groups of 'Jews' on the island, each with its own social standing."[18] The recent discovery of two new inscriptions has proved that a community of Samaritans had also been established on the island by the late third century BCE.[19]

No. 1 (*c*. 200–150 BCE)

> – – – [The] Israelites who contribute their offerings to the holy temple (of) Argarizin[20] honored Menippos son of Artemidoros from Heracleion and his offspring[21] who constructed and dedicated at their expense to the "synagogue" (*proseuchē*)[22] of God, the . . . (building?) and the walls and . . . , and crowned him with a gold wreath and . . .

No. 2 (*c*. 150–50 BCE)

> The Israelites in Delos who contribute their offerings to the temple (of) Argarizin[23] crown Sarapion[24] son of Jason citizen of Knossos with a gold wreath because of his benefactions towards them.

These Samaritans may have adopted the self-designation "Israelites" in order to express that they had come from the northern kingdom of Israel (Samaria), and to lay claim upon the term in the face of Delian Jews who wished to have sole use of it for themselves.[25] The phrase "Israelites in Delos" in the second inscription is reminiscent of Josephus' phrase, "Jews in Delos." It suggests that at least some of the Samaritans on Delos had the same status as the Delian Jews, namely, resident foreigners. These two religious associations coexisted on Delos for at least several decades, one, if not both of them, being subdivided on the basis of political status.

The Delian synagogue

Controversy has arisen over the purpose of a building discovered in 1912–13 near the gymnasium. Some scholars have identified it as a synagogue.[26] If this is indeed a synagogue, it is the oldest extant remains of a synagogue in the world. Critics of this position observe that this building has no permanent Torah shrine or Jewish symbols such as the menorah. This criticism is by no means decisive since one would not expect to find all the architectural features of the later synagogues in such an early exemplar. Moreover, this building should be interpreted in comparison with buildings used by other voluntary associations on Delos, many of which are adaptations of the Hellenistic peristyle house plan.[27] The fact that this building shares a closer genealogical relationship to Delian architecture than to synagogues in and around Israel is hardly surprising given the fact that this building predates the development of any standardized synagogal plan in the Jewish world.

Comparison with Delian architecture raises a second point, namely that the buildings of voluntary associations were also used for social and commercial purposes, as well as for religious functions. As Michael White observes, we may misinterpret the building's overall function in the life of its community if it is conceived of narrowly in terms of religious services:

> It is quite likely that an early Jewish enclave on Delos, as in other places, would have established such an ethnic association to advance their professional interests and to preserve their ancestral worship, but with little to distinguish their building from other houses and associations in the Hellenistic environment.

(1990:66)

The building's identification as a synagogue was strengthened by the discovery of several inscriptions found nearby, one of which referred to a *proseuchē*, a Greek term for "synagogue"[28] (*ID* 2329): "Agathokles and Lysimachos (dedicated this) to the synagogue." Moreover, a number of votives (small marble bases and columns) have been found in and around the same building with dedicatory inscriptions employing the epithet "the most high god."[29] This appellative is applied to the Jewish god in many Jewish Hellenistic writings.[30] The same expression also appears in two Jewish funerary inscriptions (*c.* 100 BCE) from the neighboring island of Rheneia.[31] However, this epithet is not uniquely Jewish, also being used in Graeco-Roman sources in connection with Zeus, Sabazius and other deities in Asia Minor.[32]

Critical debate continues over the identity of the building. The most recent archaeological analysis is that of Philippe Bruneau who has strongly reasserted its identification as a synagogue.[33] With his publication of the two Samaritan inscriptions (above), the debate has been put in a new light. Michael White thinks that the older inscription (no. 1) commemorates the foundation of a *Samaritan* synagogue, *not necessarily* to be identified with the excavated building under debate (*GD* no. 80).[34] Indeed, given the evidence for multiple communities of Jews and Samaritans, there may have been two or more synagogues on Delos. White speculates that the Samaritan synagogue may have been called the "house of the Israelites in Delos who pay homage to hallowed Argarizein," and the Jewish synagogue known as "the house of the Jewish *Hypsistians* in Delos."

The term *proseuchē* which generated so much controversy is attested not only in *ID* 2329 (above), but also in the Samaritan inscription no. 1. This latter inscription was discovered about 100 m from the building identified as a synagogue, and also near the site of *ID* 2329. Thus, both inscriptions were found near this building – one of which is clearly Samaritan – and both employ the phrase *epi proseuchē*.

Given the proximity of the two inscriptions, the translation of *epi proseuchē* should be consistent for both inscriptions. If *proseuchē* in both of these inscriptions refers to a "synagogue," then these inscriptions probably refer to the *same* synagogue. Since inscription no. 1 is incontrovertibly Samaritan, *ID* 2329 is probably also of Samaritan – not Jewish – provenance. This raises the real possibility that many – if not all – of the Delian inscriptions previously identified as Jewish may actually be Samaritan in origin.[35]

Two observations follow from this. First, if the inscriptions are indeed Samaritan, then there is no artefactual evidence to support the conclusion that the building is a *Jewish* synagogue. In other words, if the identity of the building is considered only with reference to the inscriptional evidence, then the unavoidable conclusion is that it must be a *Samaritan* synagogue.

Any argument in support of a Jewish identification must rely heavily on the literary testimony, especially that of Josephus, arguing that the multiple communities to which he refers had multiple synagogues, the Samaritan synagogue (referred to in inscription no. 1) being yet undiscovered. This possibility cannot be ruled out.

However, in light of the inscriptional evidence, which is both contemporaneous with the synagogue and found in close proximity to the synagogue, I suggest that the argument should be reversed: namely, if there were two synagogues on Delos, then it is the *Jewish* synagogue which has yet to be identified in the archaeological remains, and the building under discussion is a Samaritan synagogue.

Plan of the synagogue

The present structure has two adjacent rooms (A, B).[36] Entrance into both rooms is provided by a portico (C). The walls of Room A are lined with benches,

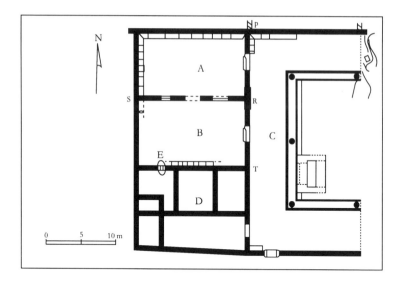

Figure 11.1 Delos Synagogue

and a marble thronos (Seat of Moses)[37] is centered on the west wall. This must have been the principal meeting room, the president sitting in the thronos. Fragments of benches have also been discovered in room B and at the northern end of the portico (C). There are three doorways in the partition wall (SR) with the adjoining room B (see Figure 11.1).[38]

Adjoining room B is a complex of smaller rooms (D) whose exact arrangement is difficult to ascertain. One of these rooms provided access to a cistern (E), though the cistern could also be reached from room B. It is unclear what other functions these smaller rooms may have served. White suggests that the internal walls may have provided storage facilities and supports for a staircase. All three rooms (A, B, D) were served by a roofed portico. An entrance is located on the south side of the portico.

The eastern termination of the portico has been destroyed by the sea. Plassart originally suggested that the portico only extended the length of the structure as a façade (1913:524–25). Taking the opposing view, Belle Mazur argued that the portico was a peristyle, extending on four sides of an open court (*c.* 18 x 18 m) (1935:17). Philippe Bruneau has discovered additional foundation walls that make both theories unlikely, arguing rather that the original portico was three-sided, that is, a tristoa (C).[39] Michael White thinks that a "grand stair" entrance may have been positioned on the long side of the portico providing a seaward entrance (1987:149–51).

History of renovations

Though the original function of the building is unknown, scholars agree that it was probably built in the early second century BCE, and only later taken over for use as a synagogue. The original structure consisted of a rectangular building (14.25 x 28.15 m) with a stoa. White thinks that the building was renovated in two stages, first in the late second century or early first century BCE, and then again following the Mithridatic raids in 88 BCE.[40]

In the first renovation, White thinks that an existing house was renovated into a synagogue, including the modification of the existing portico into a tristoa. By the construction of a central grand stair entrance, a triportal seaward entrance was created (1987:151–52). It is not possible to determine whether it was used by Jews before this renovation.

This *may* also have been the time when the partition wall (SR) was built between rooms A and B (ibid.: 151). In the earliest construction there was originally only one large hall (L:16.90 m; W:15.04 m) with three doorways in wall PT from the portico (C). This hall was subsequently subdivided by a partition wall (SR) into rooms A and B. The construction of wall SR blocked the middle doorway (2.20 m) on wall PT and required that it be filled in, leaving only the two smaller doorways (1.80 m) (ibid.:147–48).

Some of the building materials used in the renovation of rooms A and B were marble spoils from the nearby gymnasion (*GD* no. 76), including some inscriptions dating *c.* 140–110 BCE.[41] These observations led Bruneau to conclude that this stage of the renovation work was initiated sometime after the gymnasion was destroyed in the Mithridatic raids of 88 BCE, probably in the late first century BCE.[42] In this second renovation, wall PT was rebuilt and embellishments were added to rooms A and B.[43] The partition wall SR may also have been constructed at this time.

The Samaritan synagogue was probably in continuous operation from the second century BCE through to the second century CE. Thus, it is roughly contemporaneous with the House of the Poseidoniastai and Sarapeion A and B (see below). Like these other buildings, this synagogue probably served as a community centre, perhaps a place to discuss business, as well as a building for religious meetings (M. White 1987:152). However, unlike these other buildings, this synagogue made no provision for the performance of cultic rites: there is no altar or shrine. The explanation, of course, is that the congregation related to a remote external cult, namely the Samaritan cult practiced at Mount Gerizim.

CULT WITHIN THE BUILDING OF THE ASSOCIATION

A number of voluntary associations opted to incorporate their cultic rituals within the building in which they assembled. In so doing, a spatial (and perhaps ideological) continuity was created between the act of gathering and the act of offering sacrifice. One can only guess how such a reconfiguration of space might have affected the self-identity of the group. This arrangement might accord greater sanctity to the building as a whole, and perhaps even accentuate a sense of the divine presence of their god in their midst. Three examples will be discussed below: the Poseidoniastai of Berytos, Sarapeion A, and Sarapeion B. A consideration of the broader significance of these buildings will be reserved until the end of this section.

The Poseidoniastai of Berytos

This Phoenician association, known as the *koinon* of the Poseidoniastai of Berytos, Merchants, Shippers, and Warehousemen,[44] was a commercial association from Berytos (Beirut) under the patronage of Poseidon.[45] As its name would suggest, this guild united within itself the three fields of the commercial world – shipping, warehousing and merchandising. Though the origin of this association is obscure, it was certainly in existence by the second half of the second century BCE.[46] The community (*thiasitai*) of this *koinon* was headed by an eponymous *archithiasitēs*.[47] Its cultic life was presided over by an eponymous priest, assisted by a "sacrificer."[48]

Description of the building[49]

Approximately thirty years after the Heraclesiastai of Tyre sent a delegation to Athens, the Poseidoniastai of Berytos similarly sought and obtained permission to build. Construction was completed some years before 153 BCE, with at least one subsequent renovation. The excavation of this building was conducted by Charles Picard (1920; 1921).

The largest room in the structure was a peristyle court (F) (with cistern) in the north-east sector. This court faced on to two other courts, a grand court (E) in the north-east corner, and an elevated smaller court (X) in the south with an elongated shape and triportal entrance. Along the south side of the building are a series of smaller rooms (G–T) probably used for residential accommodation and the warehousing of goods (Figure 11.2).[50]

The small court (X) leads up into a stepped pronaos (V) which served as an antechamber for four rooms (V^1, V^2, V^3, V^4), at least three of which were used as shrines (*naoi*). A statue of Roma was discovered *in situ* in V^1 and an inscribed base for a statue of Poseidon was found in V^2.[51] The shrines were fitted with doors which were presumably locked most of the time, restricting access through most of the year to the priest and other cultic officials. The increasingly sacred character of this sequence of rooms is indicated by the gradually increasing elevation, the small court (X) being raised one step above the peristyle court (F), and the pronaos (V) raised by three steps above the small court (X).

Three cylindrical altars on square socles were erected in the small court (X). Two of them (f, g) were oriented along the north–south axis of the court, the third (e) was situated on the central east–west axis in line with the central

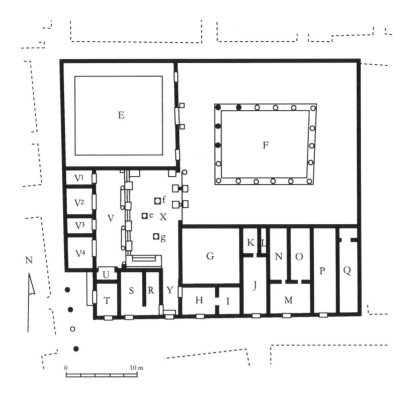

Figure 11.2 House of the Poseidoniastai

passageway into the pronaos (V). The three altars were probably dedicated to Poseidon, Astarte, and Roma. Of the three, altar f is the best preserved.[52] The placement of the altars in court X indicates that this was the cultic space where the *koinon* offered sacrifices (Figure 11.3).[53]

Correlation of the plan with ID 1520

One of the longest extant inscriptions of the Poseidoniastai (*ID* 1520) names some of the rooms of this building and sheds light on aspects of its life. Since a translation has never been published, to the knowledge of this author, a complete translation is provided:[54]

> [For good fortune. During the archonship of (Name) son of (Name). Decision] of the *Koinon* of the Berytian Poseidoniastai, Merchants, Shippers

197

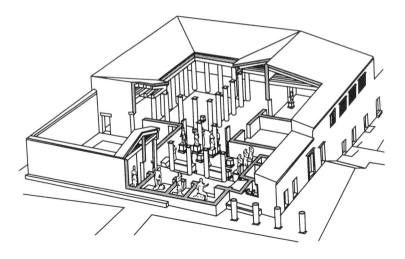

Figure 11.3 Three-dimensional artist's reconstruction

and Warehousemen [on Delos]. Whereas the *synodos* has been given funds for the completion of the headquarters and for the payment of the common account, in order that not only the things having been decreed should reach proper completion, but also that people, seeing how easy the *synodos* is to deal with, may themselves abound in contributing gladly to the things that are of benefit to the *koina* (pl.).
[*Announcement of Benefaction*: 6–20]

Marcus Minatius son of Sextus, a Roman, being a fine and good man and being well-disposed to the affairs of the gods and the affairs of the *synodos*, with regard to seeking honor, and seeking honor privately and publicly in order that the plan of the *koinon* might be strictly observed and the headquarters might be completed according to the things previously decreed, contributed as a benefaction both the accrued interest – which was much – and that which was collected, from which sum he advanced the funds for the things decided upon for the construction of the sacred enclosure, and also being a follower (of Poseidon) he made a benefaction by himself of 7,000 drachmae to the *koinon*, and has invited all of us to a sacrifice which he has prepared for the gods on behalf of the *synodos* and to a public dinner, and he also announced his intention that when holding the dinner in the future, the reason – in part – will be that it be of some benefit to the *koinon*, in order that the *synodos* may then also appear to honor those who are helpful among men and never miss at any time in returning thanks.
[*The Conferring of Honours*: 20–58]

198

For good fortune. Be it resolved by the *koinon* to commend the Roman Marcus Minatius son of Sextus and to accept the promise of him who is seeking honor for the *koinon*. And let there be given him a place in the courtyard, whichever place he wishes, for the erection of his statue, which is presently in another place, and let there be given him a place in the headquarters to set up his portrait, whichever place he wishes, with the exception of the shrines and pronaos. And on the (base of) the statue shall be inscribed: "The *Koinon* of Berytian Poseidoniastai, Merchants, Shippers and Warehousemen erected (this statue) for the Roman Marcus Minatius, son of Sextus, the banker, himself a benefactor, for the exceptional merit and goodwill which he continually has shown towards the *koinon*." The same inscription shall be written on the portrait. And let him also share the couch (of honor) with the sacrificer on the festival of Poseidon, and first seat at table at all the other assemblies. And also let a day in his honor be celebrated each year on the day following the procession of the festival of Apollo, and on this day he shall be permitted two guests of his choice. And after, a gold wreath shall be put upon him who honored the *synodos* (and) it shall be publicly proclaimed on the festival of Poseidon: "The *koinon* crowns Marcus Minatius son of Sextus with a gold wreath for his exceptional merit and goodwill which he continually has shown towards the *koinon*, for good fortune." And still on the same day (proclaim): "The *koinon* crowns Marcus Minatius son of Sextus, and it also celebrates for him a day both now and for all time for his exceptional merit and goodwill which he has continually shown towards the *koinon*, for good fortune." And (proclaim) on each month during the meetings: "The *koinon* crowns Marcus Minatius, son of Sextus, with a gold wreath, being a benefactor of the *synodos*, for good fortune." And let the public proclamation of wreaths be made among the people. And at each procession he shall be permitted to bring one guest. And he shall be exempted from service of all public appointments and all public expenditures. And let an ox be led for him in the procession each year for all time on the festival of Apollo bearing this message: "The *Koinon* of Berytian Poseidoniastai on behalf of Marcus Minatius son of Sextus." And so that the honorable things granted by the *synodos* to Marcus should continue for all time according to the law, let many become eager to seek honor for the *synodos*, knowing that it (the *synodos*) is useful, and not only votes fitting honors for benefactors, but also promotes (benefaction), which is most necessary so that the honors being given to benefactors may continue forever.

[*Penalties*: 58–69]

And it is unlawful for anyone, either a private citizen or ruler, either to say or to write that the honors which are given must be changed, nor is it lawful to take away or render of no authority anything from this decree, neither he who writes (proposed motions), nor speaks to them, nor he who reads them, or proposes them, nor he who votes on them, and may he who writes or proposes (such contrary motions) be utterly ruined and his children also, and may the use of the possessions of his estate and of his children be given to those who supervise these laws, and may its use save them who received them from (attack by) land and by sea, and whoever commits (these crimes) shall, in addition to the above, pay 6,000 sacred drachmae of Poseidon bearing a wreath on the obverse side and let him be brought to trial for wrongdoings. And likewise also the *archithiasités*, for whatever of the prescribed duties he does not accomplish, let him owe the same financial penalty and let him be brought to trial for wrongdoing.

[*Leading the Sacrificial Ox in Procession*: 69–80]

And there shall be paid to the herdsmen who have been prepared according to the law, 150 drachmae by those who have always been treasurers from the beginning for leading the ox for Marcus in procession; and for the reception which the *koinon* shall lay on for Marcus each year (the treasurers shall pay) another 150 drachmae. And the herdsmen who received the aforementioned payment shall lead the ox (both) in procession and at reception, and these things shall be accomplished according to the decree, and they (the treasurers) shall submit a written financial account of those expenses which they paid out at the first meeting which is held after the reception. And if any of the appointed herdsmen should not accomplish what is prescribed for him, he shall owe 1,000 sacred drachmae to Poseidon and let him be brought to trial for wrongdoing.

[*Responsibilities and Penalties of the Archithiasités*: 81–96]

And those who do not accomplish any of the obligations recorded in this decree shall stand subject to a curse, and also let any of the congregation who so wish denounce them in accordance with things that are lawful. And let the one who has been *archithiasités* from the beginning bring forward (both) him who makes the accusation and the defendant, and let him distribute a voting pebble to (each of) the members . . . of the defendant . . . let him be accused by the one having made the accusation . . . , by acquiring for himself one third of the fine collected. And if the *archithiasités* does not accomplish something (in this decree), let there be a prosecution against him when he becomes a private citizen, according to these things. The *archithiasités* shall engrave this decree on a stone stele and set it up publicly, and he shall place it in the courtyard . . . when Phaidrias . . . (and) those who have been treasurers from the beginning shall provide the money for these matters.

One of the challenges posed by this inscription has been to correlate the rooms named with the archaeological remains. Bruneau has made the following correlations: the temenos which the Poseidoniastai requested of the Athenians is the plot of land on which the whole edifice was constructed (*ID* 1520, ll. 11–12). The term *oikos* does not designate a particular part of the building but the entire

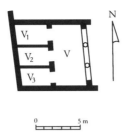

Figure 11.4 Original plan of sanctuary

structure.[55] This *oikos* was used as a multi-purpose facility or headquarters: it functioned as a sanctuary, commercial centre, and hotel for the *koinon*.

According to the inscription (l. 23), M. Minatius Sextus was permitted to have his statue erected anywhere he wished "in the courtyard." Bruneau has identified this courtyard as the small court (X) in which numerous honorific statue bases have been found. Minatius Sextus was also allowed to set up his portrait in a place of his choosing in the *oikos* with the exception of the "shrines and pronaos." These rooms correspond to the *prostoa* (V) and shrines (V^1, V^2, V^3) of the above plan.[56]

History of renovations

Though the meaning of l. 91 is unclear, the mention of the Phaidrias whose archonship was in the year 153/2 BCE is assured. Though it is unclear whether this decree should be dated before or after his archonship, the year 154/3 BCE provides an approximate *terminus ante quem* for the construction of the *oikos*.[57]

There is consensus among scholars that the building underwent at least one renovation in its history. Discussion has been focused principally on rooms V^{1-4}, especially with respect to three key questions: what was the function of these rooms? Was there was an intermediate renovation prior to the final renovation? What date should be assigned to the renovations? The main points of the debate can be summarized as follows:

In the original structure, prior to any renovations, the pronaos (V) was bounded on the south side by a wall which was the continuation of the southern boundary wall of the peristyle court (F). In this original sanctuary, there were three shrines (V^1, V^2, V^3) of approximately equal dimensions.[58] In front of these shrines was a *pronaos* (V) with two columns leading into a small court (X) (Figure 11.4; cf. Figure 11.2).[59]

In the final renovation, the western wall of the shrines was extended in a southerly direction. V^1 retained its original proportions. The wall between V^2 and V^3 was removed and this enlarged space became the new V^2. Two additional rooms were also constructed, V^3 and V^4 (Figure 11.5).[60]

201

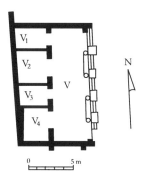

Figure 11.5 Final plan of sanctuary

The resulting structure consisted of four rooms, two small ones of approximately equal dimensions (V^1, V^3) and two larger ones, V^2 and V^4 having twice the width. Coinciding with this was the extension of the *pronaos* to the south and the addition of two more columns. Key to the debate concerning the use of these shrines is the fact that a statue of Roma and its inscribed base (*ID* 1788) were discovered in V^1, and a base for a cult statue of Poseidon in V^2 (*ID* 2325). In the opinion of Picard, the three shrines (V^{1-3}) were originally dedicated to a triad of Berytian deities assigned as follows:[61]

V^1 a Berytian god (such as Heracles–Melkart)
V^2 Poseidon
V^3 Astarte, and the "gods of the homeland"[62]

Picard concluded that in the final restoration, the Berytian god in V^1 was moved to V^4 and replaced with Roma, a loyalty cult of Berytian merchants who worked closely with the Romans. According to this argument, the occasion for the renovation was the adoption of the cult of Roma.

Bruneau interprets the evidence differently. He argues that there was never a triad of Berytian gods in V^{1-3}. Rather, there were only two national gods, Poseidon and Astarte. The remaining shrine was dedicated to Roma. According to Bruneau, Roma had been installed in V^1 from the beginning (1978a:160–90). Moreover, he thinks that V^4 was not used as a shrine, but assigned some other use such as a sacristy.[63] The purpose of the renovation was not to accommodate a new cult (Roma), but simply to enlarge the shrine of Poseidon (V^2) and create some kind of preparation room (V^4). Thus, there were three shrines (V^{1-3}) both in the original structure and in the renovated structure, dedicated to Roma, Poseidon, and Astarte respectively (Bruneau 1978a:186–89).

The debate was raised to a higher level of complexity when Hugo Meyer argued that there was an intermediate renovation prior to the final renovation (1988:203–20). According to Meyer, prior to the construction of V^4 in the final renovation, this space had been occupied by *two* rooms, V^{4A} and V^5. In other words, there were actually five rooms at the time of the intermediate renovation, with V^1 and V^5 being used as sacristies. Meyer thinks that one of the stones found *in situ* is the remainder of the partition wall which had separated V^{4A} from V^5 (1988:205–06). His argument that V^1 was *also* used as a sacristy is based on the supposition that there is a functional symmetry between V^5 and V^1. Thus, V^1 and V^5 bracketed a central block of three shrines, V^2, V^3, V^{4A}, the largest of which (V^2) was dedicated to Poseidon.[64]

Meyer argues that the cult of Roma was not represented in the shrines at this time. He thinks that V^2, V^3 and V^{4A} were dedicated to Astarte, Poseidon and a third Berytian deity respectively with V^1 and V^5 being used as sacristies. Meyer thinks that the first sacristy (V^1) was converted into a shrine of Roma in the final renovation. At this same time, the dividing wall between V^{4A} and V^5 was taken down and the shrine of the third Berytian deity (in V^{4A}) expanded into the newly renovated V^4 with the resulting loss of the sacristy space (V^5). Thus, both sacristies were lost in the final renovation.

Key to Meyer's argument that the cult of Roma was not part of the original building (or even part of the intermediate renovation), is that one of the blocks from the elongated pedestal base which supported the cult to the goddess Roma was a *spolium*. The following inscription (*ID* 1778) is carved into it:[65]

> Dedicated to the goddess Roma, our benefactor, by the *Koinon* of Poseidoniastai of Berytos, Merchants, Shippers, and Warehousemen, in recognition of her goodwill for the *koinon* and the homeland. Erected when Mnaseas son of Dionysios the benefactor was *archithiasitēs* for the second time.
> [Menandros] son of Melas the Athenian made (this sculpture).

The inscription states that the statue was erected during the second presidency (*archithiasitēs*) of Mnaseas. The base also bears the incomplete name of the sculptor: – – – *Melanos Athenaios*.[66] The personal name of the sculptor was inscribed on the adjacent block, now missing.[67] This missing name can be restored as "Menandros" on the basis of another inscription which preserves the sculptor's name intact (*ID* 2342.5–6). This same sculptor is probably responsible for the cult statue of Poseidon (cf. *ID* 2325). According to Meyer, the name Menandros refers to the original use of the block prior to its *reuse* for the Roma statue (1988:207–8). Meyer attempted to date the original usage of the block (*ID* 1778) on the basis of the sculptor's name, by cross-reference to *ID* 2342. This latter inscription can be dated precisely to 110/109 BCE.[68] He concludes that the block was inscribed with the name of Menandros towards the end of the second century BCE (1988:209).

Meyer argues that for the block to have been used a *second* time, the original statue of the late second century BCE must have been destroyed (ibid.:208–10). The nearest event in time for such a destruction is the invasion by the troops of Mithridates (88 BCE). On the basis of this conjecture he dates four events to the years following the devastation of 88 BCE, namely (a) the secondary usage of the statue base of Roma, (b) the introduction of the cult of Roma, (c) the final renovations of the *oikos*, and (d) the second presidency of Mnaseas. If Meyer is correct, then the second presidency of Mnaseas was more than sixty years after his first presidency, when he is known to have dedicated the peristyle court (F)[69] and the small court (X) (*ID* 1788).

In Bruneau's rejoinder to Meyer, he makes two main points. First, it is unlikely that the block inscribed for the base of the Roma statue was a *spolium* (1991:384–85). Meyer overlooks several important pieces of evidence. The Roma statue is stylistically datable to the third quarter of the second century BCE, not to the mid- to late first century BCE, as Meyer's theory would demand.[70] Confirmation of this is given by Marcadé's dating of Menandros' signature on the Roma base to the mid-second century BCE on the basis of paleography (1953–57, 2:67–68). Moreover, the arrangement of the Roma base with respect to the mosaic on the floor of V[1] suggests that the base is in its original position, not part of a late renovation.[71] Thus, the weight of the evidence points to Menandros as the sculptor of the statue of Roma.

Simply because *ID* 2342 bearing Menandros' name is datable *c.* 110 BCE does not mean that the statue of Roma must necessarily have been made at the same time. Menandros is probably responsible for the statue of Poseidon sculpted approximately forty years earlier (*c.* 154/3 BCE). He probably created the statue of Roma shortly after the original building was completed (*c.* 153 BCE), that is, at the same time as he sculpted the statue of Poseidon in the adjoining shrine.

Bruneau argues that the inscribed block of the Roma base was indeed reused as a *spolium*, but only *after* it had first been employed in the Roma base. The now missing name [*Menandros*] had originally been on the adjacent block when the two blocks formed part of the elongated pedestal base supporting the Roma statue.[72] When the house of the Poseidoniastai was destroyed either in 88 or 69 BCE, this adjacent block was removed and reused as a *spolium*.

Second, Bruneau also argues that the intermediate renovation proposed by Meyer is completely imaginary (1991:385–86). As noted above, Meyer interpreted block *xi* as the residue of a partition wall between V[4A] and V[5]. In his excavation report, Picard explained that this stone was actually the south boundary of a massive support at the foundation wall of V[4] (1921:72). This observation has been since verified by Bruneau who states that "there is no trace of a prolongation of '*xi*' towards the east which would allow one to speak of a dividing wall."[73]

If Meyer's proposed sacristy V[5] is fictitious, then his argument for a functional symmetry between V[5] and V[1] is no longer viable. Bruneau then argues that V[1] was never used as a sacristy. From the time of its construction, it was as a shrine to Roma.

Though the *terminus ante quem* for the construction of the original structure can be fixed *c.* 153 BCE, it is not possible accurately to determine the date of the renovation. All that can be known for sure is that it was accomplished before the first half of the first century BCE when the building was destroyed. The following chart summarizes the conclusions of Bruneau.

Original structure (before 154/3)
V^1	Roma
V^2	Poseidon
V^3	Astarte

Final structure after renovation
V^1	Roma
V^2	Poseidon
V^3	Astarte
V^4	Sacristy

Sarapeion A

The cult of Sarapis arrived on the shores of Delos from Egypt sometime during the period of Delian independence (that is, prior to 166 BCE). The Delian cult of Sarapis was connected with three other gods, Isis, Anubis, and later Harpocrates (hellenized Horace). It had a wide appeal to the local population and soon attracted followers from all nationalities such that no other Greek city has more records of the cult of Sarapis than does Delos.[74] At the height of the cult, Delos boasted three Sarapeia, all of which are located on the road which runs up the slope of Mount Cynthus, the area now known as the "terrace of the foreign gods." The devotee walking up this road would first come upon Sarapeion A, then Sarapeion B, and then higher still, on an elongated terrace, the much larger civic temple known as Sarapeion C.[75] It was managed by Athenians and served as the center of the civic cult of Sarapis from the early second century BCE through to the second century CE. Though Sarapeion C was used by many private associations, its architectural design was that of a public – not private – building and therefore will not be discussed in this study.

Sarapeion A, the oldest (*c.* 220 BCE) of the three Sarapeia, served as the center for a private cult of Sarapis for the Egyptian residents. One remarkable inscription tells the story of the introduction of the cult of Sarapis to Delos and the construction of Sarapeion A.[76] An Egyptian priest named Apollonios I migrated to Delos from Egypt bringing with him a small statue of Sarapis. Upon his arrival, he rented accommodation and conducted the worship of Sarapis in his home. Apollonios I was succeeded by his son Demetrios, and later by his grandson Apollonios II. Apollonios II relates the story of how Sarapis appeared to him one night in a dream and announced his desire to have a sanctuary built in his honor. Sarapis gave detailed instructions on how and where the sanctuary was to be built. This sanctuary (now known as Sarapeion A) was completed within six months. Upon its completion, evil men opposed the cult which resulted in a trial held in the sanctuary. As the story goes, when the moment came for the prosecution to present its case, Sarapis struck dumb the evil men and the opposition to the cult came to an abrupt end.

The inscription preserves two accounts of this story, a prose version by the priest Apollonios II (ll. 1–28) followed by a metrical version in hexameter verse by the poet Maiistas (ll. 29–94). A translation of this text (*IG* XI/4, 1299) in given here in full, since no complete English translation has yet been published:[77]

Part I: The Prose Aretalogy
[*Foundation of the Delian Cult*: 1–11]
The priest Apollonios[78] had this inscription engraved according to the command of the god.[79] Our grandfather Apollonios, an Egyptian of the sacerdotal class, having brought his god[80] with him from Egypt,[81] continued to do service[82] for his god in accordance with tradition[83] and purportedly lived to ninety-seven years of age.[84] My father Demetrios succeeded him next and likewise did service for the gods,[85] and was honored by god[86] for his piety with a bronze statue which he set up in the temple of the god.[87] He lived sixty-one years.
[*The Building of the Temple*: 12–22]
After Demetrios, I inherited the sacred images[88] and was appointed to perform diligently the divine services, and the god Sarapis revealed to me in a dream that a Sarapeion of his own must be consecrated to him, and that he should no longer be in rented rooms as before,[89] and further, that Sarapis would himself find the place where the temple should be situated and will indicate the location with a sign. And so it was. For there was a plot of land[90] filled with dung which was advertised on a placard by the pathway to the market place as being up for sale.[91] And since the god willed it, a contract of purchase was agreed upon and the construction of the sanctuary was quickly completed in six months.
[*The Law Suit*: 23–28]
And certain individuals conspired against both us and our god, and brought legal action against the temple and me in a public court, with a penalty of either corporal punishment or a fine forthcoming. But the god promised me in a dream that we would triumph. And now that legal proceedings have ended and we have won as is worthy of our god, we continued to praise the gods[92] by giving due thanks.
Part II: The Hymn of Maiistas
[*Hymnic Preamble*: 29–36]
Maiistas composed this hymn for the temple[93] on this subject: "Innumerable and wonderful are your deeds, O glorious Sarapis, with miracles being celebrated as far as the fortified cities of Egypt which is beloved of the gods, and others celebrated all over Greece, and they also praise your consort Isis. O Saviors, watch over without ceasing good men who have pure thoughts in all things. For on the island of Delos, beaten by the waves, you made famous the sacred images of Apollonios and you brought them to great praise.

206

[The Foundation of the Delian Cult of Sarapis: 37–46]

The father of my father (Apollonios I) brought them to Delos from Memphis[94] a long time ago, when they came by a ship with many oars to the city of Phoebus. He reluctantly set them up in his own rented room and he propitiated you with a generous offering of incense. When he died a very old man,[95] he left his son Demetrios in charge of your provisional sanctuary, in whom the *therapeutēs*[96] wholly rejoiced. While praying to you during the night that a bronze statue of himself be set up in the temple, you answered his prayer indeed. After you appeared to the sleeper appointed in his father's place[97] on his bed during the night, you directed him to accomplish whatever is necessary that the statue of Demetrios might be erected.

[The Building of the Temple: 46–65]

But when Demetrios was an old man, fate left him[98] and his son Apollonios II, having been taught the fine things by Demetrios, worshiped the sacred images with great devotion and daily sang praises of Sarapis' miracles, and he supplicated you without ceasing to reveal plainly one night in an oracle the place in which you wanted him to build the temple, so that your images might be installed in a sacred enclosure, not having to seek for shelter – this way and that – among foreigners. And you designated an ignominious plot of no importance, having been filled with refuse[99] of all sorts for a long time. For having approached me in bed during the night you said "Wake up, go to the entrance which is in the middle of the portico and you will see a note written on a small piece of papyrus which will instruct you – if you understand it – where you will build for me a sacred enclosure and a famous temple." And so, being astonished, he got up and left in great haste and looked joyfully at the note, and he acquired the property by paying the purchase price. In accordance with your will the sanctuary was built easily[100] along with the altars and a sacred enclosure, and all the seats and eating couches were installed in the dining hall[101] for the feast to which the god invites us.

[The Law Suit: 66–92]

But then some evil men possessed by envy were thrown into a raving madness, two of whom summoned your servant (Apollonios II) to court with an unsubstantiated indictment and they produced an evil law prescribing "either what (the lawbreaker) must suffer (i.e., death) or, what fine he would have to pay in compensation." Terror made the minister's heart tremble greatly with terrible fright morning and night. While invoking you unceasingly with tears, he begged your help, praying you to prevent the disgraceful fine, and to ward off the doom of evil death. And you, in accordance with remembrances of your mind, did not abandon him, but at night, approached the bed of the man and you said to him "Abandon fear! Be brave! No person shall cast a voting pebble against you since the charge is directed against me, moreover no one will speak more powerfully than I will.[102] Stop tormenting your soul!" But when the appointed date arrived for hearing the lawsuit, the entire city including a mixed crowd of foreigners from all nations assembled at the temple to learn about this divinely guided case. At that time both you (Sarapis) and (Isis) your wife aroused great amazement in the people. You paralyzed these wicked-minded men just as they were about to read the charge, making their tongues incapable of uttering a single word[103] such that no one could understand a word, nor were they able to provide proof for the indictment. But by divine power the accusers stood as if struck by lightning, resembling statues or stones. And the whole community marveled with dread at your miracle on that day and there was great renown for your servant on Delos, the island established by the gods.

[*Hymnic Summation*: 93–94]

Greetings to you, Blessed One, and to your consort Isis and to all the gods[104] that reside in our temple, O Glorious Sarapis!

It is difficult to reconstruct the historical detail behind this myth of origins. The precise reason for the civil case is a matter of conjecture. Nock argued that the Egyptians had failed to obtain official permission to establish a *temenos* to a foreign god (1933:50–53). Engelmann suggests two charges: (1) introducing a foreign cult; (2) building outside the assigned plot of land.[105] Michael White (1990:36) thinks that Sarapeion A encroached on the sacred spring of personified Inopos (see below).

Whatever its cause, the trial does not seem to have permanently resolved the situation. Sometime during the incumbency of a subsequent priest of Sarapeion A, Demetrios Rhenaios,[106] officials from Sarapeion C exerted pressure to have Sarapeion A closed down. This prompted Demetrios Rhenaios to appeal to Rome for a *senatus consultum*. Rome's official reply came in the form of a document sent via the Athenian *stratēgos* to the *epimelētēs* (governor) of Delos. This document upheld the right of Sarapeion A to continue. A stele bearing the text of this document was subsequently set up in the Sarapeion as a charter.[107]

Two voluntary associations are identified with Sarapeion A. The congregation as a whole was known as the *therapeuontes*.[108] A second group, known as the Contributors' Guild (*hoi symbalomenoi*), may have been chosen from among the *therapeuontes*. Their role seems to have been to make, and perhaps promote, financial contributions towards the construction and repair of the sanctuary. This group is probably connected in some way with the offertory treasury (J) set up beside one of the altars.

Description of the building

Sarapeion A was constructed in a depression below the Inopos reservoir (*GD* 97). To enter it, one must walk down a natural slope by fourteen stairs, opening out on to a paved trapezoidal court[109] forming the sacred enclosure.[110] Located

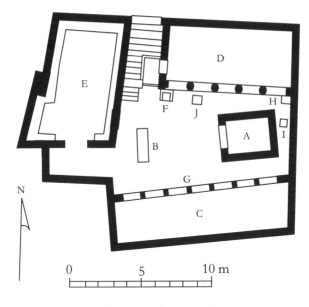

Figure 11.6 Sarapeion A

in the east end of this court is a small temple (A) (4.10 x 3.20 m) with no interior division (Figure 11.6).[111]

The temple is elevated, with three steps and a threshold leading up to its entrance (westward facing). The raised elevation of the temple communicates its greater sanctity. On its south side is a passageway leading by way of five steps down into the temple's subterranean crypt (A′) which contains a spring. This spring serves as a drain for the nearby Inopos reservoir. An underground canal conducts water into the spring from the reservoir. The spring was used as a Nilometer (that is, a sacred wellspring of the Nile) for purification rituals.[112] Water could also be drawn up from a manhole (I) to the north-east of the temple.

Three altars were erected in the court. The principal altar (B), rectangular in shape, was located between the temple and the large dining hall (E). A second altar (F) is located against the north boundary wall of the paved court near the stairs. Beside this altar is an offertory treasury (*in situ*) with a large ovaloid opening (damaged) to receive monetary donations (J).[113] This treasury probably has some connection with the activity of the contributors' guild. A third altar was positioned in the north-east corner of the paved court (H).

Walking back up the stairs again to a landing (four steps up) one has access to an elongated rectangular room (D), elevated above the level of the paved court. Two niches in its north wall and one in the east wall – at about eye-level – may have contained lamps or cult statues of lesser Egyptian deities. This space is

209

relatively independent of the remainder of the building, though it does look out on to the court through a colonnade (now destroyed).

On the south side of the court at a slightly lower level, is a second room (C), the colonnade of which was later replaced with a wall (G). Four of the original columns now serve only as decoration. To the west of the paved court is a large dining hall (E) in the shape of an irregular trapezoid, with an alcove in the south-west corner. Marble benches with inscriptions line the four walls of the dining room.[114] Two gaming boards are inscribed on one of the benches of the west wall.[115] The benches now *in situ* show signs of having been moved from their original arrangement.[116] This room was used for meetings and ritual dinners, the same room to which Sarapis invited his worshipers to a banquet (l. 65). The south side of the hall is a corridor (K) which opens out onto the central court.

History of the building

In his excavation report, Roussel made no attempt to construct a history of Sarapeion A in relation to the immediate archaeological context of the site. Michael White has since taken up this matter, describing how it was originally con-structed as an architectural extension of an existing private building (*GD* no. 91) immediately to the west (1990:35–36). The plot of land adjacent to this *insula* (no. 91) – the future site of Sarapeion A – was vacant at this time, serving as the site of the drain for the nearby Inopos reservoir.

Bruneau thinks that the House of Inopos (*GD* 95), further up the slope and across from the Inopos reservoir, was connected with the office of the "guard-ian of the (sacred) spring of the Inopos."[117] If Bruneau's deduction is correct, then as White observes:

[the] construction of the Sarapeion encroached on a local landmark, the sacred spring of personified Inopos, of which the neighbor in House 95 (i.e., the House of Inopos) was the hereditary guardian. Not only did construction of the Sarapeion divert the drain from the reservoir (so important during the dry summer months), it also transformed its religious symbolism. For the naos crypt (A´) of the Sarapeion, tied into the drain, served as a Nilometer, the sacred wellspring of the Nile.

(1990:36)

White suggests that the reference in *IG* XI/4 1299 to the neglect of the plot, that is, that it originally served as a "dung heap" (ll. 18–19) and was a despised location (l. 53), is mere hyperbole intended to counter charges that the construc-tion of the Sarapeion had debased sacred ground. By asserting that the land was *already* defiled by neglect of the guardian of the Inopos spring prior to the con-struction of Sarapeion A, they could then argue that the Sarapeion had actually sanctified the land (ibid.:36).

After study of the archaeological remains, White summarizes the construction of the Sarapeion as follows: the north wall of *insula* 91 was extended eastwards, and then south and west, thus forming the perimeter walls of the building complex.[118] The dining hall (E) was originally part of the adjoining domestic building (*insula* 91). In fact it was this building which Apollonios I had rented upon his arrival on Delos. At that time he converted his dining hall (E) into a shrine for Sarapis.[119] This dining hall was later taken over by the Sarapeion when the temple (A) and crypt (A′) were built on the adjoining undeveloped land.[120] Hall E was converted back into a dining room and the cult objects were removed to the newly constructed temple (A). This explains why *IG* XI/4 1299 does not mention the construction of the dining hall, but only its modification by the installation of seats and eating couches (ll. 63–65).[121]

White observes that the temple and crypt lie askew the main axis of the court. They are oriented along an axis perpendicular to the west wall running through corridor (K). The original drain canal from the Inopos reservoir continued past the drain along this axis, through corridor K into *insula* 91. Thus, the temple was positioned so as to tie into this drain canal and then divert it southwards (through room C).[122]

Sarapeion B

Five associations are known to have been connected with Sarapeion B. A joint dedication attests to the existence of a *koinon* of *therapeutae*,[123] a *koinon* of *melanephors*, and a *thiasos* of *Sarapistai* named after its founder, Kineas. The fact that the *therapeutae* dedicated a large number of offerings during the period of Delian independence suggests that they were of considerable importance, and should probably be identified with the primary congregation of the Sarapeion.[124] The *melanephors* were distinguished from other devotees of the Egyptian gods by wearing black linen garments in order to identify themselves with the mourning of Isis over the death of her husband Osiris.[125]

From 220 BCE onwards, inscriptions testify to two other private religious associations dedicated to the trio Sarapis, Isis, and Anubis. They were named after the day on which they met. The *koinon* of the Tenth Day met on the tenth day of each month.[126] The membership of its *koinon* which totalled sixteen (nine men/seven women) was headed by a *synagōgeus*. There was also a *koinon* of the Nineteenth Day with an *archithiasitēs* at its head.[127]

The building

On account of its general state of disrepair, it is only possible to describe the plan of Sarapeion B in general terms.[128] One enters the building by a steep set of some twenty-six stairs, interrupted by a landing (with an inscribed bench)[129] part way up. Near the top of the stairs, a passageway gives access on the left to a large meeting room (G). Against the eastern wall of this room are three altars, each with ornate marble horns. The arrangement of the western side of the room is

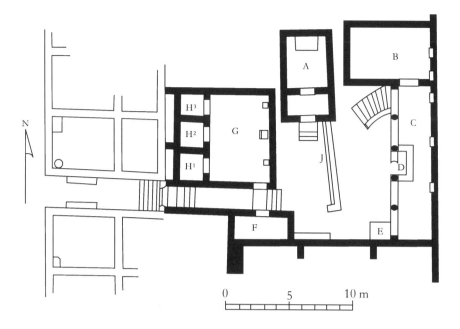

Figure 11.7 Sarapeion B

uncertain. Roussel thinks the western wall was lined with three shrines (*naoi*) (H[1], H[2], H[3]).[130] If correct, this arrangement is very similar to the *pronaos* and shrines (V[1], V[2], V[3]) of the House of the Poseidoniastai (Figure 11.7).[131]

At the very top of the stairs is a large court. A small temple (A) (7 x 4.50 m) is located in its north-west corner. The temple faces south and is elevated above ground level by several steps. Its interior is divided into a *pronaos* and *naos*, the latter being elevated by one step.

East of the temple is a slightly larger room (B) (approx. 6.50 x 3.50 m), which Roussel thinks may be a shrine dedicated to another deity. It is slightly elevated above the level of the temple. A doorway on the south side opens out onto a portico (C) running perpendicular to its façade. At the medial point of the portico (C), are the remains of a vault (D) which may have been used as a sacred cistern similar to the drain in the crypt of Sarapeion A.

Demarking a small terrace in front of the temple (A) is a row of benches (J) aligned on an axis running perpendicular from its south-east corner. The ground between the benches and the portico is on a gradual incline. In the south-east corner of the court, abutting the portico, is a large stone construction (E) which may be the remains of an altar. In the south-west corner are two more benches. The remains of two cult statues have also been found, but they cannot be identified with certainty.[132]

Summary of the buildings with internalized cult

In the above discussion, voluntary associations have been classified into two taxonomic types: associations which utilized cultic space which was *external* to the place of gathering (whether proximate or remote), and associations which incorporated their cultic space *into* their place of assembly. In an analysis of buildings of the latter type a common pattern has emerged: in each case, the space used for general assembly is adjacent to the cultic space (signified by the presence of one or more altars); this cultic space is always co-ordinated with one or more temples/shrines. The progressive sanctity of these three spaces is expressed by the gradually increasing elevation.

To be more precise, the assemblies of the general membership of the Poseidoniastai, Sarapeion A, and Sarapeion B were probably held in the largest rooms in each of these structures, the large peristyle court (F), the dining room (E), and the central court, respectively. In the latter two cases, benches *in situ* lend additional support to this deduction.

In each case, the place of sacrifice is bordering on to the meeting space. In the house of the Poseidoniastai, sacrifice was offered on the three altars in the small court (X) immediately off the peristyle court (F). In Sarapeion A, the three altars are in the central court adjacent to the dining room (E). The situation in Sarapeion B is slightly more complex. Room G with its three altars is adjacent to the central court, though access to it is somewhat indirect. A fourth altar may have been located in the central court. Thus, the meeting space was in proximity to as many as four altars, though the spatial relationship is less clearly defined than in the two previous examples.

All three structures had one or more temples or shrines which were co-ordinated with the place of sacrifice: the house of the Poseidoniastai had its *pronaos* (V) and shrines (V^{1-3}) off the small court (X); in Sarapeion A, the central temple (A) was situated in the midst of three altars; Sarapeion B had three shrines in court G (H^{1-3}) with its three altars, and a temple (and perhaps fourth shrine) in the central courtyard (perhaps with a fourth altar).

THE CHRISTIANS: THE PLACE OF CULT IN DELIAN CHURCHES

Last of the voluntary associations to establish themselves on Delos were groups of Christians, probably in the third century CE. They are known to have constructed many churches and perhaps even a monastery (Orlandos 1936). The presence of these buildings on Delos raises an interesting question: can the Christian churches profitably be analyzed with respect to the taxonomic categories of external cult versus internal cult? Clearly, church buildings cannot be classified in the former category since there is no evidence to suggest that some Christians made use of a cultic space which was external to their place of assembly. Can the Delian churches then be taxonomically grouped with voluntary associations which have an internal cult? We shall return to this question after analyzing the two best preserved Delian churches, namely the Church of Fourni and the Church of St. Kyricos.

The Church of Fourni

The Church of Fourni (Figure 11.8) is the most ancient of the churches on Delos, perhaps dating to the early fourth century CE (Orlandos 1936:86). It was constructed on the remains of a Roman house, now known as the House of Fourni,[133] taking its name from the nearby Bay of Fourni. It is approximately a fifteen-minute walk south from the centre of town, inland from the Asclepieion.

This house was built on three levels, each level being adapted to the rising slope of the terrain. The lower level consisted of a facade and several shops which opened out onto the street. This level also provided access to a small vestibule (presumably by a small set of wooden stairs) in which is located a large staircase (nine steps) leading to the upper level on which the church would subsequently be constructed.

The stairs to the upper level open onto a peristyle court,[134] off which are many small rooms. On the east side of the peristyle is the largest of these rooms, a *triclinium*. Its floor is decorated with a geometric mosaic. On the east wall of the *triclinium* is a *nymphaion*, its floor elevated by 1.23 m above the level of the *triclinium*.

The original excavators thought that a substantial part of the rear wall of the *nymphaion* had been carved out of the rock face. Since then, two water reservoirs have been discovered, constructed between the rock face and the wall of the *nymphaion* (Daux 1961:912) These reservoirs collected water which flowed down the hillside during the rains, and supplied it for use both to the *nymphaion* and (via a subterranean channel) to a stucco basin in the corner of the peristyle.

When this third level was converted into a church, the peristyle (A) served as the church's atrium. The adjoining *triclinium* was subdivided into two rooms, a narthex (B) and chancel (C), by the construction of a partition wall with a central doorway.[135] The elevated *nymphaion* was converted into an apse, access being provided by a set of six stairs from the chancel. A masonry wall, built on the western boundary of the apse, formed a low *templon*.

What Anastase Orlandos identified as an interior bench, perhaps a *synthronon*, to the rear of the apse, are the remains of the two water reservoirs. It is not clear (at least to this writer) whether or not the reservoirs were renovated into benches when the *nymphaion* was converted into an apse. The apse had a centrally located altar-table consisting of a squat column supporting a rock slab; the column was subsequently fortified with additional support.

This, the most ancient extant church on Delos, displays a rustic character. It was constructed with irregularly shaped building materials at hand. Unlike the basilica of St. Kyricos (below), there are no traces of marble sculpture relief or

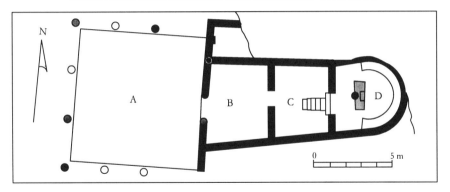

Figure 11.8 Church of Fourni

decoration. The low grade of building materials employed in renovating the structure into a church suggests that the congregation was poor. How can we account for this? Anastase Orlandos thinks that it is related to the continuance of the Graeco-Roman cults. He suggests that the church "seems to have been erected in haste, far from the centre of town, at a time when the pagan cult was perhaps still vigorous" (1936:86).

The Basilica of St. Kyricos

This church dates approximately to the mid-fifth century CE.[136] The building (16.75 × 10.70 m) has a plan typical of the basilica style and is oriented towards the east. The interior consists of a central nave (B) with two narrow side-naves or aisles (C). Opposite to the nave entrance, at the eastern end, is a raised chancel (I) and apse (A). Passageways at the eastern extremity of the two side-naves provided access for the priests and bishop to the apse.[137] In the apse is a double row of semi-circular stone benches forming the *synthronos* for the bishop and clergy (Figure 11.9).[138]

A low *templon* (F) with lattice separates the chancel (I) from the nave (B). In the chancel are the remains of an altar-table (E) whose column shaft of blue marble originally supported a larger flat surface. One of the floor tiles towards the west end of the nave is a plaque (H) with an inscription: "John, deacon, servant of holy martyr Kyricos," the latter being a reference to the cult of Kyricos,[139] not Kyriacos.[140] A second inscription was found near the apse, perhaps part of the *templom*. Its two words, "light" and "life" are arranged in a cruciform shape.[141]

An ambo (G) in the nave provided a platform for lections and preaching. The floor of the central nave is paved with tiles of white and blue marble. On two floor tiles on the north side one can see the slots in which the ambo had once been fixed.[142]

215

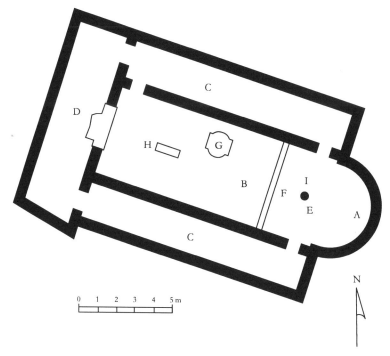

Figure 11.9 Basilica of St. Kyricos

GENERAL ANALYSIS

Before these churches can be compared with the voluntary associations sur-
veyed above, some general comment is in order with regard to the use of the
three principal spaces, the nave, chancel, and apse. The nave, of course, was the
place where the community gathered. This meeting place was annexed to a
chancel in which was set an altar-table.

The chancel and apse were vested with greater sanctity than the nave. This
gradation of sacredness from the nave to the chancel and apse is most obvious
in the Church of Fourni with its remarkable series of interconnected chambers
and highly elevated apse (1.3 m) with *templon*. In the case of the Basilica of St.
Kyricos, the increasing sanctity is indicated by the raised elevation of the chancel
and apse, and by the physical partition of the space by means of a low *templon*.
Like the temples and shrines of other associations, access to the apse was normally reserved for the cultic ministers alone, the bishop and presbyters. I shall
return to this point below.

Though the Eucharist took the form of a congregational meal in the first-
century church (for example, 1 Cor. 11:17–22), it was often interpreted as a *sacrificial* meal shared out among the congregation.[143] This is hardly surprising given

the longstanding association between the Eucharist and the Jewish Passover meal (for example, 1 Cor. 5:7).

One could speculate as to the type of sacrifice from which Gentile Christians drew their metaphor, whether bloody or bloodless. The theological interpretation of the bread as the *flesh* of Christ[144] would permit its interpretation as a fictive *bloody* sacrifice offered on an *altar*.[145] Alternatively, there were also bloodless offerings, that is, "table-offerings," which included, among other items, bread, set out on offering-tables (*trapezai*). Given the fact that bread was offered in the Eucharist, the ritual could easily be interpreted as table-offering. The ambiguity of language, symbol, and belief surrounding the Eucharist is such that it would be futile to set one interpretation over the other. What is more important is that there is no difficulty in generating a concrete correlate for the sacrificial metaphor in either case.

Though the Eucharistic beliefs of Delian Christians probably differed from those of early Christians in numerous ways, the architectural plan of both Delian churches, with their demarcated chancel, altar, and apse, demonstrates that the dominant interpretation of the Eucharist was in terms of sacrifice. If the Eucharist had been interpreted principally as a community meal, one would expect a structure similar to the Delian synagogue, with no gradation of sacredness. Similarly, such a community meal might reasonably be compared with the meal hosted by the lord Sarapis in the dining hall of Sarapeion A. However, the fact of the matter is that the architectural form of these churches clearly sets the altar apart from the space of assembly, in its own sacred space. This demonstrates that the ritual of the Eucharist was understood as a (fictive) sacrificial act.

If one accepts the premise that the Eucharist was understood as a sacrificial ritual performed on an altar, then the internal logic of the parallelism would also require a priest. Though a president may preside at a community meal, a priest is indispensable, if there is to be a sacrifice.

Though early churches experimented with a variety of titles for their various ministers, notably absent among all them is the term "priest."[146] By the beginning of the second century CE, the offices of overseer and presbyter, as well as deacon, seem to have become the dominant institutional titles, at least in the churches visited by Ignatius of Antioch.[147] None of these terms originally had cultic connotations. The "overseer/bishop," as the term would suggest, was a congregational executive officer who superintended the assembly.[148] The presbyters described in connection with the church in Jerusalem (for example, Acts 11:30) – whether real or theological constructs – bear greater resemblance to the Jewish synagogal council than they do to the Levitical priests.

At the root of the problem is the ambiguous nature of the Eucharistic meal, being interpreted both as a community banquet and as a sacrificial meal. By the end of the second century CE, the sacrificial interpretation had largely overshadowed the former. Correspondingly, overseers and presbyters became *cultic* ministers when the meal they presided over became – first and foremost – a *sacrificial* meal. Such a redefinition of their function required no synodical decision.

Simply by continuing to preside in their traditional place at the community's ritual meal – now a sacrificial meal – they were *ipso facto* performing as cultic ministers.

Delian Christian churches incorporated cultic space into their meeting space in a way analogous to that of other voluntary associations. They both display a linear progression of space: the space in which the congregation assembled (nave) is oriented in reference to a cultic space (chancel), which adjoins the most sacred space (apse), to which admittance was restricted to cultic officials. This model is identical to that of the voluntary associations with internal cults as described above. This parallelism can be schematically summarized as follows:

Delian churches
nave   chancel with altar   apse

voluntary associations with internal cults
meeting/dining room   court with altar   temple/shrine

It must be stated emphatically that there is no intention here to trace the development of the basilica-style church from the buildings of voluntary associations, much less from the Hellenistic peristyle house or atrium house. The issue is not architectural evolution but analogy. An awareness of the use of architecturally defined space in religious associations suggests new ways of describing and interpreting the corporate life of Christians. The fact that there is a shared architectural configuration which integrated the act of assembling with the act of sacrifice suggests that churches should be taxonomically grouped with voluntary associations having internal cults.

This is not to suggest that there are no significant differences (as indeed there are differences between all voluntary associations). The point is that the analogous architectural form shared by churches and voluntary associations with internal cults is an eloquent testimony to a corresponding analogy in the corporate activity of these groups. Thus, from the point of view of group activity, as it can be deduced from architectural forms, there is no radical disjunction between Christian churches and such voluntary associations.

The increasing emphasis on cult in Christian churches may have been accelerated by two sociological factors. The idea of sacrifice and sacred spaces was so deeply embedded in Graeco-Roman culture, that it is impossible to conceive of Gentile Christian converts for whom this was not part of their past religious experience. Moreover, the fact that the nascent Christian congregations had no clearly defined cultic functionaries or cultic ritual must have become a subtle pressure in the course of the natural ideological competition which arose with other voluntary associations who did have cultic functionaries and rituals. In this light, it is little wonder that the Eucharist was increasingly understood to be a *cultic* meal, and church architecture was soon adapted to include cultic space.

NOTES

1   I am very grateful for the assistance of the Social Sciences and Humanities Research Council of Canada for the provision of a grant in support of the research represented in this chapter.

2   Cf. Courby 1931; Hennig 1983.

3   Pierre Roussel assigns 60 inscriptions to the period of Delian independence (*IG* XI/4 1215–72).

4   Cf. Strabo 10.5.4; most of the evidence on the Italians at Delos is collected in *IRD*; see further *DCA* 75–84; Laidlaw 1933:201–10; on Romans in the Aegean generally, cf. Donati 1965.

5   Cf. *ID* 1711, 1712, 1713, 1714.

6   Pausanias 3.23.2; Appian, *Mithridateios* 28.

7   It is true that blood was sometimes used to purify spaces besides that of the sanctuary, especially by delineating boundaries, but this did not accord them the same inviolable sanctity (cf. Burkert 1985:81–82).

8   On the role of the magistrates see McLean forthcoming.

9   Salvait 1963: esp. 259.

10   *DCA* 272 and n. 3; cf. *GD* 75.

11   *ID* 1731; Roussel and Hatzfeld 1910:402 no. 52. Immediately to its north is a monument which they set up. It is in the shape of a *rotunda* with four columns, an Ionic architrave with dedication (*ID* 1738), and a conical roof. It is situated inside a square peribolos (Salvait 1963:259–60 n. 6 and fig. 3; Hatzfeld 1919:342–51, esp. 349; *DCA* 272; Robert 1939:88–90).

12   Vallois 1923:2–117; *GD* 76, fig. 4 ('D'); inscription: Roussel and Hatzfeld 1910:402–3 no. 53.

13   A bronze fitting in the shape of a *caduceus* served as an opening for the deposit of money. Compare the offering box discovered in Sarapeion A (p. 209).

14   Altars with ox-heads and garlands in bas-relief have been discovered in the agora (Maia [*ID* 1744]; Hermes? [*ID* 1749]; Heracles [*ID* 1746]).

15   *ID* 1519, ll. 3, 46 [pl.], 55, 56.

16   Cf. 1 Macc. 15:15–23; Strabo 10.486; *ID* 1586 (dedication of Athenians and Delians in honor of Herod Antipas); Plassart 1914; cf. *Choix* 263–65; *DCA* 94–95, 306; *CDH* 486–93.

17   Josephus, *Ant.* 14.213–14: Jews from Paros and the neighboring islands complained to the Roman proconsul in Delos that they had been forbidden "to make use of the customs of their forefathers, and their way of sacred worship." As a result of the intercession of Delian Jews on their behalf, the proconsul restored their privileges granted by Caesar.

18   White 1990:176 n. 19; cf. Baslez 1976.

19   Bruneau 1982:465–504, esp. 467–75; White 1987; cf. Horsley 1981–89, 5:138.

20   Cf. Inscr. no. 2; Plummer translates *eis hieron Argarizen* as "to the holy temple (of?) Argarizen" (1987:19–20). Though the Gerizim temple was destroyed in 129 BCE, the cult continued. On problems concerning concrete evidence for this temple see Anderson 1991. Cf. Josephus, *Ant.* 12.10; 13.74 on the controversy between Jews and Samaritans as to whether God should be worshiped at Mount Gerizim or Jerusalem.

21   White (1987:144) thinks they were non-Jews from Heracleion, Crete; Horst (1988:184–86) argues they were Jews from Crete; Bruneau, from Heracleia in Lucania, S. Italy, not the ethnic *Herakleotes* (1982: p. 481); cf. Couilloud-Le Dinahet 1978:867 no. 26 (Rheneia): this person was a *magister* of one of the Italian colleges (Hermaïstai, Apolloniastai, Poseidoniastai) in the second century BCE (cf. *IRD* 75, *Sehii* no. 3; *ID* 1754).

22   Literally, "prayer hall"; cf. no. 2; translated "synagogue," Hengel 1971; Robert 1940–65, 3:107; *epi proseuchē* can also mean "in ex-voto," that is, an offering made in fulfillment of a vow (Mazur 1935:21; cf. White 1987:142 n. 40); strangely, Bruneau (1982) translates

this "for a vow" despite the fact that he translates the same phrase in no. 1 as "to the synagogue." The proximity of the two inscriptions requires that the translations be consistent.

23 Or "to the sacred mountain Garizim" (Horst 1988:185).

24 Bruneau thinks he is a Samaritan with a hellenized name (1982:481) though the theophoric name suggests otherwise.

25 Bruneau 1982:475–77.

26 Plassart (1913) was the first to make the identification, followed by Sukenik (1934:38). Mazur argued against the identification (1935:15–24). After the study of Mazur, Sukenik reversed his thesis (1949). Others also followed Belle's conclusions (Kittel 1944:16; Robert 1958:44 and n. 7). Goodenough (1953–68, 2:71–75) offered counter arguments to Mazur and supported the identification, though with some reservations.

27 On this type, see Schultze 1895.

28 Square marble base found in House IIA (*GD* 79) immediately adjacent to the stadium dating first century BCE; Plassart 1913:205 no. 1; Plassart 1914:526 no. 1; *CIJ* 726; *ID* 2329; Lifshitz 1967:15 no. 3; *CDH* 484, pl. IX, 4; Inv. A 3052. *Proseuchē* is literally, "prayer hall"; cf. Hengel 1971a = 1975; Horsley 1981–89, 3:121–22 no. 94; 4:201–2 no. 110; 4:219–20, 249; 5:148.

29 *ID* 2328 (*CIJ* 729); *ID* 2330 (*CIJ* 728); *ID* 2331 (*CIJ* 727); *ID* 2332 (*CIJ* 730); these inscriptions are also in Lifshitz 1967.

30 The epithet *hypsistos* is a common Septuagintal translation of the Hebrew *El Elyon* (Gen. 14:18, 22; Pss. 7:18; 17:15). It also occurs in Philo, Josephus, and other Jewish inscriptions (Philo, *Legat.* 278; Josephus, *Ant.* 16.163; *CIJ* 1537; cf. Kraabel 1969; Nock, Roberts, and Skeat 1936:57 n. 27.

31 *ID* 2532 (*CIJ* no. 725). These inscriptions invoke the vengeance of God for the murder of two Jewish women, Heraclea (col. I) and Marthine (col. II): "I call and invoke the most high god, god of the spirit and of all flesh, against those who through betrayal murdered or poisoned the young, untimely departed Heraclea, and who maliciously caused her innocent blood to be shed. May the same happen to them and their children. Oh Lord, you who see everything, and you angels of god, before whom on this day every life is humbled with adversity, avenge her innocent blood, and swiftly exact blood for blood." Much of the terminology is borrowed from the Septuagint. There is also a reference to Yom Kippur (cf. Deissmann 1902).

32 Nock, Roberts, and Skeat 1936:esp. 39–54; Ustinova 1991; Horsley 1981–89, 1:25–29 no. 5; 1:101; 2:46 no. 12; 2:208; 4:128; 4:201 no. 110; 4:234; 5:136.

33 Bruneau 1982:873–74; *CDH* 480–93; followed by Kraabel 1979; 1984; cf. White 1987:133–60; *CDH* 486–91; *GD* no. 80. Contra Bruneau, Hershel Shanks argues that the building was actually a sanctuary of Zeus (1979:43).

34 According to White, *kataskeuazein* (ll. 4–5) means "to build" in the broad sense rather than "to establish" (Bruneau); *epi proseuchē* (l. 5) means "to the synagogue" not "for an ex-voto" (Bruneau 1982:142–43).

35 Dedications: *ID* 2328–2333; funerary stelai: *ID* 2532 (= *CIJ* 724; Deissmann 1908: 413–24).

36 Only fragments survive of the benches in room B.

37 A chair for the head of the synagogue (Sukenik 1934:61).

38 Adapted from M. White 1987:157, fig. 2; cf. *GD* no. 80.

39 Bruneau, *CDH* 483. White demonstrated that the portico is a simple Doric type *krēpidoma* construction which is quite common in private and public architecture on Delos (1987:149–50; White forthcoming, no. 70).

40 This stage agrees with edicts in 1 Macc. 15; cf. Bruneau, *CDH* 497; M. White 1987:151.

41 *ID* 1087, 1923 (bis), 1928 found *in situ* in wall PT; *ID* 1152 found beside wall SR (cf. Bruneau 1982:492–93 and fig. 11).

42 Bruneau, *CDH* 497.

43 This period coincides with the edict in Josephus *Ant.* 14.214.

44 *ID* 1772–96; Picard 1920; *CDH* 622–30.

45 The Poseidoniastai worshiped a form of Canaanite Baal as Poseidon. He should not be confused with Poseidon of the Italian Poseidoniastai, nor with the Delian Poseidon whose official worship did not survive the period of independence.

46 This association may have originated as the Phoenician Laodicea which made a dedication in Delos *c.* 187–175 BCE (*IG* XI/4 1114; cf. Roussel 1911; *DCA* 92–93; Picard 1920:272 n. 4, 297–98; *Choix* 96).

47 *Thiasitai* (*ID* 1520, l. 83); *archithiasitēs* (*ID* 1520, ll. 66–67, 84, 87, 89; *ID* 1778, l. 5).

48 *Hiereus* (*ID* 1780, 1796); *thytos* (*ID* 1520, l. 34).

49 *GD* 114–17 no. 57; Bruneau 1970:623–38.

50 Adapted from *GD* no. 57, fig. 20.

51 *ID* 1778 (base of Roma); 2325 (base of Poseidon); on the statue, see Marcadé 1969:386–96.

52 For photo: Picard 1921:figs 18, 21 (Inv. E 109). It is decorated with four carved ox-heads; over their heads are hung garlands of fruits and flowers, on the lower part of which are hung bunches of grapes. To the left and right of the heads hang fillets (*infulae*) terminating in round tassels. Only fragments of the cylinder of g remain, and of e only the socle survives (cf. *ID* 1791).

53 From Picard 1921:32.

54 Commentary: Robert 1973:435–89.

55 For example, *ID* 1520, ll. 3, 10; no. 1774, l. 2; Bruneau 1970:625; cf. *oikia ID* 1522, l. 4.

56 V^4 was a sacristy, not a shrine.

57 Roussel and Launey think that this decree is dated sometime after his archonship (cf. *ID* 1520). Robert's dating of the building to the second half of the second century BCE suggests that he thinks the decree predates the archonship (1973:486–88).

58 Picard 1921:13–14, 44–50; Picard 1920; Bruneau 1978a:163 (résumé in Bruneau 1978b); Meyer 1988:241.

59 Adapted from Meyer 1988:205, fig. 1.

60 Adapted from ibid. 205, fig. 2.

61 Picard 1921:13–14, 44–50.

62 i.e., the *theoi patrioi* mentioned in six dedications (*ID* 1774, 1776, 1781, 1783, 1785, 1789), though the number "three" is never specified.

63 Bruneau 1978a:160–90; 1978b; *GD* no. 57.

64 Two points are fundamental to Meyer's theory of a V^5 anteroom: first, since there is no doorway in V^5 Meyer concludes that it must have been an anteroom for V^{4A}. Second, the threshold of V^4 is off-centre as a result of the eastern wall extending northwards. That this eastern wall was constructed at the same time as the extension of V^{1-3} can be seen from the fact that it is an organic extension of both the new southern wall of V^{4A} and of the new southern wall of room T and niche U.

65 *ID* 1778; Reinach 1883:467–68 no. 1; Loewy 1885: no. 256; *OGIS* 591; Picard 1921:58 (fig. 52); Inv. E 115.

66 The signature can be restored on the basis of *ID* 2342, ll. 5–6 which preserves the name of the sculptor intact; cf. *ID* 2325, l. 2.

67 Bruneau 1991:383 (fig. 3).

68 i.e., the date of the erection of the statue of Apollo; Mnaseas also dedicated the north portico of court F (*ID* 1773) and the portico of court X (*ID* 1775); cf. Picard 1920:276.

69 Several inscriptions mention a *stoa*. This corresponds to individual sides of the colonnade of the peristyle (F). The four sides of the peristyle were paid for by different persons. Mnaseas paid for the north side (*ID* 1773). The east and south sides were paid for

by Dionysios, son of Zenon (designated by the plural *stoas* (*ID* 1772), and the *koinon* paid for the west side (*ID* 1774).

70 Bruneau 1991:384; Vermeule 1959:103; Boussac 1988:318 and fig. 18.

71 Bruneau 1978a:184–85; 1991:384.

72 See Bruneau 1991:383 (fig. 3).

73 Bruneau 1991:385; cf. n. 31.

74 Cf. Mora's prosopographical index of worshipers of Isis on Delos (1990, 1:3–178); she also discusses the participation of women in the cult and the onomastics of worshipers of Oriental cults on Delos (vol. 2). The Sarapeion in Thessalonica is the second largest depository of archaeological and epigraphical data with no fewer that thirty-five inscriptions.

75 *CE* 47–66; *GD* no. 100; Bruneau 1980.

76 *IG* XI/4 1299; *SIG*³ 663 (ll. 1–29 only); Roussel, *CE* 71–75 no. 1; Weinreich 1919:31–36; Powell 1925:68–69; Longo 1969, 1:106–16 no. 63; Engelmann 1975; Wilhelm 1934:1–8; cf. Wilamowitz-Moellendorff 1958; J. and L. Robert, *BE* 79 (1966), 404–5 no. 283.

77 Cf. Roussel's French translation in *CE* 76–78; partial English translation in Nock 1933:51–52.

78 i.e., Apollonios II, son of Demetrios, grandson of Apollonios I.

79 i.e., of Sarapis. Apollonios is reluctant to utter the name of his god (cf. ll. 4, 10, 11, 13, 21, 24, 26, 28) (p. 11).

80 "Apollonios had the god"; that is, he had a statue of Sarapis with him.

81 Apollonios came from Memphis (cf. ll. 37–38).

82 *therapeuon*: performed the ritual/served the god; the inscription mentions offerings of incense (ll. 40, 63), the chanting of divine miracles (l. 49), and a joint ritual meal (l. 65) (cf. *CE* 267–71).

83 Apollonios performed the rite like his father (cf. ll. 13, 43, 93).

84 Death of Demetrios, *c.* 205 BCE; born *c.* 266. Apollonios I lived from *c.* 312–215 BCE. Apollonios II assumed priestly office *c.* 210–205 BCE (Engelmann 1975:14).

85 Presumably statues of Sarapis, Isis, Anubis, and Harpocrates, the deities most often mentioned in Delian inscriptions (cf. *CE* 273–80).

86 Unlike Greek communities, Sarapis, not the *ecclesia*, decides to honor the devout priest. The statue is erected according to instructions received in a dream. Demetrios had been hoping for this distinction (l. 43), but neither he, nor the community could fulfill this wish. Just as Apollonios II could not embark on the construction of a temple without a specific divine directive (ll. 14–15), Sarapis must also give the command for the honorific statue (pp. 16–17).

87 "which is (now) standing in the temple": At first, the statue stood in a rented room (l. 15) which served as a temporary sanctuary.

88 *ta hiera*: the statues of the deities (cf. ll. 2, 7–8) and anything else belonging to the ritual inventory.

89 The god had been in a rented room since Apollonios I came to Delos (cf. ll. 39, 51–52).

90 The site of the new temple was in the valley of Inopus, a good residential area (cf. Bruneau 1973:111–36, esp. 135). The plot had formerly been in use as a garbage dump. This despised location is hallowed by the god.

91 The poster which advertised that the plot was for sale was displayed at the passageway through which one entered the agora from the portico which adjoined it from the south (cf. ll. 56–57).

92 Cf. ll. 7–8, 93–94.

93 The name Maiistas is not attested elsewhere. He works for the temple as an encomiographer.

94 Memphis was the centre of the cult of Isis and Sarapis.

95 Literally "life killed him as a very old man"; catachrestic usage. In ll. 46–47, *moira* (fate)

leaves him and he dies. One would expect "fate" to kill him, and "life" to leave him. Maiistas seems to have been unfamiliar with the Homeric usage and confused the meanings of *aiōn* and *moira* (Engelmann 1975:30).

96 *therapes*, poetic form of *therapeuontes*; cf. Euripides *Ion* 94. Probably the community that met in Sarapeion A which called themselves *hoi therapeuontes* (cf. ll. 5, 13, 43, 69, 93). A group known as *therapeutai* seems to have been a different group.

97 ll. 43–46 pose a number of difficulties (see Engelmann 1975:33–6). This translation follows the suggested correction of Engelmann.

98 Cf. comment on ll. 40–41.

99 Literally full of "defilements of blood" (*lythros*); a comparison with ll. 18–19 suggests that a more generalized meaning is intended.

100 So-called "Sarapeion A" was a small modest structure measuring 4.10 m deep x 3.20 m wide.

101 Dining room (E); floor space approx. 40 m² used for the ritual community meal.

102 Because none of the accusers ever speak in court (ll. 85–89).

103 Maiistas confuses *opin* "rumour" with *opa* "voice, word" (Wilamowitz-Moellendorff).

104 Especially Anubis and Harpocrates.

105 Engelmann 1975:45–47, 52; on the distrustful attitude of Delians towards the Egyptian gods see Préaux 1958:180; cf. 176–84 on Delos generally.

106 A descendant of Apollonios II.

107 *ID* 1510 (= *CE* no. 14).

108 *Therapeuōn* in the above inscription; *therapeuontes en to hiero touto* (*IG* XI/4 1217; *CE* 84 no. 2B), or simply *hoi therapeuontes* (*IG* XI/4 1290; *CE* 85 no. 3); *therapes* (poetic form of *therapeuontes*) (*IG* XI/1 1299, l. 43); membership role in *CE* 84 no. 2A = *IG* XI/4 1216–22 (cf. *CE* 249, 253–54). The *therapeuōn* are described as being *apo tōn synodōn*; for another instance of the use of *synodos* in the plural cf. no. 16, ll. 34, 44–45. This group may also be designated as the "people" (*laos*, l. 90) who marveled at the miracle, though this term may simply specify those in attendance at the trial.

109 Maximum 12 m long × 6 m wide.

110 Roussel conducted the original field survey: *CE* 19–32; cf. *GD* 136–39 no. 91; the parts of the Sarapeion are enumerated in a metrical inscription (*CE* 29).

111 Adapted from Bruneau 1990:560, fig. 1.

112 Cf. Wild 1981:34–39; Witt 1971:67–68.

113 *thēsauros*: cylindrical case with moulding mounted on a square platform. An inscription is engraved on the side of the cylinder (*CE* 87–89 no. 7; *IG* XI/4 1248). Similar examples known in Sarapeia in Thera (*IG* XII/3 443), Larisa (*IG* IX/2 590), and Priene (*I.Priene* no. 195, l. 37); cf. with offertory box of Hermaïstai in agora of the Competaliastai (above). Beside the offertory box is a marble stele (*CE* 86 no. 4; *IG* XI/4 1230).

114 *IG* XI/4 1216–1222 (= *CE* 84–85 no. 2A–G).

115 Cf. Deonna 1956:336.

116 Roussel, *CE* 29.

117 *Inopophylax/krenophylax* (Bruneau 1973:121–23).

118 White 1990:159, n. 30.

119 ibid.:160–61, n. 38.

120 ibid.:159–60, n. 31.

121 As White observes there is no description of the construction of the dining hall, but only of its decoration and outfitting (ibid.:161, n. 38).

122 ibid.:160, n. 32; on the phases of construction, 159, n. 31.

123 The *therapeutae* should be distinguished from the less frequently attested *therapeuontes* of Sarapeion A (*CE* 249, 253–54).

124 *CE* 254, n. 5. Elsewhere, some *therapeutae* are known to have rented apartments within the

sanctuary in order to be close to the deity (Apuleius, *Met.* 11.19.1). Very little is known about the purpose of the *therapeutae*. Vidman thinks they were simple worshipers united in a loose association (1970:69, 125–38); cf. *therapeutae* of Asclepius at Pergamon (Habicht 1969:114–15).

125 *melanēphoroi*; cf. Poland, s.v. *melanēphoroi*, *PW* 15:408–14; Wilcken 1927–57, 1:8, 19; Robert 1940–65, 6:9–10. Vidman suggests that the adoption of the term *synodos* in place of *koinon* as a designation of the association of *melanēphors* suggests a structural transformation (1970:72; cf. Heyob 1975:107).

126 *IG* XI/4 1227; *CE* 100 no. 25.

127 *IG* XI/4 2228, *CE* 101 no. 26.

128 *CE* 33–46; cf. *GD* no. 96.

129 *IG* XI/4 1240, 1243 (=*CE* 102 no. 28).

130 *CE* 34.

131 Adapted from *CE* 35, Pl. II.

132 Perhaps, Sarapis and Heros (*CE* 45–46).

133 *GD* 165 no. 124; Lemerle 1935:299–300; Orlandos 1936:84–86; Daux 1961:911–18; 1962:967–69.

134 *c.* 8.25 × 7.5 m, of eight columns (four *in situ*).

135 Narthex 4.05 × 4.03 m; chancel 3.18 × 4.03 m.

136 Orlandos 1936:71–82; *GD* 132 no. 86 (fig. 24); Vallois, *EAD* VII, Pt. 1, 3 no. XIV.

137 According to Bruneau (*GD*), the centre nave was for men, the two outside ones reserved for women. However, since the side chambers are only 1.70 m wide, and clearly served as passageways to the sanctuary, this seems unlikely.

138 Adapted from: *GD* 132 no. 86, fig. 24.

139 According to the legend which survives in several versions, Julitta, a widow of Iconium fled with her three-year-old son Kyrikos (Cyricus) to Tarsus where she and her son were tortured and finally executed (supposedly *c.* 304 CE). The cult had spread widely by the fourth century CE.

140 Contra Roussel, *DCA* 340 n. 4.

141 *ID* 2584 *bis*; Orlandos 1936:81 no. 1, fig. 13.

142 Reconstructed by Orlandos 1936:81, fig. 12.

143 For example, Paul's contrast of the Christian sacrificial meal with the sacrificial meals of the Graeco-Roman sacrifice suggests that he is describing not only a real, but superior sacrifice, in which the human–divine relationship was truly strengthened by a slaying. Just as the latter truly made the worshipers partners with demons, so the Christian sacrifice brings about an actual partnership with the Christ (1 Cor. 10:16–21). Similarly, the reference of Ignatius of Antioch to a Christian altar implies that the Eucharistic meal had sacrificial meaning: "Be careful, then, to observe a single Eucharist. For there is one flesh of our Lord, Jesus Christ, and one cup of his blood that makes *us* one, and one altar . . ." (Ignatius, *Phil.* 4.1–2); "Run off – all of you – to one temple of God, as it were, to one altar . . ." (Ignatius, *Magn.* 7.2).

144 e.g., Ignatius warns against those who "hold aloof from the Eucharist and from the service of prayer, because they refuse to admit that the Eucharist is the flesh of our Saviour Jesus Christ" (*Smyn.* 7.1).

145 We do not know by what term the Delian Christians referred to their altar. One might expect the term *bōmos* as in the case of altars in Graeco-Roman religion generally. However, this may not have been the case. Ignatius of Antioch refers to the Christian altar as a *thysiastērion* (*Phil.* 4.1; *Magn.* 7.2). Here, he is extending the established Christian and Septuagintal practice of using this same term for the altar of YHWH in Jerusalem (For example, Lev. 4:7, etc.; Matt. 5:23–24; 23:18–19, 35; Luke 11:51; 1 Cor. 9:13; 10:18; Heb. 7:13; Rev. 11:1; 1 Clem. 32:2; 41:2). In the Septuagint, only the altars of foreign gods are referred to as *bōmoi* (cf. 1 Macc. 1:59 for this distinction). However, by the first century

CE, this distinction is rarely observed among Jewish writers. Philo and Josephus regularly use *bōmos* to designate the Jewish altar (for example, Philo, *Spec. Leg.* 1.285ff.; *Vita Mosis* 2.106; Josephus, *Ant.* 8.88, 230).

146 e.g., overseers (bishops), deacons, apostles, prophets, teachers, miracle workers, healers, administrators, and presbyters (or "elders") (e.g., 1 Cor. 12:27–31; Eph. 2:19–21; Phil. 1:1; Acts 11:30; 15:2, 4, 6, 22–23; 16:4; 21:18).

147 e.g., Ignatius, *Phil.* preface; *Eph.* 2.2; *Magn.* 3.1, 6.1, 7.2, 13.1.

148 It was a term in use in other voluntary associations; cf. the Dionysiac *thiasos* named after its founder Ameinichos, headed by a "bishop/overseer" (*ID* 1522 8, 10, 17) who was responsible for proclaiming the honors bestowed upon benefactors.

12

JEWISH VOLUNTARY ASSOCIATIONS IN EGYPT AND THE ROLES OF WOMEN

Peter Richardson and Valerie Heuchan

One of the distinctive traits of social relations in Egypt, at least among the upper classes, is the more nearly equivalent roles of women and men. This is symbolized by the complementary roles of the Pharaoh and Queen,[1] roles recognized even by Jewish synagogues in Egypt.[2] Two Jewish groups in Egypt give evidence of the importance of women in their organizations. One is a celibate monastic group near Alexandria in which men and women participated equally, the other is a military temple-oriented community at Leontopolis, where women were involved in the priesthood.

THE TEMPLE COMMUNITY AT LEONTOPOLIS

Introduction

Tosefta *Menahot* 13.II.1 relates the following tradition about the founding of the temple of Onias at Leontopolis:

> When he [Simeon] was dying, he said to them, "My son Onias will serve in my place." Then his brother Shimei envied him, being older than he by two years and a half. He said to him, "Come, and I shall instruct you on the order of the Temple service." [Shimei] put on him a light gown and girded him with a girdle and set him up by the altar and then said to his brothers, the other priests, "See what this man has promised and carried out for his girlfriend: 'On the day on which I shall take up the office of high priest, I am going to put on your gown and gird myself with your girdle.'" His brothers the priests wanted to kill him [for coming to the altar in a woman's garments]. He fled from them and they pursued him. So he went off to Alexandria in Egypt and there he built an altar and presented on it burnt-offerings for idols.

Could this tradition connecting the cultic practice of Onias with women's garments be a reference to the presence of women priests at Leontopolis? This rather whimsical account differs substantially from the more believable accounts found in Josephus, 2 Maccabees, and the Mishnah. What is the origin of the tradition? One plausible explanation is to see it reflecting the involvement of women in cultic activities at Leontopolis. Priests connected with the temple of Onias wore women's garments. Why? Because some of them were women. This possibility, highly speculative when based only on the Talmud tradition, is corroborated by an inscription on a tombstone at the site. The inscription refers to Marin, called a priest:

> O Marin, *hierisa*, excellent one, friend of all, who caused pain to none, a friend to your neighbors, farewell. About 50 years old. In the third year of Caesar, Payni 13.
>
> (*CPJ* II 1514)

In the light of this inscription, it is possible to interpret the Talmud passage as mocking the practice of Onias' temple for including women among the priestly personnel. In what follows we review what is known about the community associated with the temple at Leontopolis and investigate the possibility of women priests at the site.

Background of the community according to Josephus

Among ancient authors, Josephus alone gives a detailed description of the Jewish community at Leontopolis and its temple. *War* and *Antiquities* give conflicting accounts of its origins. What is of importance for this paper is that Onias (III or IV?), being deprived of his right to the high priesthood, went to Alexandria, and, according to *War*, "being graciously received by Ptolemy, owing to that monarch's hatred of Antiochus, told him that he would make the Jewish nation his ally if he would accede to his proposal," which was to build a temple "somewhere in Egypt and to worship God after the manner of his fathers" (*War* 7.423–24). Ptolemy then gave him a tract of land in the nome of Heliopolis, where Onias erected a fortress and a temple, thus colonizing the district (*War* 7.421). This account implies that the area had not been settled prior to Onias' building of the fortress and temple. In *Antiquities* we are again told that while living in Alexandria Onias (here Onias IV) requested of Ptolemy and Cleopatra permission to build a temple in Egypt "similar to that at Jerusalem, and to appoint Levites and priests of his own race" (*Ant.* 13.63), but a letter purporting to be written from Onias to Ptolemy and Cleopatra gives different information from that presented in *War*:[3]

> Many and great are the services which I have rendered you in the course of the war, with the help of God, when I was in Coele-Syria and Phoenicia, and when I came with the Jews to Leontopolis in the nome of Heliopolis and to other places where our nation is settled; and I found that most of them have temples, contrary to what is proper, and that for this reason they are ill-disposed toward one another, as is also the case with the

Egyptians because of the multitude of their temples and their varying opinions about the forms of worship; and I have found a most suitable place in the fortress called after Bubastis-of-the-Fields, which abounds in various kinds of trees and is full of sacred animals, wherefore I beg you to permit me to cleanse this temple, which belongs to no one and is in ruins, and to build a temple to the Most High God in the likeness of that at Jerusalem and with the same dimensions, on behalf of you and your wife and children, in order that the Jewish inhabitants of Egypt may be able to come together there in mutual harmony and serve your interests.

(*Ant.* 13.65–7)

This letter suggests, first of all, that Onias was in the military service of Ptolemy and Cleopatra (possibly even before he went to Egypt),[4] and probably in a high position.[5] Onias was engaged in this service when he first went to Leontopolis, which location he suggested to Ptolemy as the site for a temple, rather than Ptolemy choosing it for him, as *War* implies. Further, in contrast to *War*, the letter suggests the possibility that prior to the building of the temple Leontopolis had already been settled by Jews, and Onias merely increased the population of the settlement by coming with more Jews, though it is also possible that Onias had already created a Jewish (military?) settlement prior to the writing of the letter and only added the Jewish temple later.[6] The passage tells us that a fortress and an Egyptian temple were already on the site.[7] Finally, the involvement of the Jews and Egyptians with numerous temples in the area is attested here, as well as the disputes amongst them over forms of worship. Onias expected that his temple would allow the Jews to come together in mutual harmony and serve the interests of Ptolemy and Cleopatra.

The origin of the community at Leontopolis lay in a military settlement,[8] of which Onias was the leader, to which a Jewish temple was added. It was intended to end religious disputes and unite Jews by serving all the Jews in the area surrounding it, and possibly even further abroad.

Archaeological remains

The site now known as Tel el-Yehudieh, 35 km north of Cairo in the Delta region, has been identified as the site of the temple of Leontopolis (see Figure 12.1).[9] A brick retaining wall surrounds the mound atop which the temple once stood. The temple was approached from the bottom of the hill by a large staircase on the eastern slope or from the north end where the slope was gentler, and an approach ran through an area of three or four acres which was most likely covered with houses. A road going from east to west led through the town and out to the cemetery (see below) and the desert (Petrie 1906:20–25).

At the time of Petrie's excavation only portions of the foundations of the temple walls remained, but Petrie was able to use these to reconstruct a conjectured plan of the temple. A very broad (about 65 feet wide) outer enclosure

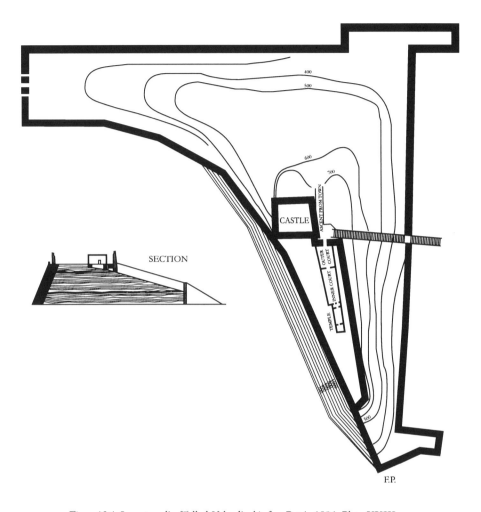

Figure 12.1 Leontopolis (Tell el-Yehudiyeh)after Petrie 1906: Plate XXIII

wall ran around the temple structures. Inside this wall is evidence of both an outer and an inner court. The outer court was wider at the front than at the back: 32 feet wide at the front and 27 feet at the back, with a length of 44 feet. The inner court is 27 feet wide in front, 21 feet wide at the back and 63 feet in length. The temple itself was rectangular, measuring 16.75 by 54.8 feet.[10] Little else can be known about its structure, except that a marble column was found which Petrie believes, based on its dimensions and material, to have been one of two columns supporting the porch (1906:22–26).

At the head of the stairway, Petrie discovered the foundation of a large rectangular building, about 52 by 73 feet, north-west of the temple. This seems to have been a defensive fortress, commanding a view of all the surrounding region, including the ascent up the stairway from the town and the entrance to the temple and its courts (1906:25).

Other finds on the site include capitals of Corinthian columns made of limestone and an ostrakon inscribed with the names Harkheb son of Zeho and Abram followed by the word "bricks." This leads to the conclusion that both Egyptians and Jews worked on the construction of the temple (Petrie 1906:26). There is also evidence of a siege: a number of limestone balls thrown by a ballista were found on the site, and the bricks of the wall on the east and the north sides, as well as the brick pier which would have supported the stairway are burnt. The ballistae are most likely from the Roman destruction of the temple in 73 CE since if they had been from an earlier siege they would not have been left around the site. Petrie also found "cylinders of pottery containing burnt offerings" in the base of the mound, usually a bed of white ashes of wood one to three inches thick with bones of lambs on top of the ashes (1906:22).

The community's military role

Some information can be gleaned about the nature of the community and the temple in the years between the building of the temple, around 160 BCE, and its closing by the Romans in 73 CE.

It was best known for its military role. Tcherikover points out that Onias led a force into Alexandria in support of Cleopatra after Philometor's death (1959:281). Chelkias and Ananias, Onias' descendants, also became generals for Cleopatra (*Ant.* 13.287). Particularly relevant for the Marin inscription, since the event occurred in her lifetime, is the encounter between Antipater's troops and the "Jews who occupied the district which took its name from Onias" (*War* 1.190 and *Ant.* 14.133), about 48 BCE. The Jews there at first barred the way of Antipater's forces but were then prevailed upon by Antipater to refrain from opposition and even to give him supplies.[11] It appears that in Marin's time the district of Onias was well populated and possessed military resources sufficient to bar the way of a force large enough to have taken Pelusium immediately beforehand (*War* 1.187–89).

The fact that the temple had to be closed in 73 CE by order of the Roman emperor suggests that its military as well as its religious importance was maintained up to this time. Josephus tells us:

> The emperor, suspicious of the interminable tendency of the Jews to revolution, and fearing that they might again collect together in force and draw others away with them, ordered Lupus to demolish the Jewish temple in the so-called district of Onias ... Lupus, the governor of Alexandria, on receipt of Caesar's letter repaired to the temple and, having carried off some of the votive offerings, shut up the building. Lupus dying soon after, Paulinus, his successor in office, completely stripped the place of its treasures, threatening the priests with severe penalties if they failed to produce them all, prohibited would-be worshipers from approaching the precincts, and, closing the gates, debarred all access, so as to leave thenceforth no vestige of divine worship on the spot.
>
> (*War* 7.421 and 433–35)

There would be little reason for the emperor or the governor to consider it necessary to close the temple at Leontopolis if it were insignificant in the life of the Jews of Egypt. The Roman officials must have been concerned that it could become a unifying institution for Egyptian Jews and a rallying point for those wishing to support the Jewish revolt. Moreover, the fact that it was necessary, even after Lupus had "shut up the building," for his successor to strip it completely, threaten the priests and force away those who wished to worship there, reveals that, even under persecution, the priests continued to keep it in operation and Jews continued to worship there. The account suggests that especially before the persecution and even after, it must have enjoyed vital importance for some Egyptian Jews. In fact, if the account is accurate, there must have been quite a large number of worshipers frequenting it for them to be a threat to Rome. It is possible that Josephus has exaggerated the details here, stressing the threat which the temple posed in order to emphasize the bravery and strength of the Jews. The discovery of limestone balls from ballistae and the burnt walls, however, support the outline of his account. They show that the temple was not overcome without military resistance, and therefore that there were people willing to defend it to the end so that a siege was necessary.

The community's cultic role

Leontopolis was a cultic community, rivaling Jerusalem. Information about cultic activities in the community can also be gleaned from archaeological, literary, and epigraphic evidence. Josephus tells us that the temple was staffed by Levites and priests of Onias' race (*Ant.* 13.63), perhaps a large number of them (*War* 7.430). As mentioned above, archaeological remains show evidence of animal sacrifices made there (Petrie 1906:22). The Mishnah, too, in referring briefly to the House of Onias, reveals its cultic practices:

[If he said,] "I pledge myself to offer a Whole-offering," he must offer it in the Temple. And if he offered it in the House of Onias he has not fulfilled his obligation. [If he said,] "I will offer it in the House of Onias," he should offer it in the Temple, but if he offered it in the House of Onias he has fulfilled his obligation ... If priests have ministered in the House of Onias they may not minister in the Temple in Jerusalem; still more does this apply to [priests who have ministered in] that other matter; for it is written, "Nevertheless the priests of the high places came not up to the altar of the Lord in Jerusalem, but they did eat unleavened bread among their brethren"; thus they were like them that have a blemish; they may share and they may eat [of the Holy Things] but they may not offer sacrifice.

(*m. Men.* 13.10)

Here it is declared acceptable to sacrifice at Leontopolis as long as the worshiper did not pledge to make the offering in the Jerusalem temple. This ruling, while not necessarily indicating an opinion about the legitimacy of the House of Onias on the part of the Jerusalem leaders, indicates that people were indeed offering sacrifices at Leontopolis. The Jerusalem leaders found themselves in the position of having to decide how to treat these sacrifices. The ruling shows that the Jerusalem leaders did not express unrelieved opposition to Leontopolis. The passage continues by saying that priests who have ministered in the House of Onias may no longer minister in the Jerusalem temple, although they do not thereby lose their levitical status. For this to be an issue priests must actually have come from the House of Onias and desired to minister in the Jerusalem temple. This was probably not an isolated incident, considering that the ruling was preserved until the compilation of the Mishnah. This point is important. First, it suggests that the Leontopolis temple was probably in regular operation for quite some time. Second, it shows that it continued to employ regular levitical priests for its operations, priests who could claim legitimacy on Jerusalem's criteria. *m. Men.* 13.10 reveals an interesting interplay between the two temples. The worship and priesthood at Leontopolis were not considered illegitimate by Jerusalem, simply inferior. Third, this situation underscores that the disqualifying element has to do with the rivalry between Jerusalem and Leontopolis, not with the conditions of service or worship.

The community's social and religious character

Leontopolis was a Jewish community with evidence of some assimilation to the surrounding culture. North-east of the temple, remains of an underground Jewish cemetery, which was excavated by E. Naville late last century, were found. According to Naville, the plan of the tombs was unlike that of usual Egyptian tombs, but closely resembled tombs found in Phoenicia and Judaea, where they are known as *fours à cercueils*.[12] Even though both Greek and Hebrew names appear on the stelae in the tombs in almost equal numbers, together with a few

Egyptian names, the arrangement of the tombs and remains of the bodies suggest that the tombs were for Jews. Several fathers with Egyptian names gave Hebrew names to their children (*CPJ* I 145). In one of the inscriptions the deceased responds to the question of her country of birth, "the famous land of Onias reared me" (*CPJ* II 1530). In most of the inscriptions the deceased is addressed in the vocative, followed by *chaire*, "farewell," and the epithet *chrsēte*, "excellent one," and *aore*, "untimely dead." The content of the stelae suggests no dominant religious or cultural outlook, most particularly no predominantly Jewish content, but neither is there any other notable leaning.[13]

Kasher analyzes the structure of the community based largely on evidence from the funerary inscriptions. The size of the cemetery and the valuable nature of the findings indicated that the community was large and economically well-established. The plots were allocated for family tombs and various qualities of rock in different sections of the catacombs suggests that there were "good" and "bad" sections. Kasher postulates that the community may have had a burial society which solved allocation problems (1985:123).

Other evidence for the formal organization of the city comes from two inscriptions, *CPJ* III 1450, and *CPJ* III 1530A. The reconstructed reading of inscription 1450 discusses a decision (*psephismata*) by the *plēthos* of the sacred district. This vocabulary agrees with that in the *Letter of Aristeas* used to refer to a *politeuma*, leading Kasher to conclude that Leontopolis was also a *politeuma*. Further evidence comes from inscription 1530A in which a man named Abramos is named the *politarchēs* of two places, a title known to have been used in Egypt for the city governor, subordinate to the *stratēgos* of the nome (1985:125). This inscription sheds light on the community organization of Leontopolis and the presence of a Jewish *politarchēs* suggests that its administration was by Jews. Abramos is said to wear "the wreath of magistracy for the whole people (*ethnikē*)," vocabulary fitting the ethnic criterion for the formation of a *politeuma* and the term applied to the Jewish community in Alexandria. Kasher concludes that Alexandria and Leontopolis seem to have both been organized as *politeumata* (1985:127). Further evidence of the organized nature of Leontopolis comes from other vocabulary found in the inscriptions, such as the plea that both "citizens and strangers" weep for Rachelis (*CPJ* III 1513), and Theon's claim to have been a "friend to all the citizens" and "renowned in council (*boulaisin*)" (*CPJ* III 1489). Perhaps Josephus himself considered Leontopolis a *politeuma*. According to Borgen, a *politeuma* was "confirmation by the king that an ethnic community was permitted – within limits – to live in accordance with its ancestral laws" (1992:1063). This description is strikingly similar to Josephus' account of the correspondence between Onias and Ptolemy. Onias requests permission of Ptolemy to build a temple to the Most High God "in order that the Jewish inhabitants of Egypt may be able to come together there in mutual harmony" (*Ant.* 13.67). Even though this correspondence is likely a fabrication of Josephus, he may be reflecting the perception (and perhaps reality) of the legal community status of Leontopolis.

This community is the context for the temple of Onias. Would such an institution have been viewed as a voluntary association? It is possible that it would have been, serving the needs of the Jewish *ethnē* in the military and cultic community. In Egypt associations usually met in a public temple (Ferguson 1987:108). Greek terms and Egyptian names in the building records of the temple and in the inscriptions at the catacombs show that Greeks and Egyptians probably also lived in the vicinity and had an influence on its culture. The Jewish temple would probably have been only one religious option in the area. Ferguson notes that foreigners in particular formed associations in Rome, in which they maintained their national identity by adherence to their own deity (1987:107). The Jews in Leontopolis, initially foreigners, would likely have been viewed as setting up their own religious association. Perhaps the organization of the catacombs was part of the work of the temple association, since most associations assumed funerary obligations.

On the other hand, if Kasher's analysis of the community as a *politeuma* is correct, the above interpretation is less tenable. The function of a *politeuma* was to create a community of people who shared the same identity. If Leontopolis was a *politeuma* according to this definition it would have had only one religious affiliation, Judaism. If this were so, and the temple was the focal point of their religious expression, the temple would probably not have been viewed as a voluntary association. Instead it would have been an integral part of the life of every member of the community.

Ultimately there is not enough information to determine the status of the temple. We can know for certain neither the cultural composition of the community (perhaps the Greek and Egyptian names simply reflect linguistic and cross-cultural influences) nor its structure. One way to reconcile the possibilities would be to posit that the Jewish community is one sector of Leontopolis (perhaps modeling their organization on the *politeuma* at Alexandria), the whole being comprised of other groups, such as Greeks and native Egyptians as well. In this scenario the temple of Onias may have been viewed by those outside of the Jewish community as a voluntary association.

The Marin inscription and the meaning of *hierisa*

Activity at Leontopolis for most of its life probably revolved largely around the Jewish temple and the military. Traditionally, then, women would not be expected to have had a large role in the administration of the city. The Marin inscription found in the catacombs at Leontopolis, however, indicates otherwise. Marin's designation *hierisa* has traditionally been translated "of priestly descent" on the grounds that no Jewish woman could be a priest.[14] There is good evidence, however, that the term should in fact be translated "priest" (Brooten 1982:78–83).

Hierisa[15] is the Greek equivalent of *kohenet*, a rabbinic term used to denote a woman who has either been born into a priestly family and is unmarried or one who has married a priest. "Such an identification," Brooten states, "would in no way imply congregational leadership or a cultic function, other than the right to eat the priestly offerings." Thus it is possible that the term simply designates Marin as the daughter or wife of a priest and that she had no cultic function in Onias' temple. For a number of reasons, however, it is not sufficient to accept this reading of the term as definitive in Marin's case.

As Brooten points out, the more common translation of *hierisa* in the Graeco-Roman world is "priest," and in any context other than a Jewish one "no scholar would have thought of arguing that 'priest' does not really mean 'priest.' The composers of [this inscription] must have been aware that they were employing a term which normally implied a cultic function" (1982:99). *Hierisa* appears not to have been as common as *hiereia*, which also designated a priestess, but there are some examples of it, including a Roman Jew, Gaudentia, designated *hierisa* (*CIJ* 315) and two uses of it in lists of Egyptian priesthoods, where *hierisson* are listed alongside *athlophorēs*, *hieron* and *canephorēs* (*P. Lond.* 880 and *BGU* 994). In Egypt, women designated *hierisa* and *hiereia* had definite cultic roles, both in indigenous Egyptian and in Hellenistic religious organizations (this will be discussed in detail below).[16] Finally there is an example in which a Jewish inscription uses the expression *Maria hē tou hiereos* to designate the wife or daughter of a priest (Brooten 1982:96). If the term *hierisa* were commonly known as the term for wife/daughter of a priest it would be highly unusual for someone to use this much more cumbersome expression for the same idea. Moreover, as Brooten points out, the expression shows "that there was a way in Greek to express such a relationship without this title [*hierisa*] which a Greek speaker would have understood as meaning 'female cultic functionary'" (1982:97).

Further evidence comes from the cultic roles of women in both Jewish and Hellenistic Egyptian religion. There are no examples in the Septuagint where *hierissa* is used and the only place where *hiereia* is used it denotes a religious assembly. There are a number of passages, however, which refer to women filling a cultic role. In both Exod. 38:8 and 1 Sam. 2:22 the same root, ŜMŜ is used for the service of women as is used for levitical service in the Tabernacle (Peritz 1898:145–46). The Targum of Judges 5:24 refers to Jael, the wife of Heber, as similar to one of the women who minister in the houses of learning. Again the word "minister" is the same as that used of the ministry of the high priest and the common priests (Brooten 1982:86). Miriam's descent is traced back to Levi (Num. 26:59; 1 Chron. 6:3) and she is also viewed as a prophet. Miriam, like Samuel, may be an example of the fusion of the offices of prophet and priest (Peritz 1898:143–44). According to Peritz, these examples of Jewish women who served a cultic function are precedents for the participation of women in priestly functions in Judaism. We wish to argue that the temple at Leontopolis participated in this tradition. The Jews at Leontopolis were a priestly community in a new setting, far from Jerusalem, and they would likely have done independent exegesis of biblical texts in defining their identity in their new cultic situation. They may particularly have adopted the Miriam tradition as a model for the women of their community since, like themselves, Miriam was closely connected with Egypt.

The possibility becomes even stronger when one looks at the priestly roles of women in classical and Hellenistic Egyptian religion. There is no question that women played a large part in cultic activities in Egypt, both in the indigenous and Ptolemaic cults. *Hiereia*, the more common term for priestess,[17] occurs in thirty-one documents from Roman Egypt, referring to priestesses of both indigenous Egyptian and Hellenistic religion (for example, Anubis, Isis). One of the more prominent roles played by *hiereiai* is that of musician–priestess. According to Blackman, "all temples in Ptolemaic times had musician–priestesses attached to them" (1921:8). Blackman gives this description of the cultic role of the musician–priestesses of the goddess Hathor:

> These musician–priestesses, when dancing and rattling their sistra in her worship, consciously impersonated the goddess ... During their performances they held out their sistra and bead-necklaces for their onlookers to touch, so imparting to them the blessing of the goddess ... The worshipers of Hathor were not merely brought into contact with her in the persons of her priestesses, but she was regarded as actually immanent also in her emblems, the sistra and bead-necklaces.
>
> (1921:14)

The musician–priestesses, then, played an important cultic role, since they symbolized the presence of the goddess in the temple. Further, inscriptions at Edfu record the name of a female officiant immediately after the high priest of the nome. Blackman comments: "that the title of the female officiant should appear side by side with that of the high-priest indicates that she occupied the same position among the women who served in the temple, i.e. the musician–priestesses, as he did among the men, and quite justifies our speaking of her as a high-priestess" (1921:9–10). Women, then, played leadership roles in Egyptian religion.

Robins comments that in the New Kingdom, women were linked to the temple cult in the role of *shemayet*, musician, a title employed by large numbers of elite women. She notes, "except for 'mistress of the house,' it must be the commonest title found for women in the Theban tombs" (1993:145). Troupes of musicians, consisting of both men and women, were in the charge of a woman called "great one of the troupe of musical performers," who was the wife of one of the high officials, or the chief priest. Robins suggests that the "great one of the musical troupe" may have been responsible for the training, practice, and rotas of the performers and for ensuring all went well during the ritual (1993:148–49). She stresses that in the New Kingdom, a distinction was made between the roles of men and women in the temple cult, with women's roles being limited to the musical aspects of worship. This does not mean, however, that their role was low-ranking. On the contrary, the "great one of the musical troupe" was of high status, and "male singers and musicians usually remained

anonymous, and clearly ranked lower than female singers from elite families"
(1993:149).

While the bulk of the evidence suggests that women's cultic role was primarily musical, there is some indication that it was not limited to music. Dunand sees
two roles for women in association with temples, one musical, one "composée
de femmes ayant une fonction sacerdotale analogue à celle des prêtres"
(1978:353–54). In one example a high priestess is depicted as pouring out a liba-
tion, in another Princess Nebttowi at Thebes is consecrating the offering. In the
Ptolemaic period women made funeral libations (Blackman 1921:25–26). Both
Dunand and Blackman interpret the evidence as indicative that women in many
cases performed the same daily temple liturgical duties as did male priests.[18]

The role of women in the priesthood in Egypt seems to have been influenced
by the roles of women monarchs. In Egyptian custom the pairing of the king
and queen was central. Because monarchs were also important cultic figures,
queens had priestly positions alongside their husbands. Blackman gives an example from pre-dynastic Egypt:

> [The] king of Heliopolis was high-priest of the sun-god and was also re-
> garded as his embodiment – Horus. The Heliopolitan queen, as wife of
> the sun-god's high-priest, would have acted as the sun-god's high-
> priestess, and would also surely have been identified with the goddess
> Hathor the sun-god's wife, both in her capacity of high-priestess and also
> in that of wife of the embodiment of the sun-god.
>
> (1921:12)

In the eighteenth dynasty, some royal women bore the title "god's wife of
Amun," for example the wife of king Ahmose, Hatshepsut, and her daughter
Neferura. The god's wife had an active role in temple ritual, as scenes from the
chapelle rouge of Hatshepsut show, and she, like male priests, entered the sanctuary
of the god (Robins 1993:151–52).

In Ptolemaic Egypt, too, it was customary for both a king and queen, often
brother and sister, to hold the throne. In many cases the monarchs were deified
and this led to other priestly positions for women. Ptolemy Philopator, for example, inaugurated a special cult in honor of his mother Berenice II and a new
eponymous priesthood, reserved for women, was created, the holder entitled *ath-
lophore*. There were other offices for women connected with female monarchs,
such as the priestess of Arsinoe Philopator and the *canephore* of Arsinoe Philadelphus (Pomeroy 1984:55–57). Egyptian priestesses apparently came from all
social classes and age was no limitation. Inscriptions record priestesses from the
age of 15 to 79 (Dunand 1978:361–62). Two priestesses are called *agrammatos*
(Dunand 1978:362) and two were the wives of weavers (Blackman 1921:22).
This last example, as well as indicating the social standing of the priestesses,
shows that they did not need to be connected with male priests, as wives or
daughters, in order to be priestesses. Dunand concludes that although there is
evidence that priests were more numerous than priestesses in Egypt, there were

many priestesses and they assumed analogous functions to those of their male colleagues, both in classical and Ptolemaic Egypt. He states that Egyptian women, "bénéficient de droits et d'avantages comparables à ceux des hommes ... Contrairement à la pratique de la plupart des sociétés antiques, leur situation apparaît presque comme une situation d'égalité" (1978:373–74). In Roman Egypt, Cleopatra is an example of the power a woman could hold. She held undisputed and sole power for a long portion of her reign, and demonstrates the degree to which women had opportunities open to them that were not contemplated in many other places.[19]

Assimilation of the Jewish community at Leontopolis

There is evidence of considerable assimilation of the Jews in Egypt to the ways of Egyptian religion, for example, documents and charms that mention the names both of the Jewish God and of various Egyptian and Greek gods in the same item. One example has a prayer to Zeus, Sarapis, and the Jewish God; another to Apollo, God, Michael, and Gabriel (Feldman 1960:232–34). The catacombs at Leontopolis themselves show some evidence of Jewish assimilation. One mentions that the departed is in Hades (*CPJ* III 1511), and one refers to the "shadowy region of Lethe" (*CPJ* III 1530). Even if, as may be possible, this vocabulary is simply that of a hired Greek poet, as the note accompanying *CPJ* III 1530 suggests, it, as well as the Egyptian names in other inscriptions, indicates the presence of non-Jews in the Leontopolis community, who would doubtless have influenced the practices of the Jews there.

This evidence for Egyptian priestesses and for assimilation of Jews in Egypt to Egyptian religious practices provides a plausible background for the claim that the temple at Leontopolis had priestesses. The *Talmudic* account of the escape of Onias from Jerusalem provides further support. The prime reason for opposition to Onias is his connection with the wearing of feminine garments during cultic practice. Perhaps the passage expresses rabbinic censure of Onias' temple because it included women in its priestly personnel.

The preceding points provide support that Marin's appellation *hierisa* indicates that she was in fact a temple functionary at Leontopolis. Unfortunately there is no indication from the inscription just what her role might have been, but, given the functions of priestesses in Egypt, it is possible that her role involved music or other daily temple duties, such as pouring libations or preparing sacrifices.

While it may initially seem implausible that Onias' temple, founded by one who held the position of high priest of the Jerusalem temple, could stray so far from Jewish orthodoxy as to have female priests, one can envision a gradual progression away from Jerusalem practice. In Egyptian practice, it was common for the priesthood to involve various members of one family. There is evidence that in some cases the office of high priestess in a temple was held by the wife of the high priest (Blackman 1921:10). In an inscription at Edfu the wife of the nomarch and high priest was the high priestess. It may be that in an Egyptian setting where it was natural for the wives or daughters of temple officiants to become involved in cultic practice, the priests at Leontopolis, after some time there, shared in this practice. The Marin inscription indicates that Marin was born in 77 BCE. By the time she would have been old enough to be a priestess, roughly 100 years had passed since the founding of the temple, and perhaps a little more since the founding of the community which supported it. This would provide plenty of time for assimilation of Egyptian practices. Further, it is possible that the many other Jewish temples in the vicinity at the time when Onias built his temple (*Ant.* 13.66), already had women priests. It is quite plausible, then, that the transition to the participation of women priests in Leontopolis would be an easy and natural one, of which Marin is an example. Perhaps cultural influences such as these, in combination with awareness of women serving in ancient Judaism, as reflected in passages such as Exod. 38:8 and 1 Sam. 2:22, pushed the Jews at Leontopolis to include women as priests as they developed religious practice in their community.

THERAPEUTAE AND THERAPEUTRIDES AT LAKE MAREOTIS

The Therapeutae/Therapeutrides formed a group known only from a lengthy and enthusiastic account in Philo.[20] Curiously, Eusebius quotes Philo's description extensively and applies it to his treatment of first-century Christians (see Richardson 1993). It seems likely that Philo's account is first-hand,[21] for the group has its principal and perhaps its only community across Lake Mareotis[22] from Alexandria.[23] He describes a number of important features of the Therapeutae, some of which are common to associations. The relevant features can be briefly listed.

1 In his introductory description "of these philosophers," and in several later references, Philo refers to the group as a *proairesis* – a word of broad meaning from "choosing" and "purpose" through to "opinion," including "sect" or "political party" or "school" of music or philosophy.[24] In several of the instances, though not in all, *proairesis* clearly implies something like a "sect." Philo also refers to them as a *systēma* (72) – a "college" or "association." This was a lifelong commitment, for new members sought "never to leave their place in this company" (12) and they gave up their property to their children or relatives, "thinking their mortal life already ended" (13, cf. 18).

2 Philo says that those who desire "justice" and "equality" (*dikaiosynē* and *isotētos*, 17) fled from society, especially to Lake Mareotis where there was a community of farm buildings (22–23) or "houses collected together" (24).[25] In Philo's opinion they were separated from the city, having joined a community and were now sharing a common purpose.

3 Each house had a *hieron/semneion*, a "shrine" in which persons were "initiated" into the "mysteries" of the sanctified life (*en hoi monoumenoi ta tou semnou biou*

mystērion telountai, 25), language that points to a voluntary association with initiatory rites and ritual provision for daily life, though much of that daily life was solitary rather than associative.

4 A number of distinct activities set the group apart: use of laws and oracles, dream activity, prayer, meditation and contemplation, reading and interpretation of scripture, singing of hymns and psalms, seventh-day assemblies, hierarchical seating, and so on (25–31).

5 The community *qua* community had a common sanctuary (*koinon semneion*, 32) with distinctive architectural features, used for meetings of the whole group, both male and female members.

6 Common meals (64–82), sharply contrasting with Roman and Greek meals (48–63), were an important feature of the group's activities. These occurred weekly, and in a special form every seventh week (65).

7 There was a sacred vigil (83–89), complementing the special festal meal every seventh week.

These elements, some definitional, some functional, leave little doubt that most Greeks or Romans observing such a group would have thought of it as a voluntary association – a collegia or a *thiasos*. There are, however, no references to other features – provision for burials, a patron or patroness – that might ordinarily have been found in certain types of voluntary associations.[26] But there are sufficient indications to suggest that the community was perceived as a voluntary association and may have perceived itself in the same way. What is more, its buildings, as described by Philo, gave built form to the unusual character of this association: a rare balance between private reflection and group activities that was a precursor for one form of Christian monasticism.[27]

There were no close contemporary parallels for this set of community buildings: synagogues and Christian monasteries came later, Qumran was contemporary but not similar in certain important respects, and most contemporary mystery religions known to us made no provision for living on the spot and in a withdrawn location.[28] We are faced here with a very unusual community, and an important one when sketching the religious variations of the Graeco-Roman and Jewish worlds.

Activities

Each day the Therapeutae prayed twice a day, at dawn and at evening (27–28). Between these times they contemplated scripture as allegory and studied the writings of their founders. They also composed hymns and psalms "in all sorts of metres and melodies," hymns suitable for processions or in libations at the altars or for the choruses. This daily activity occupied them for six days during which they ate and drank only at night, some eating only every third day and others abstaining for seven days.

On the seventh day there was a general assembly (30). The *presbytatos* gave a discourse, they ate common bread flavored with salt and hyssop, and drank water.

On the fiftieth day they were called by the *ephēmereutai* (65–66) to line up in an orderly manner and pray.[29] The *presbyteroi* reclined in rows (75) according to rank. The *proedros* discussed a question arising from scripture or one propounded by a member, treating the scripture allegorically (77–78). Then the young male attendants brought in food on tables, following which was a sacred all-night vigil (77, 81, 83). After this they all departed to their houses or cubicles to repeat the fifty-day cycle again.

Therapeutrides

As compared with Qumran[30] the most outstanding feature – apart from the different architectural provisions for life and worship – is the careful attention paid to women, the Therapeutrides.[31] In the activities described above, women had parallel, equal, and almost identical activities. While there may still be a touch of condescension or surprise in Philo's reaction to this group, what he describes offers a rare glimpse into a group in which women could be involved based on principles of equality. The Lake Mareotis community stood apart from similar religious communities dominated typically either by males (Qumran, Mithraea, most collegia) or by females (Demeter and Kore).[32] The group carried on a radical experiment in a withdrawn communal life of contemplation, characterized by equal rights and more or less equal leadership. The main features pertaining to women were these:

1 Though Philo begins in paragraph 1 referring to the "virtue of these men" he immediately thereafter refers to "Therapeutae and Therapeutrides." He does not comment on the pairing of masculine and feminine names for the group and he only once again uses the paired names, being more interested in their etymological derivation from either "heal" or "worship."[33] He certainly does not mean to imply two separate groups, for everything that follows, including the architectural and the liturgical arrangements, argues strongly for an integrated organization in which male and female were joined in an equal "fellowship." In using the separate names Philo does not drive a wedge between the two halves of the group, but uses the two forms merely in a grammatically appropriate fashion to distinguish between male and female members. Nevertheless this separate nomenclature is perhaps evidence of the unusual position women occupied.[34]

2 Between his opening reference to "men" and his reference to the two forms of the name Philo speaks of the members as "philosophers." This implies, as a couple of later passages also imply (for example, 89), that women were therefore philosophers, if not in the full Greek sense of the term at least in Philo's use of the term. To our knowledge, at the time Philo is writing only Musonius Rufus argued in the same direction.[35]

3 The seventh-day meetings (32–33; no doubt Sabbath, but this is never said) included women as equals,[36] a striking departure from synagogue practice.[37] An impression of a degree of inequality still remains in the presence – and the explanation – of the dividing wall between the sexes, the purposes of which were modesty and ease of listening. Philo seems to assume that the speakers were all male and that the open space was to enable women to hear what the men are saying. In the following descriptions, however, of food, drink, clothes, and housing (34–39) no concessions are made to any differences between men and women.[38]

4 After a long digression on feasts in pagan society (40–63) Philo turns to the community's fiftieth-day assembly that included a banquet (64–65),[39] stressing that the members of the community were "disciples" of "the prophet Moses" (64). "The feast is shared by women also, most of them aged virgins who have kept their chastity not under compulsion, like some of the Greek priestesses, but of their own free will . . ."(68).[40] Men were separated to the right and women to the left, yet that women joined with the men was the fundamental fact that must not be overlooked. Philo also describes how young male members of the community, not slaves, served the guests at the banquet.[41] Extended exposition and singing followed, punctuated by frequent chanting of closing choruses (80), during all of which men and women equally participated.[42]

5 In the vigil that followed the feast (83–89) the members formed two antiphonal choirs – one male, one female – in the middle of the dining room (*symposion*), each with its own leader and precentor. Philo makes it sound similar to a Shaker meeting,[43] a Pentecostal Assembly, or a southern church, with clapping and stomping and complex rising and falling harmonies, perhaps accompanied by wheeling dances.[44] All then joined together as a single mixed choir, "a copy of the choir set up of old beside the Red Sea in honor of the wonders there wrought" (85),[45] "so filled with ecstasy, both men and women, that forming a single choir they sang hymns of thanksgiving to God their Savior, the men led by the prophet Moses and the women by the prophetess Miriam" (87). Finally, Philo uses again the names "Therapeutae" and "Therapeutrides," here of this mixed choir, "the treble of the women blending with the basses of the men, [to] create an harmonious consent,[46] music in the truest sense." When dawn comes after their all-night singing and prayer each goes off again to his or her private sanctuary to pursue philosophy.

This was a voluntary association; unlike most voluntary associations, however, the Therapeutae/Therapeutrides formed a residential community with common meeting hall and dining room, and monastic living-*cum*-contemplative cells. The residents lived ascetic lives focused on private six-day contemplation as "philosophers," with weekly meetings of the whole group and a pentecostal feast, characterized by exposition, singing, dancing, prayer, and a night-long vigil. Women and men were equal.[47] There were almost no gender-determined roles though it is possible that most leaders and the servants at the banquet were males. There were no gender-typed roles for women. They did exactly the same things as men, having similar cells for contemplation, defined but equal space in the meeting room, and common though defined dining facilities.[48] In their choral activities men and women had completely equal and parallel roles, but it is not so clear whether this equality extended also to the spoken word. The Therapeutae had a leader who was "the prophet Moses"; the Therapeutrides were led by "the prophetess Miriam."[49] In matters of leadership, then, it is clear that there was an exact parallelism, founded on a brother and sister who played key roles in Israel's ancient history in Egypt, though we cannot say what this leadership involved. The choice of names for the leaders must have been quite deliberate.

The origins of the Therapeutae/Therapeutrides

How did a group such as this develop such equivalence? We want briefly to speculate that there were two likely sources of inspiration for the shape the Therapeutae/Therapeutrides eventually took. One likely source was the cult of Isis–Osiris, an active and influential religion during exactly this period, in which a brother and sister played the crucial roles;[50] some features of this cult reflect features of our group.[51] A second likely source was the Bible, specifically some of the stories about Moses and Miriam, another brother–sister pair with strong associations with Egypt.[52] Several features of the Biblical narratives might have prompted scriptural exegetes interested in Miriam and Moses to adapt these elements to their community needs.[53] In what follows we will briefly suggest that we should look to both these Egyptian sources – to a creative blending of certain features of each of them individually – for the impetus to create this form of community life based on a radical equality between women and men.[54]

First, Isis–Osiris. (a) In the wonderful wall-painting at Herculaneum of the cult of Isis meeting at dawn to offer sacrifice, there are two choirs ranged up either side of the stairs, apparently singing. A precentor or leader directs the choirs in the middle distance. Though the two choirs are mixed groups of males and females, the picture suggests the antiphonal choirs of the Therapeutae who are arranged partly in two separate choirs and partly as a mixed choir.[55] (b) Like the worship of Isis, the Therapeutae's worship of the God of Israel culminated in a dawn choral celebration.[56] Other similar features include: (c) the Egyptian provenance, (d) the language of initiation, (e) the provision in some instances for living within the precincts,[57] (f) dream activity, (g) celibacy, (h) periodic abstention from wine. But most important, there was a general similarity in the roles of women in the Isis cult: in some areas women participated as men did, including various priestly and lay roles,[58] and there is in some cases a rough equivalence of numbers.[59]

Second, we suggest that while some aspects of the Therapeutae may be understood against the background of the Isis cult, the Therapeutae is still a genuinely Jewish group that is something more than just a Jewish aping of an

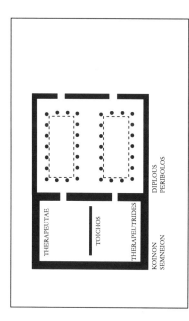

Figure 12.2 Therapeutae: Schematic Community

INDIVIDUAL HOUSES

COMMUNAL FACILITIES

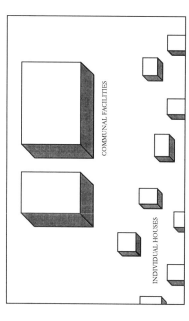

Figure 12.3 Therapeutae: Schematic "House"

MONASTERION

SEMNEION

VESTIB

GARDEN/COURTYARD

OIKIA/OIKEMA

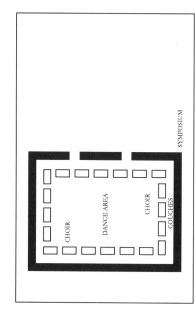

Figure 12.4 Therapeutae: Schematic Assembly Room

THERAPEUTAE

TOICHOS

THERAPEUTRIDES

KOINON
SEMNEION

DIPLOUS
PERIBOLOS

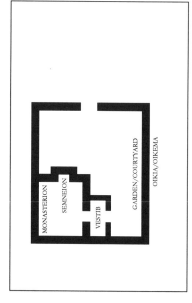

Figure 12.5 Therapeutae: Schematic Banquet Room

CHOIR

DANCE AREA

CHOIR

COUCHES

SYMPOSIUM

Egyptian cult. It draws its inspiration from Israel's ancient history. Several features of the Biblical narratives might have prompted scriptural exegetes concerned for traditions about Egypt and especially about Miriam and Moses to create this form of community life based on a radical equality between women and men.

(a) The core tradition of Miriam refers to her as a *prophetess* (Exod 15:20–21).[60] In this famous incident, set beside the Red Sea, she *danced* and *sang* to the Lord.[61] (b) Miriam was, of course, firmly rooted in *Egypt* from birth through childhood (Exod 2:4–8)[62] and adulthood. She died at Kadesh according to one tradition (Num 20:1)[63] before she could enter the Promised Land, in this respect like her brother Moses. (c) She had no children (Num 26:59); indeed she is never described as being married.[64] Though she is not referred to as a virgin in any surviving sources, she might almost have qualified as an aged virgin. (d) In the dramatic passage in Num. 12:1–15 Miriam and Aaron ganged up on Moses, claiming that the Lord had spoken to them as well as to him. When the Lord became angry and Miriam was afflicted with leprosy, Moses interceded for her and she was *healed* after seven days in the *wilderness*.[65] (e) In Philo's description of the Therapeutae only Moses and Miriam appear as prophet and prophetess. This unusual pairing of the two of them deliberately leaves Aaron to one side,[66] probably because he was the progenitor of the priesthood. At the Lake Mareotis community priesthood is barely in view,[67] unlike Qumran.[68]

In sum, the Biblical record describes Miriam as a prophetess who danced and sang to the Lord (Exod. 15:20–21) at the Red Sea (Exod. 15:23) and who spoke on behalf of the Lord (Num. 12:1–15). She had to live outside the camp for seven days before being healed (Num. 12:1–15). She was a co-leader with Moses and Aaron (Mic. 6:4) and perhaps she was an aged virgin.

We suggest that this Egyptian ascetic community in which women were so important reflected the Biblical accounts of Moses and especially of Miriam. The reason there was no reference to Aaron, and the merest glancing reference to priests, is that this was a prophetic community, not a priestly one; a non-priestly community looking for antecedents would naturally have fastened on Moses.[69] What was unusual in the case of the Therapeutae/Therapeutrides is that Miriam was paired with Moses; indeed, more of the features of the life of the community were taken from Miriam's side of the story than from Moses'. But it was a community that owed something to Egyptian religion also, specifically the Isis cult, in some of the liturgical, practical, and behavioral details of the life of the community.[70] The Miriam–Moses relationship in the leadership of the Therapeutae was especially reflective of the Egyptian setting where Isis–Osiris and the Pharaohs with their sister–consorts provided models for the strong role of Miriam. In the end, then, the leadership role claimed for the Miriam figure among the Therapeutae/Therapeutrides, though hinted at in the Bible, cannot be derived from Judaism but must be attributed in part to local influences in Egypt.[71]

SUMMARY

In two Jewish communities in Egypt, the Therapeutae and Leontopolis, women appear to have held central positions in religious life. Among the Therapeutae, women were the virtual equals of men. While this was highly unusual in Judaism at the time in which these communities flourished, it was not altogether unusual in an Egyptian setting, where women commonly held priestly and even high-priestly positions. Pomeroy attributes the high status of women in Egypt largely to a reduction in the polarity between the sexes, which in turn was caused by the monarchy, where "on the highest level, queens are to be found in the traditionally male spheres of government and warfare" (1984:xvii–xviii). Women in Egypt shared power with men in religious spheres. This sharing of power between king and queen, who also were often brother and sister, dovetails with a Jewish tradition about Moses and Miriam, a tradition also connected with Egypt. The practices of the Therapeutae/Therapeutrides and of the community at Leontopolis reduced the polarity between the sexes, with men and women at both sites sharing cultic activities. This equality, we suggest, was the result of, on the one hand, assimilation to the Egyptian environment and, on the other, interpretation of an important Jewish tradition, Moses and Miriam leading the Jews out of Egypt. Both groups, then, could view themselves as distinctly and purely Jewish.

Further, we have argued, strongly in the case of the Lake Mareotis community and less strongly in the case of the Leontopolis community, that both would have been viewed by their neighbors and by themselves as voluntary associations. In differing ways and differing degrees, the buildings, the organizational structure, the activities, and the communal features would have suggested that these were communities with distinctive and strong associative characteristics, though in both cases open to others joining them after proper initiation.

NOTES

1 "Egypt is accustomed to put up with a queen and to make no distinction of sex"; Lucan, *Civil War* 10.91–92.
2 On the important "house of prayer" inscriptions, see Peter Richardson, chapter 6 in this volume.
3 The authenticity of this letter is widely disputed. We will not try to solve this problem here, but will assume that whether or not Onias is the author of the letter it reflects a different tradition about the community and its temple from that presented in *War* and will deal with the tradition as such.
4 The allusion to Coele-Syria implies that Onias was sympathetic to Egypt's interests in the region during the troubled days in the early second century BCE.
5 As is confirmed in *Ag. Apion* 2.49, where it is stated that Ptolemy and Cleopatra placed their whole army under the control of the generals Onias and Dositheus, both Jews.
6 Possibly he was in the military service of Ptolemy and Cleopatra even before he settled in Egypt. This would be one explanation for his going to Egypt after his exile from Jerusalem. Perhaps he knew he had the support of the Egyptian monarchs and hence sought protection there.

7   The site has a long history of settlement, dating back at least to the twelfth dynasty. In the nineteenth dynasty Ramses II built a temple a little to the west of Onias' temple and Ramses III fortified the town and built a "beautiful little pavilion (?)" near it (Naville and Griffith 1890:38). In the twenty-sixth dynasty there was also a temple on the site of Ramses' town and again in Ptolemaic times (Petrie 1906:2, 8).

8   As a military settlement it acted as a border post near the point where Jewish, Idumean, and Egyptian interests met.

9   The site was originally excavated in the late nineteenth century. A re-excavation is currently in progress, but it is unlikely to reveal a great deal, according to Patricia Paice (Near Eastern Studies, University of Toronto), who has been working at the site. The raised part of the site is now almost flat; in the area below grade level (perhaps the cemetery) now stands a pool of fetid water. Thus little new information about the buildings which were once on the site is likely to be discovered.

10 These dimensions show that Josephus exaggerates when he reports Onias saying that the dimensions were the same as Jerusalem.

11 This affair, which would have occurred when Marin was about 30 years old, is the result of complex political circumstances in the area. The community would hardly have known whom to support. Presumably they were officially to support the Ptolemies, but the Ptolemies themselves were divided into pro-and anti-Roman factions. The Jews in the community, even if they were on the anti-Roman side, would have felt some motivation to support Antipater since he was a Jewish Idumean. Perhaps this is why they were easily swayed by Antipater to allow him passage and support.

12 Naville and Griffith 1890:13. The underground chamber housed horizontal niches along the sides for the bodies. Most of the niches were empty, but in a few the bodies remained. These were neither mummified nor ornamented and had a burnt brick under the head as a pillow. The tomb also contained more than eighty tombstone inscriptions.

13 *CPJ* I 145. It is interesting to note that none of the inscriptions makes any military references. This is unusual if the community was in part a military colony. It is possible, however, as Aryeh Kasher suggests (1985:126), that in the Roman period, the troops, who served the Ptolemies, had been disbanded. Because most of the inscriptions come from the late first century BCE or the early first century CE it is possible that at this time the number of people with military connections had diminished.

14 While there is a slim possibility that Marin was not Jewish, this is unlikely given that the catacombs in which her tombstone was found were Jewish. The name Marin seems, too, to have been a characteristic Jewish name. The examples of it found in *SEG* 16:887; 28:476; 33:1372 and 1499, are all Jewish epitaphs.

15 *Hierisa* appears to have been an alternative spelling for the more common *hierissa*.

16 Dunand 1978:354–55.

17 "Priestess" is used in a rather loose way to designate any temple functionaries, rather than strictly to refer to those officiating at animal sacrifices.

18 Dunand 1978:372; Blackman 1921:27.

19 Romans, for example, were horrified at the prospect of a woman holding such power. It was one of the things which turned popular opinion away from Mark Antony.

20 *De vita contemplativa*. For a good brief introduction to the group, see Kraemer 1992:113–17, 126–27.

21 Some have doubted their existence, but see Bokser 1977.

22 See Strabo 17.1.7, 10, 14, 22 for descriptions of the lake and its importance. In these passages he uses two different names for the lake: *Mareia* and *Mareotis*.

23 Philo generalizes about this type of solitary contemplative life in most of *Vita cont.* 1–20; when he begins to focus on our group he states that such persons can be found in many places, but most of all in Egypt and especially around Alexandria (21). The best of them, he claims, come to Lake Mareotis (22). Since there is nothing in the rest of his comments

that specifically alludes to another related group, we conclude that this is the only community of this kind of which he has any knowledge. For a discussion of its location, see Richardson 1993:337, 346.

24 *Proairesis* is found in 2, 17, 29, 32, 67, 79; for the various meanings see LSJ; for a discussion of translation problems see Colson and Whitaker 1929–62, 9:518–19, arguing for a broad sense.

25 The words used of these buildings are rather confusing in Philo; it is difficult to know just how to translate them and even more difficult to know how to visualize the physical character of the community. For a preliminary attempt, see p. 244

26 A synagogue at Nitria – or more correctly a house of prayer – in exactly the same area that we suppose the Therapeutae to be in (see Richardson 1993, figure 1, for a map of the possible location), had a dedicatory inscription addressed to King Ptolemy and Queen Cleopatra (dated 143–114 BCE) as "their benefactors" (see *CIJ* 1442).

27 It was this echo with developing practice in his own day that prompted Eusebius to identify the Therapeutae as Christians; it may even be that early Christian practice mimicked the Therapeutae. The earliest Christian monastic establishments were in Egypt, and the earliest of these were eremitic or quasi-eremitic, the latter being roughly how one would characterize the Therapeutae.

28 The cult of Isis might provide an inexact parallel; though not usually withdrawn as the Therapeutae were, some Isis cult centres did have living quarters for the priests. But these were not for contemplative purposes.

29 This term is used in Neh. 13:30 and in Luke 1:5 to refer to priests and Levites serving in the Temple.

30 Philo specifically draws attention to the connection with Essenes in the first paragraph; whether he intends readers to imagine that the Therapeutae are an Egyptian variant on the group in the Holy Land is not clear.

31 See Sly 1990.

32 Once again, the cult of Isis is one of the nearer analogies, for it had both male and female priests. For a visual representation of this see the important wall-painting from Herculaneum, and see further below.

33 See Vermes 1975:30–31. See LSJ on the range of meanings for *therapeia, therapeutai, therapeuō*, etc. *Therapeutria, -ides* is simply the feminine of *therapeutēs*; the latter is found of worshipers of Sarapis in inscriptions (LSJ cites *IG* XI/4 1226, second century BCE, Delos). For the significance of this, see below.

34 Strabo refers in passing (17.1.22) to a village by the name of *Gynaecopolis*, somewhere along the arm of the Nile delta between Schedia and Memphis (for his route see 17.1.16). His description is very imprecise, except for one detail: "there are on the right a very large number of villages extending as far as Lake Mareia" (i.e., Lake Mareotis). Is the name a somewhat jesting reference to the community of the Therapeutae – the town of women? In antiquity there were several attempts to explain the name, none of which was very satisfactory. See Smith *Dictionary of Geography, s.v.* For a possible location fitting Strabo's description, see Richardson 1993, figure 1.

35 It is striking that Philo and Musonius Rufus are almost exact contemporaries. Musonius reflects on whether women should study philosophy (Lutz 1947:§III, pp. 39–43). Musonius' answer is that "women as well as men have received from the gods the gift of reason . . . Likewise the female has the same senses as the male . . . both have the same parts of the body . . . not men alone, but women too, have a natural inclination toward virtue . . . and it is the nature of women no less than men to be pleased by good and just acts." His reflections on this question are sometimes still sexist, as we read them today, but there is nevertheless a very high degree of equivalence if not of equality, as the next chapter on daughters receiving the same education as sons also shows. For a broader assessment see Klassen 1984.

36 Colson's translation is slightly misleading when he refers to women making "part of the audience," as if they were passive; more correctly, "for women also habitually listen together with the same zeal . . ."; it was a shared activity of men and women – women were not merely part of an audience.

37 It is remarkable that the Temple in Jerusalem as rebuilt by Herod made provision (as I think for the first time) for participation of women in the Temple service by including specifically a court of women. This provision, however remarkable, institutionalized a subordinate position for women. In a recent paper for the Society of Biblical Literature (1994) Richardson has argued that part of the motive for paying attention to women's needs in Jerusalem was Egyptian practices.

38 Notice the difference between Philo's description of the Therapeutae and what Musonius Rufus says, especially the concessions Musonius makes to prevailing views on women, their natural tasks, stereotyped qualities, strengths and weaknesses, and so on. In the end the effect is to take away some of what he has claimed on women's behalf when he argued that women ought to study philosophy.

39 Probably a feast at Pentecost, see Colson and Whitaker 1929–62.

40 This is the same passage from Eusebius referred to earlier. Just prior to this Philo refers to those leading the community's celebrations; in all three cases (*hoi ephēmēreutoi* in 66, *hoi presbyteroi* in 67 and *ho proedros* in 75) he seems to assume that men are in control.

41 69–72, deliberately contrasting these arrangements with the use of young men – some of them ex-pederasts – in pagan feasts.

42 This is the natural meaning of the words *tote gar exēchousi pantes te kai pasai*. Since Philo has just described exposition and singing, during which "all the others" take their turns "in the proper order," Philo means that women also take their parts in the exposition and the solo singing. For *exēchoueō*, see 1 Thess. 1:8.

43 The similarities with the Shakers are striking though not complete: celibate, ecstatic, equal, founded by a woman prophet (Ann Lee). They differ in the Shakers' insistence on work, the Therapeutae's insistence on meditation and the Shakers' communal living quarters.

44 The important wall-painting of the Isis cult at worship, found at Herculaneum and dating to sometime before the eruption of Mt. Vesuvius in 79 CE, shows something along the same lines. In the centre of the picture is a stair ascending to the façade of a small temple, before which stand a male priest in the middle and a male and female priest, one on each side of him. At the bottom of the stair is an altar, with another male priest fanning the flames. Between the altar and the bottom step is yet another priest, one arm raised, apparently directing the two matched choirs that flank him on either side. The gender of the persons in the "choirs" is hard to establish, but it is reasonably clear that they are not all male and all female. Men and women are mixed on both sides, though there are occasional examples of an apparent matched pair of persons, as in the left foreground.

45 Philo describes Moses and Miriam leading choirs in *Agric.* 80–82, in somewhat similar language, but referring to the historical incident. Cf. also Philo, *Leg. All.* 2.66 and 3.103, for Miriam in a different sense.

46 *Symphonian* would be better translated "agreement," "common mind," or even "unity." That is, the act of singing together draws the men and women together into one entity expressing the group's "piety" (88).

47 Baer 1970:100–101, suggests the Therapeutrides were women in name only, since all had left behind their sexuality for a unity of the Spirit; cf. also p. 48.

48 In both latter cases we have deliberately used the word "defined" because what Philo describes is a large room with, in the one case, a barrier distinguishing women's and men's areas, in the other case merely definition by the ordering of the rows of reclining benches.

49 The text does not say "prophet *like* Moses"; such an eschatological reading could be intended, perhaps, though there is no indication elsewhere in *Vita cont.* that eschatology is a factor (cf. Deut. 18:15, 18–19; Acts 3:22–23; 7:37; 4QTest 5–8; 1QS 9.11). If it were

arguable on the basis of some similarities between Therapeutae and Qumran members that the Moses figure is an eschatologically charged, perhaps Messianic, figure, would it also follow that Miriam was a Messianic figure? On prophetic celibacy associated with Moses, see *b. Shab.* 87a; *Sifre* Num 12.1 (99); Philo, *Vita Mosis* 2.68–69; cf. Vermes 1975.

50 Another brother Set played a minor role. In the Roman period Osiris was still a significant factor in the cult, but the cult of Sarapis had to some extent become aligned with the cult of Isis to form a new pairing.

51 The inscription cited earlier from Cos, in which *therapeutēs* is a worshipper of Sarapis or Isis, is suggestive.

52 Both mirror the prevalence in Egyptian royal circles of the Pharaoh marrying his sister, another instance of the significance of brother–sister relationships. There is some evidence that Isis was the role-model for the Queen of Egypt (Lesko 1987:302). The brother–sister relationship was specifically noted in some synagogue dedications: *CIJ* 1440, "In honor of King Ptolemy and Queen Berenice, his sister and wife, and their children, the Jews built this house of prayer" (Schedia, 246–221 BCE); *CIJ* 1441, "In honor of King Ptolemy and Queen Cleopatra his sister and Queen Cleopatra his wife, the Jews from Xenephyris dedicated the portico of the house of prayer . . ." (Xenephyris, 143–116 BCE); similarly *CIJ* 1442, referred to above.

53 It is uncertain how seriously they studied and wrote. Geoltrain 1960, suggests that they may have been responsible for some or all of *T. Job*, Wis, *Joseph and Asenath*, *T. Abraham* and a papyrus hymn. See also Geoltrain 1959.

54 See in general Swidler 1976; Leipoldt 1955.

55 See Tran 1971:85–86 no. 59, plate 41; Feder 1978:128–29; Clayton 1986:85.

56 For a general description of great importance, see Apuleius, *Golden Ass.*

57 See Evans 1961:151. At Pompeii, for example, the Isis-buildings included cells for the resident priests.

58 See Heyob 1975:87, 100; in 200 of 1,089 inscriptions women are mentioned as priestesses or members of Isis-associations. From Delos come inscriptions (third century to second century BCE) referring to a loose association of worshipers as *therapeutae*; 1975:82–83, 104–5.

59 The *Dekadistai* had 9 men and 7 women, the *Navarchs* had 50 men and 45 women (in Eretria, first century BCE); see Heyob 1975:104–5.

60 Here she is referred to as Aaron's, not Moses', sister.

61 The incident is followed immediately by the account of the waters of Marah. In Pseudo-Philo 20.8 Miriam's name is associated with the waters of Marah; Marah (in the Septuagint *Merra*) is similar to the Greek for Lake Mareia/Mareotis (*Mareia* or *Mareotis*).

62 Miriam is not mentioned explicitly by name in this passage though she is in Josephus' version of the story in *Ant.* 2.221–23.

63 According to Josephus, *Ant.* 4.78, she was buried at Sin; in Jerome's tradition she was buried near Petra.

64 Cf. Josephus, *Ant.* 3.54, where Josephus represents a development of Biblical tradition, in which Miriam "acquires" a husband she didn't have in Exodus.

65 Using *iaomai*, not *therapeuō*. The Septuagint has some slight variations, including a stronger reference to her being separated outside the camp.

66 Though Moses and Aaron are commonly linked together, in some instances in the Biblical narrative Moses, Aaron, and Miriam are linked together as a threesome (for example, 1 Chron. 6:3; Mic. 6:4; Num. 12:1–15; and also in Pseudo-Philo 20.8).

67 There is only one reference, in 82, that states that the priests were the highest caste and took precedence in matters of food. This may be a historical reference to the Temple in Jerusalem (?) or at Leontopolis (?) though it seems intended to refer to some division within the Therapeutae with respect to priesthood.

68 Qumran is the nearest analogy and is demonstrably priestly in its emphases. Is the difference – a very important and underemphasized difference – directly related to the presence of another Jewish priestly community in Egypt at Leontopolis a few miles away to the south-east which had absorbed any priestly elements in the Jewish community in Egypt?

69 At about the same time the synagogue communities in Palestine also focus on Moses; note, for example, the expression in Matt. 23:2, "sit on Moses' seat."

70 See Blackman 1921:8–10.

71 Note that Philo's description of this group, focused on Moses, and possibly related to the Essenes, includes nothing about their attitude to *Torah*.

13

EVIDENCE FOR WOMEN IN THE COMMUNITY OF THE DEAD SEA SCROLLS[1]

Eileen Schuller

In 1983, in an important state-of-the-research article, Ross Kraemer reviewed an extensive list of recent studies which had explored the role and understanding of women in the pagan religions of the Graeco-Roman world and in early Christianity. However, when it came to the study of women in Judaism in the same time period, she noted the contrast: "all in all, there has been very little careful scholarly consideration of women in the varieties of Judaism in late antiquity" (1983:131). Now just over a decade later, the situation has changed somewhat, and we have seen a steady stream of books and articles which combine both historical and feminist concerns in the study of women in Diaspora Judaism, Philo, Josephus, and the literature of the Apocrypha and Pseudepigrapha.[2]

However the one area for which there is still virtually no bibliography is study about women in the type(s) of Judaism which produced the Dead Sea Scrolls.[3] A number of factors help to explain this lacuna. Most obvious is the simple fact that not all of the Dead Sea Scroll material has been published as yet.[4] Although scholars now have access on microfiche to photos of all the fragments (Tov, Pfann, and Reed 1993), we still await a basic *editio princeps* of a number of important texts. On the basis of preliminary reports and from a rapid survey of obvious vocabulary items in the Concordance of Cave Four texts (Strugnell 1988), it is clear that there are some significant texts which deal with women still to be published and studied in detail.

Beyond the issue of unpublished material is the larger reality that Qumran studies as a whole are in a state, if not of turmoil, certainly of fluidity and change. Many factors have come together to bring about this volatile situation almost fifty years after the discovery of the Scrolls – and this, in itself, could be the subject of a paper. The recent publication of some long-awaited texts (especially the much-discussed 4QMMT)[5] along with a steady stream of shorter texts has given us previously unknown material from which to work. But the increase of information has rendered the overall picture more complex and confusing; rather than solving problems, increased data have brought new questions and made it less easy to relate and integrate the texts we do have. In recent years Qumran scholars have become more self-conscious and critically aware of fundamental presuppositions and religious, political and sociological factors which have influenced the course of scholarship on the Scrolls.[6] Thus, the "prevailing consensus," developed by Cross and Milik in the late 1950s and popularized by Vermes,[7] which closely identified both the archaeological remains and the manuscripts found at Qumran with the Essenes of classical sources (Pliny, Josephus and Philo), and viewed the authors of the Scrolls as a dissident group originating in the aftermath of the "Hellenistic crisis" because of disputes over priesthood, calendar, or halakah (or some combination of all of these), has come under attack in the scholarly as well as the popular forum. Radically different proposals have been put forward about the origin and nature of the group(s) which produced the scrolls, while at the same time, the traditional "Essene hypothesis" has been vigorously reiterated and refined.[8] Thus, while the data are not yet "all in" and there is no consensus about fundamental questions, it is difficult, if not impossible, to make definitive pronouncements about the specific question of the role and place of women.

This chapter can be, at best, an initial exploration. It was undertaken, in part, simply to explore if the study of women in the voluntary associations of the Graeco-Roman world can be extended to the Scrolls. It attempts to raise certain questions and highlight fundamental texts without making any claim to be comprehensive or to enter into a discussion of the larger issues under dispute in current Qumran scholarship. We need to begin, in fact, with the most basic question. Were women part of the group within Second Temple Judaism which produced the Scrolls or did the Scrolls come from a community of male celibate ascetics? Was this group married, or celibate, or a mixture of both? Were there any female celibate ascetics? In the second part of the chapter I will attempt to collect and examine briefly those texts which do speak specifically of women. Finally, I raise the question of whether there are other types of questions or other ways of configuring the data so as to provide indirectly some further information about either the role of women or attitudes towards women.

MARRIED OR CELIBATE?

The question of whether the Scrolls reflect a married or celibate community has been part of scholarly discussion since their first publication. While a complete survey of discussion is not possible here, certain aspects of the evidence or lack of evidence and of how the question has been formulated need to be highlighted.

The Cross–Vermes hypothesis, in postulating a close link, if not identity, between the Essenes and the authors of the Scrolls, paid particular attention to passages in Josephus and Philo that stated that the Essenes were males who did not marry, that they shunned pleasure, strove for self-control, and avoided contact with female "wantonness" and "egoism."[9] Certain major scrolls, especially the Community Rule (1QS), seemed to corroborate the Greek authors. 1QS makes no explicit mention of women[10] or children or marriage and was thus interpreted as the rule of life for a group of male celibates who withdrew to the desert wilderness to live "without women . . . with only the palm trees for company."[11] The preponderance of male graves in the main section of the cemetery excavated by de Vaux in 1953 served to reinforce this reconstruction (de Vaux 1954).

In this picture of the community (which is the standard description found in most handbooks on the Scrolls) there is little to say about women. Women were simply not part of the *yaḥad*, that is, the group usually considered as the founders and core of the movement and centered geographically at the site of Khirbet Qumran.[12] Scholars have, of course, always recognized that Josephus speaks of another group of Essenes who did marry for the sake of propagation of life (*War* 2.160–161). Texts (such as the Cairo Damascus Document) which do talk plainly of wives and children were interpreted as describing this form of the life. But in fact, most of the interest and study, both popular and scholarly, has been focused on those who were often described as the "monks,"[13] while the "marrying Essenes" have been treated – on analogy with Christian monasticism – as a kind of "third order," subordinate to the dominant celibate group. Yet we should recall that Josephus, in describing the two groups, emphasizes rather their similarity; he writes about "another order of Essenes" who "have the same views as the rest in their way of life, customs and laws" (*War* 2.160).

We should not underestimate how important the order of discovery and publication of the scrolls has been in our conceptualization. 1QS, a text in which women are conspicuous by their absence, was one of the first of the Qumran texts published; as a relatively complete and readable document it took on a somewhat normative status. However, now it is becoming increasingly clear that when we consider *all* the material, both published and unpublished, the image of "monk" or male celibate ascetic is not sustained. A significant number of major texts of differing genres speak plainly of women (and often children) and assume a community in which marriage was the norm.

Although I will treat these texts at greater length in the second part of the chapter, it is the very existence of these many texts which speak of women and children which now raises questions for the dominant hypothesis, or at least challenges us to rethink how we should conceptualize the relationship between a celibate and a married group. The issues are larger than this single question. How do all these texts we now have relate? Do they all refer to a single group, or to different groups or different times? How do we explain apparent contradictions in community organization and legal prescriptions? To give a specific example in terms of our topic: those who see celibacy as the norm emphasize that 1QS makes no mention of women or relationship between the sexes, or sexual offenses (not even in the penal code in 1QS vi 4–vii 25; the prohibition of indecent exposure in vii 13 is addressed to males). However, 1QS makes no mention of laws for the observance of the sabbath either; yet no one would want to claim that the sabbath was not observed. Are women not mentioned in the prescriptions of 1QS precisely because they are treated in CDC? Such basic questions about the relationship of documents still require have not been resolved.

Given that so often discussion of the Scrolls begins by assuming a celibate group, it is important to remember that there has long been another stream of scholarship, less well known perhaps, that worked with the opposite assumption, namely, that the group behind the Scrolls was married. In 1970 Hans Hübner (1970–71) attempted to show that all of the published Qumran texts could be read without postulating a rule of celibacy; in particular, he drew attention to a number of expressions which must, in fact, be explained away as figurative if the authors are thought to be celibate (for example, 1QS iv 7 PRWT ZRʿ, 1QH xvii 14 ZRʿM; 4QpPsᵃ 1–10 iii 2 WLZRʿM). Scholars such as Schiffman[14] have long taken as a fundamental premise that the people who wrote the Scrolls married and lived "in each city" (*War*. 2.124) throughout the land. Since Schiffman interpreted 1QSa as a rule for the eschatological "last days," its mention of women and children simply reinforced the continuum between the present way of life and what is envisioned for all Israel at the end times. Baumgarten has also maintained that marriage was the norm for the community, though he acknowledged that certain thrusts in their strict views on marriage and purity may have developed over time into a de facto practice of celibacy for those who desired a "perfection of holiness" (CDC vii 6), particularly in the later years of a person's life (1990). Others have postulated the opposite movement in the history of the community, that is, from an initial period of eschatological fervor in which celibacy was the norm to a settling down into married life.[15] In recent discussion of the question, Stegemann is convinced that the authors of the Scrolls were married and Essenes, and undertakes to explain how it came about that Philo, Josephus, and Pliny all thought that the Essenes were unmarried (1992).

One way of approaching the discussion is to ask whether the adoption of celibacy is either demanded or explainable in light of the specific theological orientation of this community. Scholars have proposed a variety of reasons why celibacy might have been adopted: the desire for a high degree of ritual purity,[16] a preparation for the eschatological holy war,[17] or a prerequisite to receive special prophetic inspiration (Guillaumont 1971). Josephus and Philo explain the Essenes' choice not to marry in terms which are clearly misogynist: for example, "no Essene takes a wife, because a woman is a selfish creature, excessively jealous and an adept at beguiling the morals of her husband . . ." (*Hypothetica* 11.14–15). However, such statements may well tell us more about Josephus and Philo and their attitudes![18] But it is difficult to find a single text in the Scrolls which specifically discusses, advocates, or praises celibacy. One relevant text might be a section in CDC vii 5–7, but the passage is, admittedly, less than clear.[19] It appears to set up a contrast: on the one hand are "those who walk in perfect holiness" who are promised that "the covenant of God shall stand faithfully with them to keep them alive for thousands of generations." The next sentence goes on: "and if they live in camps according to the rule of the land, marrying and begetting children . . .". If this interpretation of two contrasting groups is correct, we have here the only reference in the Scrolls themselves for a distinction between those who marry and have children, and those who, having no physical children, are promised posterity through the continuity of the community through all generations.

If we allow that some, perhaps a core, of the community were celibate, it has generally been assumed that these were men. However, there have recently been some attempts to look to Qumran for an example of early Jewish female ascetics, somewhat analogous to the Therapeutrides described by Philo in Egypt, and to find celibate Essene women, that is "women who decided not to marry and came there to live in complete chastity, like Christian nuns."[20] Indeed Kraemer has pointed out that the search for such communities within Second Temple Judaism may have a certain apologetic dimension; in as much as feminists have suggested that such groups can provide advantages and opportunities for women that are absent in the larger society, there is a desire to find such women in Second Temple Judaism as well as in early Christianity (1989:367). Certainly feminist scholarship has alerted us to the possibility that women can be present in a group but almost entirely invisible in written documents which reflect an entirely androcentric perspective. Does perhaps language such as "men of perfection" (CDC vii 4–5 HMTHLKYM B'LH BTMYM QDŠ) hide the female ascetics, and should it in fact be translated according to the same inclusive principles which have become commonplace in the translation of Biblical texts?

Given the lack of concrete evidence, we are reduced to searching out any possible traces and arguments for the presence or absence of female ascetics. Attempts to explain that the conditions and climate at Qumran were too harsh for women betray more about the stereotypes of the proponent than anything else. Kraemer suggests that "the entire cosmology, theology and symbolic universe of Qumran was so pervasively male that no women would have found it acceptable, let alone compelling" (1989:365); yet this seems basically unprovable given that women have found a home in communities whose literature (whether the Hebrew Bible, New Testament, or Koran) is very male-orientated. The discovery of female skeletons[21] in the graveyard is open to a multitude of conjectures about who these women were;[22] the presence of children's graves (including one grave of a woman and child) argues against the explanation of celibate women. 4Q502 is one text which seems to speak of groups of women within the *yahad*, designating them as "elderly women" (ZQNWT) and "sisters" ('HYWT); these may be honorific titles describing a position. Other small fragments in this text speak of "his wife" and "his companion" (4Q502 1 3, 7), and include an exchange of blessings between man and woman (4Q502 24); Baumgarten has suggested that we have here an "old-age ritual" for men and women who undertake a life of celibacy in their later years, but this is all highly conjectural.[23]

To draw this section to a close: most of the discussion about women in the Scrolls which has taken place up to this time has been within the framework of the larger discussion of whether the authors of the Scrolls were married or celibate – and on this point there is no consensus. Publication of further texts, more extensive excavation of the cemetery and re-evaluation of all the archaeological remains from the site are necessary to advance the discussion.

TEXTS THAT SPEAK OF WOMEN

Apart from the question of marriage or celibacy, it is clear that we do have texts in the scrolls which talk specifically of women and that these need to be studied in and of themselves. Within the confines of this chapter, I can only give a brief overview of the major documents. Many of these are fragmentary and often there are difficulties simply on the level of decipherment, arrangement of fragments, and interpretation. Yet even to make a start on collecting these texts is a first step. Since the list is not meant to be comprehensive, I confine myself to published texts, and unpublished texts where we have at least a preliminary description. Given the lack of certainty about the precise relationship among the documents, it seems premature to adopt a thematic approach (for example, marriage in the Scrolls, purity in the Scrolls) lest this result in an artificial conflation of documents which are really quite distinct.

The Damascus Document

This text, of which we have the medieval version from the Cairo Genizah, fragmentary copies from Caves 5 and 6, and eight copies from Cave 4, contains both a hortatory appeal to remain faithful to the covenant and a legal code. Both sections assume the presence of women: there is mention of wives (CDC vii 7); women servants (CDC xi 12; xii 10); widows (4Q271 1 12); "young girl" (CDC xiv 15 BTWLH); and "mothers" (probably an honorific title in 4Q270 11 14). Yet the perspective and formulation of the text is androcentric; for example, they "take wives and beget children" (CDC vii 7); they are "not to lie with a woman in the city of the sanctuary to defile the city of the sanctuary with their uncleanness" (CDC xii 1–2). Following the Biblical pattern, the laws are formulated in masculine terms even though many certainly apply to women, and some perhaps specifically to women as, for example, the prohibition against wearing perfumes or carrying an infant on the Sabbath (CDC xi 9–11).[24] Thus, given that the community includes both men and women, the initial summons W'TH BNYM ŠM'W LY (CDC ii 14) is surely to be read inclusively.

In one of the key passages in the Admonitions section (iv 15–v 11), this group defines itself in opposition to "the builders of the wall" who are ensnared in the "three nets of Belial." Three of the four points of conflict are halakic proscriptions involving women: marriage of an uncle with a niece, intercourse with a menstruant, and "taking two wives in their lifetime." Although some have read the latter as a prohibition of polygamy,[25] most commentators interpret the passage as evidence of a prohibition against divorce or, more specifically, remarriage after divorce.[26] Given that we are dealing here with a Jewish group which, in contrast to the practice among the Pharisees and Sadducees, may have prohibited divorce, questions can be raised about how the restriction would have been experienced by women, whether as a safeguard or a constraint. We have too little knowledge about the actual life situation of the family to answer; certainly the derivation of the prohibition from Scripture (on the basis of exegesis of Gen. 1:27; 7:9, and Deut. 17:17) gives no hint that concern for rights and care of the woman was the motivating force.

The derivation of the prohibition of marriage between uncle and niece is especially interesting (v 8–11). There is explicit acknowledgement that the laws of incest are written with reference to men (WMŠPṬ HʿRYWT LZKRYM HWʾ KTWB) but that they apply in the same way to women (WKHM HNŠYM). How much more widely this principle was applied in the development of halakah needs to be explored further.

Though the Damascus Document presumes marriage, there are strict restrictions on sexual intercourse. CDC v 6–7, as mentioned above, implies a stricter halakah with regard to intercourse and menstruation, although it is impossible to establish the details.[27] CDC xii 1–2 appears to prohibit intercourse in all of Jerusalem (the city of the sanctuary) though ʿYR HMQDŠ may apply only to the Temple Mount.[28] In a broken context within a catalogue of transgressions in 4Q270 9 ii 16, there is a reference to ʾŠH HRH; Baumgarten suggests that this is the conclusion of a law prohibiting sexual intercourse during pregnancy. This would correspond to Josephus' comment about the marrying Essenes: "they do not have intercourse with them [their wives] during pregnancy, demonstrating that they marry not for self-gratification but for the necessity of children" (War 2.161). In the penal code, there is reference to a man committing "fornication" with his wife ([WŠ]R YQR[B] LZNWT LʾŠTW, 4Q270 11 i 12–13); although the precise nature of the offense is unclear, some type of sexual activity between a man and his wife is judged serious enough to merit expulsion from the community (Baumgarten 1992a:270).

Although the full publication of the 4QD fragments is not yet available, Baumgarten has pointed out a number of other passages in these fragments which pertain to women and are without parallel in CDC.[29] These include a discussion of the ordeal of the Soṭah (4Q270 8), the responsibilities of the father of the bride and issues concerning the blemishes of the bride (4Q271 1 7–15), and reference to "mothers" (ʾMWT, probably as an honorific title, with the penalty for offending them and the puzzling comment "they do not have authority (?) in the midst of [the congregation]" (KY ʾYN LʾM[W]T RWQMH BTWK [HʿDH]) (4Q270 11 i 13–14) (Baumgarten 1992a:270–71).

There are a number of interesting but complex questions – which can only be raised here – around the issue of the process of initiation and membership in the Damascus Document. Could women become full members of the community in their own right? Did they take the "oath of the covenant . . . to return to the law of Moses" (CDC xv 5–10); that is, is Vermes correct in translating "when the children of all those who have entered the Covenant (BNYHM. . . reach the age of enrollment" or is it only "their sons" as Rabin translates? Schiffman, for instance, has argued that the men took the oath, and "the status of women in the sect . . . was determined only insofar as their husbands took on membership" (Schiffman 1983:57). Here we should recall the section in War 2.161 (in a passage where the Greek phraseology is admittedly less than clear)[30] in which Josephus says "they put their wives to the test for a three-year period." Josephus had used the same verb (*dokimazō*) earlier for the testing period for men (*War* 2.138) as he uses here for women; might this suggest that the testing of women was not only in terms of sexual fertility but involved a probation parallel to that of the men, leading to full and independent membership? The whole question will require much more detailed study, especially when all the manuscripts of the Damascus Document are edited.

1QSa: The Rule of the Congregation

This short document of which we have only a single copy appended to the end of 1QS is a rule (*serek*) for "all of the congregation of Israel in the end of days," treating duties of members at various ages and the structure and tasks of the formal assembly. The document has been understood in different ways depending on the interpretation of the initial phrase B'ḤRYT HYMYM. Given that this expression elsewhere refers to the present time of the community's existence, this rule must be for now, not for some far-distant eschatological future,[31] though it is not easy to specify with any certainty the precise relationship between this rule and 1QS and the Damascus Document.

1QSa i 4–19 gives instruction for the life-stages of both men and women at various ages. According to i 4–5, "all those who come including children and women" are gathered together for the reading of the "precepts of the covenant" and instructed (LHBYNM) in "all their statutes" so that "they will no longer stray in their [errors]." I suggest that we continue reading with this same subject until the text itself alerts us to change; this means that all children are to be instructed in the mysterious book of Hagu (i 6–7) and the precepts of the covenant, and at the age of 20 to come into the holy congregation (i 8–9). Then follow two parallel statements, one about the age of marriage for men (WLW' Y[QRB] 'L 'ŠH) and one about women (i 11 "she [TQBL] will be received to bear witness of him concerning the judgment of the law and to take her place in proclaiming the ordinances." That is, women are to give testimony, probably with respect to menstrual purity. This reading respects the structure of the text and does not require the purely gratuitous emendation of the perfectly clear Hebrew feminine verb TQBL to a masculine YQBL, "he will bear witness."[32]

1QSa i 27–ii 11 describes the Council of the Community ('ṢT HYḤD) and its tasks, with particular attention to those who are excluded by reasons of impurity, physical deformity, or age because "holy angels [are in their coun]cil." Interestingly, women are not on the list, in contrast to 1QM vii 3–4 where women are shut out from the camp in the final battle where the angels are present.

Legal texts

Among the substantial body of texts of a legal nature, some of which are only now being published, there are a considerable number of proscriptions concerning women. Again we can only highlight some examples here, beginning with some of the smaller texts. 4Q159, 513 and 514 may be from the same document, although the relationship between them is complicated.[33] 4Q159 2 6–10 groups together two laws from Deut. 22, the prohibition against wearing women's clothing (Deut. 22:5) and the accusation of unchastity (22:13–21); in the latter, the phrase "if at [the time of] his taking her, he should say so" is added to the Biblical text, and serves to limit the time in which the husband can make the accusation against his wife.[34] 4Q513 treats a variety of matters about ritual purity and the calendar;[35] fg. 2 ii 2 is concerned with "women married to foreigners and all fornication" (B'LWT LBNY HNKR WLKWL HZNWT); given the context (eating the *terumah*), this could refer to illicit marriages between women of the household of the priests and foreigners. The first line of 4Q514 1 i contains the word 'ŠH, but the fragment is badly broken here and the precise context lost; the following lines are concerned with the first-day ablutions of the *zab*. 4Q251, a halakic work with many parallels to CDC, 1QS and 11QTS, has sections on the prohibited degrees of marriage (12 1–7), and 4Q265 specifies the length of the period of impurity after the birth of a male and female child (7 ii 14–17) (Baumgarten 1994:3–10). Many issues of purity rules for the time of menstruation are treated in Tohara* (4Q274) (Baumgarten 1995) and Serek Ha-Niddot (4Q284).

Purity rules are also a major focus in the list of halakot in the recently published 4QMMT, Miqsat Ma'ase Ha-Torah (4Q394–399). Some of the issues of conflict among the groups in dispute ("we say . . . you say . . .") concerned prohibited sexual unions (B 39–49 and 75–82)[36] and relate to women in the context of marriage laws. Qimron suggests that another fragmentary section (C 4 = 4Q397 17) was introduced by W'L HNŠY[M] "and concerning the wo[men]," and treated laws relating to incest; however both the placement of this fragment and the reconstruction are very uncertain.[37]

Finally, there is considerable treatment of women in the Temple Scroll. The document describes a group in which women were clearly a part (for example, laws about the accusation of unchastity, rape, and incest [lxv–lxvi]; marriage to a captured woman [lxiii 10–15], vows and oaths of women [lii 16–liv 5]). In terms of the Temple, women are to be excluded from the middle court (xxxix 7–9) but allowed in the outer court (xl 6). According to most interpreters, it is implied that women cannot dwell in Jerusalem.[38] In other cities, a place is provided for them outside the city during menstrual uncleanness and after childbirth (xlviii 15–17) – the only example from Second Temple Judaism of the isolation of the menstruant from society (Cohen 1991:278). There is a lengthy section, not paralleled in Biblical law, about the woman whose child dies in her womb; she is "unclean like a grave" (110–19) all the time the foetus is within her and she defiles the house where she stays. Within the specific section of the Laws of the King, both polygamy and divorce are prohibited for the king (lvii 17–19).[39] However, this does not appear to be the general norm, since there is a passing reference to the vow of the divorced woman (liv 4), and col. lxiv (in the missing section) apparently quoted Deut. 21:15 on the loved and hated wife. This highlights the fundamental question about the Temple Scroll – was it authored by the same group as the other scrolls or only part of their library?[40] The answer given to this question will obviously affect how we can make use of the information about women contained therein.

Liturgical texts

A few liturgical-type texts mention women. 4Q512, for instance, is a badly preserved papyrus manuscript of blessings to be said at rituals of purification in conjunction with various types of impurity. In fg. 41, a second hand has added "a man or a woman" (['Y]Š 'W 'ŠH) before the words of blessing. That women are involved with purificatory ablutions calls to mind Josephus' comment about the Essenes (*War* 2.161) "in the baths the women are covered with a garment . . .".

A very puzzling but fascinating text is 4Q502, made up of 344 very small fragments. At least part of these are liturgical in nature with blessing formularies and ritual directions (for example, [W'NW] W'MRW 19 6). There are frequent references to women ('ŠTW, 1 3; WBTWLWT N'RYM WN'[RWT], 19 3; L'ḤYWT, 96 1) and fertility (L'ŚWT ZR', 1 4; ZR' BRKH, 19 2; LPRY B[TN], 20 3; 163 3). Sometimes the viewpoint is that of the male ("his wife" 1 3, 309 1; "his companion" R'YYTW, 1 7), but in other fragments a woman is the subject of verbs (24 4 [W]'MDH BSWD ZKNY[M]) and perhaps the speaker (24 5 YMYKH BŠLWM). As a parallel to the standard BN 'MT, "son of truth," women are described as BT 'MT (2 3) "daughter of truth," possessing knowledge and intelligence (ŚKL WBYNH, 2 4). Throughout the fragments the language of rejoicing is repeated (ŚMḤ, ŚMḤH). In the *editio princeps* Baillet proposed that we have here a "Ritual of Marriage" and linked it specifically with the "marrying Essenes" described by Josephus.[41] Baumgarten places more emphasis on the ZQNYM and ZQNWT, and suggests that this is a ritual for the celebration of the entrance into the community of older men and women who now will spend their final years in study, pious observance and celibacy. Again, this is a text which requires further study.

CONCLUDING EXPLORATIONS

To this point we have concentrated on texts which specifically mention women or are related to issues of marriage and/or celibacy. However, as scholars working on the Bible from a feminist perspective have discovered, both the lived-world of women and prevalent ideas about women can sometimes be illuminated from texts which do not deal specifically with women or which speak of them only indirectly. Though sometimes this approach has been used to arrive at misleading conclusions about the Scrolls (as I will illustrate below), there is much to be learned by further study with more sophisticated attention to method.

Whether the presence or absence of certain texts in the library at Qumran can tell us anything about attitudes toward women is a difficult question. For example, discussions about the Biblical manuscripts found at Qumran always note that there are no copies of the book of Esther. Since this is the only book of what we now know as the Hebrew canon not attested in the caves,[42] there has been speculation whether a celibate or misogynist group had deliberately excluded the one Biblical book with a woman as heroine. However there is little evidence of this kind of "censorship" of texts dealing with women; one would have to wonder, for example, why the full and detailed poem describing the beauty of Sarah (Genesis Apocryphon 20:2–8) escaped the censor's notice! There could be many explanations for the non-appearance of Esther, the most likely being simply the size of the book – given that only one small fragment (4Q118) remains of a lengthy work such as 1–2 Chronicles, the absence of Esther is probably related more to statistical probability than to misogynist intent.[43]

In contrast to the absence of Esther, the appearance of certain works in the Qumran library deserves comment. In addition to the poem about Sarah in the Genesis Apocryphon, there is an expanded version of the Song of Mariam which was added at Exodus 15 in a reworked Pentateuch manuscript.[44] Milik (1981) has suggested that a small Aramaic fragment may come from the story of Susanna (though the identification is less than certain). In 11QPs[a] there is an acrostic poem to Wisdom (xxi 11–xxii 1) known to us already (in a rather innocuous Greek translation and in a Hebrew form in a Cairo Genizah manuscript) from Sir. 51:13–30. It describes the psalmist's search for Lady Wisdom, . his nurse, teacher, and mistress who comes to him in her beauty as he burns with desire for her (xxi 15–17). In preparing the *editio princeps*, Sanders interpreted this poem within the context of a celibate male community at Qumran, and saw in it a reflection of the young man's effort to dedicate "his normally developing passions and desires to the pleasures of life with Wisdom" and thus "a commendable manner of sublimation in celibacy" (1965:84). Whether such across-the-ages psychologizing can help us to understand the people at Qumran may be less than convincing, but again the inclusion of this poem in praise of Lady Wisdom is worth noting.

Another text which sometimes has been used as a window onto attitudes toward women at Qumran is 4Q184. This poem has been read as a vivid description of the harlot (according to Allegro's restoration of [HZWN]H as the first word)[45] and her seductions of the righteous. Even when she has been allegorized (the harlot = false teaching, or the evils of Rome, or the personification of evil)[46] or if she is seen as a demonic Lilith figure (Baumgarten 1991), the fact remains that it is a female figure which is described so graphically and negatively. However, given that this text stands directly in the tradition of Prov. 7, Zech. 5:11, and Isa. 34:14, I am not sure that it proves that the group in whose library it was found was necessarily particularly misogynist.

A close analysis of the imagery in the Thanksgiving psalms (the Hodayot) may provide some indirect clues – but that is a project for another paper.[47] Attention needs to be paid both to what Biblical language is used and particularly to where phraseology is subtly changed and modified. It can be noted that the Hodayot maintain the Biblical precedent of speaking directly of God only as father (1QH ix 35), and not as mother, but are not hesitant in drawing upon female imagery (for example, the woman in travail, 1QH iii 7–12, v 30) or balancing male and female illustrations (ix 30, 35–36).

FINAL COMMENTS

The nature of this paper has been so wide-reaching and exploratory that it seems to me premature to attempt to draw any overall conclusions. I have attempted to explore certain questions that might be asked and to draw attention to the major texts which need that might be brought into the discussion. Much work remains to be done both on individual documents in and of themselves, and then by drawing together and comparing different documents which treat the same topic (for example, purity rules, membership, marriage, divorce and prohibition of divorce, oaths, and vows of women). The discussion about women cannot take place in isolation from the larger discussion of the nature and origin of the community of the Scrolls and the archaeology of the site of Khirbet Qumran. And in all these areas, much work lies ahead of us!

NOTES

1 This paper was presented to the Voluntary Association Seminar at the Canadian Society of Biblical Studies meeting in 1992 and updated, particularly in terms of bibliography, in the summer of 1994. Some of the material was further reworked for a Conference of the New York Academy of Sciences and the Oriental Institute of the University of Chicago in December 1992; see Schuller 1994.
2 The bibliography is far too extensive to be comprehensive here, but I would mention in particular: Kraemer 1992; Levine 1991; Brown 1992; Sly 1990; Wegner 1988; for a more uncritical compilation of sources, see Archer 1990.
3 Brief discussions of a page or two can, of course, be found in most standard discussions of the Dead Sea Scrolls, usually consisting of the statements in Philo, Josephus, and Pliny that the Essenes do not marry, plus some remarks on the oddity of finding a few female skeletons in the cemetery. The standard information is put together succinctly in a note by Meeks 1973–74:178–79, n. 70.
4 Estimates of the amount of published versus unpublished material vary. Sometimes figures are computed on the basis of total lines of extant material; since many of the largest scrolls are already published, it is calculated that 20 per cent still await publication. If the calculations are made on the basis of number of manuscripts, the figure is approximately 60 per cent published, 40 per cent unpublished.
5 Qimron and Strugnell 1994. The text has been the subject of much interest since a preliminary report was released in 1984; see Qimron and Strugnell 1985; Schiffman 1990b.

6 Schiffman 1991a. P. R. Davies (1987:9) suggests that some of what we are experiencing might be described as "a reversion to some aspects of adolescent behavior" that can mark middle age!

7 Milik 1959; Cross 1980; Vermes 1977.

8 Some scholars have emphasized Sadducean links, particularly in halakic matters (Schiffman 1990b:68–71); others have sought to find the origin of the group behind the Scrolls in a movement returning from Babylon (Murphy-O'Connor 1977), or a Palestinian apocalyptic movement (Garcia Martinez and van der Woude 1990); still others link the Scrolls with the Jerusalem temple (Golb 1989). In support of the Essene hypothesis, see VanderKam 1991; and Stegemann 1994.

9 Josephus, *War* 2.120–21; *Ant.* 18.21; Philo, *Hypothetica* 11.14–17. For a discussion of Josephus' texts, see Beall 1988:37–42.

10 The only use of the word "woman" is in the Biblical phrase (Job 14:1, 15:14, 25:4) "born of a woman" (WYLWD 'ŠH) in 1QS xi 21.

11 Pliny, *Hist. nat.* 5.73.

12 For an interpretation which sees the group living at Qumran as a splinter breakaway group, see P. R. Davies 1987:47–49.

13 The language of Christian monasticism permeates much of the discussion; note even the title of the book by Sutcliffe 1960.

14 Schiffman 1983:12–13; 1991b:117.

15 Milik 1959:96; to quote P. R. Davies (1987:85) "a century, after all, is a long time to wait for the eschaton."

16 Brownlee 1964:80–81; Qimron 1992.

17 Marx 1969–71; Coppens 1978.

18 For a comparison between statements about the Essenes and Philo's general language about women, see Sly 1990:207–9.

19 Baumgarten 1990:18–19. Qimron seems to have come independently to much the same interpretation; see Qimron 1986:86–87 and 1992; and already Ginzberg 1976:32–33. For a different interpretation which reads the problematic text as referring to the children born within the group, see Davies 1983:142.

20 Flusser 1989:31; Elder 1994.

21 Out of 50 graves now excavated, 36 are of men, 9 of women and 6 of children. De Vaux found 1 female grave among 26 in the main cemetery; the other 6 were in the east section of the main cemetery or the second cemetery (1973:47–49). Steckoll (1968–69) reports to have found 2 other women's graves in the main cemetery. Thus, 30 per cent of the total graves examined belong to women and children (Elder 1994:223–225). However, since only 50 out of the approximately 1,200 graves have been examined, the statistical basis is too small to draw any conclusions.

22 One recurrent suggestion is that Qumran was the site of an annual gathering of all diverse groups, and that during the time of an assembly some women and children died there (see Sanders 1992:529, n. 6).

23 See p. 261 for further discussion of this puzzling text.

24 See Schiffman 1975:116–17, 119–20.

25 For example, Vermes 1974. Another minority view sees the passage as forbidding a second marriage at any time, even after the wife's death, for example, Murphy-O'Connor 1970:220, and P. R. Davies 1987:73–86.

26 e.g., Fitzmyer 1978. CDC xiii 17 may mention "the one who divorces" (LMGRŠ). These lines in the Rule for the Overseer (CDC xii 7) are broken and difficult to read in CDC but more fully preserved in 4Q266 18 ii 1–11. This text requires more study.

27 Ginzberg 1976:22 "what halakic controversy is alluded to here one cannot say with certainty."

28 For a discussion of the very complex issues around "the city of the sanctuary" see Schiffman 1985.

29 Baumgarten (1992a) gives an initial description of the 4QD material. My numbering of fragments and lines is according to the earlier transcription of J. T. Milik, and may be somewhat different in the final edition.

30 See Schuller 1994:121–22; Kraemer 1989 and the bibliography in n. 20.

31 As argued by Stegemann 1994:159–62, contra the interpretation of Schiffman 1989.

32 Many translators, following the suggestion of Baumgarten (1957:266–69) have emended the text, sometimes without even a note to give the original.

33 For a negative judgment about their identity as one text, see Schiffman 1994:148.

34 Following the interpretation of Weinert 1974:202.

35 Baillet (1982:292) suggested that fg. 13 might have included material on incestuous marriage (reading WM'RWT 'BY') in line 1 "the nudity of the father," but Baumgarten's reading GB' "rock-pool" seems preferable in context (1985:391–92).

36 Qimron and Strugnell 1994:158–60 and 171–72.

37 In oral communication, Stegemann indicated that he is convinced of a totally different placement and reconstruction – so that the fragment is not at all relevant to the discussion of women.

38 See Yadin 1977–83, 1:289, 306–7; for a somewhat different approach, see Schiffman 1985:301–20.

39 This is the usual interpretation, though it has been disputed, for example, Vawter 1977:533.

40 For a brief survey, see Brooke 1989:13–19 where he describes the widely divergent theories which attempt to place the scroll anywhere from the early post-exilic period as a sixth book of the Torah (Stegemann) to an actual composition of the Essenes (Yadin).

41 Against this is the observation made by Schiffman (1987:43) that the text has no points of contact with the amoraic marriage blessings (*b. Ket.* 7b–8a) while other liturgical texts in the scrolls have some links of vocabulary and themes with later liturgy.

42 Taking Ezra–Nehemiah as a single book; there is no trace of Nehemiah either.

43 Milik (1992) has published an Aramaic text which he considers closely related to the Hebrew book of Esther; this is certainly a court-tale but links to Esther *per se* are less than certain.

44 White 1992; Brooke 1994.

45 Though this reading is hardly possible; see Strugnell 1970:264.

46 Carmignac 1965; Allegro 1964; Moore 1981.

47 For an examination of the Hodayot from the perspective of the fatherhood of God, Strotmann 1991:337–59.

14

WHERE WOMEN SAT IN ANCIENT SYNAGOGUES

The archaeological evidence in context[1]

Sharon Lea Mattila

The story of women in the ancient synagogue is a difficult one to reconstruct, not least because synagogue studies today are in a state of flux, with new material forcing much re-evaluation and many of the old theories foundering (Meyers 1992:259). This chapter will begin with a brief survey of the archaeological evidence for synagogues in the Graeco-Roman world – evidence that undermines the setting up of women in the ancient synagogue as a foil for women in the early house-church. Two questions will then be addressed: (1) Were women's galleries or barriers between the sexes common in ancient synagogues? (2) How was seating arranged with respect to the sexes? An effort will be made to keep the archaeological evidence *in context* – that is, to correlate it as much as possible with the relevant literary and inscriptional data. In order to address the question of seating arrangements, it will be necessary to examine some of the evidence on women in public settings from the wider Graeco-Roman context, both pagan and Christian.

THE ANCIENT SYNAGOGUE BEFORE AND AFTER 70 CE

The archaeological evidence for Second-Temple synagogues is scanty. No hard evidence exists for basilical synagogues in this period and most synagogues probably reflected the local architecture of their particular regions, often being indistinguishable from domestic architecture and therefore not liable to identification (Gutmann 1975b:xii–xiii). It has been plausibly proposed by L. Michael White (1990) that many Jewish synagogues – like many pagan shrines and churches – were installed in private homes donated by patrons or benefactors who were either members of the community or sympathizers. The earliest synagogue excavated so far (first century BCE) was originally a house in a residential quarter near the seashore on the isle of Delos in the Aegean Sea (White 1990:64–67; 1987). Initially, the interior remodelling of these homes would do little to change their basic domestic character, and sometimes the owners would continue to live in certain parts of the house. In the larger and wealthier communities, further adaptation and renovation in successive stages could occur. Besides houses, other buildings could be converted into synagogues. Both the

Masada and the Herodium synagogues initially were buildings that were part of Herod's fortress palaces, improvised into assembly halls during the First Jewish Revolt.[2]

Some pre-70 synagogues, however, seem to have been built as public assembly halls from their foundations. The synagogue at Gamla (dated 23 BCE–41 CE) is significantly larger than those at Masada and Herodium[3] and displays "an advanced architecture with proficiency in Hellenistic building techniques" (Ma'oz 1981:40) with fine workmanship and ornamentation.[4] The Ophel or Theodotus inscription (Jerusalem, first century CE) refers to a synagogue complex founded and constructed over several generations, and includes the words *oikodomeō* and *themelioō*, indicating that it was built from its foundations as a public building set aside for "purposes of reciting the Law and studying the commandments."[5] Philo singles out an Alexandrian synagogue as being "the greatest and most famous," perhaps the predecessor of the monolithic second-century Alexandrian Diplostoon mentioned in the Tosefta.[6]

The destruction of the Temple in 70 CE certainly had a profound impact on the Jewish synagogue, but it is not feasible – either logically or on the basis of the evidence – to argue for *too* abrupt a transition in the nature of the synagogue from the pre-70 to the post-70 period. Significant changes did take place architecturally and liturgically, but they probably happened gradually, especially in the Diaspora. For instance, not even after Constantine did basilical architecture universally and immediately supersede all existing synagogues or church buildings, and the renovated religious domus continued to exist alongside the basilica. This was particularly the case in the Diaspora where the Jewish communities constituted minorities (albeit sometimes significant ones) in the various Graeco-Roman cities in which they lived (White 1990:21, 23). Of the five post-70 Diaspora synagogue buildings that have been excavated extensively – Priene (fourth century), Sardis (third to fifth century), Stobi (second to third century), Ostia (first to fourth century), and Dura-Europos (second to third century) – all but one seem to have been renovated from private dwellings typical of the domestic architecture of their particular locale. The massive Sardis synagogue stands out as the single exception, and even its monumental basilical hall had not been originally designated as a synagogue, but was installed in the long south-eastern wing of a mammoth Roman bath–gymnasium complex.[7]

From the post-Second-Temple period in Palestine a plethora of new data on synagogues has been unearthed,[8] to which rigid typological–chronological schemes cannot be applied. For a substantial minority of these synagogues, even the issue of orientation towards Jerusalem is not clear-cut. Nevertheless, the majority can still be classed roughly into three basic types: (1) the basilica with a monumental façade facing Jerusalem; (2) the broadhouse; and (3) the basilica with an apse or niche facing Jerusalem.[9] In the post-70 period, basilical synagogues seem to have dominated the architectural landscape in Palestine far more than in the Diaspora.[10] This is not unexpected, given that in Palestine the concentration of Jews was higher than in the Diaspora. It is not yet certain, however, when basilicas became the predominant type of Palestinian synagogue, as the dating of many synagogues is still being debated. It is possible that the basilica did not become widespread until after Constantine.[11] Nor can it be determined whether or not house-synagogues also continued to exist in Palestine during this period. In the smaller communities, it is likely enough that they did.

GENERAL IMPLICATIONS FOR WOMEN IN BOTH ANCIENT SYNAGOGUE AND EARLY CHURCH

Several general implications regarding women not only in the ancient synagogue but also in the early church can be drawn from this evidence. Most importantly, the data challenge the view that the role of women in the house-church was by its "privatized" nature intrinsically something quite different from that of women in the ancient synagogue. The labeling of house-churches as "private" or "quasi-private" has suggested greater autonomy for women within their precincts, since women generally had freer reign in the private domain.[12] But to call a house-church "private" and an ancient synagogue "public" is a false dichotomy. No longer can the house-church be depicted as something unique, for the renovation of private homes was a common way of turning over property for public use. Many synagogues were also installed in homes, especially in the Diaspora – where, incidentally, the majority of house-churches were also established. Women in the ancient synagogue can no longer be set up as a foil for women in the house-church.[13]

White has cautioned that a distinction must be drawn between house-churches and a later *domus ecclesiae* such as the Dura-Europus Christian building (1990:7–8, 20–22). The extent of architectural overhaul to which a house-church would have been subjected would probably not have compared to that observed in the church *domus* at Dura. Yet we have no way of knowing to what extent the earliest Christian communities remodeled the interiors of the homes they gave over for church use in order to accommodate them to their new public function. Given that such renovation of private property for public use was common among religious and collegial groups, at least some remodeling is likely. For instance, despite the hurried and makeshift nature of the renovations effected on the Herodian halls at Masada and Herodium, the Jewish insurgents still subjected them to a fair degree of structural overhaul,[14] and this despite the fact that they did not expect to use them on a permanent basis. These examples of the insurgents' industry should give us pause before we assume that all early Christians left the domestic character of their house-churches intact. But even the humblest house-synagogue or house-church, while it may have been more intimate than a larger, overhauled structure, was not for this reason any less public.

What this would have meant for women is this: both in the synagogue and in the house-church, they would have been expected to behave as they would in any respectable, Graeco-Roman *public* forum. Both the synagogue and the house-church were understood to be *public* spaces devoted to *public* use, and this notwithstanding the particular stage of their renovation from private homes. Thus, not only is a rigid portrayal of women in the synagogue called into question, but a "privatized," informal, egalitarian model of the house-church must also be re-evaluated.[15]

GALLERIES OR BARRIERS BETWEEN THE SEXES IN ANCIENT SYNAGOGUES?

Already in 1975, Joseph Gutmann cautioned, "the existence of women's galleries in Galilean synagogues is far from established and demands re-examination" (1975b:xiii). Bernadette Brooten has since demonstrated definitively that in the vast majority of the excavated synagogue sites in the Diaspora and in Palestine there exists no solid evidence for women's galleries (1982:103–38). According to Brooten, only five synagogue sites offer plausible evidence for a gallery – Capernaum, Chorazin, 'En-Gedi, Khirbet Shema', and Khirbet Susiya (1982:121–22). In Marilyn Chiat's *Handbook of Synagogue Architecture* only the last two – Khirbet Shema' and Khirbet Susiya – are listed unambiguously as having galleries of some sort.[16] Chiat does not include Capernaum in this list because reports by V. Corbo and S. Loffreda (two principal excavators of the site) have indicated that the synagogue's foundations are too weak to support an upper floor.[17] She makes no mention at all of a gallery at Chorazin, but documents only a stairway on the synagogue's south (and possibly one on the east) ascending to a "terrace that runs the full length of the building's façade" (1982:98). At 'Ein Gedi, the remains of a stairway and the thickness of the western piers suggest the possibility of a gallery above the narthex and the western aisle, but neither the excavators nor Chiat judge this to be certain.[18]

The archaeological remains of the synagogue at Khirbet Shema' in Upper Galilee (see Figure 14.1) do seem to indicate that it contained a gallery of some sort, as the reconstructed plan shows (see Figure 14.2). The synagogue is a broadhouse, with its broad southern wall facing Jerusalem. It underwent two building stages (third century and fourth century CE), the earlier synagogue being more elaborate than its successor, but very similar in plan, orientation, and size.[19] The western end of the synagogue is built into the side of a hill, with a monumental staircase entering down along the southern wall into the main hall from the west. A second entrance to the synagogue is located on the northern wall, level with the main hall, while the *bema* is situated on the southern wall. The gallery is level with the upper landing of the western staircase. Directly underneath the gallery, cut into the bedrock, is a gaily frescoed chamber which opens into the center of the main hall's western wall. This chamber has direct access to a small room to its south, under the western staircase, possibly a *genizah*. Directly beside the north-western wing of the synagogue, level with the gallery and separated from it by a narrow passage leading down from the street to the lower entrance, is a building whose architectural features suggest a study hall. This passageway was improved with a regular flight of stairs at the second stage. The

Figure 14.1 Restored prayer hall of Khirbet Shema' synagogue, looking south-west (from: *Ancient Synagogues Revealed*, ed. Lee I. Levine. Jerusalem: The Israeli Exploration Society, 1981:70)

gallery has a northern doorway (cut at the second stage) opening onto this side-alley stairway, as well as a small entrance off the landing of the western staircase.[20]

This reconstruction of the Khirbet Shema' synagogue does not very plausibly lend itself to the hypothesis that its gallery was reserved for women. Brooten reports that one of the excavators, Meyers, admitted that he is "not inclined to call the gallery a 'women's gallery'" (1982:254 n. 64). Its floor-space is less than 20 per cent that of the main hall and its location with respect to the focus of worship would have made it an awkward place from which to participate in the service.[21] The narrow side-alley steps between the synagogue and study hall also seem an inappropriate entrance-way for women, especially in contrast to the spacious western and northern entrances supposedly reserved for the men. As for the gallery's entrance off the landing of the western staircase, women would have had to enter the landing with the men before reaching it, defeating the gallery's putative purpose of separating women from men in the synagogue (Safrai 1993:5).

Perhaps menstrual regulations and the exemption of women from a number of cultic obligations, including the obligation to attend synagogue,[22] resulted in

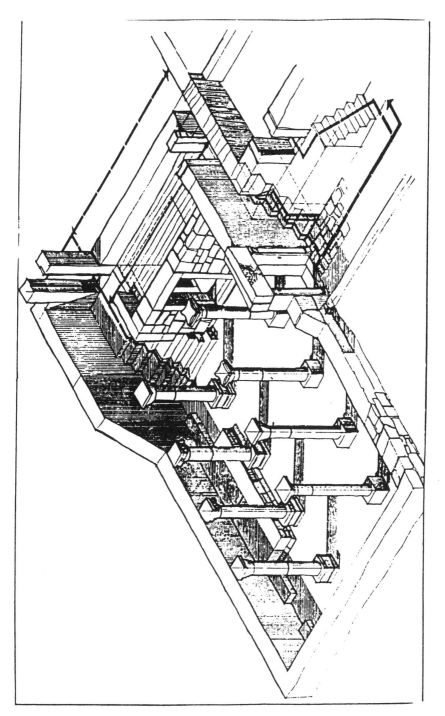

Figure 14.2 Isometric reconstruction of Khirbet Shema' synagogue looking south-west, with study hall at right (from: *Ancient Synagogues: The State of Research*, ed. Joseph Gutmann, BJS 22. Chico, Calif: Scholars, 1981:118)

fewer women being present at any given time than men. But the exact nature of these rules in this period and in different geographical regions, as well as their effects on women's actual synagogue attendance, are difficult to ascertain.[23] Even if fewer women did as a rule attend this synagogue than men, their confinement to such a space so awkwardly positioned with respect to the focus of worship seems unlikely. A more reasonable hypothesis is that this small space was some sort of storage area. The northern door opening onto the side-alley steps next to the study hall would suggest that this storeroom contained the scrolls used by the rabbis, scribes, and students who regularly gathered next door to study them. The installation of the door and regular flight of stairs at the second stage could have been to facilitate access to this storeroom from the study hall. Various synagogue implements could also have been kept there.

The Khirbet Susiya synagogue (fourth to fifth century CE) is also a broad-house, with its two *bemas* located along its broad northern wall, facing Jerusalem (see Figure 14.3). There is an enclosed courtyard to the east of the main hall, with five wide steps ascending 1.5 m through a colonnade to the narthex. Along the synagogue's southern wall are two auxiliary rooms. The main hall is lined with triple-tiered benches along its southern and western walls, and along the northern wall up to the main *bema*. The synagogue plan shows two flights of stairs, separated by almost the full breadth of the prayer hall.[24] According to the excavator's report, the steps at the southern end of the narthex "led up to a second story which lay above the southern wing," while the "hall itself probably rose the full two-story height of 8–9 m" (Gutman, Yeivin, and Netzer 1981:124). Was this second story a women's gallery? Chiat reports that Ze'ev Yeivin (in two personal interviews with her in 1975 and 1977) proposed that at a later stage of construction a gallery was "built over the hall's western wall, which was reinforced to support the added weight" (1982:231–32, 234, n. 1). The second set of stairs was installed to lead up to this gallery in the south-western auxiliary room. These steps ascend "over a small vaulted storeroom" to their left (Gutman, Yeivin, and Netzer 1981:124).

The case for a gallery over the southern wing and possibly over the narthex of the synagogue (Brooten 1982:118), later extended over the western wall as well, is reasonably strong here. After its extension, such a gallery would have supported a fair number of women congregants who would have been able to observe the worship service quite conveniently. Moreover, access to the gallery would have been separated from the men's three entrances off the narthex. Still, it cannot be said that the evidence for a women's gallery at Khirbet Susiya is conclusive. The extension of the gallery over the western wall is hypothetical, and the narrow second story over the southern wing could well have served as a storage area, accessible via these two flights of stairs.

In the Rabbinic literature, there is only one women's gallery to which unambiguous reference is made – the gallery specially erected to surround the Women's Court of the Jerusalem Temple (*b. Sukk.* 51b–52a; cf. *m. Mid.* 2:5, Josephus, *War* 5.198–200, *Ag. Apion* 2.102–4). But this was used by the women

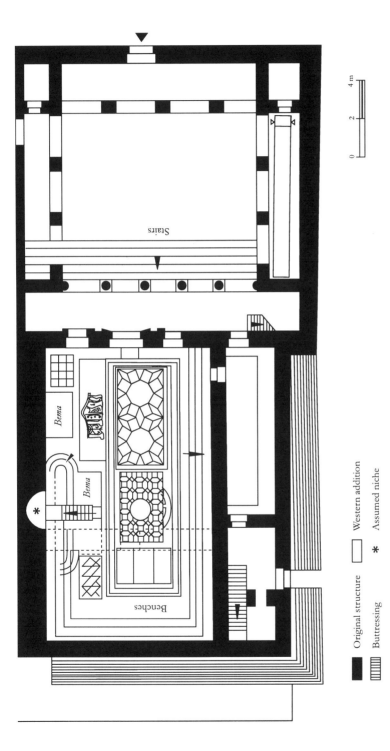

Figure 14.3 Reconstructed plan of Khirbet Susiya synagogue (from: *Ancient Synagogues Revealed*, ed. Lee I. Levine, Jerusalem: The Israeli Exploration Society, 1981:123)

Original structure   Western addition

Buttressing   * Assumed niche

Stairs

Bema

Bema

Benches

0   2   4 m

only during the Water-Drawing Festival held annually on the Feast of Taber-
nacles, when dancing went on all night and it was feared that the spirit of levity
would bring about licentious conduct between the sexes.[25] The Jerusalem
Talmud (*y. Sukk.* 55b.14–23) *may* refer to a women's gallery in the enormous
second-century "double colonnade" *Diplostoon* (DPLSTWN = *diplē stoa*) of Alexandria. This magnificent edifice was destroyed by Trajan. After slaughtering all
the men, the emperor offered the women mercy on condition of obedience, to
which they responded, "Do to those above ('YYLY') as you have done to those
below ('YY'R')."[26] Jacob Neusner offers an alternative translation of this passage: "What you did to the ones who have fallen do also to us who are yet standing" (1984:119). Despite its ambiguity, this passage *may* imply the existence of a
women's gallery in the Alexandrian Diplostoon.

On the subject of physical barriers between the sexes, the Rabbinic literature
has little to say. One passage in the Babylonian Talmud (*b. Kid.* 81a) makes reference to a partition of jugs set up between the sexes by Abaye and a partition of
canes by Raba, but the precise context in which these partitions were made is not
clear. There is, however, one certain instance of a physical barrier between the
sexes in a Jewish worship setting attested by Philo. In *Vita cont.* Philo describes a
monastic Jewish sect living near Lake Mareotis outside Alexandria – the Therapeutai and Therapeutrides.[27] During the week these people lived in individual
cells, devoting their lives to philosophical contemplation and prayer, but on the
Sabbath they assembled for prayer and study in their own specially designed
"gathering place":

> This common sanctuary (*to de koinon touto semneion*) in which they come to-
> gether every seventh day is a double enclosure (*diplous esti peribolos*), one
> section set apart for the men, the other for the women (*ho men eis andrōna,
> ho de eis gynaikōnitin apokritheis*). For women too customarily form part of
> the audience, possessed by the same fervor and sense of purpose. The par-
> tition [lit., "wall"] between the two chambers (*ho de metaxy tōn oikōn toichos*)
> is built up to three or four cubits above the floor in the form of a breast
> work, while the space above up to the roof is left open. This serves two
> purposes: that the modesty proper to women's nature (*tēi gynaikeiai physei*)
> be maintained and that the women seated within ear-shot with nothing to
> obstruct the voice of the speaker may obtain easy apprehension.
>
> (32–33)[28]

Other first-century sources, however, militate against the notion that physical
barriers between the sexes were common in ancient synagogues. In a Lukan miracle story (Luke 13:10–17), Jesus heals a crippled woman while "teaching in one
of the synagogues on the sabbath" (13:10). When "seeing her," "he called her to
himself" (13:12) in order to "place his hands on her" and heal her (13:13). The
setting of this miracle story in a synagogue would have jarred the imaginations
of the Lukan community had women been commonly restricted to galleries.
Moreover, had physical barriers between the sexes been familiar in the

synagogue, the audience would have wondered how Jesus was able to "see" the infirm woman.[29] As for the *archisynagōgos* who protests the miracle, he sees nothing indecorous in Jesus' contact with the woman, but only in his healing on the Sabbath (13:14).

A much-debated passage in the book of Acts (16:11–15) speaks of a *proseuchē* on the outskirts of Philippi by a river, in which Paul and Silas find a group of women who had "come together" (*tais synelthousais gynaixin*) for prayer (16:13). There seems to be no impediment to the men joining this all-female congregation. Among the women is a wealthy godfearer (*sebomenē ton theon*), Lydia, a seller of purple who becomes a convert when she hears Paul's preaching. This is the only place where Acts refers to a *proseuchē*. The term *synagōgē* is far more common (Acts. 6:9; 9:2, 20; 13:5, 14–15, 43; 14:1; 15:21; 16:13, 16; 17:1, 10, 17; 18:4, 7–8, 17, 19, 26; 19:8; 22:19; 26:11). In Egypt, the term *proseuchē* was commonly used for synagogue buildings or assembly halls, but the solo appearance of this term in Acts, especially in contrast to the abundant occurrence of the term *synagōgē*, does give us pause in interpreting this *proseuchē* to be a building. One possible explanation for the occurrence of this *hapax legomenon* is that vv. 11–15 may represent a travel narrative incorporated into the book of Acts (Gillman 1990:70). It is certainly not inconceivable that a synagogue building could have existed outside the city near a river. Josephus cites a "decree of the people of Halicarnassus" by which the Jews were permitted to "build places of prayer near the sea, in accordance with their native custom" (*tas proseuchas poieisthai pros tēi thalattēi kata to patrion ethos*).[30] The early synagogue at Delos was built near the sea, as was an amphitheater-style synagogue in Berenice, together with synagogues in several other cities, such as Miletus, Ephesus, and Caesarea Maritima (Applebaum 1979:162). The presence of a reasonably influential Jewish community in the prominent Macedonian Roman colony of Philippi is suggested by Phil. 3:1–10, in which Paul warns his followers against "those mutilators of the flesh" (3:2). It is true that Acts 16:20 dramatically depicts the Philippian Romans rejecting the customs of the Jews, but this does not necessarily mean that Jews were marginal in Philippi. Romans in the mother-city were not always overly receptive to Jewish customs either, and this did not prevent the Jews from founding a substantial community in Rome.[31] If this *proseuchē* was understood by the first- and second-century audience of Acts to have been a building, this passage would have presented a singularly absurd scene to their imaginations had women's galleries or physical barriers between the sexes been familiar to them.

It can also be asked whether the architectural plans and artistic ornamentation of many ancient synagogues conveniently allowed for the erection of barriers between the sexes. It is difficult to imagine, for instance, where in the Gamla synagogue – given its theater-like design and focus at the center – such a partition would have been installed. In the later basilical-style synagogues, such barriers would have been eyesores. Moreover, such obtrusive dividers would not have permitted some of the mosaics – an important feature of a synagogue's interior décor – to be properly viewed. Some mosaics are clearly designed for display over the entire space of the main floor-area. For example, the mosaic pavement of the Beth Alpha basilical synagogue, laid out in the nave, includes a zodiac cycle occupying a large portion of its central area. The two sizeable rectangular scenes flanking the zodiac cycle at either end of the nave, one depicting the sacrifice of Isaac and the other the ark surrounded by religious objects, also span most of the nave's width. Any partition installed either horizontally or vertically in this hall would have obstructed the presentation of this mosaic's design.[32] A full display of the main mosaic floor of the synagogue at 'En Gedi likewise would have been impeded by the erection of a barrier, although this synagogue *may* have had a gallery.[33] Similarly, the elaborate cycle of Biblical scenes covering all four walls of the Dura synagogue would not have readily allowed for a partitioned room.[34]

It cannot be argued definitively that, aside from the instance of the ascetic Therapeutai, partitions were never raised in Jewish assembly halls, nor can it be asserted that not a single women's gallery ever existed in an ancient synagogue. Nevertheless, the evidence manifestly indicates that *if* women's galleries did exist in some ancient synagogues, they were rare. Nor can we generalize from the assembly-hall of the ascetic Therapeutai to the average prayer-hall used by less ascetic Jews.

SEATING ARRANGEMENTS IN ANCIENT SYNAGOGUES

While the evidence suggests that women were rarely (if ever) confined to galleries and that physical barriers between the sexes may not have been common, this does not answer the question as to whether or not segregated seating arrangements were adopted in ancient synagogues. Clearly, this is not a question that the archaeological evidence can answer on its own. It is thus necessary to turn elsewhere for illumination in order to set the archaeological data in context. A range of data from the Graeco-Roman environment within which synagogue assemblies took place must be considered.

It is widely accepted that in comparison to their Athenian counterparts Roman women enjoyed considerable autonomy in this period – even more than Macedonian and Dorian women who, among the Greeks, were the most autonomous.[35] In their private homes, the Romans were not segregated as were the Greeks. Floor plans of wealthy Roman domiciles, in which the various rooms of a given house surround the central atrium, stand in contrast to Greek/Hellenistic homes of comparable wealth, typically divided into separate men's and women's quarters (Cotter 1994:359–60). Visitors would find the Roman *materfamilias* in the atrium where they could converse with her. Nor were respectable Roman women barred from the market-place, as were their Athenian counterparts (Clark 1981:201).

Roman women were also in the habit of attending public banquets with their husbands (unthinkable for Greek women). However, it should be stressed that this was only for the *deipnon*, or meal proper. After the meal itself had ended and the *symposion* or drinking-party had begun, respectable Roman matrons were expected to leave. For at this point the prostitutes and courtesans (*hetairai*) joined in to enhance the men's entertainment. It goes without saying that the prostitutes and *hetairai* mingled freely enough with the men at the *symposion*. But at the *deipnon*, Roman matrons and their husbands reclined *separately*, men with men, women with women, couch by couch. Women were sometimes given a couch or section of couches completely set apart from the men, particularly at weddings. As for unmarried young girls, these did not as a rule attend public banquets, except for the carefully segregated wedding feasts (Corley 1993:24–31).

Not even at the theater or the games did Roman men and women mingle freely. Beryl Rawson reports:

> We know . . . that from Augustus's time separate sections of the theatre or amphitheatre were set aside for different groups. For the watching of plays, gladiatorial contests, animal shows and other games, married men, women and schoolboys all sat in different places (the schoolboys' slave attendants – the *paedagogi* – who were responsible for their conduct sitting in a section adjoining the boys').[36]

According to an inscription from the second century BCE, a group of six freedmen constructed a block of seats specifically for women at a theater in Capua.[37] The *Acts of Thecla* 32 depicts women as sitting separately from men in the arena at Pisidian Antioch where Thecla was cast to the beasts (Kraemer 1992:107).

Upper-class Jewish women also seem to have attended public banquets, where they too were segregated from the men. At the fortress of Herod at Machaerus, archaeological excavations have revealed two dining rooms immediately alongside one another – one for women and one for men. Sir. 9:9 implies that, although it was not unheard of, it was considered to be "mortally" dangerous for a man to recline next to a woman at a public feast: "With a married woman dine not, recline not at table to drink by her side, lest your heart be drawn to her and you go down in blood to the grave" (NAB). The sole exception seems to have been the Passover seder, at which women were required to recline next to their husbands, no doubt in imitation of the families who gathered together to eat the Passover lamb in Exodus 12. Note, however, that this is not tantamount to a free mingling of the sexes, as only husband and wife were permitted to recline together. Moreover, the women were barred from participating in the after-dinner liturgical celebrations, just as Roman women were excluded from the *symposion* (Corley 1993:66–79).

The New Testament evidence also supports the argument that in public settings respectable women tended to be segregated from men. Kathleen E. Corley has recently completed a comparative study of women in the context of public meals in the three synoptic gospels. Only Matthew portrays women as present with men at public meals (1993:178–79); neither Mark nor Luke explicitly depict

women as eating or reclining with men (1993:106–9). Except at the wedding of
Cana (John 2:1–11), the gospel of John also does not depict women reclining
with men at public meals. At weddings, even young virgins would have been
present (Matt. 25:1–13). However, following the Graeco-Roman custom at weddings – even in the case of Roman women – it is very probably understood in
this narrative that the women reclined separately from the men.

Matthew is the only gospel to mention the presence of women and children at
the feeding miracles (Matt. 14:13–21 / Mark 6:32–44 / Luke 9:10b–17 / John
6:1–15; Matt. 15:32–39 / Mark 8:1–10) (Corley 1993:160–64). Corley's suggestion that the Matthean feeding miracles are "eucharistic family meals" representing an "egalitarian community" (ibid.:178) is questionable, however. This is
demonstrated by the fact that in neither of the Matthean miracles do the women
and children number among the count for the men. All four versions of the
feeding of the five thousand *men* speak specifically of *pentakischilioi andres* (Matt.
14:21=Mark 6:44=Luke 9:14=John 6:10), and the Matthean version of the feeding of the four thousand is more specific than the Markan version[38] in stipulating
that there were present *tetrakischilioi andres* (four thousand *men*) (Matt. 15:38). The
phrase *chōris gynaikōn kai paidiōn* (besides women and children, Matt. 14:21;
15:38) is simply tacked on. While it is true that the gospel of Matthew is more
inclusive than the others in its representation of the feeding miracles, the portrait is hardly one of an "egalitarian community." Furthermore, one must be
careful not to assume that Matthew intends to depict a free mingling of women
and children with men, after the manner of a modern-day church picnic.[39]

There is also no reason to assume that Paul's letters imply the free intermingling of men and women in house-church gatherings. Indeed, Paul more
than once insists on decorum with respect to women's public comportment, a
decorum reflecting typical Hellenistic values (for example, 1 Cor. 11:2–16; 14:33–
36).[40] One might even say that Paul, clearly more Hellenistic than Roman (notwithstanding his Roman citizenship), is relatively conservative in his attitude towards women in public. Averil Cameron has gone so far as to call Paul's attitude
"reactionary" (1980:63–66), and she may not be entirely off the mark.

While Paul clearly had significant contact with Romanized women,[41] rendering due honor to those who were patronesses of the church,[42] his diatribe
against bare-headed women in 1 Cor. 11:2–16 reveals that in his estimation some
Roman customs were not to be tolerated. The Corinth of Paul's time was very
much a Roman colony,[43] and it was observed by the biographer, Plutarch, that
it was "more the custom for women to be veiled" in the Greek half of the
Mediterranean world than in the Roman.[44] In the Priscilla fresco or "Fractio
Panis," a Eucharistic fresco from the Roman catacombs, only one of the seven
women depicted dons a veil. The rest wear their hair upswept, with a hint of
earrings, arranged in a manner comparable to the hairstyles of emperor's wives
depicted on coins datable to the end of the first century CE.[45] Paul's diatribe is
thus best understood as resulting from a cultural clash with Romanized Corinthian women, and his conservative, Hellenistic attitude is plain. It is altogether

unlikely that a man of traditional sentiments like Paul would have countenanced the free intermingling of the sexes at Eucharistic celebrations.

It must be underscored that even the "emancipated," unveiled women represented in the Roman fresco do not recline together with men when celebrating the Eucharist. In the several other Roman Eucharistic scenes similar to the "Fractio Panis" from the same early period, the participants (always seven in number) are all male.[46] Thus, the scenes depict segregated Eucharistic gatherings. This is not in the least bit surprising, as we have seen. Their segregation simply reflects a concern for propriety in public settings that pervaded all of Graeco-Roman society in this period (Corley 1993:76–77).

Later Christian literature also confirms that men and women did not intermingle in church. The Christian father, Tertullian, alludes to gender-segregated seating in the churches.[47] Detailed orders for appropriate seating arrangements in church are elaborated in the (fourth century CE?) *Constitutions of the Holy Apostles* (2.57). Besides being segregated according to gender, people are organized according to age and status. Even separate entrances for women and men, duly guarded, are required: "Let the Porters stand at the entries of the men, and observe them. Let the Deaconesses also stand at those of the women, like shipmen." Moreover, the women are commanded to approach the altar "with their heads covered, as is becoming the order of women."[48]

While the archaeological evidence undermines the notion that women's galleries or other structural barriers between the sexes were common in ancient synagogues, a good deal of evidence indicates that seating arrangements in respectable, Graeco-Roman public settings – pagan, Jewish, and Christian – were segregated. Clearly, ancient synagogues in the Roman empire are to be classified as respectable, Graeco-Roman public forums. Barriers or galleries would not have been necessary for such separation of the sexes. In any of the synagogues from the Diaspora or Palestine – whether from the Second-Temple period or well after it, whether the humblest house-synagogue or the most monumental structure – segregated seating could have been implemented with ease. If women in the ancient synagogue mingled freely with men, then the synagogue was a most unusual, liberal, and countercultural Graeco-Roman public institution indeed. Not only was it less conservative than the Pauline house-church, it was also looser than the Roman public banquet, and even more libertine than the Roman arena and theater! Needless to say, this is not a likely scenario. Therefore, it is highly probable that women, with few exceptions if any, sat separately from men in ancient synagogues throughout the Roman empire.

There is one argument recently offered against segregated seating in ancient synagogues that should be addressed. An inscription from Phocaea in Ionia (third century CE?) speaks of a benefactress, Tation, who was rewarded by the Jewish synagogue for her generosity with a golden crown and the privilege of sitting in a seat of honor (*proedria*).[49] Ross Kraemer claims that this inscription "violates the assumption that men and women sat separately in ancient synagogues" (1992:119). Referring to the imposing triple-tiered semi-circle of marble benches in the apse of the Sardis synagogue, which could seat about seventy people (see Figure 14.4) – no doubt reserved for various leaders, donors, and other important congregants – Kraemer speculates that Tation might have sat, "together with men and other women honored by the community," in "precisely such a seat" (1992:107). But the magnificent Sardis synagogue, the largest synagogue excavated from the ancient world (substantially larger than the largest excavated Palestinian synagogue, Beth Yerah), was hardly typical of synagogues in western Asia Minor. According to Andrew R. Seager, the semi-circular benches in the apse are "unique among ancient synagogues" (Seager 1983:177). More importantly, while there is a fair amount of evidence scattered throughout the empire for women patrons and leaders in various synagogues,[50] it is not certain that the Sardis evidence itself offers much to encourage the probability of Kraemer's speculation. Because the Sardis inscriptions have not yet been fully published,[51] we must rely on the reports of those who have seen them, together with the few scattered inscriptions that are in print. Among the approximately 80 Sardis synagogue inscriptions, women do not figure very prominently – only 12 are mentioned, all in conjunction with their husbands.[52] The majority of these wives are not even named![53] On the other hand, the 80 inscriptions apparently have a great deal to say about the positions held by the men. According to the reports, civilian titles are especially common, attesting to the prestige of the Sardis Jews, and religious titles also appear.[54] Thus, the dearth of evidence for women leaders at Sardis cannot be said to be due to a lack of evidence from this synagogue regarding its prestigious members.

When one compares the Sardis inscriptions to a roughly contemporary set of inscriptions from the mosaic-floor remains of the synagogue at Apamea, Syria (dated to 391 CE), the role of women in the Sardis synagogue seems to have been quite subdued. Of the 19 Apamean donor inscriptions, no less than 9 were dedicated by women whose names appear without any mention of either husband or father.[55] One of these independent women donors contributed 150 feet of mosaic pavement[56] – the same amount as the *archisynagōgos* of Antioch (Lifshitz 1967:38)! These Apamean women may have belonged to the same household, but this does not negate their obvious prominence in contrast to the women of Sardis. When women were prominent in a given synagogue community, therefore, the inscriptional evidence seems to show it.

Which of the Sardis women, then, would have been invited to sit among the 70 men of honor? The 12 wives, most of whom their husbands had neglected to name? In short, the Sardis evidence simply does not proffer any serious women candidates for its imposing semi-circle of marble seats.

The Sardis case notwithstanding, women leaders from other parts of the empire – for whom we do have evidence – such as Tation, were probably given seats of honor in their synagogues. And there is one respect in which the Phocaean synagogue (albeit on a humbler scale) *may* have resembled the Sardis building: according to Renov, synagogue dignitaries generally sat in a conspicuous location, facing the congregation (1975:235–36). But it is not clear that these

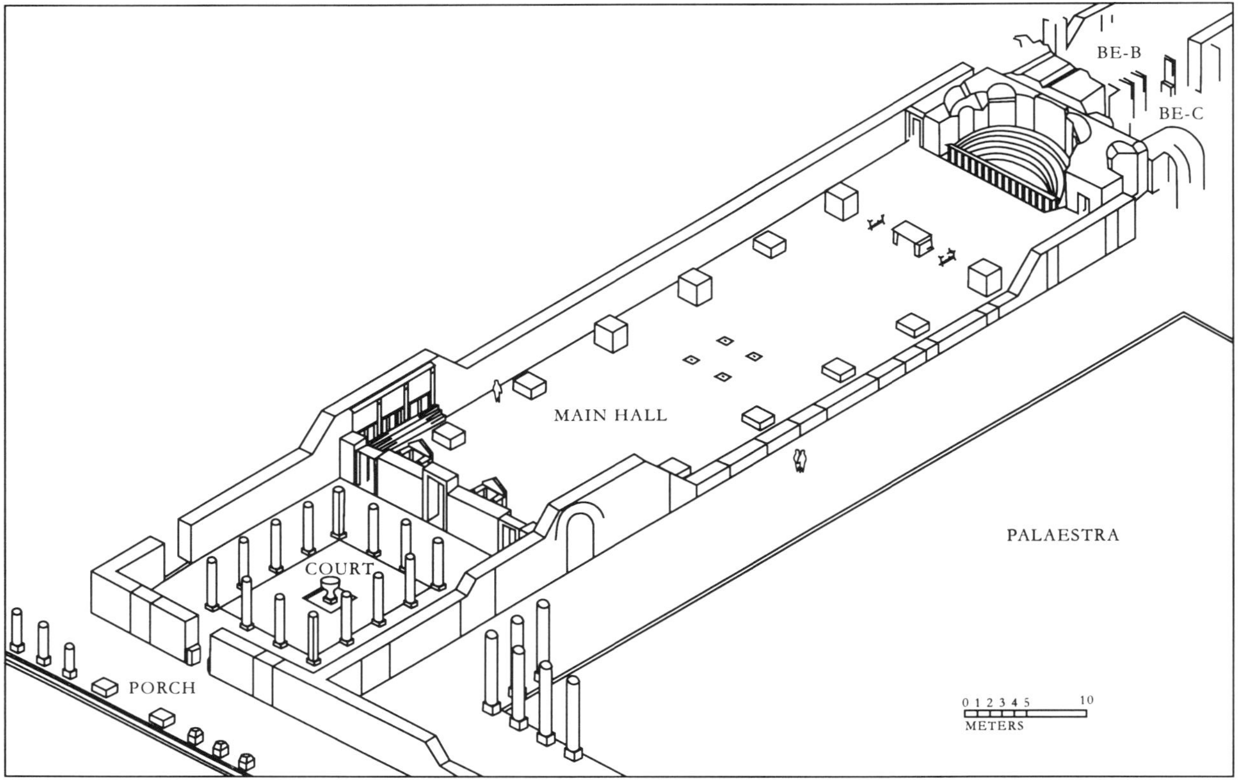

Figure 14.4 Isometric reconstruction of Sardis synagogue (from: *The Synagogue: Studies in Origins, Archaeology and Architecture*, New York: KTAV, 1975:189)

BE-B

BE-C

PALAESTRA

0 1 2 3 4 5   10
METERS

MAIN HALL

COURT

PORCH

conspicuous seats always formed a single unit, as at Sardis. Tation may have sat facing the congregation, but from a separate location near the women's area. Kraemer seems to assume that seats of honor could not have been segregated, an assumption that is quite unwarranted.

While the ascetic Jewish monastics described by Philo cannot be generalized to the average synagogue community, the practice of this sect does demonstrate how readily seats of honor could be segregated. When the Therapeutrides gathered with the Therapeutai every fifty days for their special banquet celebration, it is not surprising to find that the men and women reclined separately – the men to the right of the refectory, and the women to the left (Philo, *Vita cont.* 69). Both sexes reclined according to their rank within the community, based on the length of time they had been members, a clear example of segregated seats of honor.[57]

Even if, by chance, a woman dignitary did sit among her male peers, it is simply not reasonable – in face of the evidence presented here – to generalize such special cases to the main body of women in the assembly hall. Not only did the vast majority of women in the ancient synagogue *not* sit in a seat of honor – the vast majority, if not all, probably sat separately from the men.

CONCLUSION

The artistic and architectural diversity that the evidence exhibits does not allow us to assume that the status and role of women from synagogue to synagogue in the various rural and urban areas of the Roman Empire were identical. Jewish women – then as now – cannot be classified as a homogeneous group without regard to social class or ethnic influence, and the archaeological evidence reinforces the fact, already manifest in the literary sources, that Judaism itself was far from uniform. In the Second-Temple period, the experience of a woman who attended a house-synagogue in a residential block must have differed significantly from that of a woman in the well-crafted, theater-like synagogue of Gamla, and her experience in turn would have differed from that of a woman in "the greatest and most famous" Alexandrian synagogue described by Philo. In the post-70 period, the woman who attended a modest Diaspora synagogue-*domus* would have had a very different experience from the woman in the massive second-century Alexandrian Diplostoon.[58] The woman contemplating the Biblical cycle of paintings surrounding her on all four walls of the Dura-Europos synagogue would have sat in a very different atmosphere than did the woman gazing down the enormous and opulent hall of the Sardis synagogue. In Palestine, the "extroverted" basilical synagogue with its monumental façade would not have left the same impression as the "introverted" basilica with its lavish interior décor.[59] The broadhouse would have left another impression again, as would the simpler ornamentation of the rural synagogue.[60]

Thus, there seems to have been a constant of Graeco-Roman culture characteristic of almost all ethnic and religious groups within the boundaries of the Roman empire, including those who attended synagogues – that is, segregated seating arrangements in respectable public settings. Superimposed on this, however, is a rich multiplicity of variables. For the women who sat in ancient synagogues, we see both a diversity and a commonality of experience – a multi-faceted phenomenon whose many facets are part of the same crystal, for they are all part of Judaism in the Graeco-Roman world, yet they reflect a kaleidoscope of color.

NOTES

1 I would like to thank Adèle Reinhartz for the opportunity to make this contribution.
2 Yadin 1981 and Foerster 1981c. While there has been some debate as to whether or not these were actually synagogues, their identification as such has been widely accepted (see Grabbe 1988:405–7). [On pre-70 synagogues, see Richardson, chapter 6 in this volume – ed.]
3 See Chiat 1981:57 (Table 1) and Foerster 1981c:24.
4 Ma'oz 1981:35–41; Gutman 1981:30–34.
5 Lifshitz 1967: no. 79; Kloner 1981:11.
6 Philo, *Legat.* 134; *t. Sukk.* 4.6.
7 White 1990:7–8, 62. For convenient surveys of these Diaspora synagogues, see White 1990:60–101; Hachlili 1992; Foerster 1981b and Kraabel 1979. On the Sardis synagogue, see Bonz 1993; Seager 1981, 1983; and Kraabel 1983.
8 Meyers 1992:253–55. For a survey of Palestinian synagogues, see Kloner 1981. On Galilean synagogues, see Meyers 1987.
9 Chiat 1982:4–5, Table 7, 338.
10 In Chiat's *Handbook* (1982) on Palestinian synagogues (Table 2, 333), there are twice as many basilical synagogues listed as there are broadhouses and other architectural types.
11 Disagreements on typology and chronology plague the field of synagogue studies in Israel (Meyers 1987:127–28). In the first half of this century, scholars proposed a second- to third-century dating for the earliest "Galilean" basilical synagogues, but these dates have been called into question by recent and ongoing excavations at Capernaum, Gush Halav, Khirbet Shema', and Meron. Many of the Galilean synagogues may require a later, fourth-century dating (Chiat 1982:4–5, 356; Gutmann 1975b:xiii). The synagogue at Capernaum in particular has occasioned vigorous debate with regard to its dating, and may have been founded as late as the fifth century. For both sides of the debate, see Loffreda 1981; Foerster 1981a; and Avi-Yonah 1981.
12 Karen Jo Torjesen's (1993) hypothesis that women in the early church enjoyed considerable leadership because the house-church operated in the private domain – leadership of which women were later deprived as the church moved out into the public realm – may require modification. There would have been differences, to be sure, between the house-church and the basilica, and these no doubt had some effect on women's roles in church. But precisely what these differences were requires further examination in light of the evidence for the parallel architectural development of synagogues, house-churches, and pagan shrines in this period – all of which were understood to be *public* forums.
13 As has recently been pointed out by Brooten (1986) and Plaskow (1993), it has been the unfortunate tendency of some Christian feminist scholarship to engage in what are effectively anti-Semitic arguments in order to depict "pristine" Christianity as uniquely non-sexist.
14 At Masada, the partition between the initial vestibule and hall was torn down by the insurgents, two of the pillars were repositioned, and a small cell (possibly a *genizah*) was constructed in the northern corner. Three rows of benches, tier upon tier, were constructed

along all the walls of the assembly hall. The Herodium synagogue was reconstructed out of a *triclinium*, to which four new columns and rows of benches were added (Yadin 1981; Foerster 1981c).

15 It is not the place to address this question here, but I suspect that the model of earliest Christianity as a "discipleship of equals," such as that proposed by Fiorenza (1983), is problematic.

16 Chiat 1982:34, 232, Table 5, 336.

17 Ibid. 1982:92, 96 nn. 2 and 3.

18 Barag, Porat, and Netzer 1981:116–19; Chiat 1982:221, 224 n. 1.

19 Meyers 1981; 1992:257–58. The first structure was destroyed in a massive earthquake in 306 CE; the second more modest building met a similar end under the tremors of another earthquake in 419 CE.

20 Meyers 1981; Brooten 1982:121–22, 254, n. 57; Chiat 1982:31–36; Meyers, Kraabel, and Strange 1976:56–58, 80–82, 85, 86, 89–91. The excavators admit that the south-western entrance is not certain: "There may have been a barrier or wall at the south end of the gallery, blocking any access via the west door" (ibid.: 58).

21 Brooten 1982:254 n. 63, modifying Chiat 1982:33; Meyers, Kraabel, and Strange 1976:58.

22 For a discussion of the Mishnah's exemption and exclusion of women from many aspects of public cultic practice, see Wegner 1988:145–67. Convenient summaries of women in Rabbinic sources include Wegner 1991a; Kraemer 1992:93–105; Baskin 1985.

23 On the difficulties associated with the subject of menstruants in the synagogue, see Cohen 1991; 1992.

24 Chiat 1982:230–35; Gutman, Yeivin, and Netzer 1981.

25 Safrai 1993:5–6; Brooten 1982:130–32; Grossman 1992.

26 The ambiguity of this passage is reinforced by the fact that the parallels in *Lam. Rab.* 1:45 (on 1:16) and 4.22 (on 4.19) have the terms reversed: "Do to those below as you have done to those above" (Brooten 1982:132–33).

27 For a feminist analysis of Philo on the Therapeutrides, see Kraemer 1989.

28 Trans. Winston 1981:47, with some modifications.

29 While it may be the case that no member of the Lukan community had seen a Galilean synagogue like the one depicted in Luke 13, it is likely that most members were better acquainted with first-century Diaspora synagogues than we are.

30 *Ant.* 14.10.23.258 (LCL).

31 Personal interview with Steve Mason, October 1994.

32 See the drawing and description of this mosaic in Kloner 1981:15–16.

33 See the photograph of the mosaic and diagram of the hall in Barag, Porat, and Netzer 1981:117, 119.

34 The literature on the Dura wall-paintings is copious. Interesting discussions are offered by Gutmann 1975a; 1987.

35 For example, unlike their Athenian counterparts, Gortynian women could inherit and control property. However, the inheritance of a daughter was less than that of a son (Pomeroy 1975:39). By contrast, Roman society generally divided property equally between all heirs of the same blood and same rank, regardless of their sex (Corbier 1991:185). On Macedonian women, see Pomeroy 1975:121–25; Gillman 1990:62–63. On Dorian women, see Pomeroy 1975:35–42; Cantarella 1987:42–43. On upper-class Roman women, see Pomeroy 1975:149–89; Clark 1981; Hallett 1984; Evans 1991:26–100.

36 Rawson 1986:31. Only at the circus, according to Suetonius (*Augustus* 44–45), could respectable Roman families sit together to watch the horse-races.

37 *CIL* I² 2506 as repr. by Evans 1991:88, n. 3.

38 Mark 8:9 simply states *ēsan de hōs tetrakischilioi* – "there were about four thousand (people)."

39 Here I trust that Corley would agree.

40 There is some debate as to whether 1 Cor. 14:33–36 was actually penned by Paul. A number of scholars, including Kraemer (1992:149), argue that it is a later interpolation. I remain unconvinced by this argument.

41 Cotter (1994) has shown that of the six women leaders mentioned in Paul's letters – Apphia (Philem. 2), Chloe (1 Cor. 1:11), Prisca (1 Cor. 16:19; Rom. 16:3,4), Phoebe (Rom. 16:1–2), Euodia and Syntyche (Phil 4:2) – all but one (Apphia from Colossae) are un-equivocally connected with cities that were heavily Romanized (Corinth, Cenchreae, Philippi, Ephesus, and Rome).

42 See Winter 1988:87–103. On Phoebe as patroness, see Whelan 1993.

43 Julius Caesar refounded Corinth as a Roman colony in 44 BCE, after it had been razed to the ground in 146 BCE by the Roman general Mummius. On the Roman nature of Cor-inth, see Gill 1993.

44 Plutarch (*Moral.* 267 A) as repr. by MacMullen 1982:208.

45 Irvin 1980:81–84. Mosaics in Syria, Lebanon, and Palestine also depict women with their heads uncovered, so it is clear that not *all* women in the eastern provinces went about veiled. MacMullen plausibly resolves the conflict in the evidence by suggesting that in Italy Romanized women of all classes generally went about with uncovered heads. But in the eastern provinces only the wealthier, more "modern" women who were adopting the new Roman ways went bare-headed; the more conservative women of the humbler classes went veiled (1982:217–18, 217 n. 40). Women in the Roman colonies of the provinces were probably also not in the habit of wearing veils.

46 Irvin 1980:83–84. Some have argued that one or more of the figures in the fresco are men. After examining the photograph of the fresco in Irvin's article, I find it difficult to understand how any of these figures could be construed as men.

47 Kraemer 1992:107. The relevant reference is Tertullian, *On the Veiling of Virgins* 9.2–3.

48 Kraemer 1988:241–42 (no. 109).

49 Lifshitz 1967: no. 13, trans. Brooten 1982:157.

50 See Brooten 1982: *passim*; Kraemer 1992:106–27; Cohen 1980.

51 Bonz (1993:140 nn. 3 and 6) reports a forthcoming article by John H. Kroll, "The Greek Inscriptions," in Seager, Kraabel, and Kroll, *The Synagogue at Sardis* (Archaeological Explor-ation of Sardis 5; Cambridge, Mass.: Harvard University Press).

52 According to Seager 1981:184. Brooten cites three of these inscriptions (1982: Appendix I, 25–27), and so does Lifshitz, along with eight other Sardis inscriptions not mentioning women (1967:17–27). Louis Robert discusses a few of the inscriptions (including two of those which mention wives) in Robert 1964–89, 1:37–58.

53 According to John H. Kroll in a personal interview, 22 May 1995.

54 The civilian and religious titles that appear among the men are listed in White 1990:99; Kraabel 1983:280; and Kraabel 1992a:262–63. White cites his *The Christian Domus Ecclesiae and Its Environment: A Collection of Texts and Monuments* as a sourcebook for the inscriptions, but I have not been able to gain access to it. [The volume is still forthcoming – ed.]

55 Brooten 1982: Appendix I, nos. 7–15; Lifshitz 1967:41–46, 51, 54–55.

56 Brooten 1982: Appendix I, no. 12; Lifshitz 1967:46.

57 At first glance, Philo seems to describe a mingling of the sexes at the sacred vigil that took place after the banquet. The men and women would form two choirs, each of which gave its own performance in turn, and then the male and female choirs would "mix (*anamignyn-tai*), and the two choirs became one (*kai ginontai choros heis ex amphoin*)" (*Vita cont.* 85; trans. Winston). As one reads further, however, the precise outlines of this "mixing" become clearer. The single choir formed is "a copy of the choir organized at the Red Sea on the occasion of the wonders there wrought . . . men and women alike were filled with divine ecstasy, formed a single choir . . . the men led by the prophet Moses and the women by the prophetess Miriam" (*Vita cont.* 85–87; trans. Winston). In other words, the two choirs have joined to sing as a single choir but men and women remain in separate sections, led by

their respective choir-leaders. [See Richardson and Heuchan, chapter 12 in this volume – ed.]

58 This hall was so enormous that an assistant had to wave flags from the *bema* which stood in the middle of the hall so that the people would know when to say "amen" (*t. Sukk.* 4:6).

59 Tsafrir (1987) insists that these differences represent a transition in synagogue architecture in the Byzantine period, and that this transition can be used to establish chronology. But the data, while supporting this transition as a *general trend*, offer striking exceptions to this trend – in particular, the Capernaum synagogue which has a monumental façade facing Jerusalem, and which is probably Byzantine.

60 Decorative practices in ancient synagogues seem to have varied regionally (Meyers 1987:133).

WORKS CITED

Adams, B. N. 1968. *Kinship in an Urban Society*. Chicago, Ill.: Markham Publ. Co.

Afanassieff, N. 1974. "L'Assemblée eucharistique unique dans l'église ancienne." *Kleronomia* 6:1–36.

Allegro, J. M. 1964. "The Wiles of the Wicked Woman." *PEQ* 96:53–55.

Amitai, J., ed. 1985. *Biblical Archaeology Today*. Jerusalem: Israel Exploration Society and the Israel Academy of Sciences and Humanities.

Anderson, G. M. 1974. *Networks of Contact: The Portuguese and Toronto*. Waterloo, Ont.: Wilfrid Laurier University Press.

Anderson, R. T. 1991. "The Elusive Samaritan Temple." *BAR* 54(2):104–7.

Applebaum, S. 1976a. "The Organization of the Jewish Communities of the Diaspora." In Safrai and Stern 1974–76:464–503.

———. 1976b. "The Social and Economic Status of the Jews in the Diaspora." In Safrai and Stern 1974–76:701–27.

———. 1979. *Jews and Greeks in Ancient Cyrene*. SJLA 28. Leiden: E. J. Brill.

Archer, L. J. 1990. *Her Price is Beyond Rubies: The Jewish Woman in Graeco-Roman Palestine*. JSOT Sup. 60. Sheffield: Sheffield Academic Press.

Ascough, R. S. 1995. "Local and Translocal Relationships Among Voluntary Associations in Antiquity." Paper presented at the annual meeting of the Canadian Society of Biblical Studies, University of Montréal, Montréal, Québec.

Attridge, H. W. 1976. *The Interpretation of Biblical History in the Antiquitates Judaicae of Flavius Josephus*. HDR 7. Missoula, Mont.: Scholars Press.

Aune, D. E. 1991. "Romans as a Logos Protreptikos." Pp. 278–96 in *The Romans Debate*. Revised edn, ed. K. P. Donfried. Peabody, Mass.: Hendrickson.

Avi–Yonah, M. 1981. "Some Comments on the Capernaum Excavations." In Levine 1981:60–62.

———. 1993. "Caesarea: Excavation of the Synagogue." In *NEAEHL* 1:278–80.

Baer, R. A. 1970. *Philo's Use of the Categories Male and Female*. ALGHJ 3. Leiden: E. J. Brill.

Baer, Y. F. 1961. "Israel, the Christian Church and the Roman Empire from the Time of Septimius Severus to the Edict of Toleration of A.D. 313." *Scripta Hierosolymitana* 7:79–149.

Baillet, M., ed. 1982. *Qumran Grotte 4, III: (4Q482–4Q520)*. DJD 7. Oxford: Clarendon Press.

Baker, J. A. 1975. "The Myth of the Church: A Case Study in the Use of Scripture for Christian Doctrine." Pp. 165–77 in *What About the New Testament? Essays in Honour of Christopher Evans*, ed. M. D. Hooker and C. J. A. Hickling. London: SCM.

Banks, R. J. 1980. *Paul's Idea of Community: The Early House Churches in Their Historical Setting*. Grand Rapids, Mich.: Wm. B. Eerdmans.

Banton, M. 1968. "Voluntary Associations: Anthropological Aspects." *In International Encyclopedia of the Social Sciences*, ed. D. L. Sills, 16:357–62. New York: Macmillan & Co.

Barag, D., Y. Porat, and E. Netzer. 1981. "The Synagogue at 'En-Gedi." In Levine 1981:116–19.

Bardtke, H. 1961. "Der gegenwärtige Stand der Erforschung der in Palästina neu gefundenen hebräischen Handschriften, 44: Die Rechtsstellung der Qumran-Gemeinde." *TLZ* 86:93–104.

Bartchy, S. S. 1973. *Mallon Chresai: First-century Slavery and the Interpretation of 1 Corinthians 7:21.* SBLDS 11. Missoula, Mont.: Society of Biblical Literature.

Barton, S., and G. H. R. Horsley. 1981. "A Hellenistic Cult Group and the New Testament Churches." *JAC* 24:7–41.

Baskin, J. 1985. "The Separation of Women in the Rabbinic Judaism." Pp. 3–18 in *Women, Religion, and Social Change,* ed. E. B. Findly and Y. Y. Haddad. Albany, NY: State University of New York Press.

Baslez, M.–F. 1976. "Déliens et étrangers domiciliés à Délos (166–155)." *REG* 89:343–60.

Baumgarten, J. M. 1957. "On the Testimony of Women in 1QSa." *JBL* 76:266–69.

———. 1985. "Halakhic Polemics in New Fragments from Qumran Cave 4." In Amitai 1985:390–99.

———. 1990. "The Qumran–Essene Restraints on Marriage." In Schiffman 1990a:13–24.

———. 1991. "On the Nature of the Seductress in 4Q184." *RevQ* 15:133–43.

———. 1992a. "The Cave 4 Versions of the Penal Code." *JJS* 43:268–76.

———. 1992b. "The Laws of the Damascus Document in Current Research." Pp. 51–62 in *The Damascus Document Reconsidered,* ed. M. Broshi. Jerusalem: The Israel Exploration Society and the Israel Museum.

———. 1994. "Purification after Childbirth and the Sacred Garden in 4Q265 and Jubilees." In Brooke and Garcia Martinez 1994:3–10.

———. 1995. "The Laws about Fluxes in 4QTohara³ (4Q274)." In Dimant and Schiffman 1995:1–8.

Beall, T. S. 1988. *Josephus' Description of the Essenes Illustrated by the Dead Sea Scrolls.* SNTSMS 58. Cambridge and New York: Cambridge University Press.

Bean, G. E., and T. B. Mitford. 1970. *Journeys in Rough Cilicia 1964–1968.* Denkschriften der Österreichen Akademie der Wissenschaften, Phil.–hist. Klasse, Bd. 102 = Tituli Asiae Minoris, Ergänzungsband no. 3. Wien, Graz, and Köln: Hermann Böhlaus.

Beck, R. L. 1976. "Interpreting the Ponza Zodiac." JMS 1:1–19.

———. 1978. "Interpreting the Ponza Zodiac." JMS 2:87–147.

———. 1979. "Sette Sfere, Sette Porte, and the Spring Equinoxes of A.D. 172 and 173." In Bianchi 1979:515–30.

———. 1988. *Planetary Gods and Planetary Orders in the Mysteries of Mithras.* EPRO 109. Leiden: E. J. Brill.

———. 1992. "The Mithras Cult as Association." *SR* 21:3–13.

———. 1994a. "In the Place of the Lion: Mithras in the Tauroctony." In Hinnells 1994:29–50.

———. 1994b. "Cosmic Models: Some Uses of Hellenistic Science in Roman Religion." *APEIRON* 27(4): 99–117.

Behr, C. A., 1968. *Aelius Aristides and The Sacred Tales.* Amsterdam: A. M. Hakkert.

———. ed. and trans. 1973. *Aristides.* Volume 1: *Panathenaic Oration and In Defence of Oratory.* LCL. London: Wm. Heinemann; Cambridge, Mass.: Harvard University Press.

———. ed. and trans. 1981–86. *P. Aelius Aristides: The Complete Works:* Vol. 1: *Orations 1–16 with an Appendix Containing the Fragments and Inscriptions;* Vol. 2: *Orations 17–53.* Leiden: E. J. Brill.

Bell, H. I. 1953. *Cults and Creeds in Graeco-Roman Egypt.* New York: Philosophical Library; Liverpool: Liverpool University Press.

Berger, K. 1976. "Volksversammlung und Gemeinde Gottes: Zu den Anfängen der christlichen Verwendung von 'ekklesia'" *ZTK* 73:167–207.

Berger, P. L., and T. Luckmann. 1966. *The Social Construction of Reality: A Treatise in the Sociology of Knowledge.* Garden City, NY: Doubleday.

Berkman, L. F., and S. L. Syme. 1979. "Social Networks, Host Resistance, and Mortality: A Nine–year Followup Study of Almeida County Residents." *American Journal of Epidemiology* 109:186–204.

Beskow, P. 1980. "The portorium and the Mysteries of Mithras." *JMS* 3:1–18.

Beyer, H. W. 1965. "κατηχέω" *TDNT* 3:638–40.

Bianchi, U., ed. 1979. *Mysteria Mithrae*. EPRO 80. Leiden: E. J. Brill.

Bickerman, E. J. 1980. "La chaîne de la tradition pharisienne." Pp. 256–69 in *Studies in Jewish and Christian History, Part II*. AGJU 9. Leiden: E. J. Brill.

Blackman, A. M. 1921. "On the Position of Women in the Ancient Egyptian Hierarchy." JEA 7:8–30.

Blanchetière, F. 1989. "Au coeur de la cité: le chrétien philosophe selon l'*à Diognète* 5–6." *RSR* 63:183–94.

Blasi, A. J. 1989. *Early Christianity as a Social Movement*. Toronto Studies in Religion 5. New York: Peter Lang.

Blue, B. B. 1991. "The House Church at Corinth and the Lord's Supper: Famine, Food Supply, and the Present Distress." *Criswell Theological Review* 5:221–39.

Boak, A. E. R. 1937. "The Organization of Gilds in Greco-Roman Egypt." *TAPA* 68:212–20.

Boissevain, J. 1978. *Friends of Friends: Networks, Manipulators and Coalitions*. Oxford: Basil Blackwell.

Bokser, B. M. 1977. *Philo's Description of Jewish Practices*. Protocol of the Center for Hermeneutical Studies in Hellenistic and Modern Culture 30. Berkeley, Calif.: The Center for Hermeneutical Studies in Hellenistic and Modern Culture.

Bonz, M. P. 1993. "Differing Approaches to Religious Benefaction: The Late Third–Century Acquisition of the Sardis Synagogue." *HTR* 86(2):139–54.

Borgen, P. 1965. *Bread from Heaven: An Exegetical Study of the Concept of Manna in the Gospel of John*. NovTSup 10. Leiden: E. J. Brill.

———. 1983a. "The Early Church and the Hellenistic Synagogue." *ST* 37:55–78.

———. 1983b. *Paul Preaches Circumcision and Pleases Men: And Other Essays on Christian Origins*. Trondheim: Tapir.

———. 1984a. "Philo of Alexandria: A Critical and Synthetical Survey of Research Since World War II." *ANRW* II.21.1:98–154.

———. 1984b. "Philo of Alexandria." Pp. 233–82 in *Jewish Writings of the Second Temple Period: Apocrypha, Pseudepigrapha, Qumran, Sectarian Writings, Philo, Josephus*, ed. M. E. Stone. CRINT 2/2. Assen: Van Gorcum; Philadelphia, Pa.: Fortress.

———. 1987. *Philo, John, and Paul: New Perspectives on Judaism and Early Christianity*. BJS 131. Atlanta, Ga.: Scholars Press.

———. 1992. "Judaism in Egypt." In *ABD* 3:1061–72.

Boussac, M.-F. 1988. "Sceaux Déliens." *RA* n.s. 69:307–40.

Bowersock, G. W. 1969. *Greek Sophists in the Roman Empire*. Oxford: Clarendon Press.

———. 1975. *Julian the Apostate*. Cambridge, Mass.: Harvard University Press.

Brawley, R. L. 1987. *Luke–Acts and the Jews: Conflict, Apology and Conciliation*. SBLMS 33. Atlanta, Ga.: Scholars Press.

Breiger, R. L. 1988. "The Duality of Persons and Groups." Pp. 83–98 in *Social Structures: A Network Approach*, ed. B. Wellman and S. D. Berkowitz. Cambridge and New York: Cambridge University Press.

Brooke, G. J., ed. 1989. *Temple Scroll Studies: Papers Presented at the International Symposium on the Temple Scroll, Manchester, December 1987*. JSPSup 7. Sheffield: JSOT Press.

———. 1994. "A Long-Lost Song of Miriam." *BA* 20:62–65.

Brooke, G. J., and F. Garcia Martinez, eds. 1994. *New Qumran Texts and Studies: Proceedings of the First Meeting of the International Organization for Qumran Studies, Paris, 1992*. Studies on the Texts of the Desert of Judah 15. Leiden and New York: E. J. Brill.

Brooten, B. J. 1982. *Women Leaders in Ancient Synagogues: Inscriptional Evidence and Background Issues*. BJS 36. Chico, Calif.: Scholars Press.

———. 1986. "Jewish Women's History in the Roman Period: A Task for Christian Theology." Pp. 22–30 in *Christians among Jews and Gentiles: Essays in Honor of Krister Stendahl on his Sixty-fifth Birthday*, ed. G. W. E. Nickelsburg and G. W. MacRae. Philadelphia, Pa.: Fortress.

———. 1991. "Iael προστάτης in the Jewish Donative Inscription from Aphrodisias." Pp. 149–62 in *The Future of Early Christianity: Essays in Honor of Helmut Koester*, ed. Birger Pearson. Minneapolis, Minn.: Fortress.

Brown, C. A. 1992. *No Longer be Silent: First Century Jewish Portraits of Biblical Women*. Louisville: Westminster/John Knox.

Brownlee, W. H. 1964. *The Meaning of the Qumran Scrolls for the Bible*. New York: Oxford University Press.

Bruneau, P. 1965. *Guide de Délos*. Paris: E. de Boccard.

———. 1970. *Recherches sur les cultes de Délos à l'époque hellénistique et à l'époque impériale*. BEFAR 217. Paris: E. de Boccard.

———. 1973. "Le Quartier de L'Inopos à Délos et la Fondation du Sarapeion A." Pp. 111–36 in *Etudes déliennes: publiées à l'occasion du centième anniversaire du début des fouilles de l'Ecole française d'Athènes à Délos*, ed. André Plassart. BCHSup 1. Athens: Ecole française d'Athènes; Paris: E. de Boccard.

———. 1978a. "Les cultes de l'établissement des Poseidoniastes de Bérytos à Délos." Pp. 160–90 and plates V–VIII in *Hommages à Maarten J. Vermaseren*, ed. M. B. De Boer and T. A. Edridge. EPRO 68. Leiden: E. J. Brill.

———. 1978b. "Deliaca (II): 19. L'établissement des Poseidoniastes de Bérytos: contributions récentes." *BCH* 102:133–34.

———. 1980. "Le dromos et le temple C du Sarapeion C du Délos." *BCH* 104:161–88.

———. 1982. "'Les Israélites de Délos' et la Juiverie délienne." *BCH* 106:465–504.

———. 1990. "Deliaca (VIII): 58. La crypte du Sarapeion A." *BCH* 114:559–63.

———. 1991. "Deliaca (IX): 67. Encore le sanctuaire et les cultes des Poseidoniastes de Bérytos." *BCH* 115:379–86.

Brunt, P. A., and J. M. Moore, eds. 1967. *Res Gestae Divi Augusti: The Achievements of the Divine Augustus*. London: Oxford University Press.

Buckler, W. H. 1923. "Labour Disputes in the Province of Asia." Pp. 27–50 in *Anatolian Studies, Presented to Sir William Mitchell Ramsay*, ed. W. H. Buckler and W. M. Calder. Manchester: Manchester University Press.

Burford, A. 1972. *Craftsmen in Greek and Roman Society*. London: Thames & Hudson; Ithaca, NY: Cornell University Press.

Burkert, W. 1979. *Structure and History in Greek Mythology and Ritual*. Sather Classical Lectures 47. Berkeley: University of California Press.

———. 1985. *Greek Religion: Archaic and Classical*. Oxford: Basil Blackwell; Cambridge, Mass.: Harvard University Press.

Cameron, A. 1980. "Neither Male nor Female." *G&R* 27:60–68.

Cantarella, E. 1987. *Pandora's Daughters: The Role and Status of Women in Greek and Roman Antiquity*. Baltimore and London: Johns Hopkins University Press.

Carmignac, J. 1965. "Poème allégorique sur la secte rivale." *RevQ 5:361–74.*

Carney, T. F. 1975. *The Shape of the Past: Models and Antiquity*. Lawrence, Kans.: Coronado Press.

Carpenter, H. 1978. *The Inklings: C. S. Lewis, J. R. R. Tolkien, Charles Williams and Their Friends*. London: Unwin.

Cenival, F. de. 1972. *Les associations religieuses en Egypte d'après les documents démotiques*. Publications de l'Institut français d'archéologie orientale du Caire. Bibliothèque d'étude 46. Le Caire: Institut français d'archéologie orientale.

Chapman, J. W. 1969. "Voluntary Association and the Political Theory of Pluralism." In Pennock and Chapman 1969:87–118.

Charlesworth, J. H., ed. 1985. *The Old Testament Pseudepigrapha*. Vol. 2. *Expansions of the "Old Testament" and Legends, Wisdom and Philosophical Literature, Prayers, Psalms and Odes, Fragments of Lost Judaeo–Hellenistic Works*. Garden City, NY: Doubleday.

—— ed. 1994. *The Dead Sea Scrolls: Rule of the Community and Related Documents*. The Dead Sea Scrolls: Hebrew, Aramaic, and Greek texts with English translations 1. Tübingen: J. C. B. Mohr (Paul Siebeck); Louisville: Westminster/John Knox.

Chiat, M. J. 1981. "First Century Synagogue Architecture: Methodological Problems." In Gutmann 1981:49–60.

——. 1982. *Handbook of Synagogue Architecture*. BJS 29. Chico, Calif.: Scholars Press.

Clark, A. C., ed. 1918. *Orationum Ciceronis*. Oxford: Clarendon Press.

Clark, E. A. 1992. "Elite Networks and Heresy Accusations: Towards a Social Description of the Origenist Controversy." In White 1992b:79–117.

Clark, G. 1981. "Roman Women." *G&R* 28:193–212.

Clauss, M. 1990a. Mithras: Kult und Mysterien. München: C. H. Beck.

——. 1990b. "Die sieben Grade des Mithras-Kultes." ZPE 82:183–94.

——. 1992. *Cultores Mithrae: die Anhängerschaft des Mithras-Kultes*. Heidelberger althistorische Beiträge und epigraphische Studien 10. Stuttgart: Franz Steiner Verlag.

Clayton, P. 1986. *Treasures of Ancient Rome*. New York: Gallery.

Clemente, G. 1972. "Il Patronato nei collegia dell'imperio romano." *Studi Classici e Orientali* 21:142–229.

Coenen, L. 1975–78. "Church." In *New International Dictionary of New Testament Theology*, ed. Colin Brown, vol. 1:291–307. Exeter and Grand Rapids, Mich.: Paternoster; Zondervan.

Cohen, A. 1969. *Custom and Politics in Urban Africa: A Study of Hausa Migrants in Yoruba Towns*. Berkeley: University of California Press.

Cohen, S. J. D. 1980. "Women in the Synagogues of Antiquity." *Conservative Judaism* 34:23–29.

——. 1987a. *From the Maccabees to the Mishnah*. Philadelphia, Pa.: Westminster.

——. 1987b. "Pagan and Christian Evidence on the Ancient Synagogue." In Levine 1987:159–81.

——. 1991. "Menstruants and the Sacred in Judaism and Christianity." Pp. 273–99 in *Women's History and Ancient History*, ed. S. B. Pomeroy. Chapel Hill: University of North Carolina Press.

——. 1992. "Purity and Piety: The Separation of Menstruants from the Sancta." Pp. 103–15 in *Daughters of the King: Women and the Synagogue: A Survey of History, Halakhah, and Contemporary Realities*, ed. S. Grossman and R. Haut. Philadelphia, Pa.: Jewish Publication Society.

Collingwood, R. G. 1933–40. "Roman Britain." In *An Economic Survey of Ancient Rome*, ed. T. Frank, vol. 3:1–118. Baltimore, Md.: Johns Hopkins University Press.

Collins, J. J. 1983. *Between Athens and Jerusalem: Jewish Identity in the Hellenistic Diaspora*. New York: Crossroad.

Colson, F. H. 1917. "Philo on Education." *JTS* 18:151–63.

Colson, F. H., and G. H. Whitaker, eds. and trans. 1929–62. *Philo, with an English Translation*. LCL. Cambridge, Mass.: Harvard University Press.

Combet-Farnoux, B. 1980. *Mercure romain: Le culte public de Mercure et la fonction mercantile à Rome de la république archaïque à l'époque augustéene*. BEFAR 238. Paris: E. de Boccard.

Conzelmann, H. 1966. "Luke's Place in the Development of Early Christianity." Pp. 298–316 in *Studies in Luke–Acts: Essays Presented in Honor of Paul Schubert*, ed. L. E. Keck and J. L. Martyn. Nashville, Tenn.: Abingdon.

——. 1975. *1 Corinthians: A Commentary on the First Epistle to the Corinthians*. Hermeneia. Philadelphia, Pa.: Fortress.

Cooley, C. H. 1922. *The Two Major Works of Charles H. Cooley: Social Organization: Human Nature and the Social Order*. Revised ed. Glencoe, Ill.: Free Press.

Coppens, J. 1978. "Le célibat essénien." Pp. 295–303 in *Qumrân: sa piété, sa théologie et son milieu*, ed. M. Delcor. BETL 46. Paris: Duculot.

Corbier, M. 1991. "Family Behavior of the Roman Aristocracy, Second Century B.C.–Third Century A.D." Pp. 173–96 in *Women's History and Ancient History*, ed. S. B. Pomeroy. Chapel Hill: University of North Carolina Press.

Corley, K. E. 1993. *Private Women, Public Meals: Social Conflict in the Synoptic Tradition*. Peabody, Mass.: Hendrickson Publishers.

Cotter, W. 1989. "The Collegia and Roman Law: The State Restrictions on Private Associations 64 BCE–200 CE." Paper presented at the annual meeting of the Canadian Society of Biblical Studies, Université Laval, June 1989.

———. 1994. "Women's Authority Roles in Paul's Churches: Countercultural or Conventional?" *NovT* 36:350–72.

Couilloud-Le Dinahet, M.–Th. 1978. "Rhénée: Tombes d'Anô–Générale." *BCH* 102:853–77.

Courby, F. 1931. *Les temples d'Apollon. EAD* 12. Paris: E. de Boccard.

Craffert, P. F. 1993. "The Pauline Movement and First-century Judaism: A Framework for Transforming the Issues." *Neot* 27:233–62.

Cross, F. M. 1980. *The Ancient Library of Qumran and Modern Biblical Studies*. Rev. ed. Grand Rapids, Mich.: Baker Book House.

Culpepper, R. A. 1975. *The Johannine School: An Evaluation of the Johannine-school Hypothesis*. SBLDS 26. Missoula, Mont.: Scholars Press.

Cumont, F. 1911. *The Oriental Religions in Roman Paganism*. Chicago: Open Court Publishing.

———. 1975. "The Dura Mithraeum." In Hinnells 1975:151–214.

Dahl, N. A. 1941. *Das Volk Gottes: eine Untersuchung zum Kirchenbewusstsein des Urchristentums*. Skrifter utg. av det Norske videnskaps–akademi i Oslo. II. Hist.–filos. klasse, 1941 2. Oslo: J. Dybwad.

———. 1977. *Studies in Paul: Theology for the Early Christian Mission*. Minneapolis, Minn.: Augsburg Pub. House.

Danker, F. W. 1982. *Benefactor: Epigraphic Study of a Graeco-Roman and New Testament Semantic Field*. St. Louis, Mo.: Clayton Pub. House.

Dar, S., and Y. Mintzker. 1995. "The Synagogue of Horvat Sumaqa, 1983–1993." In Urman and Flesher 1995:157–65.

Daux, G. 1961. "Chronique des fouilles et découvertes archéologique en Grèce en 1960." *BCH* 85:601–953.

———. 1962. "Chronique des fouilles et découvertes archéologiques en Grèce en 1961." *BCH* 86:629–974.

Davies, J. G. 1987. "Architecture." In *The Encyclopedia of Religion*, ed. Mircea Eliade, vol. 1:382–92. New York and London: Macmillan; Collier Macmillan.

Davies, P. R. 1983. *The Damascus Covenant: An Interpretation of the "Damascus Document"*. JSOTSup 25. Sheffield: JSOT Press.

———. 1987. *Behind the Essenes: History of and Ideology of the Dead Sea Scrolls*. BJS 94. Atlanta, Ga.: Scholars Press.

Dawson, L. L. 1990. "Reflections on Sociological Theories of Sects and New Religious Movements." Paper read at the 1990 annual meeting of the Canadian Society of Biblical Studies, Victoria, B.C.

———. 1992. "Church/Sect Theory: Getting it Right." *North American Religion* 1:5–28.

Deichmann, F. W. 1983. *Einführung in die christliche Archäologie*. Darmstadt: Wissenschaftliche Buchgesellschaft.

Deissmann, A. 1902. "Die Rachegebete von Rheneia." *Philologus* 91:262–65.

———. 1908. *Licht vom Osten: Das Neue Testament und die neuentdeckten Texte der hellenistisch–römischen Welt*. Tübingen: J. C. B. Mohr (Paul Siebeck).

———. 1927. *Light from the Ancient East: The New Testament Illustrated by Recently Discovered Texts of the Graeco-Roman World*. London: Hodder & Stoughton.

Deonna, W. 1956. *Le mobilier délien. EAD* 18. Paris: E. de Boccard.

DeRobertis, F. M. 1934. *Storia delle corporazioni e del regime associativo nel mondo romano.* Repr. 1973. Bari: Adriatica Editrice.

———. 1938. *Il diritto associativo romano dai collegi della repubblica alle corporazioni del Basso Impero.* Storia delle corporazioni, collana di studi. Sezione 1: Le Corporazioni e il fenomeno associativo nel mondo romano 1. Bari: Laterza.

———. 1955. *Il fenomeno associativo nel mondo romano: dai collegi della repubblica alle corporazioni del Basso Impero.* Naples: Libreria Scientifica Editrice; repr. *Il fenomeno associativo nel mondo romano: dai collegi della reppublica alle corporazioni del Basso Impero.* Studia historica ("L'Erma" di Bretschneider) 126. Roma: "L'Erma" di Bretschneider, 1981.

Desjardins, M. 1991. "Bauer and Beyond: On Recent Scholarly Discussion of Hairesis in the Early Christian Era." *Second Century* 8:65–82.

Dessau, H. 1892–1916. *Inscriptiones latinae selectae.* 3 vols in 5. Berlin: Weidmann.

DeVaux, R. 1954. "Fouilles au Khirbet Qumran." *RB* 61:206–36.

———. 1973. *Archaeology and the Dead Sea Scrolls.* London: Oxford University Press.

DeWitt, N. 1967. *Epicurus and His Philosophy.* Cleveland and New York: Meridian.

Dibelius, M. 1937. *An die Thessalonicher I–II. An die Philipper.* 3d edn. HNT 11. Tübingen: J. C. B. Mohr (Paul Siebeck).

Dill, S. 1905. *Roman Society from Nero to Marcus Aurelius.* 2d edn. New York: Macmillan & Co.

Dimant, D., and L. H. Schiffman, eds. 1995. *Time to Prepare the Way in the Wilderness: Papers on the Qumran Scrolls.* Studies on the Texts of the Desert of Judah 16. Leiden and New York: E. J. Brill.

Dion, P. E. 1977. "Synagogues et temples dans l'Égypte hellénistique." *ScEs* 29:45–75.

Dittenberger, W., ed. 1915–24. *Sylloge Inscriptionum Graecarum.* Nunc tertium edita. Lipsiae: S. Hirzel.

Dölger, F. J. 1929–50. "Der Heiland." Pp. 241–72 in *Antike und Christentum: Kultur- und religionsgeschichtliche Studien,* vol. 6. Münster: Aschendorff.

Dombrowski, B. W. 1966. "*HYHD* in 1QS and *to koinon*: An Instance of Early Greek and Jewish Synthesis." *HTR* 59:293–307.

Donaldson, T. L. 1993. "Thomas Kuhn, Convictional Worlds, and Paul." In McLean 1993b:190–98.

Donati, A. 1965. "I Romani nell'egeo i documenti dell'eta republicana." *Epigraphica* 27:3–59.

Dörpfeld, W. 1892. "Die Ausgrabungen an der Enneakrunos." *MDAIA(A)* 17:439–45.

———. 1894. "Die Ausgrabungen an der Enneakrunos." *MDAIA(A)* 19:143–51.

Dunand, F. 1978. "Le Statut des 'Hiereiai' en Egypte romaine." Pp. 352–74 in *Hommages à Maarten J. Vermaseren,* ed. Margreet B. De Boer and T. A. Edridge. EPRO 68. Leiden: E. J. Brill.

Durkheim, E. 1964. *The Division of Labor in Society.* Trans. G. Simpson. New York: Free Press.

Durrbach, F. 1926. *Choix d'inscriptions de Délos, avec traduction et commentaire.* Subsidia epigraphica 6. Paris: E. de Boccard.

Durrbach, F., P. Roussel, M. Launey, A. Plassart, and J. Coupry, eds. 1926–73. *Inscriptions de Délos.* 7 vols. Paris: Librairie ancienne Honoré Champion.

Edelstein, E. J., and L. Edelstein. 1945. *Asclepius: A Collection and Interpretation of the Testimonies.* 2 vols. Baltimore: The Johns Hopkins Press.

Eisenstadt, S. N., and L. Roniger. 1984. *Patrons, Clients, and Friends.* Cambridge and New York: Cambridge University Press.

Elder, L. B. 1994. "The Woman Queston and Female Ascetics Among Essenes." *BA* 57:220–34.

Eliachevitch, B. 1942. *La personnalité juridique en droit privé romain.* Paris: Sirey.

Elliott, J. H. 1981. *A Home for the Homeless: A Sociological Exegesis of 1 Peter, its Situation and Strategy.* Philadelphia, Pa.: Fortress.

Engelmann, H. 1975. *The Delian Aretalogy of Sarapis.* EPRO 44. Leiden: E. J. Brill.

—— ed. 1979–84. *Die Inschriften von Ephesos.* Inschriften griechischer Städte aus Kleinasien 11–17. Bonn: Rudolf Habelt.

Epstein, A. L. 1969. "The Network and Urban Social Organization." In Mitchell 1969b:77–116.

Evans, C. A., and J. A. Sanders. 1993. *Luke and Scripture: The Function of Sacred Tradition in Luke–Acts.* Minneapolis, Minn.: Fortress.

Evans, J. A. S. 1961. "The Social and Economic History of an Egyptian Temple in the Greco-Roman Period." YCS 7:149–283.

Evans, J. K. 1991. *War, Women, and Children in Ancient Rome.* London and New York: Routledge.

Feder, T. H. 1978. *Great Treasures of Pompeii and Herculaneum.* New York: Abbeville.

Feldman, L. H. 1960. "The Orthodoxy of the Jews in Hellenistic Egypt." *Jewish Social Studies* 22:215–37.

——. 1993. *Jew and Gentile in the Ancient World: Attitudes and Interactions from Alexander to Justinian.* Princeton, NJ: Princeton University Press.

Ferguson, E. 1987. *Backgrounds of Early Christianity.* Grand Rapids, Mich.: Wm. B. Eerdmans; 2d ed. 1993.

Finger, R. H. 1994. "Open Homes and Fictive Kin Groups: Jesus Reinvents the Family." *Daughters of Sarah* 20(1):18–22.

Finney, P. C. 1988. "Early Christian Architecture: The Beginnings (A Review Article)." *HTR* 81:319–39.

Fiorenza, E. S. 1983. *In Memory of Her: A Feminist Theological Reconstruction of Christian Origins.* New York: Crossroad.

Firth, R. W. 1954. "Social Organization and Social Change." *Journal of the Royal Anthropological Institute* 84:1–20.

Fisher, N. R. E. 1988a. "Greek Associations, Symposia, and Clubs." Pp. 1167–97 in *Civilization of the Ancient Mediterranean: Greece and Rome,* ed. M. Grant and R. Kitzinger. New York: Charles Scribner's Sons.

——. 1988b. "Roman Associations, Dinner Parties, and Clubs." Pp. 1199–225 in *Civilization of the Ancient Mediterranean: Greece and Rome,* ed. M. Grant and R. Kitzinger. New York: Charles Scribner's Sons.

Fitzmyer, J. A. 1978. "Divorce Among First-Century Palestinian Jews." *Eretz Israel* 14:103–10.

Flap, H. D. 1988. *Conflict, Loyalty, and Violence.* Beiträge zur Gesellschaftsformung 4. Frankfurt am Main: Peter Lang.

Flesher, P. V. M. 1995. "Palestinian Synagogues Before 70 C.E. A Review of the Evidence." In Urman and Flesher 1995:27–39.

Flusser, D. 1989. *The Spiritual History of the Dead Sea Sect.* Tel Aviv: MOD.

Foerster, G. 1981a. "Notes on Recent Excavations at Capernaum." In Levine 1981:57–59.

——. 1981b. "A Survey of Ancient Diaspora Synagogues." In Levine 1981:164–71.

——. 1981c. "The Synagogues at Masada and Herodium." In Levine 1981:24–29.

——. 1995. "Dating Synagogues with a 'Basilical' Plan and Apse." In Urman and Flesher 1995:87–94.

Forbes, C. A. 1933. *Neoi: A Contribution to the Study of Greek Associations.* Philological monographs pub. by the American Philological Association 2. Middletown, Conn.: American Philological Association.

Foucart, P. 1873. *Des associations religieuses chez les Grecs – thiases, éranes, orgéons, avec le texte des inscriptions rélatives à ces associations.* Paris: Klincksieck.

Fox, R. L. 1987. Pagans and Christians. New York: Knopf.

Francis, E. D. 1975. "Mithraic Graffiti from Dura-Europos." In Hinnells 1975:424–45.

Frank, T. 1940. "Rome and Italy of the Empire." Vol. 5 in *An Economic Survey of Ancient Rome,* ed. T. Frank. Baltimore, Md.: Johns Hopkins University Press.

Fraser, P. M. 1977. *Rhodian Funerary Monuments.* Oxford: Clarendon Press.

Gafni, I. 1995. "Synagogues in Babylonia in the Talmudic Period." In Urman and Flesher 1995:221–31.

Gager, J. G. 1975. *Kingdom and Community: The Social World of Early Christianity*. Englewood Cliffs, NJ: Prentice-Hall.

Gal, Z. 1995. "Ancient Synagogues in the Eastern Lower Galilee." In Urman and Flesher 1995:166–73.

Garcia Martinez, F., and A. S. van der Woude. 1990. "A 'Groningen' Hypothesis of Qumran Origins and Early History." *RevQ* 14:521–41.

Garnsey, P., and R. Saller. 1987. *The Roman Empire: Economy, Society and Culture*. London and Berkeley: Duckworth; University of California Press.

Gaster, T. H. 1956. *The Dead Sea Scriptures in English Translation*. Garden City, NY: Doubleday.

Gaston, L. 1987. *Paul and the Torah*. Vancouver: University of British Columbia Press.

Geertz, C. 1973a. *The Interpretation of Cultures: Selected Essays*. New York: Basic Books.

———. 1973b. "Thick Description: Toward an Interpretive Theory of Culture." Pp. 3–30 in *The Interpretation of Cultures: Selected Essays*. New York: Basic Books.

Geoltrain, P. 1959. "La Contemplation à Qoumran et chez les Thérapeutes." *Semitica* 9:49–57.

———. 1960. "Le traité de la vie contemplative de Philon d'Alexandrie: introduction, traduction et notes." *Semitica* 10:5–66.

Gierke, O. F. von. 1977. *Associations and Law: The Classical and Early Christian Stages*. Toronto and Buffalo: University of Toronto Press.

Gill, D. W. J. 1993. "Corinth: A Roman Colony in Achaea." *BZ* 37:259–64.

Gillman, F. M. 1990. "Early Christian Women at Philippi." *Journal of Gender in World Religions* 1:59–79.

Gilson, E. 1938. *Reason and Revelation in the Middle Ages*. New York: Charles Scribner's Sons.

Ginzberg, L. 1976. *An Unknown Jewish Sect*. New York: Jewish Theological Seminary of America.

Goffman, E. 1971. *Relations in Public: Microstudies of the Public Order*. New York: Harper & Row.

Golb, N. 1989. "The Dead Sea Scrolls: A New Perspective." *The American Scholar*:177–207.

Goodenough, E. R. 1953–68. *Jewish Symbols in the Greco-Roman Period*. New York: Pantheon Books.

Goodman, M. 1994. *Mission and Conversion: Proselytizing in the Religious History of the Roman Empire*. Oxford and New York: Clarendon Press; Oxford University Press.

Goodman, P. 1959. *The Empire City*. Indianapolis, Ind.: Bobbs-Merrill.

Gordon, R. L. 1972. "Mithraism and Roman Society: Social Factors in the Explanation of Religious Change in the Roman Empire." *Religion* 2:92–121.

———. 1976. "The Sacred Geography of a Mithraeum: The Example of Sette Sfere." *JMS* 1:119–65.

———. 1978. "The Date and Significance of CIMRM 593." *JMS* 2:148–74.

———. 1980. "Reality, Evocation and Boundary in the Mysteries of Mithras." *JMS* 3:19–99.

———. 1988. "Authority, Salvation and Mystery in the Mysteries of Mithras." Pp. 45–80 in *Image and Mystery in the Roman World*, ed. P. Zanker. Gloucester: Alan Sutton.

———. 1994. "Mystery, Metaphor and Doctrine in the Mysteries of Mithras." In Hinnells 1994:103–24.

Grabbe, L. L. 1988. "Synagogues in Pre–70 Palestine: A Reassessment." *JTS* 38:401–10.

———. 1995. "Synagogues in Pre–70 Palestine: A Reassessment." In Urman and Flesher 1995:17–26.

Graeber, A. 1983. *Untersuchungen zum spätrömischen Korporationswesen*. Frankfurt am Main, New York, and Bern: Peter Lang.

Graser, E. R. 1933–40. "The Edict of Diocletian on Maximum Prices." Pp. 305–421 in *An Economic Survey of Ancient Rome*, ed. T. Frank, vol. 5. Baltimore, Md.: Johns Hopkins University Press.

Green, W. S. 1983. "Reading the Writing of Rabbinism: Toward an Interpretation of Rabbinic Literature." *JAAR* 51:191–206.

Greene, W. C. 1933. *The Achievement of Rome: A Chapter in Civilization.* Cambridge, Mass.: Harvard University Press.

Griffiths, J. G. 1995. "Egypt and the Rise of the Synagogue." In Urman and Flesher 1995:3–16.

Groh, D. E. 1995. "The Stratigraphic Chronology of the Galilean Synagogue from the Early Roman Period Through the Early Byzantine Period (*c.* 420 CE)." In Urman and Flesher 1995:51–69.

Grossman, S. 1992. "Women and the Jerusalem Temple." Pp. 22–27 in *Daughters of the King: Women and the Synagogue: A Survey of History, Halakhah, and Contemporary Realities,* ed. S. Grossman and R. Haut. Philadelphia, Pa.: Jewish Publication Society.

Guillaumont, A. 1971. "A propos du célibat des Esséniens." Pp. 395–404 in *Hommages à André Dupont-Sommer.* Paris: Adrien-Maisonneuve.

Gülzow, H. 1974. "Soziale Gegebenheiten der altkirchlichen Mission." Pp. 194–226 in *Kirchengeschichte als Missionsgeschichte,* ed. H. Frohnes and U. W. Knorr, vol. 1. *Die alte Kirche.* München: Chr. Kaiser.

Guterman, S. L. 1951. *Religious Toleration and Persecution in Ancient Rome.* London: Aiglon.

Gutman, S. 1981. "The Synagogue at Gamla." In Levine 1981:30–34.

Gutman, S., Z. Yeivin, and E. Netzer. 1981. "Excavations in the Synagogue at Horvat Susiya." In Levine 1981:123–28.

Gutmann, J. 1975a. "Programmatic Painting in the Dura Synagogue." In Gutmann 1975b:210–32.

——— ed. 1975b. *The Synagogue: Studies in Origins, Archaeology, and Architecture.* New York: Ktav Publishing House.

——— ed. 1981. *Ancient Synagogues: The State of Research.* BJS 22. Chico, Calif.: Scholars Press.

———. 1987. "The Dura Europos Synagogue Paintings: The State of Research." In Levine 1987:61–72.

Habicht, C. 1969. *Die Inschriften des Asklepieions.* Altertümer von Pergamon 8/3. Berlin: Walter de Gruyter.

Hachlili, R. 1992. "Diaspora Synagogues." *ABD* 6:260–63.

Hadas, M. 1959. *Hellenistic Culture: Fusion and Diffusion.* New York: Columbia University Press.

Hallett, J. P. 1984. *Fathers and Daughters in Roman Society: Women and the Elite Family.* Princeton, NJ: Princeton University Press.

Hamilton, M. 1906. *Incubation or The Cure of Disease in Pagan Temples and Christian Churches.* London: Simpkin, Marshall, Hamilton, Kent & Co.; St. Andrews: St. Andrews University Press.

Hammond, M. 1959. *The Antonine Monarchy.* Papers and Monographs of the American Academy in Rome 19. Rome: American Academy in Rome.

Hanell, K. 1935. "Neokoroi." *PW* 16/2:2422–28.

Hansen, M. H. 1983. *The Athenian Ecclesia: A Collection of Articles 1976–1983.* Opuscula Graecolatina 26. Copenhagen: Museum Tusculanum.

Harnack, A. von. 1906. *Die Mission und Ausbreitung des Christentums in den ersten drei Jahrhunderten.* Leipzig: J. C. Hinrichs.

Harrington, D. J. 1980. "Sociological Concepts and the Early Church: A Decade of Research." *TS* 41:181–90.

Hatch, E. 1881. *The Organization of the Early Christian Churches: Eight Lectures.* Bampton Lectures, 1880. London: Rivingtons.

Hatch, E., and H. A. Redpath. 1897–1906. *A Concordance to the Septuagint and the Other Greek Versions of the Old Testament.* Oxford: Clarendon Press.

Hatzfeld, J. 1912. "Les Italiens résidant à Délos." *BCH* 36:5–218.

———. 1919. *Les trafiquants italiens dans l'Orient hellénique. BEFAR* 115. Paris: E. de Boccard.

Heinrici, G. 1876. "Die Christengemeinden Korinths und die religiösen Genossenschaften der Griechen." *ZWT* 19:465–526.

———. 1896. *Der erste Brief an die Korinther*. 8. Aufl. KEK 5. Göttingen: Vandenhoeck & Ruprecht.

Hengel, M. 1971a. "Proseuche und Synagoge: Jüdische Gemeinde, Gotteshaus und Gottesdienst in der Diaspora und in Palästina." Pp. 157–84 in *Tradition und Glaube: das frühe Christentum in seiner Umwelt. Festgabe für Karl Georg Kuhn*, ed. G. Jeremias, H.-W. Kuhn, and H. Stegemann. Göttingen: Vandenhoeck & Ruprecht.

———. 1971b. "Die Ursprünge der christlichen Mission." *NTS* 18:15–38.

———. 1974. *Judaism and Hellenism: Studies in Their Encounter in Palestine During the Early Hellenistic Period*. 2 vols. London: SCM; Philadelphia, Pa.: Fortress.

———. 1975 [=1971a]. "Proseuche und Synagoge: Jüdische Gemeinde, Gotteshaus und Gottesdienst in der Diaspora und in Palästina." In Gutmann 1975b:27–54.

Hennig, D. 1983. "Die 'heiligen Häuser' von Delos." *Chiron* 13:411–95.

Henrichs, A. 1982. "Changing Dionysiac Identities." In Meyer and Sanders 1982:137–60, 213–36.

Hermansen, G. 1982. *Ostia: Aspects of Roman City Life*. Edmonton: University of Alberta Press.

Herrmann, P. 1978. "Genossenschaft. A. Griechisch." *RAC* 10:83–99.

Heyob, S. K. 1975. *The Cult of Isis Among Women in the Graeco-Roman World*. EPRO 51. Leiden: E. J. Brill.

Hicks, R. D. 1925. *Diogenes Laertius, Lives of Eminent Philosophers*. LCL. 2 vols. Cambridge. Mass.: Harvard University Press; London: W. Heinemann.

Hinnells, J. R., ed. 1975. *Mithraic Studies*. Manchester: Manchester University Press; Totowa, NJ: Rowman & Littlefield.

——— ed. 1994. *Studies in Mithraism*. Storia delle religioni 9. Rome: Bretschneider.

Hock, R. F. 1980. *The Social Context of Paul's Ministry: Tentmaking and Apostleship*. Philadelphia, Pa.: Fortress.

Holmberg, B. 1990. *Sociology and the New Testament: An Appraisal*. Minneapolis, Minn.: Fortress.

Homolle, T., M. Holleaux, G. Fougères, C. Picard, and P. Roussel. 1909–85. *Exploration archéologique de Délos*. BEFAR 1–35. Paris: Fontemoing et Cie.; E. de Boccard.

Hoppe, L. J. 1989. "Synagogue and Church in Palestine." *Bible Today* 27:278–84.

Horsley, G. H. R. 1981–89. *New Documents Illustrating Early Christianity: A Review of the Greek Inscriptions and Papyri*. 5 vols. North Ryde, Australia: Ancient History Documentary Research Centre, Macquarie University.

———. 1987. *New Documents Illustrating Early Christianity: A Review of the Greek Inscriptions and Papyri Published in 1979*. New Documents Illustrating Early Christianity 4. North Ryde, Australia: Ancient History Documentary Research Centre, Macquarie University.

Horst, P. W. van der. 1988. "The Jews of Ancient Crete." *JJS* 39:183–200.

———. 1989. "Jews and Christians in Aphrodisias in the Light of Their Relations in Other Cities of Asia Minor." *NedTTs* 43:106–21.

———. 1991. *Ancient Jewish Epitaphs: An Introductory Survey of a Millennium of Jewish Funerary Epigraphy (300 BCE–700 CE)*. Kampen, The Netherlands: Kok Pharos.

Hübner, H. 1970–71. "Zölibat in Qumran?" *NTS* 17:153–67.

Hultgren, A. J. 1994. "The Church in the New Testament: Three Polarities in Discerning Its Identity." Dialog 33:111–17.

Hutter, H. 1978. *Politics as Friendship: The Origins of Classical Notions of Politics in the Theory and Practice of Friendship*. Waterloo, Ontario: Wilfrid Laurier University Press.

Ilan, Z. 1995. "The Synagogue and the Study House at Meroth." In Urman and Flesher 1995:256–80.

Irvin, D. 1980. "The Ministry of Women in the Early Church: The Archaeological Evidence." *Duke Divinity Review* 45:76–86.

297

Jewett, R. 1993. "Tenement Churches and Communal Meals in the Early Church: The Implications of a Form-Critical Analysis of 2 Thessalonians 3:10." BR 38:23–43.
——. 1994. "Tenement Churches and Pauline Love Feasts." *Quarterly Review* 14:43–58.
Johnson, A. C. 1936. "Roman Egypt to the Reign of Diocletian." Vol. 2 in *An Economic Survey of Ancient Rome*, ed. T. Frank. Baltimore, Md.: Johns Hopkins University Press.
—— ed. 1961. *Ancient Roman Statutes: A Translation, with Introduction, Commentary, Glossary, and Index*. The Corpus of Roman Law 2. Austin: University of Texas Press.
Jones, A. H. M. 1957. *Athenian Democracy*. Oxford: Basil Blackwell.
Jordan, M. D. 1986. "Ancient Philosophic Protreptic and the Problem of Persuasive Genres." *Rhetorica* 4:309–33.
Judge, E. A. 1960. *The Social Pattern of Christian Groups in the First Century: Some Prolegomena to the Study of New Testament Ideas of Social Obligation*. London: Tyndale.
——. 1960–1. "The Early Christians as a Scholastic Community." *JRH* 1:4–15, 125–37.
——. 1980. "The Social Identity of the First Christians: A Question of Method in Religious History." *JRH* 11:201–17.
Kadushin, C. 1966. "The Friends and Supporters of Psychotherapy: On Social Circles in Urban Life." *ASR* 31:786–802.
Kane, J. P. 1975. "The Mithraic Cult Meal in its Greek and Roman Environment." In Hinnells 1975:313–51.
Kasher, A. 1985. *The Jews in Hellenistic and Roman Egypt: The Struggle for Equal Rights*. Rev. English ed. Texte und Studien zum antiken Judentum 7. Tübingen: J. C. B. Mohr (Paul Siebeck).
——. 1995. "Synagogues as 'Houses of Prayer' and 'Holy Places' in the Jewish Communities of Hellenistic and Roman Egypt." In Urman and Flesher 1995:205–20.
Kayser, F. 1994. *Recueil des inscriptions grecques et latines (non funéraires) d'Alexandrie Impériale (I*[er]*–III*[e] *s. apr. J.-C.)*. Bibliothèque d'étude 108. Cairo: Institut français d'archéologie orientale du Caire.
Kee, H. C. 1990. "The Transformation of the Synagogue after 70 CE: Its Import for Early Christianity." *NTS* 36(1):1–24.
Keil, B., ed. 1898. *P. Aelii Aristidis Opera quae exstant omnia*. Berlin: Weidmann.
Kirsopp Michaels, A. 1953. "III. – The Topography and Interpretation of the Lupercalia." *TAPA* 84:35–59.
Kittel, G. 1944. "Das kleinasiatische Judentum in der hellenistisch–römischen Zeit." *TLZ* 69:9–20.
Klassen, W. 1984. "Musonius Rufus, Jesus and Paul: Three First Century Feminists." Pp. 185–206 in *From Jesus to Paul: Studies in Honour of Francis Wright Beare*, ed. J. C. Hurd and G. P. Richardson. Waterloo: Wilfrid Laurier University Press.
Klauck, H.-J. 1986. *Herrenmahl und hellenistischer Kult: eine religionsgeschichtliche Untersuchung zum ersten Korintherbrief*. 2. Aufl. NTAbh NF 15. Münster: Aschendorff.
Kloner, A. 1981. "Ancient Synagogues in Israel: An Archeological Survey." In Levine 1981:11–18.
Kloppenborg, J. S. 1987. *The Formation of Q: Trajectories in Ancient Wisdom Collections*. Philadelphia, Pa.: Fortress.
——. 1989. "The Phenomenology of Graeco-Roman Private Associations." Paper presented at the annual meeting of the Canadian Society of Biblical Studies, Université Laval, June 1989.
——. 1992. "*Exitus Clari Viri*: The Death of Jesus in Luke." Pp. 106–20 in *Scriptures and Cultural Conversations: Essays for Heinz Guenther at 65*. = *Toronto Journal of Theology* 8/1, ed. J. S. Kloppenborg and L. E. Vaage. Toronto: University of Toronto Press.
——. 1993. "Edwin Hatch, Churches, and *Collegia*." In McLean 1993b:212–38.
Kloppenborg, J. S., M. W. Meyer, S. Patterson, and M. G. Steinhauser. 1990. *Q Thomas Reader*. Sonoma, Calif.: Polebridge.
Kornemann, E. 1901. "Collegium." *PW* 4:380–480.

Kraabel, A. T. 1969. "Hypsistos and the Synagogue at Sardis." *GRBS* 10:81–86.

——. 1979. "The Diaspora Synagogue: Archaeological and Epigraphic Evidence since Sukenik." *ANRW* II.19.1:477–510.

——. 1983. "Impact of the Discovery of the Sardis Synagogue." Pp. 178–90, 284–85 in *Sardis from Prehistoric to Roman Times: Results of the Archaeological Exploration of Sardis, 1958–1975*, ed. G. M. A. Hanfmann, C. Foss, and W. E. Mierse. Cambridge, Mass.: Harvard University Press.

——. 1984. "New Evidence of the Samaritan Diaspora has been Found on Delos." *BAR* 10(2):44–46.

——. 1987. "Unity and Diversity among Diaspora Synagogues." In Levine 1987:49–60.

——. 1992a. "Social Systems of Six Diaspora Synagogues." Pp. 257–67 in *Diaspora Jews and Judaism: Essays in Honor of, and in Dialogue with, A. Thomas Kraabel*, ed. J. A. Overman and R. S. MacLennan. South Florida Studies in the History of Judaism 41. Atlanta, Ga.: Scholars Press.

——. 1992b. "Unity and Diversity among Diaspora Synagogues." Pp. 21–33 in *Diaspora Jews and Judaism: Essays in Honor of, and in Dialogue with, A. Thomas Kraabel*, ed. J. A. Overman and R. S. MacLennan. South Florida Studies in the History of Judaism 41. Atlanta, Ga.: Scholars Press.

——. 1995. "The Diaspora Synagogue: Archaeological and Epigraphic Evidence since Sukenik." In Urman and Flesher 1995:95–126.

Kraemer, R. S. 1983. "Women in the Religions of the Greco-Roman World." *RSR* 9(2):127–39.

—— ed. 1988. *Maenads, Martyrs, Matrons, Monastics: A Sourcebook on Women's Religions in the Greco-Roman World*. Philadelphia, Pa.: Fortress.

——. 1989. "Monastic Jewish Women in Greco-Roman Egypt: Philo Judaeus on the Therapeutrides." *Signs: Journal of Women in Culture and Society* 14:342–70.

——. 1992. *Her Share of the Blessings: Women's Religions among Pagans, Jews, and Christians in the Greco-Roman World*. New York: Oxford University Press.

Krautheimer, R. 1969. *Studies in Early Christian, Medieval, and Renaissance Art*. New York: New York University Press.

——. 1975. *Early Christian and Byzantine Architecture*. 2d ed. Harmondsworth and Baltimore: Penguin Books.

Laidlaw, W. A. 1933. *A History of Delos*. Oxford: Basil Blackwell.

Lajtar, A. 1992. "Dedication of the *Prostates* of a *Synodos* from Alexandria." *JJP* 22:29–36.

La Piana, G. 1927. "Foreign Groups in Rome during the First Century of the Empire." *HTR* 20:183–354.

Leipoldt, J. 1955. *Die Frau in der Antiken Welt und Im Urchristentum*. 2. Aufl. Leipzig: Köhler und Ameland.

Lemerle, P. 1935. "Chronique des fouilles: Cyclades, îles d'Asie Mineure." *BCH* 59:297–303.

Lenz, F. W., and C. A. Behr, eds. 1976–80. *P. Aelii Aristidis Opera quae exstant omnia*. Vol. 1: *Orations 1–16*. Leiden: E. J. Brill.

Leon, H. J. 1960. *Jews of Ancient Rome*. Philadelphia, Pa.: Jewish Publication Society of America.

Lesko, L. H. 1987. "Isis." In *The Encyclopedia of Religion*, ed. Mircea Eliade, vol. 7:302. New York and London: Macmillan; Collier Macmillan.

Levine, A.-J., ed. 1991. *"Women Like This": New Perspectives on Jewish Women in the Greco-Roman World*. Early Judaism and its Literature 1. Atlanta, Ga.: Scholars Press.

Levine, L. I., ed. 1981. *Ancient Synagogues Revealed*. Jerusalem: Israel Exploration Society.

—— ed. 1987. *The Synagogue in Late Antiquity*. Philadelphia, Pa.: American Schools of Oriental Research.

Lewis, C. S. 1949. "The Inner Ring." Pp. 55–66 in *The Weight of Glory and Other Addresses*. New York: Macmillan.

———. 1955. *Surprised by Joy: The Shape of My Early Life*. London: Geoffrey Bles.

Lewis, N., and M. Reinhold, eds. and trans. 1966a. *The Empire*. In *Roman Civilization: Sourcebook II*. New York: Harper & Row.

———. eds. and trans. 1966b. *The Republic*. In *Roman Civilization: Sourcebook I*. New York: Harper & Row.

Liebenam, W. 1890. *Zur Geschichte und Organisation des römischen Vereinswesens: 3 Untersuchungen*. Leipzig: B. G. Teubner.

Liebeschuetz, J. H. W. G. 1994. "The Expansion of Mithraism among the Religious Cults of the Second Century." In Hinnells 1994:195–216.

Lietzmann, H. 1969. *An die Korinther I/II*. 5. Aufl. Revised by W. G. Kümmel. HNT 9. Tübingen: J. C. B. Mohr (Paul Siebeck).

Lieu, J. M. 1987. "The Social World of the New Testament." *Epworth Review* 14:47–53.

Lifshitz, B. 1967. *Donateurs et fondateurs dans les synagogues juives*. Cahiers de la Revue biblique 7. Paris: J. Gabalda et Cie.

Lightstone, J. N. 1988. *Society, the Sacred, and Scripture in Ancient Judaism: A Sociology of Knowledge*. Studies in Christianity and Judaism / Etudes sur le christianisme et le judaïsme 3. Waterloo, Ont.: Published for the Canadian Corporation for the Study of Religion by Wilfrid Laurier University Press.

Lindner, H. 1972. *Die Geschichtsauffassung des Flavius Josephus im Bellum Judaicum*. AGJU 12. Leiden: E. J. Brill.

Lissi-Caronna, E. 1986. *Il mitreo dei Castra Peregrinorum (S. Stefano Rotondo)*. EPRO 104. Leiden: E. J. Brill.

Loewy, E. 1885. *Inschriften griechischer Bildhauer*. Leipzig: B. G. Teubner.

Loffreda, S. 1981. "The Late Chronology of the Synagogue at Capernaum." In Levine 1981:52–56.

Long, A. A. 1974. *Hellenistic Philosophy: Stoics, Epicureans, Sceptics*. London and New York: Duckworth; Scribner.

Longo, V. 1969. *Aretalogie nel mondo greco*. Pubblicazioni dell'Istituto di filologia classica dell'Universita di Genova 29. Genova: Istituto di filologia classica e medioevale.

Lührmann, D. 1981. "Neutestamentliche Haustafeln und antike Ökonomie." *NTS* 27:83–97.

Lutz, C. E. 1947. *Musonius Rufus, "The Roman Socrates"*. YCS 10. New Haven, Conn.: Yale University Press.

McCready, W. O. 1985. "A Second Torah at Qumran." *SR* 14:5–15.

———. 1990. "Johannine Self-Understanding and the Synagogue Episode of John 9." Pp. 147–66 in *Self-definition and Self-discovery in Early Christianity: A Study in Changing Horizons: Essays in Appreciation of Ben F. Meyer from Former Students*, ed. D. J. Hawkin and T. A. Robinson. Lewiston, NY: Edwin Mellen.

MacIver, R. M. 1970. *On Community, Society and Power: Selected Writings*. Ed. L. Bramson. Chicago and London: University of Chicago Press.

MacIver, R. M., and C. H. Page. 1949. *Society: An Introductory Analysis*. New York: Holt, Rinehart, & Winston.

McLean, B. H. 1993a. "The Agrippinilla Inscription: Religious Associations and Early Christian Formation." In McLean 1993b:239–70.

———. ed. 1993b. *Origins and Method: Towards a New Understanding of Judaism and Christianity: Essays in Honour of John C. Hurd*. JSNTSup 86. Sheffield: JSOT Press.

———. Forthcoming. "Voluntary Associations on Delos." In *Voluntary Associations in the Hellenistic World: A Sourcebook*, ed. J. S. Kloppenborg and B. H. McLean.

MacMullen, R. 1966. *Enemies of the Roman Order: Treason, Unrest, and Alienation in the Empire*. Cambridge, Mass.: Harvard University Press.

———. 1974. *Roman Social Relations, 50 B.C. to A.D. 284*. New Haven, Conn.: Yale University Press.

———. 1981. *Paganism in the Roman Empire*. New Haven, Conn.: Yale University Press.

———. 1982. "Woman in Public in the Roman Empire." *Historia* 31:484–502.

Magie, D. 1950. *Roman Rule in Asia Minor.* 2 vols. Princeton, NJ: Princeton University Press.

Maier, H. O. 1991. *The Social Setting of the Ministry as Reflected in the Writings of Hermas, Clement, and Ignatius.* Dissertations SR 1. Waterloo, Ont.: Published by the Canadian Corporation for the Study of Religion by Wilfrid Laurier University Press.

———. 1995. "The Topography of Heresy and Dissent in Late-Fourth-Century Rome." *Historia* 44:232–49.

Malherbe, A. J. 1970. "Gentle as a Nurse: The Cynic Background to I Thess II." *NovT* 12:203–17.

———. 1977. *Social Aspects of Early Christianity.* Baton Rouge: Louisiana State University Press.

———. 1982. "Self–Definition among Epicureans and Cynics." In Meyer and Sanders 1982:46–59, 192–97.

———. 1983. *Social Aspects of Early Christianity.* 2d ed. Philadelphia, Pa.: Fortress.

———. 1987. *Paul and the Thessalonians: The Philosophic Tradition of Pastoral Care.* Philadelphia, Pa.: Fortress.

———. 1989. *Paul and the Popular Philosophers.* Minneapolis, Minn.: Fortress.

———. 1990. "'Pastoral Care' in the Thessalonian Church." *NTS* 36:375–91.

Malina, B. J. 1986a. *Christian Origins and Cultural Anthropology: Practical Models for Biblical Interpretation.* Atlanta, Ga.: John Knox.

———. 1986b. "Religion in the World of Paul." *BTB* 16:92–101.

Malingrey, A. M. 1961. *Philosophia: étude d'un groupe de mots dans la littérature grecque, des présocratiques au IV* siècle après J.C.* Etudes et commentaires 40. Paris: C. Klincksieck.

Ma'oz, Z. 1981. "The Synagogue at Gamla and the Typology of Second-Temple Synagogues." In Levine 1981:35–41.

Marcadé, J. 1953–7. *Recueil des signatures de sculpteurs grecs.* Paris: E. de Boccard.

———. 1969. *Au musée de Délos: étude sur la sculpture hellénistique en ronde bosse découverte dans l'île.* BEFAR 215. Paris: E. de Boccard.

Marrou, H. I. 1956. *A History of Education in Antiquity.* Madison: University of Wisconsin Press.

Marx, A. 1969–71. "Les racines du célibat essénien." *RevQ* 7:323–42.

Maser, P. 1990–91. "Synagoge und Ecclesia – Erwägungen zur Frühgeschichte des Kirchenbaus und der christlichen Bildkunst." *Kairos* 32–33:9–26.

Mazur, B. D. 1935. *Studies on Jewry in Greece.* Athens: Hestia.

Meeks, W. A. 1973–74. "The Image of the Androgyne: Some Uses of a Symbol in Earliest Christianity." *HR* 13:165–208.

———. 1983. *The First Urban Christians: The Social World of the Apostle Paul.* New Haven, Conn.: Yale University Press.

Mendelson, A. 1982. *Secular Education in Philo of Alexandria.* Monographs of the Hebrew Union College 7. Cincinnati: Hebrew Union College Press; New York: Ktav Publishing House.

Meredith, A. 1991. "Later Philosophy." Pp. 288–307 in *The Oxford History of the Roman World,* ed. J. Boardman, J. Griffin, and O. Murray. Oxford and New York: Oxford University Press.

Merkelbach, R. 1984. *Mithras.* Königstein: A. Hain.

———. 1990. "Priestergrade in den Mithras-Mysterien." *ZPE* 82:195–97.

Merton, R. K. 1967. *On Theoretical Sociology: Five Essays, Old and New.* New York: Free Press; London and Toronto: Collier-Macmillan.

Meyer, B. F. 1986. *The Early Christians: Their World Mission and Self-discovery.* Good News Studies 16. Wilmington, Del.: Michael Glazier.

Meyer, B. F. and E. P. Sanders, eds. 1982. *Jewish and Christian Self-definition. Volume 3: Self-definition in the Graeco-Roman World.* Philadelphia, Pa.: Fortress.

Meyer, H. 1988. "Zur Chronologie des Poseidoniastenhauses in Delos." *MDAIA(A)* 103:203–20.

Meyers, E. M. 1981. "The Synagogue at Horvat Shema'." In Levine 1981:70–73.

———. 1987. "The Current State of Galilean Synagogue Studies." In Levine 1987:127–37.

———. 1992. "Synagogue." *ABD* 6:251–60.

Meyers, E. M., A. T. Kraabel, and J. F. Strange. 1976. *Ancient Synagogue Excavations at Khirbet Shema', Upper Galilee, Israel, 1970–1972.* Meiron excavation project 1. Annual of the American Schools of Oriental Research 42. Durham, NC: Published for the American Schools of Oriental Research by Duke University Press.

Meyers, E. M., and L. M. White. 1989. "Jews and Christians in the Roman World." *Archaeology* 42(2):26–33.

Michels, R. 1959. *Political Parties: A Sociological Study of the Oligarchical Tendencies of Modern Democracy.* New York: Dover Publications.

Milik, J. T. 1959. *Ten Years of Discovery in the Wilderness of Judea.* Naperville, Ill.: Allenson; London: SCM.

———. 1981. "Daniel et Susanne à Qumrân?" Pp. 337–59 in *De la Torah au Messie: Etudes d'exégèse et d'herméneutique bibliques offertes à Henri Cazelles,* ed. M. Carrez. Paris: Desclee.

———. 1992. "Les modèles araméens du livre d'Esther dans la Grotte 4 de Qumrân." *RevQ* 15:321–408.

Minear, P. S. 1962. "Church, Idea of." *IDB* 1:607–17.

Mitchell, J. C. 1969a. "The Concept and Use of Social Networks." In Mitchell 1969b:1–50.

———. ed. 1969b. *Social Networks in Urban Situations, Analyses of Personal Relationships in Central African Terms.* Manchester: Manchester University Press.

Moehring, H. R. 1975. "The Acta Pro Judaeis in the Antiquities of Flavius Josephus. A Study in Hellenistic and Modern Apologetic Historiography." Pp. 124–58 in *Christianity, Judaism and Other Greco-Roman Cults: Studies for Morton Smith at Sixty,* ed. J. Neusner. SJLA 12. Leiden: E. J. Brill.

Momigliano, A. 1969. "Seneca Between Political and Contemplative Life." Pp. 239–56 in *Quarto Contributo alla Storia degli Studi Classici e del Mondo Antico.* Storia e Letteratura 115. Rome: Edizioni di Storia e Letteratura.

Mommsen, T. 1843. *De Collegiis et sodaliciis romanorum.* Kiliae: Libraria Schwersiana.

Moore, G. F. 1929. "Fate and Free Will in the Jewish Philosophies According to Josephus." *HTR* 22:371–89.

Moore, R. D. 1981. "Personification of the Seduction of Evil: 'The Wiles of the Wicked Woman'." *RevQ* 10:505–19.

Mora, F. 1990. *Prosopografia isiaca.* EPRO 113. Leiden and New York: E. J. Brill.

Mott, S. C. 1978. "Greek Ethics and Christian Conversion: The Philonic Background of Titus II, 10–14 and III, 3–7." *NovT* 20:22–48.

Moulton, W. F., and A. S. Geden. 1963. *A Concordance to the Greek Testament.* 4th ed. rev. Edinburgh: T. & T. Clark.

Moxnes, H. 1991. "Patron–Client Relations and the New Community in Luke–Acts." Pp. 241–68 in *The Social World of Luke–Acts: Models for Interpretation,* ed. J. H. Neyrey. Peabody, Mass.: Hendrickson Publishers.

Mühll, P. von der. 1976. "Das griechische Symposion." Pp. 483–505 in *Ausgewählte kleine Schriften.* Schweizerische Beiträge zur Altertumswissenschaft 12. Basel: Friedrich Reinhardt.

Murphy-O'Connor, J. 1970. "An Essene Missionary Document? CD II 14–VI 1." *RB* 77:200–29.

———. 1977. "The Essenes in Palestine." *BA* 40:100–24.

Muszynski, M. 1977. "Les associations religieuses en Egypte d'après les sources hiéroglyphiques, démotiques et grecques." *OLP* 8:145–74.

Naville, E., and F. L. Griffith. 1890. *The Mound of the Jew and the City of Onias. Belbeis, Samanood, Abusir, Tukh el Karmus.* London: Kegan Paul, Trench, Trübner.

Naydenova, V. 1994. "Un sanctuaire syncrétisé de Mithra et Sol Augustus découvert à Novae (Mésie Inférieure)." In Hinnells 1994:225–28.

Netzer, E. 1981. "The Herodian Triclinia – A Prototype for the 'Galilean-Type' Synagogue." In Levine 1981:49–51.

———. 1987. "The Synagogues in Massada, Herodium, Gamla and Magdala (?) from the Architect's Viewpoint." Pp. 167–72 in *Synagogues in Antiquity* (Hebrew), ed. A. Kasher, A. Oppenheimer, U. Rappaport, and H. Goldberg. Yerushalayim: Yad Yitshak Ben-Tsevi.

———. 1993. *Masada III: The Yigael Yadin Excavations 1963–1965. Final Reports. The Buildings: Stratigraphy and Architecture.* The Masada Reports 3. Jerusalem: Israel Exploration Society; The Hebrew University of Jerusalem.

Neusner, J., ed. and trans. 1984. *Tractate Sukkah.* The Talmud of Babylonia 6. Chico, Calif.: Scholars Press.

———. 1988–9. *The Philosophical Mishnah.* 4 vols. BJS 158, 163–64, 172. Atlanta, Ga.: Scholars Press.

———. 1991. *Judaism as Philosophy: The Method and Message of the Mishnah.* Columbia, SC: University of South Carolina Press.

Nilsson, M. P. 1967. *Geschichte der griechischen Religion.* 3. Aufl. Handbuch der Altertumswissenschaft. 5. Abt., 2. Teil, 1. Band. München: C. H. Beck.

Nisbet, R. A. 1970. *The Quest for Community.* Reprint of 1953 ed. With a revised Preface (1962). New York: Oxford University Press.

Nock, A. D. 1924. "The Historical Importance of Cult-associations." *CR* 38:105–08.

———. 1933. *Conversion: The Old and the New in Religion from Alexander the Great to Augustine.* London: Oxford University Press.

———. 1972. *Essays on Religion and the Ancient World.* ed. Zeph Stewart. Oxford: Clarendon Press.

Nock, A. D., C. Roberts, and T. C. Skeat. 1936. "The Guild of Zeus Hypsistos." *HTR* 29:39–88.

O'Neil, E., trans. 1977. *Teles (the Cynic Teacher).* SBLTT 11. Graeco-Roman Religion series 3. Missoula, Mont.: Scholars Press.

Oppenheimer, A. 1995. "Babylonian Synagogues with Historical Assocations." In Urman and Flesher 1995:40–48.

Orlandos, A. C. 1936. "Délos chrétienne." *BCH* 60:68–100.

Painter, R. J. 1994. *Mithraism and the Religious Context at Caesarea Maritima.* Ph.D. Diss. Southern Baptist Theological Seminary.

Panciera, S. 1979. "Il materiale epigrafico dallo scavo del mitreo di S. Stefano Rotondo (con un addendum sul verso terminante . . . sanguine fuso)." In Bianchi 1979:87–112.

Pennock, J. R., and J. W. Chapman, eds. 1969. *Voluntary Associations.* Nomos: Yearbook of the American Society for Political and Legal Philosophy 11. New York: Atherton.

Peritz, I. J. 1898. "Women in the Ancient Hebrew Cult." *JBL* 17:111–48.

Perowne, S. 1961. *Hadrian.* New York: W. W. Norton.

Petersen, J. M. 1969. "House-Churches in Rome." *VigChr* 23:264–72.

Petrie, W. M. Flinders. 1906. *Hyksos and Israelite Cities.* London: Office of the School of Archaeology.

Picard, C. 1920. "Fouilles de Délos (1910): Observations sur la société des Poseidoniastes de Bérytos et sur son histoire." *BCH* 44:263–311.

———. 1921. *L'Etablissement des Poseidoniastes de Bérytos. EAD* 6. Paris: E. de Boccard.

Piccottini, G. 1994. *Mithrastempel in Virunum.* Aus Forschung und Kunst, 28. Klagenfurt: Verlag des Geschichtsvereines für Karnten.

Pilisuk, M., and C. Froland. 1978. "Kinship, Social Networks, Social Support and Health." *Social Science and Medicine* 12:273–80.

Plaskow, J. 1993. "Anti–Judaism in Feminist Christian Interpretation." Pp. 117–29 in *Searching the Scriptures. Volume One: A Feminist Introduction,* ed. Elisabeth Schüssler Fiorenza. New York: Crossroad.

Plassart, A. 1913. "Le synagogue juive de Délos." Pp. 201–15 and plates 5, 12 in *Mélanges*

Holleaux: Recueil de mémoires concernant l'antiquité grecque offert à Maurice Holleaux. Paris: Auguste Picard.

——. 1914. "Mélanges: Le synagogue juive de Délos." *RB* 11:523–34.

Pleket, H. W. 1964. *Epigraphica Vol. 1: Texts on the Economic History of the Greek World*. Leiden: E. J. Brill.

Plummer, R. 1987. *"ARGARAZIN:* A Criterion for Samaritan Provenance?" *JSJ* 18:18–23.

Pohlenz, M. 1953. "Nomos und Physis." *Hermes* 81:418–38.

Poland, F. 1909. *Geschichte des griechischen Vereinswesens*. Leipzig: B. G. Teubner; repr. Leipzig: Zentral-Antiquariat der Deutschen Demokratischen Republik, 1967.

Pomeroy, S. B. 1975. *Goddesses, Whores, Wives, and Slaves: Women in Classical Antiquity*. New York: Schocken Books.

——. 1984. *Women in Hellenistic Egypt: From Alexander to Cleopatra*. New York: Schocken Books.

Potter, D. S. 1992. "Pergamum." *ABD* 5:228–30.

Powell, J. U., ed. 1925. *Collectanea alexandrina: reliquiae minores poetarum graecorum aetatis ptolemaicae 323–146 A.C.* Oxonii: E Typographeo Clarendoniano.

Préaux, C. 1958. "Les étrangers à l'époque hellénistique (Egypte–Délos)." Pp. 141–93 in *L'Etranger*. Recueils de la Société Jean Bodin 9–10. Bruxelles: Editions de la Librairie Encyclopédique.

Qimron, E. 1986. "Davies' *The Damascus Covenant*." JQR 77:84–87.

——. 1992. "Celibacy in the Dead Sea Scrolls and the Two Kinds of Sectarians." In Trebolle Barrera and Vegas Montaner 1992:287–94.

Qimron, E., and J. Strugnell. 1985. "An Unpublished Halakhic Letter from Qumran." In Amitai 1985:400–7.

——. 1994. *Qumran Cave 4. V: Miqsat Maase Ha-Torah*. DJD 10. Oxford: Clarendon Press.

Rabin, C. 1958. *The Zadokite Documents*. 2d rev. ed. Oxford: Clarendon Press.

Rader, R. 1983. *Breaking Boundaries: Male/Female Friendships in Early Christian Communities*. New York and Mahwah: Paulist.

Rajak, T. 1985. "Jewish Rights in the Greek Cities under Roman Rule." Pp. 19–35 in *Approaches to Ancient Judaism: Theory and Practice. Volume 5: Studies in Judaism and its Greco-Roman Context*, ed. W. S. Green. BJS 32. Missoula, Mont.: Scholars Press.

Rawson, B. 1986. "The Roman Family." Pp. 1–57 in *The Family in Ancient Rome: New Perspectives*, ed. Beryl Rawson. Ithaca, NY: Cornell University Press.

Reich, R. 1995. "The Synagogue and the *Miqveh* in Eretz–Israel in the Second-Temple, Mishnaic and Talmudic Periods." In Urman and Flesher 1995:289–97.

Reicke, B. I. 1951. *Diakonie, Festfreude und Zelos in Verbindung mit der altchristlichen Agapenfeier*. Uppsala: A.-B. Lundequistska Bokhandeln; Wiesbaden: Otto Harrassowitz.

Reinach, S. 1883. "Fouilles de Délos (I): I. Temple des Poseidoniastes." *BCH* 7:462–76.

Remus, H. 1983. *Pagan–Christian Conflict over Miracle in the Second Century*. Patristic Monograph Series 10. Cambridge, Mass.: Philadelphia Patristic Foundation.

Renov, I. 1975 (1955). "The Seat of Moses." In Gutmann 1975b:233–38.

Reynolds, J. M., R. Tannenbaum, and K. T. Erim. 1987. *Jews and God-fearers at Aphrodisias: Greek Inscriptions with Commentary*. Proceedings of the Cambridge Philological Society, Supplementary series 12. Cambridge: The Cambridge Philological Society.

Riccobono, S., G. Baviera, C. Ferrini, G. Furlani, and V. Arangio-Ruiz, eds. 1940–43. *Fontes iuris romani antejustiniani*. Editio altera aucta et emendata. Florentiae: G. Barbera.

Richardson, G. P. 1993. "Philo and Eusebius on Monasteries and Monasticism: The Therapeutae and Kellia." In McLean 1993b:334–59.

——. 1994. "'A Most Pious Enterprise': The Herodian Temple's Architecture, Innovations and Social Setting." Paper presented at the Annual Meeting of the Society of Biblical Literature, Chicago, Ill., 21 November.

——. Forthcoming, 1996. *Herod, King of the Jews and Friend of the Romans*. Studies on Personalities of the New Testament. Columbia, SC: University of South Carolina Press.

Richardson, G. P., and V. Heuchan. 1992. "Jewish Voluntary Associations in Egypt and the Roles of Women." Paper presented at the annual meeting of the Canadian Society of Biblical Studies, Charlettetown, Prince Edward Island.

Robert, F. 1939. *Thymélè: recherches sur la signification et la destination des monuments circulaires dans l'architecture religieuse de la Grèce.* BEFAR 147. Paris: E. de Boccard.

Robert, L. 1940–65. *Hellenica: recueil d'épigraphie de numismatique et d'antiquités grecques.* Limoges: A. Bontemps.

———. 1958. "Inscriptions grecques de Sidè en Pamphylie." *Revue de Philologie* 32:15–53.

———. 1964–89. *Nouvelles inscriptions de Sardes.* Hautes études du monde gréco-romain 15. Paris: Adrien Maisonneuve.

———. 1973. "Sur les inscriptions de Délos." Pp. 435–89 in *Etudes deliennes,* ed. A. Plassart. BCHSup 1. Athènes: Ecole française d'Athènes; Paris: E. de Boccard.

Robertson, D. B., ed. 1966. *Voluntary Associations: A Study of Groups in Free Societies: Essays in Honor of James Luther Adams.* Richmond, Va: John Knox.

Robins, G. 1993. *Women in Ancient Egypt.* London: British Museum.

Robinson, J. A. T. 1952. *The Body: A Study in Pauline Theology.* Philadelphia, Pa.: Westminster.

Robinson, T. A. 1990. "Self-Definition, Voluntary Association, and Theological Diversity in Early Christian Communities." Paper presented at the annual meeting of the Canadian Society of Biblical Studies, University of Victoria, June 1990.

Rordorf, W. 1964. "Was wissen wir über die christlichen Gottesdiensträume der vorkonstantinischen Zeit?" *ZNW* 55:110–28.

Rosenau, H. 1979. *Visions of the Temple. The Image of the Temple of Jerusalem in Judaism and Christianity.* London: Oresko.

Rostovtzeff, M. I. 1926. *The Social and Economic History of the Roman Empire.* 2d ed. 1963. Oxford: Clarendon Press.

Roussel, P. 1911. "Laodicée de Phénicie." *BCH* 35:433–40.

———. 1916a. *Les cultes égyptiens à Délos du IIIe au Ier siècles av. J. C.* Paris: Berger; Nancy: Levrault.

———. 1916b. *Délos, colonie athénienne.* BEFAR 111. Paris: E. de Boccard.

Roussel, P., and J. Hatzfeld. 1910. "Fouilles de Délos exécutées aux frais de M. le Duc Loubat: Inscriptions (1905–1908)." *BCH* 34:355–423.

Safrai, S. 1976. "Jewish Self-Government." In Safrai and Stern 1974–76:377–419.

———. 1993. "The Place of Women in First-Century Synagogues." *Jerusalem Perspective* 5 (Sept.–Oct.):3–6.

Safrai, S., and M. Stern, eds. 1974–76. *The Jewish People in the First Century: Historical Geography, Political History, Social, Cultural and Religious Life and Institutions.* CRINT Section One. Assen: Van Gorcum; Philadelphia, Pa.: Fortress.

Safrai, Z. 1995. "The Communal Functions of the Synagogue in the Land of Israel in the Rabbinic Period." In Urman and Flesher 1995:181–204.

Salvait, F. 1963. "Dédiaces d'un *Tryphaktos* par les Hermaïstai Déliens." *BCH* 87:252–64.

Sandbach, F. H. 1975. *The Stoics.* Ancient Culture and Society. London: Chatto & Windus.

Sandelin, K.-G. 1991. "The Danger of Idolatry According to Philo of Alexandria." *Temenos* 27:109–50.

Sanders, E. P. 1977. *Paul and Palestinian Judaism: A Comparison of Patterns of Religion.* Philadelphia, Pa.: Fortress.

———. 1983. *Paul, the Law, and the Jewish People.* Philadelphia, Pa.: Fortress.

———. 1991. *Paul.* New York: Oxford University Press.

———. 1992. *Judaism: Practice and Belief 63 BCE–66 CE.* Philadelphia, Pa.: Trinity Press International.

Sanders, J. A., ed. 1965. *The Psalms Scroll of Qumran Cave 11 (11QPsA).* DJD 4. Oxford: Clarendon Press.

San Nicolò, M. 1913–15. *Ägyptisches Vereinswesen zur Zeit der Ptolemäer und Römer. I: Die Vereinsarten; II: Vereinswesen und Vereinsrecht.* Münchener Beiträge zur Papyrusforschung und antiken Rechtsgeschichte. 2. Heft. München: C. H. Beck; 2. Aufl. mit Nachtragen von J. Herrmann. München: C. H. Beck, 1972.

Sarason, R. S. 1980. "Mishnah and Scripture: Preliminary Observations on the Law of Tithing in *Seder Zera'im*." Pp. 81–96 in *Approaches to Ancient Judaism. Volume 2*, ed. W. S. Green. BJS 9. Chico, Calif.: Scholars Press.

Saulnier, C. 1981. "Lois romaines sur les Juifs selon Flavius Josèphe." *RB* 88:161–98.

Schiess, T. 1888. *Die römischen Collegia Funeraticia nach den Inschriften*. München: T. Ackermann Königlicher Hof-Buchhandler.

Schiffman, L. H. 1975. *The Halakhah at Qumran*. SJLA 16. Leiden: E. J. Brill.

——. 1983. *Sectarian Law in the Dead Sea Scrolls: Courts, Testimony and the Penal Code*. BJS 33. Chico, Calif.: Scholars Press.

——. 1985. "Exclusion from the Sanctuary and the City of the Sanctuary in the Temple Scroll." *Hebrew Annual Review* 9:301–20.

——. 1987. "The Dead Sea Scrolls and the Early History of the Jewish Liturgy." In Levine 1987:33–48.

——. 1989. *The Eschatological Community of the Dead Sea Scrolls: A Study of the Rule of the Congregation*. SBLMS 38. Atlanta, Ga.: Scholars Press.

—— ed. 1990a. *Archaeology and History in the Dead Sea Scrolls: The New York University Conference in Memory of Yigael Yadin*. JSPSup 8. Sheffield: JSOT Press.

——. 1990b. "The New Halakhic Letter (4QMMT) and the Origins of the Dead Sea Sect." *BA* 53(2):64–73.

——. 1991a. "Confessionalism and the Study of the Dead Sea Scrolls." *Forum of the World Union of Jewish Studies* 31:3–14.

——. 1991b. *From Text to Tradition: A History of Second Temple and Rabbinic Judaism*. Hoboken, NJ: Ktav Publishing House.

——. 1994. "Ordinance and Rules." In Charlesworth 1994:145–75.

Schmithals, W. 1972. *Paul and the Gnostics*. Trans. J. E. Steely. Nashville, Tenn.: Abingdon.

Schmitt-Pantel, P. 1990. "Collective Activities and the Political in the Greek City." Pp. 199–213 in *The Greek City from Homer to Alexander*, ed. Oswyn Murray and S. R. F. Price. Oxford: Clarendon; New York: Oxford University Press.

Schuller, E. 1994. "Women in the Dead Sea Scrolls." Pp. 115–32 in *Methods of Investigation of the Dead Sea Scrolls and the Khirbet Qumran Site: Present Realities and Future Prospects*, ed. M. O. Wise. New York: New York Academy of Sciences.

Schultze, V. 1895. *Archäologie der altchristlichen Kunst*. München: C. H. Beck.

Schürer, E. 1973–87. *The History of the Jewish People in the Age of Jesus Christ (175 B.C.–A.D. 135)*. New English edition revised by G. Vermes, F. Millar, M. Black, and M. Goodman. Edinburgh: T. & T. Clark.

Scott, S. P., ed. 1932. *The Civil Law, Including the Twelve Tables, the Institutes of Gaius, the Rules of Ulpian, the Opinions of Paulus, the Enactments of Justinian, and the Constitutions of Leo*. Cincinnati: The Central Trust Company.

Seager, A. R. 1981. "The Synagogue at Sardis." In Levine 1981:178–84.

——. 1983. "The Building." Pp. 168–78 in *Sardis from Prehistoric to Roman Times: Results of the Archaeological Exploration of Sardis, 1958–1975*, ed. G. M. A. Hanfmann, Clive Foss, and W. E. Mierse. Cambridge, Mass.: Harvard University Press.

——. 1989. "The Recent Historiography of Ancient Synagogue Architecture." Pp. 85–92 in *Ancient Synagogues in Israel: Third–seventh Century C.E.* Proceedings of Symposium, University of Hafia [i.e. Haifa], May 1987, ed. Rachel Hachlili. BAR international series 499. Oxford: BAR.

Segal, A. F. 1993. "Conversion and Universalism: Opposites That Attract." In McLean 1993b:162–89.

Seland, T. 1984. "Collegium kai Ekklesia: Nyere synspunkter på de gresk-romerske foreninger som modell for og paralell til de urkristne forsamlinger." *Ung Theologi* 17:49–65.

Shanks, H. 1979. *Judaism in Stone: The Archaeology of Ancient Synagogues.* New York: Harper & Row; Washington: Biblical Archaeology Society.

Sherk, R. K., ed. and trans. 1988. *The Roman Empire: Augustus to Hadrian.* Cambridge: Cambridge University Press.

Sherwin-White, A. N. 1966. *The Letters of Pliny: A Historical and Social Commentary.* Oxford: Clarendon Press; London: Oxford University Press.

Sills, D. L. 1959. "Voluntary Associations: Instruments and Objects of Change." *Human Organizations* 18:17–21.

———. 1968. "Voluntary Associations: Sociological Aspects." In *International Encyclopedia of the Social Sciences,* ed. D. L. Sills, vol. 16:362–79. New York: Macmillan & Co.

Simmel, G. 1923. "Die Krenzung Sozialer Kreise." Pp. 305–44 in *Soziologie: Untersuchungen über die Formen der Vergesellschaftung.* 3d ed. Gesammelte Werke 2. Berlin: Duncker & Humblot.

———. 1955. "The Web of Group Affiliations." Pp. 125–95 in *Conflict.* Glencoe, Ill.: Free Press.

Sly, D. 1990. *Philo's Perception of Women.* BJS 209. Atlanta, Ga.: Scholars Press.

Smallwood, E. M. 1976. *The Jews under Roman Rule from Pompey to Diocletian: A Study in Political Relations.* SJLA 20. Leiden: E. J. Brill.

Smith, J. Z. 1990. *Drudgery Divine: On the Comparison of Early Christianities and the Religions of Late Antiquity.* London: The School of Oriental and African Studies; Chicago: University of Chicago Press.

Smith, M. 1956. "Palestinian Judaism in the First Century." Pp. 67–87 in *Israel: Its Role in Civilization,* ed. M. Davis. New York: Israel Institute of the Jewish Theological Seminary.

———. 1960–1. "The Dead Sea Sect in Relation to Ancient Judaism." *NTS* 7:347–60.

Smyth, H. W. 1956. *Greek Grammar.* Rev. ed. Cambridge, Mass.: Harvard University Press.

Sohm, R. 1907. *The Institutes: A Text-book of the History and System of Roman Private Law.* 3d ed. Oxford, London, and New York: Clarendon Press.

Sokolowski, F. 1955. *Lois sacrées de l'Asie Mineure.* Ecole française d'Athènes. Travaux et mémoires, fasc. 9. Paris: E. de Boccard.

Stambaugh, J. E., and D. L. Balch. 1986. *The New Testament in its Social Environment.* Philadelphia, Pa.: Westminster.

Staveley, E. S. 1972. *Greek and Roman Voting and Elections.* Ithaca, NY: Cornell University Press.

Steckoll, S. H. 1968–69. "Preliminary Excavation Report in the Qumran Cemetery." *RevQ* 6:323–36.

Stegemann, H. 1992. "The Qumran Essenes – Local Members of the Main Jewish Union in Late Second Temple Times." In Trebolle Barrera and Vegas Montaner 1992:83–166.

———. 1994. *Die Essener, Qumran, Johannes der Täufer und Jesus: ein Sachbuch.* 4. Aufl. Freiburg im Breisgau: Herder.

Stendahl, K. 1978. *Paul among Jews and Gentiles, and Other Essays.* Philadelphia, Pa.: Fortress.

Stern, M. 1974. *Greek and Latin Authors on Jews and Judaism I: From Herodotus to Plutarch.* Jerusalem: Israel Academy of Sciences and Humanities.

Stowers, S. K. 1984. "Social Status, Public Speaking and Private Teaching." *NovT* 26:59–82.

Strange, J. F. 1979. "Archaeology and the Religion of Judaism in Palestine." *ANRW* II.19.1:646–85.

Strotmann, A. 1991. *"Mein Vater bist Du!" (Sir 51,10): zur Bedeutung der Vaterschaft Gottes in kanonischen und nichtkanonischen frühjüdischen Schriften.* Frankfurter theologische Studien 39. Frankfurt am Main: Josef Knecht.

Strugnell, J. 1970. "Notes en marge du volume V des Discoveries in the Judaean Desert." *RevQ* 7:163–276.

———. 1988. *A Preliminary Concordance to the Hebrew and Aramaic Fragments from Qumran Caves II– X Including Especially the Unpublished Material from Cave IV.* With Raymond E. Brown, J. A. Fitzmyer, W. G. Oxtoby, J. Teixidor, and H. P. Richter. Göttingen: Distributed by H. Stegemann on behalf of J. Strugnell.

Struve, V. V., ed. 1965. *Corpus inscriptionum Regni Bosporani (CIRB): Korpus bosporskikh nadpisei.* Moskva and Leningrad: Nauka.

Sukenik, E. L. 1934. *Ancient Synagogues in Palestine and Greece.* London: Published for the British Academy by Oxford University Press.

———. 1949. "The Present State of Ancient Synagogue Studies." *Louis Rabinowitz Bulletin for the Exploration of Ancient Synagogues:*21–23.

Süssenbach, U. 1977. *Christuskult und kaiserliche Baupolitik bei Konstantin: Die Anfänge der christlichen Verknüpfung kaiserlichen Repräsentation am Beispiel der Kirchenstiftungen Konstantins.* Abhandlungen zur Kunst-, Musik- und Literaturwissenschaft 241. Bonn: Bouvier.

Sutcliffe, E. F. 1960. *The Monks of Qumran as Depicted in the Dead Sea Scrolls.* Westminster, Md.: Newman.

Swidler, L. 1976. *Women in Judaism: The Status of Women in Formative Judaism.* Metuchen: Scarecrow.

Talbert, C. H. 1975. *Literary Patterns, Theological Themes, and the Genre of Luke–Acts.* SBLMS 20. Cambridge, Mass. and Missoula, Mont.: Society of Biblical Literature; Scholars Press.

Tcherikover, A. 1959. *Hellenistic Civilization and the Jews.* Philadelphia, Pa.: Jewish Publication Society of America.

Theissen, G. 1982. *The Social Setting of Pauline Christianity: Essays on Corinth.* Philadelphia, Pa.: Fortress.

Thompson, J. 1982. *The Beginnings of Christian Philosophy: The Epistle to the Hebrews.* CBQMS 13. Washington: Catholic Biblical Association of America.

Thrams, P. 1992. *Christianisierung des Römerreiches und heidnischer Widerstand.* Heidelberg: Carl Winter Universitätsverlag.

Tod, M. N. 1932. *Sidelights on Greek History: Three Lectures on the Light thrown by Greek Inscriptions.* Oxford: Basil Blackwell.

Torjesen, K. J. 1993. "Reconstruction of Women's Early Christian History." Pp. 290–310 in *Searching the Scriptures. Volume One: A Feminist Introduction,* ed. Elisabeth Schüssler Fiorenza. New York: Crossroad.

Tov, E., S. J. Pfann, and S. A. Reed, eds. 1993. *The Dead Sea Scrolls on Microfiche: A Comprehensive Facsimile Edition of the Texts from the Judean Desert.* Leiden and New York: E. J. Brill.

Tran, V. T. T. 1971. *Le culte des divinités orientales à Herculanum.* EPRO 17. Leiden: E. J. Brill.

———. 1982. "Sarapis and Isis." In Meyer and Sanders 1982:101–17, 207–10.

Trebolle Barrera, J. C., and L. Vegas Montaner, eds. 1992. *The Madrid Qumran Congress: Proceedings of the International Congress on the Dead Sea Scrolls, Madrid 18–21 March, 1991.* Studies on the texts of the desert of Judah 11. Leiden and New York: E. J. Brill.

Tsafrir, Y. 1987. "The Byzantine Setting and its Influence on Ancient Synagogues." In Levine 1987:147–57.

———. 1995. "On the Source of the Architectural Design of the Ancient Synagogues in the Galilee: A New Appraisal." In Urman and Flesher 1995:70–86.

Turcan, R. 1981. "Le sacrifice mithriaque: innovations de sens et de modalités." Pp. 341–80 in *Le sacrifice dans l'Antiquité classique: huit exposés suivis de discussions.* Entretiens sur l'antiquité 27. Vandoeuvres–Genève: Fondation Hardt.

Turner, C. H. 1918. "Apostolic Succession." Pp. 93–214 in *Essays on the Early History of the Church and the Ministry,* ed. Henry Barclay Swete. London: Macmillan & Co.

Turner, H. W. 1979. *From Temple to Meeting House: The Phenomenology and Theology of Places of Worship.* Religion and Society 16. The Hague: Mouton.

Turner, V. 1969. *The Ritual Process: Structure and Anti-structure.* Chicago: Aldine Pub. Co.

Urman, D. 1995a. "Early Photographs of Galilean Synagogues." In Urman and Flesher 1995:174–77.

———. 1995b. "The House of Assembly and the House of Study: Are They One and the Same?" In Urman and Flesher 1995:232–55.

Urman, D., and P. V. M. Flesher, eds. 1995. *Ancient Synagogues: Historical Analyses and Archaeological Discovery*. SPB 47/1–2. Leiden, New York, and Köln: E. J. Brill.

Ustinova, J. 1991. "The Thiasoi of Theos Hypsistos in Tanais." *HR* 31:150–80.

Vallois, R. 1923. *L'exploration archéologique de Délos VII: Le Portique de Philippe*. Paris: E. de Boccard.

VanderKam, J. C. 1991. "The People of the Dead Sea Scrolls: Essenes or Sadducees?" *BR* 7(2):42–47.

Vawter, B. 1977. "Divorce and the New Testament." *CBQ* 39:528–42.

Vermaseren, M. J. 1956–60. *Corpus Inscriptionum et Monumentorum Religionis Mithriacae*. The Hague: Martin Nijhoff.

———. 1963. *Mithras, the Secret God*. London: Chatto & Windus; New York: Barnes & Noble.

———. 1971. *Mithriaca I: The Mithraeum at S. Maria Capua Vetere*. EPRO 16. Leiden: E. J. Brill.

Vermaseren, M. J., and C. C. van Essen. 1965. *The Excavations in the Mithraeum of the Church of Santa Prisca in Rome*. Leiden: E. J. Brill.

Vermes, G. 1962. *The Dead Sea Scrolls in English*. Harmondsworth: Penguin.

———. 1974. "Sectarian Matrimonial Halakah in the Damascus Rule." *JJS* 25:197–202.

———. 1975. "Essenes and Therapeutae." Pp. 30–36 in *Post-Biblical Jewish Studies*. Leiden: E. J. Brill.

———. 1977. *The Dead Sea Scrolls: Qumran in Perspective*. London: Collins.

Vermeule, C. 1959. *The Goddess Roma in the Art of the Roman Empire*. Cambridge, Mass.: Spink.

Vidman, L. 1970. *Isis und Sarapis bei den Griechen und Römern*. RGVV 29. Berlin: Walter de Gruyter.

Wadell, P. J. 1989. *Friendship and the Moral Life*. Notre Dame, Ind.: University of Notre Dame Press.

Walke, S. C. 1950. "The Use of *Ecclesia* in the Apostolic Fathers." *ATR* 32:39–53.

Waltzing, J. P. 1895–1900. *Étude historique sur les corporations professionnelles chez les Romains depuis les origines jusqu' à la chute de l'Empire d'Occident*. 4 vols. Louvain: Peeters; repr. Hildesheim: Georg Olms, 1970.

Walzer, R. 1949. *Galen on Jews and Christians*. Oxford Classical and Philosophical Monographs. London: Oxford University Press.

Wankel, H. and H. Engelmann. 1979–84. *Die Inschriften von Ephesos*. Inschriften griechischer Städte aus Kleinasien 11–17. 8 vols. Bonn: Rudolf Habelt.

Waszink, J. H. 1978. "Genossenschaft. B. Römisch." *RAC* 10:99–117.

Weber, M. 1968. *Economy and Society: An Outline of Interpretive Sociology*. New York: Bedminster.

Wegner, J. R. 1988. *Chattel or Person? The Status of Women in the Mishnah*. New York: Oxford University Press.

———. 1991a. "The Image and Status of Women in Classical Rabbinic Judaism." Pp. 68–93 in *Jewish Women in Historical Perspective*, ed. J. R. Baskin. Detroit, Mich.: Wayne State University Press.

———. 1991b. "Philo's Portrayal of Women – Hebraic or Hellenic?" In Levine 1991:41–66.

Weinert, F. D. 1974. "4Q159: Legislation for an Essene Community Outside of Qumran?" *JSJ* 5:179–207.

Weinfeld, M. 1986. *The Organizational Pattern and the Penal Code of the Qumran Sect: A Comparison with Guilds and Religious Associations of the Hellenistic-Roman Period*. NTOA 2. Fribourg: Editions Universitaires; Göttingen: Vandenhoeck & Ruprecht.

Weinreich, O. 1919. *Neue Urkunden zur Sarapis-Religion*. Sammlung aus dem Gebiet der Theologie und Religionsgeschichte 86. Tübingen: J. C. B. Mohr (Paul Siebeck).

Weiss, H.-F. 1979. "Pharisäismus und Hellenismus: Zur Darstellung des Judentums im Geschichtswerk des jüdischen Historikers Flavius Josephus." *OLZ* 74:421–34.

Wellman, B. 1988. "Structural Analysis: From Method and Metaphor to Theory and Substance." Pp. 19–61 in *Social Structures: A Network Approach*, ed. B. Wellman and S. D. Berkowitz. Cambridge and New York: Cambridge University Press.

Wellman, B., and S. D. Berkowitz. 1988. "Introduction: Studying Social Structures." Pp. 1–14 in *Social Structures: A Network Approach*, ed. B. Wellman and S. D. Berkowitz. Cambridge and New York: Cambridge University Press.

Westermann, W. L. 1932. "Entertainment in the Villages of Graeco-Roman Egypt." *JEA* 18:16–27.

Wheeldon, P. D. 1969. "The Operation of Voluntary Associations and Personal Networks in the Political Processes of an Inter-ethnic Community." In Mitchell 1969b:128–80.

Whelan, C. F. 1993. "*Amica Pauli*: The Role of Phoebe in the Early Church." *JSNT* 49:67–85.

White, L. M. 1987. "The Delos Synagogue Revisited: Recent Fieldwork in the Graeco-Roman Diaspora." *HTR* 80(2):133–60.

——. 1988. "Shifting Sectarian Boundaries in Early Christianity." *BJRL* 70(3):7–24.

——. 1990. *Building God's House in the Roman World: Architectural Adaptation among Pagans, Jews and Christians*. Baltimore, Md.: Johns Hopkins University Press.

——. 1992a. "Finding the Ties That Bind: Issues from Social Description." In White 1992b:3–22.

—— ed. 1992b. *Social Networks in the Early Christian Environment: Issues and Methods for Social History*. Semeia 56. Atlanta, Ga.: Scholars Press.

—— Forthcoming. *The Christian Domus Ecclesiae and its Environment: A Collection of Texts and Monuments*. Harvard Theological Studies 36. Minneapolis, Minn.; Fortress.

White, S. A. 1987. "A Comparison of the 'A' and 'B' Manuscripts of the Damascus Document." *RevQ* 12(48):537–53.

——. 1992. "4Q364 and 365: A Preliminary Report." In Trebolle Barrera and Vegas Montaner 1992:217–28.

Whittaker, M. 1984. *Jews and Christians: Graeco-Roman Views*. Cambridge and New York: Cambridge University Press.

Wide, S. 1894. "Inschrift der Iobakchen." *MDAIA(A)* 19:248–92.

Wilamowitz-Moellendorff, U. von. 1958. *Griechische Verskunst*. 2. Aufl. Darmstadt: H. Gentner.

Wilcken, U. 1927–57. *Urkunden der Ptolemäerzeit (Ältere Funde)*. Berlin: Walter de Gruyter.

Wild, R. A. 1981. *Water in the Cultic Worship of Isis and Sarapis*. EPRO 87. Leiden: E. J. Brill.

Wilhelm, H. 1934. "Zu dem Gedichte des Maiistas." Symbolae Osloenses 13:1–8.

Wilken, R. L. 1972. "Collegia, Philosophical Schools and Theology." Pp. 268–91 in *The Catacombs and the Colosseum: The Roman Empire as the Setting of Primitive Christianity*, ed. S. Benko and J. J. O'Rourke. London and Valley Forge, Pa.: Oliphants.

——. 1980. "The Christians as the Romans (and Greeks) Saw Them." Pp. 100–25 in *Jewish and Christian Self-definition. Vol. 1: The Shaping of Christianity in the Second and Third Centuries*, ed. E. P. Sanders. Philadelphia, Pa.: Fortress.

——. 1984. *The Christians as the Romans Saw Them*. New Haven, Conn.: Yale University Press.

Wilkinson, J. D. 1984. "Orientation, Jewish and Christian." *PEQ* May–June, 13–30.

Williams, M. H. 1992. "The Jews and Godfearers Inscription from Aphrodisias – A Case of Patriarchal Interference in Early 3rd Century Caria?" *Historia* 41:297–310.

Willoughby, H. R. 1929. *Pagan Regeneration*. Chicago: University of Chicago Press.

Wilson. B. R. 1970. *Religious Sects: A Sociological Study*. World University Library. New York: McGraw-Hill; London: Weidenfeld & Nicolson.

Wilson, S. G. 1973. *The Gentiles and the Gentile Mission in Luke–Acts*. SNTSMS 23. Cambridge: Cambridge University Press.

Winston, D. 1981. *The Contemplative Life. The Giants. Selections*. Classics of Western Spirituality. New York: Paulist.

Winter, B. W. 1988. "The Public Honouring of Christian Benefactors: Romans 13.3–4 and 1 Peter 2.14–15." *JSNT* 34:87–103.

Witt, R. E. 1971. *Isis in the Graeco-Roman World*. London: Thames & Hudson.

Wolfson, H. A. 1947. *Philo: Foundations of Religious Philosophy in Judaism, Christianity, and Islam.* Rev. ed. Cambridge, Mass.: Harvard University Press.

Yadin, Y. 1966. *Masada: Herod's Fortress and the Zealots' Last Stand.* London: Weidenfeld & Nicolson.

——. 1977–83. *The Temple Scroll.* Jerusalem: Israel Exploration Society.

——. 1981. "The Synagogue at Masada." In Levine 1981:19–23.

Zeitlin, S. 1930–31. "The Origin of the Synagogue." *Proceedings of the American Academy of Jewish Research* 2:69–81.

Ziebarth, E. G. L. 1896. *Das griechische Vereinswesen.* Stuttgart: S. Hirzel; repr. Wiesbaden: M. Sändig, 1969.

INDEX OF MODERN AUTHORS

Magie, D. 148
Maier, H. O. 15, 170, 171
Malherbe, A. J. 57, 58, 63, 69, 71, 72, 126
Malina, B. J. 27, 126, 135, 144
Malingrey, A. M. 55, 57
Ma'oz, Z. 267, 283
Marcadé, J. 204, 221
Marrou, H. I. 39, 56, 156
Martinez, F. Garcia 264
Marx, A. 264
Maser, P. 71
Mason, S. 3, 4, 6, 10, 15, 284
Mazur, B. 108, 194, 220
Meeks, W. A. 62, 64, 65, 66, 67, 69, 70, 72, 126, 127, 134, 144, 263
Mendelson, A. 122, 127
Meredith, A. 32, 57
Merkelbach, R. 183, 184
Merton, R. K. 172
Meyer, H. 202, 203, 204, 221
Meyers, E. M. 71, 104, 266, 270, 283, 284, 286
Michaels, A. Kirsopp 169
Michels, R. 143
Milik, J. T. 253, 262, 264, 265
Minear, P. S. 70
Mitchell, J. C. 149, 171, 172
Moehring, H. R. 107
Momigliano, A. 37, 57
Mommsen, T. 20, 28, 70, 87, 89, 104
Moore, G. F. 57
Moore, R. D. 265
Mora, F. 222
Mott, S. C. 121
Moulton, W. F. 70
Moxnes, H. 126
Mühll, P. von der 116
Murphy-O'Connor, J. 264
Muszynski, M. 125

Naville, E. 232, 247
Naydenova, V. 184
Netzer, E. 101, 104, 108, 272, 284
Neusner, J. 46, 57, 274
Nilsson, M. P. 164
Nisbet, R. A. 169, 170
Nock, A. D. 6, 10, 27, 32, 33, 35, 37, 38, 42, 56, 57, 72, 89, 126, 208, 220, 222

O'Neil, E. 56
Oppenheimer, A. 92
Orlandos, A. C. 213, 214, 224

Painter, R. J. 183
Panciera, S. 184
Pennock, J. R. 14, 170
Peritz, I. J. 235
Perowne, S. 89
Petersen, S. M. 71
Petrie, W. M. F. 228, 230, 231, 247
Piana, G. La 28
Picard, C. 196, 202, 204, 221, 222
Piccottini, G. 184
Pilisuk, M. 164
Plaskow, J. 283
Plassart, A. 194, 219, 220
Pleket, H. W. 28
Plummer, R. 219
Pohlenz, W. 174
Poland, F. 22, 23, 24, 25, 27, 29, 30, 63, 71, 107, 111, 113, 125, 126, 127, 224
Pomeroy, S. B. 237, 246, 284
Potter, D. S. 174
Powell, J. U. 222
Préaux, C. 223

Qimron, E. 260, 263, 264

Rabin, C. 144, 258
Rader, R. 171
Rajak, T. 115
Rawson, B. 277, 284
Reich, R. 92
Reicke, B. I. 126, 127
Reinach, S. 221
Remus, H. 5, 10, 165, 174
Renov, I. 280
Reynolds, J. M. 30
Riccobono, S. 88
Richardson, G. P. 4, 12, 15, 104, 105, 107, 108, 109, 127, 239, 246, 248, 249, 283, 286
Robert, L. 219, 220, 221, 222, 285
Robertis, F. M. De 89, 126
Robertson, D. B. 14, 143, 170
Robins, G. 236, 237
Robinson, J. A. T. 72
Robinson, T. A. 63, 71, 72
Rordorf, W. 72
Rosenau, H. 109
Rostovtzeff, M. I. 23, 26, 29
Roussel, P. 210, 212, 219, 221, 222

Safrai, S. 142, 270, 284
Safrai, Z. 92

INDEX OF TEXTS

325

PAPYRI